PRAGMATISM AND FEMINISM

Charlene Haddock Seigfried

Pragmatism and Feminism

REWEAVING THE
SOCIAL FABRIC

THE UNIVERSITY OF CHICAGO PRESS   *Chicago & London*

Charlene Haddock Seigfried, professor of philosophy and American studies at Purdue University, is the author of *Chaos and Context: A Study in William James* (1978) and *William James's Radical Reconstruction of Philosophy* (1990).

The University of Chicago Press, Chicago 60637
The University of Chicago Press, Ltd., London
© 1996 by The University of Chicago
All rights reserved. Published 1996
Printed in the United States of America
05 04 03 02 01 00 99 98 97 96   1   2   3   4   5

ISBN: 0-226-74557-0 (cloth)
0-226-74558-9 (paper)

Library of Congress Cataloging-in-Publication Data

Seigfried, Charlene Haddock, 1943–
    Pragmatism and feminism : reweaving the social fabric / Charlene Haddock Seigfried.
        p.   cm.
    Includes bibliographical references and index.
    1. Pragmatism.   2. Feminist theory.   3. James, William. 1842–1910.   4. Dewey, John, 1859–1952.   I. Title.
    B832.S45   1996
    144'.3'082—dc20   95-46879
                                                                            CIP

⊗ The paper used in this publication meets the minimum requirements of the American National Standard for Information Sciences—Permanence of Paper for Printed Library Materials, ANSI Z39.48-1984.

To all the friends, colleagues, and students,

and especially to Hans and Karl,

whose sympathetic understanding so well expresses

what pragmatist feminists mean by social intelligence.

When women who are not mere students of other persons' philosophy set out to write it, we cannot conceive that it will be the same in viewpoint or tenor as that composed from the standpoint of the different masculine experience of things.

John Dewey, 1919

Contents

Acknowledgments   *ix*

Abbreviations   *x*

I
WHERE HAVE ALL THE WOMEN GONE?

1   The Theory of Practice   *3*

2   The Missing Perspectives: Where Are All the
Pragmatist Feminists and Feminist Pragmatists?   *17*

3   Reclaiming a Heritage: Women Pragmatists   *40*

4   Acknowledging Mutual Influences: The Chicago Years   *67*

5   Educational Experiments in Cooperation   *90*

II
LIBERATING THEORY

6   The Feminine-Mystical Threat to
Scientific-Masculine Order   *111*

7   Who Experiences? Genderizing Pluralistic Experiences   *142*

8   What's Wrong with Instrumental Reasoning? Realizing the
Emancipatory Potential of Science   *174*

9   Who Cares? Pluralizing Gendered Experiences   *202*

10   Social Ethics   *224*

11   Cooperative Intelligence   *259*

Notes   *277*

Bibliography   *317*

Index   *333*

Acknowledgments

Earlier versions of some of the chapters have appeared elsewhere. Two articles included in chapter 2 are "Where Are All the Pragmatist Feminists?" published in *Hypatia* 6/2 (1991), 1–20, and "The Missing Perspective: Feminist Pragmatism," published in *Transactions of the Charles S. Peirce Society* 27/4 (1991): 405–16. Chapter 3 was originally published as an essay with the title "Classical American Philosophy's Invisible Women," in *Canadian Review of American Studies* Special Issue, Part I (1992), 83–116. Chapter 7 is an expanded version of an essay called "Validating Women's Experiences Pragmatically," in *Philosophy and the Reconstruction of Culture,* edited by John J. Stuhr; reprinted by permission of the State University of New York Press, © 1993. Chapter 9 first appeared under the title "Pragmatism, Feminism, and Sensitivity to Context," in *Who Cares? Theory, Research, and Educational Implications of the Ethic of Care,* edited by Mary M. Brabeck; reprinted by permission of Praeger, an imprint of Greenwood Publishing Group, Inc., Westport, CT, © 1989. I am grateful for permission to reprint them here.

I am also happy to acknowledge that my research was aided by a semester at the Purdue University Center for Humanistic Studies and by the friendly help received at the Dewey Center and the Special Collections of the Southern Illinois University at Carbondale Library.

Abbreviations

JOHN DEWEY

The series abbreviation is followed by volume number and page. The first volume of the *Early Works*, page 5, for example is (EW 1:5).

EW   *The Early Works of John Dewey, 1882–98.* Edited by Jo Ann Boydston. 5 vols. Carbondale and Edwardsville: Southern Illinois University Press, 1969–72.

MW   *The Middle Works of John Dewey, 1899–1924.* Edited by Jo Ann Boydston. 15 vols. Carbondale and Edwardsville: Southern Illinois University Press, 1976–83.

LW   *The Later Works of John Dewey, 1925–53.* Edited by Jo Ann Boydston. 17 vols. Carbondale and Edwardsville: Southern Illinois University Press, 1981–90.

Index   *Index to The Collected Works, 1882–1953.* Edited by Anne S. Sharpe. Carbondale and Edwardsville: Southern Illinois University Press, 1991.

WILLIAM JAMES

The Works of William James. Edited by Frederick H. Burkhardt, Fredson Bowers, and Ignas K. Skrupskelis. Cambridge: Harvard University Press. The original date of publication is given in parentheses.

PP   *The Principles of Psychology,* 3 vols., 1981 (1890)

PBC   *Psychology: Briefer Course,* 1984 (1892)

WB   *The Will to Believe,* 1979 (1897)

TT   *Talks to Teachers on Psychology,* 1983 (1899)

VRE   *The Varieties of Religious Experience,* 1985 (1902)

PM   *Pragmatism,* 1975 (1907)

MT   *The Meaning of Truth,* 1975 (1909)

PU   *A Pluralistic Universe,* 1977 (1909)
SPP   *Some Problems of Philosophy,* 1979 (1911)
ERE   *Essays in Radical Empiricism,* 1976 (1912)
EPH   *Essays in Philosophy,* 1978
ERM   *Essays in Religion and Morality,* 1982
EPS   *Essays in Psychology,* 1983
EPR   *Essays in Psychical Research,* 1986
ECR   *Essays, Comments, and Reviews,* 1987
MEN   *Manuscript Essays and Notes,* 1988
ML   *Manuscript Lectures,* 1988

1

Where Have All the Women Gone?

One

The Theory of Practice

This book attempts to serve as an introduction to an area much beyond the scope of a dozen books, let alone one. In it I can only gesture toward the largely unwritten history of pragmatism and feminism, indicate the broad sweep of overlapping pragmatist and feminist issues in theory and practice, and illustrate the depth of analysis possible by a few detailed reconstructions. At this stage the explanation can only be preliminary and suggestive. What William James says of science applies also to the development of theories: "At a certain stage in the development of every science a degree of vagueness is what best consists with fertility."[1] This is itself a fact that needs explanation, since feminist theory and practice have already developed enough to produce lengthy bibliographies on Marxist feminism, liberal feminism, radical feminism, psychoanalytic feminism, socialist feminism, and many other varieties of feminism. My book is strangely out of sync with the times and in some ways belongs with the earlier, tentative phases of feminism. It is preliminary compared with many more sophisticated studies responding to years of analysis and debate.

On the other hand, it is late work, which does have the advantage of hindsight. Many problems growing out of earlier feminist formulations have now become more obvious and the alternatives more sharply defined.[2] Just how a pragmatist perspective fits into the conceptual landscape can be more exactly articulated. Furthermore, although pragmatist feminism is still in its infancy, many analyses that developed under the aegis of other traditions have obvious affinities with it. Nancy Fraser has developed a pragmatic feminism out of Marxist critical theory, for instance, and there is a growing body of literature in pragmatist feminist legal theory and in literary theory.[3] There are also many pragmatist interpretations scattered throughout feminist theory. When gathered together and seen from the perspective of Classical American Philosophy, a designation often simply shortened to *pragmatism,* these scattered insights take on new meanings and possibilities.[4]

The need both to provide the basic parameters for a still undeveloped field of inquiry as well as to respond to the present state of feminist theory threatens to subvert the work by multiplying what ought to be covered beyond the possibility of closure. To avoid the specter of such a never-ending task, I therefore conceive of this effort as an invitation rather than as a systematic treatise. I seek to develop and open up a promising, mutually beneficial discussion between pragmatists and feminists that I believe has the potential for changing the theoretical analyses and concrete practices of both.[5] The categories used are preliminary and descriptive rather than analytic, more in the essay style of William James than in the labored architectonic style of Charles Sanders Pierce. This is just as well, since, like James, I am more comfortable with exploratory efforts than with the systematic expositions that inevitably follow, being among those "whose ideal of mental nature is best expressed by the word 'richness'" and for whom "statistical and cognitive intelligence will seem insufferably narrow, dry, tedious and unacceptable."[6]

My intent is to sketch out a research program sufficiently promising to be further revised and developed by others. For both practical and theoretic reasons the project envisioned must be a collaborative endeavor if it is to succeed at all: practically, it is beyond my powers to develop such a large project on my own; and theoretically, it is axiomatic to both feminism and pragmatism that knowledge is developed interactively among communities of inquirers and given conditions. The method proposed is a pragmatist hermeneutics of cooperation as called for by Jane Addams and William James and developed into community-based theories of inquiry by George Herbert Mead and John Dewey.[7]

There is both a historical and a conceptual dimension to feminism, and they do not neatly cohere. I can conceptually define feminism as any of multiple theories or perspectives either based on the premise that women have been and continue to be oppressed, in which case the emancipation and empowerment of women is taken as a goal, or based on the premise that gender is a fundamental category of analysis. Or I can identify feminism with the beginning of an organized women's movement and seek some precipitating event, such as the women's rights convention at Seneca Falls in 1848, or a period of organized protest, such as the nineteenth-century struggle for enfranchisement. It is sometimes suggested that it is anachronistic to call a woman a feminist if she disputed her assigned role before a particular organized movement was in existence. But in every era for which we have sufficient records to make a judgment, there is evidence that women have used feminist arguments to challenge suffocating social, economic, and political arrangements.[8]

Denying the label *feminism* to their efforts might help to clarify a theoretical issue in that it allows for the definition and distinction of feminism as a specific historical movement. But it does not solve the practical issue that there were women making eloquent protests against their situation *as women* even when there was no movement to support them. It has the unfortunate effect of further isolating and leaving in a conceptual limbo those women who were feminists "before their time," as if this were possible.[9]

An analogous situation obtains with regard to pragmatism. It can be dated as a specific historic movement, which began with the Metaphysical Club in Cambridge, Massachusetts, in the 1870s; was announced as a new philosophical perspective by both Peirce and James; and expanded considerably with Dewey's Chicago School of pragmatism. However, scattered expressions of positions already existed, which came to be organized by academic philosophers into variant but coherent pragmatist theories that consolidated into a philosophic movement. Even setting aside the reductionist tendency to call pragmatist any position that has a strong practical or even unprincipled dimension, there still remains a considerable number of positions recognizably pragmatist in the germane sense but which developed and continue to develop independently of the pragmatist movement in philosophy. Since many of these pragmatists who are not affiliated with the historical movement of pragmatism are women and feminists, I must specify what makes a position pragmatist in the sense being used in this book.

As with feminism, defining what qualifies as a pragmatist position means adopting a particular perspective, which some call political but which in any case already instantiates value judgments. To avoid the a priori limitation of the field that essentialist definitions require, I therefore begin by defining as pragmatism the positions developed by the members of the historically recognized movement of American pragmatism. But this is only a beginning meant to be left behind. One problem that immediately arises is that many writers defining the movement have focused almost exclusively on the pragmatic method and pragmatic theories of meaning and truth and have drawn their inferences from articles and books specifically addressed to this cluster of issues.[10] James's "What Pragmatism Means" is often reproduced in collections of pragmatist philosophy, for instance, but not his *Essays in Radical Empiricism;* Dewey's "Supremacy of Method" is reproduced, but not his *Art as Experience.* Their focus on methodology is rejected because it is too narrow. On the other hand, Richard Rorty's dismissal of pragmatist methodology, right along with the Dewey of *Experience and Nature* and the James of *Essays in Radical Empiricism,* also unacceptably narrows the resources pragmatism has to offer feminist theory.

Another problem is that a historical definition privileges certain philosophers as founding a movement, which is then limited to variations on their positions, without questioning either the cogency of the persons chosen or the adequacy of positions thus privileged. Since I intend to question both, and yet recover and extend an actual tradition, I have adopted the following procedure. To situate pragmatism as a historical movement, I have taken as my starting point for reflection those who have traditionally been designated as Classical American philosophers, primarily Charles Sanders Peirce, William James, Josiah Royce, John Dewey, and George Herbert Mead. From their writings I have developed an initial formulation of pragmatist theory. Notably absent from this group are women and minorities, and notably absent from pragmatist analyses are any systematic discussions of sexism or racism.

The next stage of analysis is to extend the original group to include women who directly or indirectly influenced the historically recognized pragmatists, as well as women who were influenced by them. I examine their writings to show in what sense they are pragmatist according to the classical expressions of pragmatism and to what extent they diverged, particularly insofar as they incorporated reflections on their own lives as women and developed feminist analyses. Doing so forces a reconstruction of pragmatism, both historically, by making visible women's contributions even to the original formulations of pragmatist theory and by recovering a tradition of women pragmatists; and conceptually, by developing pragmatist positions informed by feminist perspectives and feminist positions revisioned from pragmatist perspectives.

Finally, I hope that eventually this reconstructed model of feminist pragmatism and pragmatist feminism can itself be interrogated from the perspective of feminist versions of pragmatism that developed independently. Not only will such an analysis permit a more differentiated and less simplistic understanding of what it means to call a position pragmatist, but it will continue the process of understanding the interrelationship of self and world through multiple perspectives.

The problem remains, however, as to what is identifiably pragmatist about the writings of the pragmatists. We need a working hypothesis to get the whole process started. Are there some premises they all share, even though they might differ considerably in how they express those premises and what they mean by them? Pragmatism, as a philosophy that stresses the relation of theory to praxis, takes the continuity of experience and nature as revealed through the outcome of directed action as the starting point for reflection.[12] Experience is the ongoing transaction of organism and environment; in other words, both subject and object are constituted in the process. When intelligently ordered, initial conditions are deliberately transformed according to ends-in-view, that is, intentionally, into a subsequent state of affairs thought to be more desirable. Knowledge is therefore guided by interests or values. Since the reality of objects cannot be known prior to experience, truth claims can be justified only as the fulfillment of conditions experimentally determined—that is, clearly the outcome of inquiry. Emphasis on the reciprocity of theory and praxis, knowledge and action, facts and values follows from its post-Darwinian understanding of human experience, including cognition, as a developmental, historically contingent process.

Knowledge is instrumental, not in the sense of merely linking means to predetermined ends, but in the sense of a tool used, along with other tools, for organizing experiences satisfactorily. Concepts are habits of belief or rules of action. Truth cannot be determined solely by epistemological criteria because the adequacy of these criteria cannot be determined apart from the goals sought and the values instantiated. Values, which arise in historically specific cultural situations, are intelligently appropriated only to the extent that they satisfactorily resolve problems and are judged worth retaining. According to pragmatic theories, truths are beliefs confirmed in the course of experience and are therefore fallible, subject to further revision. True beliefs for Peirce represent real objects as successively confirmed until they converge on a final determination; for James, they are leadings that are worthwhile; and, for Dewey, the transformation of an indeterminate situation into a determinate one that leads to warranted assertions.

Pragmatist ethics is naturalistic, pluralistic, developmental, and experimental. It reflects on the motivations influencing ethical systems, examines the individual developmental process wherein an individual's values are gradually distinguished from those of society, situates moral judgments within problematic situations irreducibly individual and social, and proposes as ultimate criteria for making decisions the value for life as growth. In any given case, what counts as growth ought to be intelligently determined by all those affected by the actual or projected outcomes, insofar as they can be included in the decision-making process.

John J. Stuhr, who prefers the label *Classical American Philosophy* to *pragmatism*, also defines it historically and thematically, and lists the following defining characteristics: (1) the rejection of the central problems of modern philosophy, which presuppose such dichotomies as percept/concept, reason/will, thought/purpose, intellect/emotion, appearance/reality, experience/nature, belief/action, theory/practice, facts/values, and self/others; (2) fallibilism, or the impossibility of attaining unrevisable, certain empirical knowledge as an irreducible dimension of the human condition; (3) pluralism of experiences, values, and meanings; (4) radical empiricism, according to which experiencing subject and experienced object constitute a primal, integral, relational unity; (5) treatment of the results of experimental inquiry as the measure of theory; (6) meliorism, the view that human action can improve the human condition; and (7) the centrality of community and the social, such that the individual is intrinsically constituted by and in her or his social relations, thus linking the attainment of individuality with the creation of community.[13]

These theoretically necessary but artificial definitions and distinctions, which aim to embody the essence of feminism and pragmatism, can also function to obscure important dimensions of each. Experience and theory are intricately, dynamically interrelated. Take women's experiences of being treated as less than human, naming the sources of the unequal treatment and even of life-threatening actions, yet resisting the distortions and threats. Definitions of feminism seek to reflectively appropriate many different processes of recognition and conviction that cannot be reduced without distortion to any single formulation. As James argues from his position of pluralistic perspectivism, "Something escapes the best of us—not accidentally, but systematically and because we have a twist."[14] This is why there are as many different feminist and pragmatist theories as there are distinctive points of view. There exists an unresolvable tension between feminism as experienced by different persons, members of varied ethnic groups, classes, sexual identities, and so forth, and as reflectively and theoretically appropriated. It is a fruitful tension insofar as lived experiences and theoretical appropriations continually challenge and enrich each other. It is a harmful tension insofar as either distorts or unfairly denies the validity of the other.

I know now, for instance, that feminist ideas and practices extend far into the past, but there was no feminist movement that I was aware of during my high school years, which ended in 1960. To say that I was part of an older movement stretching back in time falsifies my experience of participating in the reinvention of feminism in the sixties and seventies. To say that my generation's experiences were unrelated to earlier feminist struggles is, however, also false. Part of our understanding of our own movement has come from rediscovering and reappropriating a past, the ignorance of which contributed to some false starts and dead ends but also to the exhilaration of the times. In coming to a clearer understanding of what feminism means I do not want to distort the actual path by which particular individuals become feminist. These paths are related but not identical. Hence, my understanding of feminism and pragmatism will differ from that of others. I cannot assume an omniscient point of view even if I wanted to, and therefore I will necessarily distort as well as disclose. It is, nevertheless, the function of public discourse to supply missing points of view and to strive for a mutually satisfactory understanding of the issues involved, or at least to understand and express more clearly what areas of disagreement still remain.

As a general overview, Simone de Beauvoir's remark in *The Second Sex* that "women do not contest the human situation, because they have hardly begun to assume it," captured both the felt restrictions within which I grew up and, at the same time, issued a welcome challenge to me to take my rightful place in the world.[15] Today the challenge has been met, and women are contesting the human situation all over the world, as in Ursula K. Le Guin's statement that her books "were written from the fragile but real security of women's solidarity—the assurance that our perception is valid and our experience authentic, and that our imagination of how things might be different, or better, is urgently wanted; the assurance that, after all, this world is our world."[16]

My aversion to being reduced to a label extends back at least to my Ph.D. dissertation defense. When asked by a member of the committee how I, as a pragmatist, would answer a particular question, I responded that I was defending a pragmatist thesis, but that did not turn me into a pragmatist. Conceptual categories cannot contain lived experience. I was both more than and less than a pragmatist. Clearly, though, not to be identified as a pragmatist or as a feminist works against concerted action. Again an unresolvable tension emerges. One must both assume labels to act effectively and reject them in order to retain the dynamic sense of self that cannot be reduced to any one dimension. Pragmatist philosophy explores this tension between conceptualization and experience as problematic in ways that can contribute to the further development of feminist theory.

On the other hand, feminist theory can critique, extend, and transform pragmatism. In response to a symposium on pragmatism and feminism in 1991 of the Society for the Advancement of American Philosophy, a member of the audience said that while a pragmatist feminism made sense to her, a feminist pragmatism did not. Among possible implications of this remark are that while feminists could certainly learn from pragmatists, the reverse was not the case; and that though feminists could broaden their perspective by adopting a pragmatist approach, pragmatists could only narrow their perspective by adopting a feminist approach. The response raises the question of how a philosophical perspective like pragmatism, a philosophy founded on the centrality of praxis with its emancipatory goals, a philosophy that is theoretically pluralistic and anti-dogmatic, could historically come to the point where feminism, one of the most distinctive contemporary theories of liberation, would appear to be irrelevant to its own future development.

Pragmatism, possibly more than any other philosophic movement, defends the legitimacy and irreducibility of multiple perspectives. But it does so generically, as it were, by not committing itself to any one of them. Such privileging of only one perspective would be counterproductive to its defense of everyone's right to be heard. Feminist analyses have, however, shown that even a defense of pluralism proceeds from some particular ground and set of commitments. In making explicit its own interpretive space, feminism can help to identify the hidden assumptions of pragmatist analyses and to demonstrate the crucial difference between merely acknowledging other perspectives and coming to terms with the consequences of such recognition. This confrontation of a particular perspective with the defense of perspectivism opens the possibility for new insights into the effort to both privilege the unique struggles of women, of different ethnic groups, of the economically deprived, of homosexuals and lesbians, and to affirm a common struggle.

There is growing evidence that women scholars are more comfortable than men in fields or departments that cross and transcend disciplinary boundaries.[17] One could see this simply as an eclecticism often found in those whose careers have not followed the usual pattern of strict, uninterrupted education geared to a well-defined disciplinary paradigm. If so, women's penchant for interdisciplinary research will disappear in direct proportion to their mainstreaming into the professions. This would be a pity, since intellectual growth requires challenging accepted paradigms. But there are as well good theoretical grounds for the interdisciplinary nature of feminist studies, whether by women or men. Since feminist analysis involves specific criticism of existing social orders that transcend any one discipline, it must remain open to all appropriate evidence and inquiry involving women and women's issues, no matter where they originate.

Feminist theory has often been divided into three areas according to its origins and major emphases. The social and political branch is traced back either to Marxist or liberal analyses and to the nineteenth-century abolitionist and suffrage movements or to the twentieth-century civil-rights movement; the literary and cultural branch to psychological theories, notably Freud's, or to existentialist theory; and the radical or cultural branch to women's experiences, particularly lesbian and other writings identified as by women. Pragmatism seems so promising for revisioning by feminists because it develops all three areas of concern and methodologically requires evidence that only interdisciplinary research can satisfy. These areas of concern are variously integrated by the classical American pragmatists, each of whom emphasizes one more than the others. Social, economic, and political transformations are central to Dewey's and Mead's philosophies, while psychology, religion, and literary style are central to James's. While neither James nor Dewey explores sexuality in his psychology texts, Dewey explicitly links psychological development to social, political, and economic conditions.[18] All the pragmatists choose experience as the starting point for reflection, and all criticize the neo-Kantian and logical positivist turns to epistemology.

Feminist educators have been in the forefront of curriculum reform in higher education, seeking to reunite into a holistic approach what has been fragmented into separate, often hostile, disciplines. Giles Gunn defines interdisciplinary studies as "a distinctive predisposition to view all fields as potentially vulnerable to re-creation in the partial image of some other or others," and he gives as examples American studies, feminist criticism, and African-American criticism or postcolonial criticism.[19] From the first, Women's Studies programs were interdisciplinary, and recent writings place a group of Black feminist intellectuals "at the centre of the theorizing about race, class and gender in the USA."[20] Pragmatist philosophy reflects the interdisciplinary approach of its founders, since their careers developed before the hardening of disciplinary boundaries. James was a professor of physiology and psychology at Harvard before he was appointed professor of philosophy. Dewey was head of the departments of psychology, education, and philosophy at the University of Chicago and later continued in philosophy and pedagogy at Columbia University and Teachers College. He worked closely with economists and anthropologists; and he contributed, along with Mead and Jane Addams, to the emergence of the discipline of sociology.[21] James Hayden Tufts, James Rowland Angell, Dewey, and Mead originated a new school of pragmatist philosophy at the University of Chicago in the 1890s. "From the beginning of the school, Tufts, Dewey, and Mead believed that philosophy and psychology should have either a direct or an indirect bearing on social, educational, political, economic, industrial, and moral problems, in that philosophy should furnish the theory to be put in direct practice."[22]

But the holistic, interdisciplinary, and emancipatory character of the early pragmatists was not just an accident of history; it was adopted deliberately. James, Dewey, and Mead directly attacked the growing professionalizing of philosophy insofar as it increasingly favored merely verbal solutions, abstractions, and pretended absolutes over concrete analyses of the human condition. They argued for a pluralism of nonreductively multiple points of view. As doctoral programs, professional meetings, and journals proliferated, the public forum for discussion became devalued as popularizing or trivializing issues too complicated for those not initiated into increasingly technical discussions of epistemology and logic. James called his empiricism radical because it turned away from such scholastic preoccupations "towards concreteness, and adequacy, towards facts, towards action, and towards power."[23] Dewey calls his "type of pragmatic anti-intellectualism" one that "starts from acts, functions, as primary data, functions both biological and social in character" and "treats the knowledge standpoint, in all its patterns, structures, and purposes, as evolving out of, and operating in the interests of, the guidance and enrichment of these primary functions."[24]

James announced a new dawn for philosophy, one which turns away from philosophizing as the development of merely technical expertise to a recognition that each person already senses, however inarticulately, the meaning of life. Instead of empty abstractions, what would be most helpful to those searching for deeper understanding of the meaning of life would be insight into joining the world of facts and scientific developments with the realm of values, personal worth, and spontaneity. In this shared inquiry, no one could claim "superior discernment or authority" as to what makes life worth living for others. Philosophy should thus be returned to the people, and professional philosophers should see themselves as facilitators rather than as experts in ever more arcane theory construction. Overintellectualism James criticized as escapism, a search for those "simple, clean and noble" classic sanctuaries that wall us off from the muddy particularities of everyday existence. "The world of concrete personal experiences to which the street belongs," he said, "is multitudinous beyond imagination, tangled, muddy, painful and perplexed."[25]

Given this pragmatic turn toward experience and the pressing problems of everyday life, it would be surprising if women influenced by it had not reflected on and theorized about their own experiences and problems as women. But although scholars have recovered original sources showing that for W. E. B. Du Bois and Alain Locke, who studied with William James and other Classical American philosophers, the issue of race was central to their theoretical analyses, there has been little published showing that women pragmatists influenced the course of feminist theory—or even of pragmatism, for that matter.[26] This study begins by accounting for this anomaly and challenging its accuracy.

None of the founding pragmatists made women's experiences central to their own discourse, although their examples are often taken from spheres traditionally assigned to women, such as the family, early childhood education, and (for James, at least) mysticism. They did explicitly, frequently, and consistently encourage their students to develop their own experiential basis for reflection and discouraged them from simply taking over philosophical positions they themselves held. Dewey, especially, repeatedly testified to learning from women's experiences and points of view as women, and he fought publicly for women's issues, such as women's right to coeducation, birth control, and a living wage. Women studying with the pragmatists were empowered to trust their own experiences and to challenge the system. They commonly saw the first-generation male pragmatists as allies against entrenched prejudices and misogynistic institutional practices. It seems that from the beginning feminism and pragmatism have been mutually transformative, though this relationship has not yet been adequately recovered.

When not dismissed as a philosophical justification for unprincipled action, pragmatism is often merely identified with a methodology and theory of truth. It is therefore a misleading term for a rich and varied tradition that includes Peirce's semiotics; James's existential, phenomenological hermeneutics; Dewey's deconstructive and reconstructive social and political philosophy, radical educational proposals, and paradigm of experience as art; and Mead's explanation of the development of the individual through responsive transformation of the generalized Other. Apt comparisons can be made with other philosophical movements, but these are also misleading because of the unique configuration of Classical American pragmatic philosophy. Like Nietzsche, James has a genealogical deconstruction of values embedded in interpretive structures that have come to be taken as simply factual; but unlike Nietzsche, he argues for an inclusive, nonhierarchical pluralism. Like Marx, Dewey criticizes the hegemonic control of the means of production by industrialists and urges a democratically socialist government; but unlike Marx he develops a theory and strategy by which all disaffected groups, including but not limited to persons as workers, can and should actively contribute to a radical reconstruction of society. Again, unlike Marx, he has a carefully worked out psychology, logic, theory of knowledge, pedagogy, ethics and value theory, and aesthetics, all integral to his social and political philosophy.

Each of the classical American philosophers is remembered as much for his own original angle of vision as for what unites him to the others, thus making it very difficult to give any definition of pragmatism that does not falsify as much as it enlightens. To take an example, over the years Thelma Z. Lavine has connected American culture and classical American philosophy in a way that contrasts with Rorty's postmodernist approach. Her thesis is that pragmatism can best be understood as a sustained attempt to integrate what other contemporary philosophical perspectives have striven to separate, namely the two streams of modernism: enlightenment modernism and romantic modernism. She says that "within a nation whose national identity is established upon Enlightenment Modernist rationalistic principles of natural rights, democracy and science," American pragmatist philosophers attempted "to appropriate and integrate the dialectically opposite cognitive structure of Romantic Modernism."[27] They creatively and critically appropriated "the Enlightenment instrumentalism of science and technology and the Romantic expressiveness of personal and group life," changing the emphases of both in the process. "Organic unity, wholeness, community, group cohesion, communication, collectivism—by this language Dewey expresses the romantic quest for unification, for human community, and for communion with nature." Untypically, though, "he does not share the Romantic contempt for the bourgeoisie, for mass education or for democratic process." [28]

Since the two streams of modernity have sought to delegitimatize and demystify the claims of the other, it is no wonder that contemporary perspectives, such as positivism, phenomenology, analytic and other linguistic philosophies, existentialism, critical theory, action theory, hermeneutics, and postmodernism, which selectively emphasize one or the other, criticize pragmatism for contradictory reasons. For critical theorists its democratic inclusiveness insufficiently privileges a higher or transcendental moral order that ought to provide a check on the conclusions reached by less than ideal speaking communities. For analytic philosophers, on the other hand, its thesis that values configure even perception unacceptably renders subjective an epistemology that claims to be a view from nowhere. All such criticisms from extremes that are already synthesized in pragmatist philosophy miss the distinctiveness of the pragmatist turn.

Given the breadth and depth of this living tradition, I can select only a few themes that might be of interest to feminists and hope that the reader will be encouraged to pursue some of these insights further. Given most feminists' insistence that our theories should be continuous with our experiences and practices, it is at least plausible that one of the few philosophies to have developed in the United States should differentially reflect aspects of this North American culture and history that can be criticized, revalued, extended, but not simply ignored. Thinkers like Martin Heidegger, Michel Foucault, and Jürgen Habermas begin their philosophies by reworking and criticizing European philosophy, culture, and politics as a basis for developing their own unique insights. Many philosophers have been strangely reluctant to do the same with philosophies developed in the United States. Surely our analyses would be enriched and deepened by rediscovering one of our own philosophic traditions. Postmodernists have sought to deconstruct, not privilege, Eurocentric culture, but they have not simply ignored it. Recovering pragmatism would put the rediscovery and development of local, national, and international feminist theoretical and practical traditions in a usable context. In the process we would discover valuable resources that have been neglected, along with androcentric biases that should be exposed and rejected.

A case in point is feminist's revisioning of psychoanalysis. Through various critical transformations virtually all of them trace back to Freud and his followers or dissidents. That French feminists such as Luce Irigaray and Julia Kristeva should do so is to be expected. It is part of their cultural heritage. As Betty Friedan pointed out in *The Feminine Mystique*, it is also part of ours and is responsible for some dimensions of women's oppression. But despite hyperbolic claims, neither Freud nor Lacan, nor anyone else for that matter, can represent Western ontology as such. An alternative cultural, person-centered model of psychology is developed in William James's *Principles of Psychology*. The neglect it has suffered is all the more surprising in view of the fact that one of "psychology's preeminent historian[s], E. G. Boring, listed James as one of the four greatest psychologists, along with Darwin, Helmholtz, and Freud." [29] From the beginning, the book had an international as well as a national reputation and influenced such diverse philosophers as Husserl and Wittgenstein.

Perhaps its neglect is due to the fact that, unlike Freud, James did not make sexuality the central issue of his psychology. Its absence is indeed conspicuous and might well invite feminist analysis. For feminists eager to develop a psychology that does not reduce human consciousness to sexual consciousness, however, there is still much of interest, including his rejection of Humean atomism in favor of a holistic view of consciousness, his rejection of reductionism and defense of the many worlds of experience, his anti-essentialism, his stress on relations, and his process view of the self as developing interactively with historical, cultural, and social conditions. [30] On the other hand, his sexist views on women are also—fortunately—not so well known as Freud's, nor have they been as influential. Consequently they have not yet received a thorough feminist criticism, such as I begin to develop in chapter 6.

Since feminist consciousness-raising depends on linking the particularity of each participant's point of view to the larger social dimensions in which it is embedded, thus redirecting personal blame for dysfunctionalism to social and political analysis of the multidimensionality of sexism, the neglect of Dewey's trenchant social criticism is even more surprising. Jürgen Habermas examines German philosophy and ideology, and he extends his critique of German society to other postindustrial societies. Foucault makes a similar move from French to other postmodern societies. By contrast, most American feminists in social and political philosophy look exclusively to European philosophers for models, even when applying them to our national scene in the United States. This would be understandable if we had no philosophical predecessors who engaged in social and political discourse. But since we have a vigorous pragmatist tradition of philosophical critique of American culture and institutions, feminist analyses are impoverished by neglecting it, just as pragmatist analyses are impoverished by neglecting the many groundbreaking feminist social and political analyses. Dewey's writings span every major and many minor social, political, cultural, and economic issues from the 1880s to the 1950s.[31] Unless we respond to them, to criticize, appropriate, or transform the analyses, those of us who do philosophy in the United States or who are affected by its decisions and its power risk falling into the essentialism and false universalism that follows from neglecting our own historical circumstances.[32]

I will emphasize throughout those aspects of pragmatism that have the most to offer an evolving feminism and those aspects of feminist theory that can best reconstruct an evolving pragmatism. Because of the transactive character of any such engaged communicative encounter, these positions cannot simply be taken over. As we appropriate what is valuable in each other's perspective, the distortions in our own perspective, as viewed from theirs, must also be acknowledged, and this recognition will affect the character of what remains.

$\mathscr{T}wo$

The Missing Perspectives:
Where Are All the Pragmatist Feminists
and Feminist Pragmatists?

"Is Liberal Feminism Oxymoronic?" The student in an American studies graduate course who gave her term paper this title answered her own question affirmatively. Liberal feminism is oxymoronic, she said, because "it is both internally inconsistent and severely restrictive in the pursuit and achievement of feminist goals." [1] The shortcomings all applied to the individualistic liberalism that John Dewey also cogently attacked in *Individualism Old and New*, one of the course texts (*LW* 5:41–123). But although she used extensively feminist criticisms of liberalism from the perspective of Marxist socialism, pragmatist criticisms were virtually absent from her paper. The reason soon became obvious: none of the feminist literature that served as the basis of her critique appropriated or referred to Dewey's writings. Why not?

This question parallels another that has long bothered me: Why aren't there more pragmatist philosophers writing on feminist issues? Five years ago, in a search for articles combining feminist and pragmatist perspectives in philosophy I could not find enough to put together an edited volume. [2] This chapter was occasioned by my disappointing search for other pragmatist feminist voices. It is exploratory and tentative— more a plea born of frustration than a sustained defense of a thesis. The issue of the paucity of pragmatist feminist analyses is not being raised merely to convict pragmatism of the same shortcomings exhibited by any theory that is not explicitly feminist. Rather, the very suitability of pragmatism to feminist reconstruction leads me to raise the issue. My explicit agenda is to arouse interest in exploring the mutual benefits of a feminist pragmatism and a pragmatist feminism. I am convinced that pragmatist theory has resources for feminist theory untapped by other approaches and that feminism, in turn, can uniquely reinvigorate pragmatism.

In the first section of this chapter I point out the absence of the

American tradition of pragmatism in most feminist discourse and make some suggestions to account for this fact. The equally puzzling lack of a tradition of feminist theorizing from a pragmatist perspective is explained in the second section by the lack of references to women's writings in histories and collections of philosophy in America—or their marginalization when they are acknowledged—and to the absence of any theory of sexual discrimination or recognition of gender bias in the works of the Classical American philosophers. I then seek to encourage the rediscovery of women pragmatists as a first step in examining their contributions to both feminism and pragmatism. Pragmatism seems to me to exhibit a recognizably feminine style, a point developed in the fourth section of the chapter, partly in order to help account for its marginalization but also to encourage feminist interest in this exception to what has been called the exaggerated masculinity of much of the Western philosophical tradition. Finally, I mention a few features that feminism and pragmatism share. Particularly significant is their recourse to the practices and institutions of everyday life, both to dismantle the social and political structures of oppression and to develop better alternatives.

1. THE ECLIPSE OF PRAGMATISM

It is sometimes incorrectly assumed that pragmatism is missing from formal classifications of feminism because it continues to make liberal assertions about the isolated individual, because it advocates the public-private split, or because it is scientistic. Richard Rorty's neopragmatism gives some substance to the first two assumptions, but he has also been criticized by other pragmatist philosophers for rejecting, among other things, the social and political dimensions of the pragmatist tradition.[3] A more likely hypothesis is that the ascendancy of logical positivism after World War II eclipsed pragmatism for reasons that feminists would reject. Pragmatism never disappeared. It was marginalized. Generations of philosophy students grew up mostly ignorant of it or, worse, were inoculated against it by the newly dominant philosophical mainstream of analytic philosophy, the assumption being that anything worthwhile about pragmatism had already been assimilated into the very different agendas of Wilfred Sellars, W. V. O. Quine, Nelson Goodman, and Hilary Putnam.[4]

On the other hand, it has sometimes been claimed that all feminists are pragmatists.[5] This assertion could be explored as part of feminist reconstructions of pragmatism, but in this book *pragmatism, pragmatic,* and *pragmatist* refer to a historically specific philosophical movement. Since pragmatism is a living tradition and not a deductive system, there are many varieties of pragmatist theory, ranging from the more architectonic semiotics based on Peirce to a fallibilist pluralism derived from James.[6] Specific claims will be more true or more false of some pragmatists than others. But in order to begin recovering both the developmental history of feminism and pragmatism and varying degrees of awareness of that history, I will continue using the general definitions of pragmatism given in the first chapter as constituting its core set of family resemblances in Wittgenstein's sense.

Pragmatism influenced the development of the humanities and social sciences in America, particularly philosophy, psychology, sociology, political science, American studies, and education. Therefore, feminists seeking to ground analyses in their historical cultural context can further develop the objective basis of the feminist revisioning of these same disciplines by examining pragmatism's theoretical contributions. Like Marxism, what has been developed in its name has sometimes been antithetical to its best original insights. Just as feminists are questioning the assumptions and omissions of the various disciplines, so are contemporary pragmatists questioning the disciplinary developments falsely attributed to pragmatist theory.[7]

From the beginning, pragmatism appealed to women thinkers and activists who found in it a movement within which they could work for a new intellectual and social order. Katherine Camp Mayhew and Anna Camp Edwards hasten to allay suspicions of male dominance that might be aroused by the title of their book, *The Dewey School*. They chose the title in gratitude for Dewey's having made possible the Laboratory School of the University of Chicago "by his objective and impersonal attitude of faith in the growing ability of every individual, whether child or teacher." They deny that Dewey was ever dominating and testify that he respected the opinions of even the youngest and least experienced members of his staff. They speak from their own experience. Mayhew was vice principal and head of the science department, while Edwards was a teacher of history and later a special tutor, interacting with all the disciplinary departments for the older students. The intellectual appeal of pragmatism was grounded in an absolute respect of one for the other: "Only a person who has worked in such an atmosphere can understand what inspiration to creative work such freedom gives."[8]

If pragmatism has so much to offer feminist theory, one may well wonder at its nearly total absence in contemporary feminist discourses. A handful of articles bring together pragmatism and feminism, but until quite recently there was no general recognition that such a concretely different angle of vision existed.[9] One will look in vain in books on feminist theory to see it even listed as one among other positions. Alison Jaggar, for instance, organizes her book *Feminist Politics and Human Na-*

ture around "the major versions of contemporary feminism," which are taken to be liberal feminism, Marxist feminism, radical feminism, and socialist feminism.[10] Although Rosemarie Tong recognizes eight classifications of feminism in *Feminist Thought,* she makes no mention of pragmatist feminism.[11]

Such categories are certainly based on an analysis of the content of actual writings, but categorization itself is political or normative; that is, these categories appear obvious given a certain perspective, with its assumptions, values, and goals. Jaggar, in fact, clearly frames her presentation with the recognition that general agreement on "the appropriate criteria for evaluating normative and scientific theories" does not lead to universal judgments because of disagreements over "what counts as evidence, on what are the data that need explanation and on which explanations are illuminating." She argues that "the most politically appropriate and theoretically illuminating interpretations of theoretical desiderata are those associated with socialist feminism."[12] It is not a criticism to point out that the cogency of her own arguments depends on the acceptance of the same socialist feminist framework of legitimation that is adopted in the text.

I also think that some version of social feminism best captures feminism's political goals and theoretical interpretations. Unfortunately, Jaggar's categories have rendered invisible my version of social feminism, which is pragmatist feminism. According to her schema, pragmatism would perhaps be classified as a version of liberalism, but by the same logic Marxism would be categorized as a version of idealism. Only if Marx can be accused of being an idealist because he drew on Hegelian philosophy could pragmatism be reductively viewed simply as a version of liberalism. But Marx "materialized" Hegel, just as the pragmatists "socialized" liberalism. In both cases the changes were significant enough to merit a new classification. Moreover, the biggest influence on Dewey and Mead was Hegel, not Hume or Locke. James, for his part, radicalized empiricism by starting with the concrete situation in which relationships are given and sense data are abstracted through selective interests.

The problem with any classification is that, as the French sociologist Pierre Bourdieu points out, it gives too much power to the theorist to hierarchize positions, privileging one's own at the top or the center and subordinating or marginalizing the rest.[13] James recognized as "vicious intellectualism" the related problem of "the treating of a name as excluding from the fact named what the name's definition fails positively to include."[14] According to this practice, if there are other aspects of pragmatism that do not fit under the labels of liberalism or reformism, or even contradict these two, they can be ignored.

But Jaggar cannot be blamed for marginalizing pragmatism, which was already in eclipse long before she began to write. It may seem strange to talk about the marginalization of pragmatism in the wake of its resurgence, largely in response to Rorty's dramatic rejection of the bankruptcy of analytic philosophy. But these recent developments cannot obscure the fact of widespread ignorance of the major theories and texts of pragmatism, a philosophical position that was once acknowledged as central to "the golden age of American philosophy." There is a bit of the social Darwinist in all of us that assumes it was a tradition tried and found wanting and had therefore ceased to be a central part of the philosophy curriculum. But from my perspective it seems to have been criticized and eventually relegated to the margins for holding the very positions that feminists today would find to be its greatest strengths. These include early and persistent criticisms of positivist interpretations of scientific methodology; disclosure of the value dimension of factual claims; reclaiming aesthetics as informing everyday experience; linking of dominant discourses with domination; subordinating logical analysis to social, cultural, and political issues; realigning theory with praxis; and resisting the turn to epistemology and instead emphasizing concrete experience.[15] Thomas McCarthy, for one, notes the enormous influence of the human sciences and the liberating potential of sociohistorical research on Continental philosophy and American pragmatism, and he suggests that James and Dewey were ignored by analytic philosophers because "it was not always possible to overlook [their] appropriation of the human sciences," as was possible in the case of Peirce.[16]

The early pragmatists located reflection in its actual historical, psychological, economic, political, and cultural context and defined its goal as the intelligent overcoming of oppressive conditions. According to Cornel West, they influenced engaged public philosophers as much as they did professional philosophers. The pragmatist belief that theory unrelated to practice is moribund inspired some of their more radical students to abandon purely conceptual philosophical analysis. West points out that C. Wright Mills, a student of Dewey, gave up philosophy after earning his M.A. and turned to social theory, declaring war on Talcott Parsons's sociology because it supported the corporate liberal establishment. W. E. B. Du Bois "also gave up philosophy after studying under William James at Harvard, turning to the study of history and society."[17] The retreat of academic philosophers to their ivory towers and away from the pragmatists' active engagement in the problems of their day is an indictment not of pragmatism but of academic philosophy. James anticipated this development and warned against it to no avail in "The Ph.D. Octopus."[18] If the pragmatists had succeeded in stopping philosophers from turning their backs on active engagement in solving society's most pressing problems, then feminists of our generation would not have had to endure the continuing struggle both to break into academia and to deinstitutionalize and open up academic deliberations to the wider community.

Against the newly ascendant positivist model legislating value neutrality for the social sciences, the pragmatists called for active engagement.[19] They both attacked the supposed neutrality as a self-deceptive mask for unacknowledged interests and advocated a radical social agenda. The social sciences themselves were to be advocates for transformation rather than upholders of the status quo and instruments for the enhancement of power of one segment of the society against another. The subtitle to Dewey's *Human Nature and Conduct* is *An Introduction to Social Psychology*. The great issues of self-determination, exploration of values, and problems of community living are not taken as addenda to the science of social psychology; they are at its very heart. In Dewey's words: "Why employ language, cultivate literature, acquire and develop science, sustain industry, and submit to the refinements of art? To ask these questions is equivalent to asking: 'Why live?' The only question having sense which can be asked is *how* we are going to use and be used by these things, not whether we are going to use them. Reason, moral principles, cannot in any case be shoved behind these affairs, for reason and morality grow out of them" (*MW* 14:57–58). The first internationally acclaimed book in American psychology, James's *Principles of Psychology* (1890), was also criticized in early reviews for importing moral issues into a book whose purpose was to distinguish a separate, empirical psychology from armchair philosophical psychology.

Since the pragmatists aimed at democratic inclusiveness, they—with the notable exception of Peirce—fought the development of a specialized disciplinary jargon inaccessible except to a specialist elite.[20] Marilyn French shows how such mechanisms of exclusion have unfairly impacted on women over the centuries.[21] In connecting "high style" with patriarchy, she renders plausible my contention that this is one more factor in the displacement of pragmatism by theories elaborated in increasingly technical vocabularies. One need only compare Dewey's *Logic: The Theory of Inquiry* with the dominant position now accorded symbolic logic (LW 12). James held that "*technical* writing on *philosophical* subjects . . . is certainly a crime against the human race."[22] And Dewey criticized science for being highly abstract and technically specialized and for utilizing vocabularies and symbol systems that are impenetrable to the uninitiated. He calls this state of affairs a disaster because it renders "the things of the environment unknown and incommunicable by human beings in terms of their own activities and sufferings."[23]

In seeking to answer the question of why pragmatism was marginalized from mainstream philosophy, I have drawn on my feelings and my recollections of how feminism was rediscovered a few decades after World War II. The first responses to accusations that there were no great women artists, scientists, writers, and so forth, was to point out their exclusion from the social, educational, and professional ambience of male productivity. This early response led to critical and detailed studies of the mechanisms of exclusion. Closely following on this early response was the claim that there were talented women in the past, perhaps even women of genius, but they tended to be exceptionally situated and served as spokeswomen for the establishment, such as Queen Elizabeth I. By now the search was on. Mary Wollstonecraft's *Vindication of the Rights of Woman*, published in 1792, was at first thought to be one of the earliest voices raised in explicit protest. But by dint of research to recover our heritage, we have come to see that she did not spring up out of nowhere; she was herself part of a long line of feminist voices that receded into the dim past.[24] Each new discovery raised new questions. If feminist women existed in the past, why didn't we know about them? How had they become invisible? The answers have given concrete content to the theoretical claim that women's intellectual contributions were not just forgotten but were actively suppressed.[25]

The recovery of a history of feminist writings has also contributed to defining some common features of feminist thought, which is otherwise extremely diverse. These two features are (1) the identification and investigation of the oppressive structures that contribute to women's subordination in order to actively dismantle them; and (2) the development of analyses of women's experiences that are not systematically distorted by sexist assumptions. Moreover, like most socially conscious philosophical theorizing, feminist philosophy engages in two distinct but interrelated tasks: negative criticism and positive theory construction. It points out the ways women have been excluded from philosophy, both as practitioners and as subject matter and the misogyny or unquestioned male prerogative that is both the cause and the effect of such exclusion. It further reveals how the absence and denigration of women have affected both the profession and its work by disguising a masculine perspective as a neutral, human one. Positively, feminist philosophers have made numerous contributions to virtually every area of philosophy, sometimes by building on traditional positions after they have been purged of androcentric assumptions, sometimes by developing original analyses, and always by recovering women whose work has been neglected or ignored in the public transmission of the exemplary contributions of the discipline.

I am not arguing that the loss of our pragmatic heritage is comparable to the suffering of women under various forms of patriarchal domination and millennia of misogynist beliefs and practices. But I am suggesting that unless we continue to explore the reasons for the omission of pragmatism from core curricula of philosophy, the myth will persist that something vital is lacking in pragmatism itself, rather than in the philosophical milieu.[26] It would be a shame if the same forces that succeeded for so long in denying that feminist issues were properly philosophical were to succeed in convincing feminists to neglect that very part of our American philosophical tradition that radically joined theory with praxis. If it is true that pragmatism declined in influence just to the extent that it challenged the rejection by professional philosophers of their role as cultural critic and scorned the pseudoscientism that reduced philosophy to supposedly value-free epistemology, then feminists have good reasons for reclaiming it as an ally.[27] Moreover, if the history of feminism is any precedent, we should also expect to generate an evolving redefinition of pragmatism, one that explicitly raises feminist issues and includes women's contributions.

2. NOW YOU SEE THEM, NOW YOU DON'T: WOMEN IN THE HISTORY OF AMERICAN PHILOSOPHY

Feminist philosophers could not have ignored pragmatism for so long if pragmatist philosophers had not demonstrated a comparable blindness to female philosophers and feminist philosophy. To illustrate the absence of women in the history of classical American philosophy, I have cursorily examined the indexes of three major history books of philosophy in America by pragmatist philosophers.[28] For many philosophers the introduction to and standard history of American philosophy was Herbert W. Schneider's *History of American Philosophy*.[29] Schneider's index is primarily, but not exclusively, a name index. Out of approximately 608 entries I counted seven who were recognizably women. The page numbers listed for four of those women refer only to bibliographical entries in the "Guide to Recent Literature," which was compiled with the assistance of Gerald Runkle. Elizabeth Flower, Anne V. Schlabach, and Ola E. Winslow each have one page reference to a bibliographical entry, and Adrienne Koch has three references. One woman listed in the index, Mary Whiton Calkins, cannot be found on the page given.

Of the remaining two women whose page listings refer to the body of the text, Jane Addams is allotted one line for applying John Dewey's theory of democracy to urban society and international relations. The ideas of only one woman, Frances Wright, are discussed, and she has five entries, the most listed for a woman. By way of comparison, a random selection for references to males yields the names of three French romanticists said to have influenced Orestes Augustus Brownson. There are four entries for Cousin, one for Constant, none for Leroux, and twelve for Brownson.

We might guess that the recognition of women's philosophical achievements and intellectual influence gets better the closer we come to our own time. The first sentence of the first chapter of Elizabeth Flower and Murray G. Murphey's two-volume history is not promising: "The men who settled America were not philosophers." [30] Does this perhaps imply that the women were? Or does it mean that no women settled America? The answer to both questions is negative, of course, but the fact that the absence of women from the history of philosophy in America is so obviously taken for granted provides evidence of the pernicious effects of even an unconscious bias against, or blindness toward the possibility of, women as philosophers. [31]

In Flower and Murphey's "Index of Names," which contains approximately 720 entries, I found ten entries for women. Nine had a single page reference. The exception is Margaret Fuller, with two references. In the first she is listed as one among other transcendentalists who were Unitarians but not ministers (1, 400); in the other, we are told that Emerson wrote to her (2, 506). Jane Addams is mentioned in a single sentence in connection with Dewey (2, 825), and Alice Chipman is credited with broadening her husband's outlook (2, 823). Mrs. Cheney appears as one name on a list of lecturers at the Concord School (2, 506). Christine Ladd-Franklin is on a list of people who had been contacted by Peirce, and Gertrude Stein appears on a list of people James knew (2, 568, 636). Esther Stoddard is given as the mother of Jonathan Edwards (1, 139). Although Beatrice Webb is listed in the index, her name does not actually appear on page 486; instead, she is subsumed in the phrase "the Fabian Society of the Webbs."

Dale Carnegie, Adrianus Heereboord, and Christopher Columbus are important enough to the history of philosophy in America to be listed in the index, but Charlotte Perkins Gilman, Matilda Joslyn Gage, Susan B. Anthony, Sojourner Truth, Mary Whiton Calkins, Antoinette Brown Blackwell, Ida B. Wells-Barnett, Emma Goldman, and Margaret Sanger are not. Leonhard Euler has three entries, Mary Wollstonecraft none. John Stuart Mill gets twenty-nine references, Harriet Taylor Mill none. And women's invisibility in the histories of philosophy in America has to do with more than relative numbers. It also involves what is said about them when they do make an appearance. Except for one lecturer and two queens, Mary and Elizabeth I, the women mentioned in Flower and Murphey's book are included for their contributions as wives, mothers, acquaintances, and supporters of famous men. There is not a single line about the substance of any woman's contribution to philosophy in the three hundred years covered.

Fifty-two columns of a combined subject and name index yielded the names of twelve women in H. S. Thayer's *Meaning and Action: A Critical*

History of Pragmatism. Gertrude Ezorski, Evelyn U. Shirk, and Susan L. Stebbing are mentioned in footnote references to their books, which are listed in the bibliography.[32] Four are mentioned in their relations to the classical American pragmatists: Jane Addams and Ella Flagg Young (not indexed) as close friends of Dewey, and Harriet Fay and Juliette Froissy as wives of Peirce. Mrs. Humphrey Ward's "popular novel" is given because Dewey wrote to correct her picture of Green's philosophy. Maria Theresa, empress of Austria, takes a bow, and a woman figures as one of a pair of fictional characters, Pyramus and Thisbe. As in the other two books, women appear chiefly as appendages to men.

Two women philosophers do share most of the references to women: eight for Christine Ladd-Franklin, and seven for Lady Victoria Welby (one listing of each having misprints). But only Welby's philosophy is actually discussed. An entry for Ladd-Franklin names her as one in a list of Peirce's students, and the six other references are actually to a letter written to her by Peirce, which was published in an article of hers. Three footnote references to Lady Victoria Welby point out letters sent to her by Peirce, Bradley, and Vailati. The other four references, one covering four pages, contain substantial discussion of her philosophical importance. Lest one conclude that women fare no better than lesser-known men, or that only philosophers or only Americans are included, it should be pointed out that such obscure figures as Berengarius of Tours, an eleventh-century dialectician, E. P. B. Waible, and James Harvey Robinson were judged to be worth noting and indexing.

These three books have not been selected because they are shockingly bad examples of the academic neglect of women's intellectual contributions or because histories of American philosophy or philosophy in America are any worse than general histories of philosophy.[33] On the contrary, they were picked because they are typical and central to our understanding, as American philosophers, of our own history. The fact that of the hundreds of philosophers collectively mentioned in the three books, only two women's contributions (Wright's and Welby's) were judged significant enough to merit more than a passing reference, tells us something about our perception of women's roles in general and about women as philosophers in particular. It is time we examined that something, which has for too long gone unrecognized. Thanks to the post-World War II revival of feminism it is now possible to question a whole range of hidden assumptions involving women and culturally transmitted views of masculinity and femininity. Feminists have shown how these assumptions infect even such supposedly gender-free analyses as metaphysics, epistemology, and logic.

Pragmatist philosophy has not yet been adequately subjected to feminist criticism or transformed by feminist revisioning.[34] As a first step, this would entail examining the attitudes toward women, women's issues, and the feminine in the writings of the classical American pragmatists and their successors in order to determine how these attitudes have influenced the substance of their philosophies. Without this first step of acknowledging and rejecting in pragmatist writings (and in ourselves) attitudes toward women that range from benign neglect to outright misogyny, we have no basis from which to develop a positive pragmatist feminism. We still have to wait for such a fundamental evaluation of pragmatism as Robin May Schott, for instance, has provided in regard to Kant.[35]

A good place to begin is with Dewey's occasional remarks about women and the philosophical relevance of analyses of gender. He said in 1911 that "there is no important adjustment in society into which the proper relation of the sexes does not enter."[36] If this rather startling assertion is the case, then it would follow that the examination of the relations of women and men must be central to social and political philosophy. But although John Dewey did, in fact, make the assertion, he did not follow it up in his own philosophy. The reason can be found in the context of the remark. It is given as a justification for his support of coeducation in the *Ladies' Home Journal.* Much like John Stuart Mill, who also argued that society would not be fully liberated until women were, but who did not incorporate his arguments in *On the Subjection of Women* into his other works, Dewey's examination of women's roles in society was mostly limited to brief remarks in his polemical writings. It has been left to feminist theorists to move women and women's issues from the margins to the center of philosophic discourse.

Even though women and issues concerning women were not central to the philosophical reflections of the classical American pragmatist philosophers, their unexamined preconceptions about women nonetheless affect their arguments and therefore should be made explicit. This can be demonstrated by expanding the context of the publication of Dewey's article on coeducation to include its theoretical framework. The relation of the sexes is said to affect all of society's adjustments because of the place of women in the family and the importance of the family to the well-being of society. But her primary identity within the family is given from the male point of view: "As a wife the woman is in relation to a man" (*MW* 6:161). The correlative fact that, as husbands, men are in relation to women is not drawn because men do not define themselves in relation to women or receive their primary identity as husbands or fathers.

In his *Journal* article Dewey stresses that all social advances depend on the mutual cooperation of men and women in their shared interests and that this cannot come about unless both women and men sympathetically grasp "the point of view and method of the other" (*MW* 6:162). Moreover, coeducation is said to be advantageous to society because it prepares women for vocations and social careers outside the home, while not neglecting their role within it. Whether Dewey's progressive views or his traditional ones are emphasized depends both on one's own point of view and goal in doing so.[37]

For my part, I would point out that although he contributed to undermining many prejudices against women, Dewey still seems to have viewed them primarily as homemakers. My criticism is not just that he ends his article by praising the scientific preparation coeducational colleges give women for "parenthood and household management" but that this domestic framework prevented him from exploring the many other ways that the unequal relations between women and men affect society. The issue of women's unequal and less powerful position in the family and in the larger society is not even raised as an issue that needs to be addressed, although he hints that some men oppose women's coeducation because they fear that women's intellectual abilities are so superior to theirs that young men will be discouraged from pursuing academic studies (*MW* 6:159). It seems to me that Dewey successfully challenged some prejudices against women and supported specific women's rights, but he did not deepen his analyses of the causes of women's oppression nor extend these insights into his thinking in general because, like many other male philosophers, he neither shared in women's experiences nor was sufficiently motivated to focus on women's issues.[38] The unfortunate outcome was that women remained on the margins of pragmatism.

I am not criticizing Dewey for being of his time and place, especially since he so often exposed commonly held prejudicial assumptions and actively campaigned for women's rights. In fact, I think that he satisfies the criteria Sandra Harding gives for being counted a feminist at least as well as do her other instances of male philosophers who have made important contributions to feminist thought, namely, Mill, Marx, and Engels. Like them, too, his "writings are certainly controversial and, at best, imperfect; but so, too, are the writings of the most insightful women thinkers of these periods or, for that matter, in the present day."[39] My intention is to encourage recognition of the transformations that must occur when pragmatism is rethought from the perspective of decades of recent feminist analyses. Assumptions about women affected not only the personal relations of individual pragmatists; they entered into the very fabric of their philosophical thought. The precise ways that these assumptions about women affected pragmatist metaphysical and epistemological issues as well as social and political ones must be explored in depth before the positive aspects of pragmatist analysis can be fully appropriated by feminists. And unless pragmatists recognize that something is lacking or distorted in their own theoretical analyses, there can be no incentive for remedying the situation.

In *The Promised Land: The Great Black Migration and How It Changed America,* Nicholas Lemann examines the enormous migration of African-American people from the rural South to the metropolitan North—over a million and a half between the First World War and the Great Depression.[40] He uses the life of Ruby Lee Daniels to personalize and unify the historical narrative. But he nearly missed doing so because her initial interviews did not stand out from the rest. While routinely rechecking a fact with her, even more interesting ones came to light. She explained why the earlier interview was unproductive: "You didn't ask me the right questions. I've had a very interesting life and have lots of stories to tell."

Thanks to feminist research of the last decades, we can now challenge Dewey's 1919 statement in "Philosophy and Democracy" that "women have as yet made little contribution to philosophy." The sentence that follows it, however, is as relevant today as when it was written: "But when women who are not mere students of other persons' philosophy set out to write it, we cannot conceive that it will be the same in viewpoint or tenor as that composed from the standpoint of the different masculine experience of things" (*MW* 11: 45). Women have led interesting lives and have lots of stories to tell. Pragmatism has more resources than have yet been tapped. We just need to ask the right questions.

3. CHALLENGING THE CANON: WOMEN PRAGMATISTS

If my assumption that pragmatism is congenial to feminism is correct, then one would expect to find enthusiastic women pragmatists in the heyday of pragmatism in the late nineteenth and early twentieth centuries. My limited research indicates that this is indeed the case but that these women have fallen through the cracks of patriarchal public memory and need to be rediscovered. In the absence of any feminist biography of Jane Addams, "the most outstanding progressive activist in the U.S.," how can we assess her influence on Dewey and vice versa?[41] Pragmatism's white male pantheon needs to be expanded to include women's contributions, including those of people of color, much as West does in *The American Evasion of Philosophy.*

I expect that my own attempts to recover women whose pragmatism bolstered their feminism will be superseded by further research. It is well known that James, Dewey, and Mead had many enthusiastic women students, but their names are barely known, let alone their philosophic positions. Lucy Sprague was a student at Radcliffe College in the 1890s, studied with James at Harvard, and went on to a distinguished career in education. It is better known that Gertrude Stein studied with James. But so did Mary Whiton Calkins, who was not only the first woman to be president of the American Philosophical Association, but was elected president of the American Psychological Association. She also studied with Josiah Royce. And Christine Ladd-Franklin was a member of Peirce's first class at Johns Hopkins.

The influence was not one-sided. Lynn D. Gordon tells us that "Sprague's student themes demonstrate that she challenged her teacher's views on the grounds that they excluded women's experiences from their discussions and approached such issues as free will versus determinism from a male-oriented perspective." [42] Mary Mahowald points out that Peirce's first wife, Melusina Fay Peirce, was a feminist who "called for cooperative housekeeping as essential to the establishment of sexual equality" and that Dewey credited Jane Addams with educating him about women's rights.[43] Emma Goldman was a friend of Dewey's, one whom he publicly defended against scurrilous attacks. Lynne Adrian suggests that Goldman's concept of artful living may have influenced Dewey's aesthetics.[44] Like Dewey, Mead actively supported women's suffrage and worked with Jane Addams and Ellen Gates Starr at Hull House. He discussed his manuscripts with Irene Tufts Mead, who also assisted in their publication.[45] Continuity with these pioneers was broken because of a double marginalization. Women's theoretical contributions were not acknowledged by pragmatists, and by the time feminism was reborn yet again in the 1960s few women philosophy students had much acquaintance with pragmatism.

I suspect that the pragmatist influence on some current feminist positions is not so much absent as invisible. Just recently I serendipitously discovered such a hidden connection. Only when Sidney Ratner received the Herbert Schneider Award in 1989 for his contributions to American philosophy did I learn that his wife, Louise M. Rosenblatt, was the first person to develop the reader-response theory of literature in her 1938 book, *Literature as Exploration,* later more systematically presented in *The Reader the Text the Poem: The Transactional Theory of the Literary Work.*[46] It is an interesting case of degrees of marginalization and the mechanisms of disappearance. Rosenblatt is virtually unknown in philosophy, either to feminist or pragmatist philosophers, despite the fact that her literary theory is based on pragmatism, specifically on Dewey's theory of transaction, and despite the fact that reader-response theory is so central to one branch of feminist literary theory.[47]

Dewey's theory of transaction replaces that of the Cartesian isolated ego that inaugurated the modern alienation of subject and object. Both subject and object are interactively constituted within a horizon of social praxis. Changing the gender in Dewey's explanation gives us the following:

> An experience is always what it is because of a transaction taking place between an individual and what, at the time, constitutes her environment, whether the latter consists of persons with whom she is talking about some topic or event, the subject talked about being also a part of the situation; or the toys with which she is playing; the book she is reading . . . ; or the materials of an experiment she is performing. The environment, in other words, is whatever conditions interact with personal needs, desires, purposes, and capacities to create the experience which is had.[48]

Rosenblatt herself did not fully explore the radical consequences of either pragmatism or feminism, but this alone cannot account for her neglect. Her virtual disappearance is a salutary reminder that not only does the dominant philosophic discourse marginalize other discourses, such as feminism, pragmatism, phenomenology, and Marxism, but that the groups so marginalized also have their centers and margins.[49]

The very effort needed to recover women pragmatists points to a more substantial reason for the dearth of pragmatist feminists. With the exception of Dewey's brief polemical addresses supporting women's issues, women as such do not figure much in pragmatist writings, not even in those of women writing in the pragmatist tradition. Moreover, James's views of women were consistent with the Victorian era's patriarchal tradition, rather than with the more radical movements of the time. Pragmatists often criticize the social and political oppressions of class, race, nationalism, ethnic origin, and monopolistic capitalism, but not of sex. This absence may be partially ameliorated by widening the circle of those who are considered pragmatists, as Maureen L. Egan does by including Charlotte Perkins Gilman because she shared some of the ideas and interests that would eventually be known as pragmatist.[50] However, the lack of specific analyses of women's oppression in pragmatism will only be overcome by explicitly feminist reconstructions of pragmatist theory.

4. FEMININE STYLE

Two aspects of pragmatist theory that I suspect contributed to the marginalizing of pragmatism should also make the theory particularly attractive to feminist reconstruction. One is its explicit linking of categorizations with value judgments. The pragmatists' position that human knowledge always instantiates particular perspectives, including values, ran strongly counter to the rising tide of positivist ideology espousing the neutrality of science and the objectivity of pure observation. Claims about reality are political. The power to name is exercised most extensively by the dominant forces—individual and institutional—in powerful economic and social positions, but it rightly belongs to every human being.

The other feature of pragmatism is more subtle. Indeed, without recent feminist analyses uncovering the gender assumptions and relations influencing modes of discourse, it could not even be recognized or named. On a scale of traits, assumptions, and positions that range from stereotypically masculine to stereotypically feminine, pragmatism (again excepting Peirce) appears far more feminine than masculine. Among the various aspects contributing to this feeling are a penchant for indirect, metaphorical discourse rather than a deductive and reductively symbolic one and the concreteness of pragmatist methodology. Such concreteness stresses the experiential basis of theory and problematic situations over traditional textbook puzzles and abstract conceptual distinctions. The pragmatist goal of philosophical discourse, which is shared understanding and communal problem solving rather than rationally forced conclusions, is more feminine than masculine, as is its valuing of inclusiveness and community over exaggerated claims of autonomy and detachment. The same can be said for its developmental rather than rule-governed ethics.

This feminine rather than masculine style may help account for why I was drawn to pragmatism in the first place and have continued to find it emotionally sustaining as well as intellectually attractive. I would not go so far as Gilman does in her statement that "the whole feminine attitude toward life differs essentially from the masculine, because of her superior adaptation to the service of others." The differences are not essential, but socially constructed, and women are not always superior to men in their service to others. Nonetheless, social differences are real—if contestable—differences, and women's generally greater sensitivity to the nuances of relationships is by now well documented. Their greater presence in the service sector of the economy does not reflect greater adaptation to service but social patterns of deliberate exclusion from prestigious and well-paying jobs as well as the devaluation of service skills by those with the power to avoid sharing in their more onerous aspects. Still, Gilman's belief that women's philosophy and religion will differ from men's because of their different attitudes toward life seems borne out in the varieties of feminist philosophies and religious theories that have developed since her time. She attributes the differences between women's and men's attitudes toward life to two contrasting principles. On the side of men, "the principle of struggle, conflict, competition, the results of which make our 'economic problems.' On the other, the principle of growth, of culture, of applying service and nourishment in order to produce improvement."[51] Not only are her feminine principles remarkably similar to pragmatist ones, but her characterization of the alternative, masculine principles sounds like pragmatist criticisms of theories and social and political arrangements that express a will to dominate instead of a will to cooperate.

I am not the only one to make these connections. Mahowald finds feminine elements in pragmatism and suggests that this may have been due to direct feminist influence. She cites Royce's emphasis on community, which refers "more to the relationships that exist among individuals than to their collective or aggregate status," as what attracted her to his writings.[52] She also cautions against confusing feminine characteristics with feminist analyses, which explicitly expose and reject the sexist oppression of women. Challenging the naturalness of the cluster of traits attributed to the feminine in various cultures and examining the negative consequences for women of such beliefs has constituted a significant aspect of feminist theories. Such theories in turn have been criticized for ignoring other factors, such as race and class. Many of the traits associated with femininity in Europe and the United States reflect the cultural, social, and economic characteristics of whites rather than of blacks, and this can also account for feelings of familiarity with or alienation from the perceived feminine aspects of pragmatism. This encoding of whiteness in stereotypical models of femininity leads to doubly stigmatizing many black women who are criticized for not fulfilling a white feminine ideal but who are also not praised for fulfilling traits found positive when attributed to men.[53]

Femininity and masculinity are social and psychological interpretations of gender that both exhibit and mask unequal power relations. Feminism exposes the negative impact of such stereotypical attributions of gender characterizations. However, some aspects of experience that have been associated with women, labeled *feminine,* and consequently devalued in patriarchal cultures have also been positively revalued by feminists. A nonauthoritarian leadership style comes to mind as an example of feminine behavior that has been revalued and redefined as a feminist method. That I find James's metaphorical and suggestive style more congenial to my own way of thinking than an analytic and explicit style can be understood as the expression of a feminine style without implying that all women think this way or that no men do. James, for instance, rejects the polemically virulent style of philosophic argumentation that seeks to triumph over opponents by convicting them of errors and argues instead for shared understanding as the goal of philosophic discourse.[54] From my point of view, he is rejecting a prevalent form of masculine style for a feminine one.

Before filling in the claim that pragmatism seems more feminine than masculine, something more needs to be said about how an intellectual schema can be gendered. What constitutes femininity or masculinity varies over time and among cultures, even taking on opposite characteristics according to what is most valued at particular times and places. The kernel of gender differences may be biological, but the nature and extent of this biological substratum are difficult, perhaps impossible to determine, given the context of beliefs, values, and expectations that inform the differential psychological developmental patterns that are discussed.[55] Therefore, what seems masculine or feminine varies cross-culturally as well as between subcultures, including variations among races, ethnic groups, and classes. It would perhaps be better to talk about a variety of feminine and masculine styles as long as it is remembered that these styles are also aspects of lived experience that influence how one perceives the world. According to the stereotypical gender characteristics often associated with or imposed on women and men in late nineteenth- and twentieth-century America, pragmatism appears far more feminine than what replaced it. But since for both pragmatism and many versions of feminism, masculinity and femininity are not reductively biological essential natures but culturally mediated assumptions of gender, as soon as the gendered nature of a theoretical position such as pragmatism is pointed out, what is held to constitute its gendered attributes is already being subverted and pluralized.

In *The Flight To Objectivity* Susan Bordo draws on Carol Gilligan, Evelyn Fox Keller, and Nancy Chodorow to attribute the configuration of masculine traits she identifies as prominent in modern, western rationalism to the "more rigorous individuation from the mother demanded of boys (as a requisite to their attaining a 'masculine' identity in a culture in which masculinity is defined in opposition to everything that the mother represents)." Whether one agrees with this psychological explanation or finds the origins of misogyny in specific cultural, economic, and political conditions, the list of stereotypically masculine traits that results is recognizably plausible as values prominently exhibited in elite as well as popular culture. They are "detachment, autonomy, and a clear sense of boundaries between self and world, self and others. This has resulted, in our male-dominated intellectual traditions, in the fetishization of detachment and 'objectivity' in ethical reasoning and scientific rationality."[56]

Thomas Nagel's *View from Nowhere* is the logical conclusion of a long process, which extends back to Descartes, of such distancing of self from world.[57] He is also heir to a shift in mainstream philosophizing that was inaugurated by the arrival of members of the Vienna school of logical positivism in America. It is this movement that eventually displaced pragmatism. Bordo connects the extreme mind/body dualism in Descartes's philosophy to separation anxiety. The disconnectedness of a male from both the natural world and his own body reflects "separation from the *maternal*—the immanent realms of earth, nature, the authority of the body—and a compensatory turning toward the *paternal* for legitimation through external regulation, transcendent values, and the authority of law." [58]

Against such a background understanding of the polarizing of masculinity and femininity in Western thinking, it is possible to see how pragmatism would be implicitly categorized with feminine rather than masculine traits, even if such a connection were not made in print or on a conscious level. Descartes reacted to the Galilean and Newtonian displacement of the human species away from the center of cosmic history. Dewey, on the other hand, responded to the Darwinian reconnection of humans with all of organic life. When separation, generalization, sharp boundaries, and the drive to reduce the multiplicity of experience are categorized as masculine, then inclusiveness, concreteness, vagueness, tolerance of ambiguities, and pluralism are seen as feminine. But this latter constellation of traits is also characteristic of pragmatist thinking.[59] Compare Bordo's description of Cartesian separation anxiety, for instance, with one of Dewey's early articles, explaining his "New Psychology" as a better starting point for philosophizing than abstract analysis of language or of theoretical terms:

> The New Psychology is content to get its logic from . . . experience, and not do violence to the sanctity and integrity of the latter by forcing it to conform to certain preconceived abstract ideas. It wants the logic of fact, of process, of life. It has within its departments of knowledge no psychostatics, for it can nowhere find spiritual life at rest. For this reason, it abandons all legal fiction of logical and mathematical analogies and rules; and is willing to throw itself upon experience, believing that the mother which has borne it will not betray it. But it makes no attempts to dictate to this experience, and to tell it what it *must* be in order to square with a scholastic logic. Thus the New Psychology bears the realistic stamp of the contact with life.[60]

Whereas contemporary philosophers often privilege physics or computational analysis as the most rational models of science, ones which should be imitated by philosophers, pragmatists consistently use biological models and examples drawn from ordinary experience and the human sciences.[61] Pragmatists' pervasive metaphors are often as characteristic of women's experiences as of men's. Dewey's are organic and developmental; many were drawn from his involvement with early childhood education, while James's metaphors, which are as striking as Nietzsche's, include the stream of thought, truth as the marriage function of our beliefs with sensory experiences, and the organization of experience as weaving chaos into order.[62] Imagine the reaction of philosophers of the late nineteenth century, who not only prided themselves on their rigorous argumentative form but were also suffering from an acute case of science envy, to James's use of homely metaphors in his exposure of the false objectivity of positivist science:

> It is absurd for Science to say that the egoistic elements of experience should be suppressed. The axis of reality runs solely through the egotistic places—they are strung on it like so many beads. To describe the world with all the various feelings of the individual pinch of destiny, all the various spiritual attitudes, left out from the description . . . would be something like offering a printed bill of fare as the equivalent for a solid meal. . . . A bill of fare with one real raisin in it instead of the word "raisin," with one real egg instead of the word "egg," might be an inadequate meal, but it would at least be a commencement of reality.[63]

It may seem odd that I am pointing out some feminine aspects of pragmatism when it is so often dismissed as an irresponsible instrumentalism. Martin Heidegger, for instance, once contemptuously decried it as a "*Weltanschauung* for engineers and not for human beings in the full sense of the word."[64] But this is a self-indictment, both of his ignorance of pragmatism as a philosophy and of his indifference to social and political reconstruction. One need only recall Dewey's definition of philosophy as "reconstruction through criticism" to recognize that he aligned himself with neither a reductionist instrumentalism nor a fatalistic openness to being.[65] He says in "Context and Thought" that "philosophy is criticism; criticism of the influential beliefs that underlie culture; a criticism which traces the beliefs to their generating conditions as far as may be, which tracks them to their results, which considers the mutual compatibility of the elements of the total structure of beliefs. Such an examination terminates, whether so intended or not, in a projection of them into a new perspective which leads to new surveys of possibilities" (*LW* 6:19). Far from blindly advocating a ruthless application of the most efficient means to accomplish predetermined ends, Dewey's pragmatic instrumentalism advocates criticizing the beliefs that have led to presently unsatisfactory conditions in order to radically reconstruct our society according to nonoppressive and cooperative standards. A feminine style does not preclude critical reconstruction. But as the presence of what I'm calling feminine traits in the works of male pragmatists shows, belief in stereotypically masculine and feminine traits masks the complex ways both these clusters of traits are instantiated in individuals and the complex ways power and valuations are expressed through determinations of which traits are embodied in which gender, race, and class.

5. THE CONTEXT OF OPPRESSION

I would like to conclude with pragmatism's criticism of philosophy as traditionally practiced and its plea to turn away from problems found only in academic philosophy journals and toward problems that arise in actual experience. For pragmatists, philosophical reflection begins and ends with experience, as it does for many feminists. For both, experience is inextricably personal and social. Pragmatism needs feminism to carry out its own stated program, since feminists are in the forefront of philosophers addressing the social and political issues that affect women. On the other hand, the three features that Sandra Harding suggests best characterize feminist analysis have also been developed in pragmatism as ones that should characterize any defensible inquiry. They are related as the specific to the general. Feminist theory is about women, even when more recent revisions have rejected the essentialism implicit in making claims about women *as such* and have emphasized the plurality of women's situated experiences. Pragmatism argues for the inclusion of diverse communities of interest, particularly marginalized ones.

Harding lists three distinctive features of feminist research: (1) it begins with women's experiences as the basis for social analysis; (2) its aim is to benefit women; and (3) the researcher is not a neutral observer, but is on the same critical plane as the subject matter. Support for and development of these three themes can be found throughout pragmatist philosophy, which emphasizes that reflection ought to begin with experience, which is irreducibly plural; that the goal of reflection is to satisfactorily resolve the problematic situations that arise within particular experiences, as these are defined by those involved; and that knowledge is always shaped by—in Harding's words—the "concrete, specific desires and interests" of the investigator.[66]

Pragmatism and feminism reject philosophizing as an intellectual game that takes purely logical analysis as its special task. For both, philosophical techniques are means, not ends. The specific, practical ends are set by various communities of interest, the members of which are best situated to name, resist, and overcome the oppressions of class, sex, race, and gender. The problem with philosophy's enchantment with "the logic of general notions" is that it forces specific situations into predetermined, abstract categories. Pragmatism's fundamental criticism of traditional philosophy is that it "substitutes discussion of the meaning of concepts and their dialectical relationship to one another" for knowledge of specific groups of individuals, concrete human beings, and special institutions or social arrangements (*MW* 12:188).[67]

Dewey says that "we want to know about the worth of the institution of private property as it operates under given conditions of definite time and place" (*MW* 12:189). Instead, we get discussions of "*the* state, *the* individual, the nature of institutions as such, society in general" (*MW* 12:188). Instead of assisting inquiry, the disregard of specific historical phenomena for general answers with supposedly universal meaning closes it. "In transferring the issue from concrete situations to definitions and conceptual deductions, the effect . . . is to supply the apparatus for intellectual justification of the established order" (*MW* 12:189–190). Women are members of all the categories mentioned, but how specific is pragmatist analysis of the diversity of women's situatedness, individually, socially, and institutionally? According to its own logic, to the extent to which pragmatists do not actually reflect on the status of women and the oppressions of race, class, sexual orientation, and economic forces that women suffer, they are contributing to the justification of the established order.

Feminists, on the other hand, can benefit from such specific theoretical analyses as those by which pragmatism radically revisions the task of philosophy. Dewey, for instance, argues that "neglect of context is the greatest single disaster which philosophic thinking can incur" (*LW* 6:11). Philosophy and other reflective endeavors have their own context of discourse, which is narrowly constrained within disciplinary concerns and only tenuously, if at all, connected with everyday life. He insists that the strategic research of the sciences and other disciplines gains its meaning and value from its relation to what is taken to be the purpose of human life as such. What this purpose is cannot be imposed from above, by experts, but must be decided from below, by all those affected. Disciplinary contexts are necessarily narrowly strategic, and strategic thinking becomes dangerous to the extent that it is not guided by more encompassing purposes agreed upon as being mutually beneficial. It is dangerous for the disciplines to neglect context in a way that is not the case in less explicitly structured situations: "In the face to face communications of everyday life, context may be safely ignored . . . [because] it is irrevocably there" (*LW* 6:5). In everyday life it is taken for granted, for it can be explicitly retrieved when the need arises. "But in philosophizing there is rarely an immediately urgent context which controls the course of thought" (*LW* 6:6).

This "neglect of specific acknowledgement" of context in philosophizing "is, then, too readily converted into virtual denial" (*LW* 6:6). Context includes selective interest as well as both the temporal and spatial backgrounds which are not consciously attended to. It includes the horizon of meaning and value that gives point to everything said. If context is being denied, then the actually informing meanings and values remain unrecognized, uncriticized, and thus unreconstructed. We then passively acquiesce in the operative structures of power rather than participate in setting the conditions for our own being-in-the-world.

In fighting the entrenched belief that it is "derogatory to link a body of philosophic ideas to the social life and culture of their epoch," pragmatism is a helpful ally of feminist criticism (*LW*6:17). I think feminism and pragmatism have much to offer each other. Pragmatist philosophy, for instance, explains why the neglect of context is the besetting fallacy of philosophical thought.[68] Feminism cogently and extensively shows how gender, race, class, and sexual preference are crucial parts of context that philosophy has traditionally neglected.

To answer the question posed in the title of this chapter: Pragmatist feminists and feminist pragmatists exist among us, but in surprisingly small numbers. Pragmatist philosophers might be predisposed to be sympathetic to feminism, but too often they do not directly engage in feminist analysis. This is a loss for both pragmatist and feminist theory and praxis. Likewise, many feminist philosophers know little about pragmatism. West, unfortunately, exhibits a widespread pragmatist ignorance of feminist analyses of the pervasiveness of gender when he expresses the opinion that American culture "cuts deeper than sexual identity." But he also expresses pragmatism's openness to revision, its recognition of cultural specificity, and its refusal to speak for those who can more authentically speak for themselves when he follows this statement by saying that "the issue is how American women will reshape and revise pragmatism" through reflections on their own experiences. "For the difference pragmatism makes is always the difference people make with it."[69]

Three

Reclaiming a Heritage:
Women Pragmatists

> Humanity, thus considered, is not a thing made at once and unchangeable, but a stage of development; and is still . . . "in the making." Our humanness is seen to lie not so much in what we are individually, as in our relations to one another; and even that individuality is but the result of our relations to one another. It is in what we do and how we do it, rather than in what we are. Some, philosophically inclined, exalt "being" over "doing." To them this question may be put: "Can you mention any forms of life that merely "is," without doing anything?"

This passage by an American writer in 1910 captures such characteristic pragmatist themes as those of process, evolutionary development, the self defined in relation to others, and praxis as determinative of being. It could have been written by any of the classical American pragmatists. What follows it, however, could not have been, namely, that during the comparatively short period of written history, "we have had almost universally what is here called an Androcentric Culture. The history, such as it was, was made and written by men. The mental, the mechanical, the social development, was almost wholly theirs. We have, so far, lived and suffered and died in a man-made world."[1]

For someone immersed in pragmatist philosophy, the contrast is especially striking. The irruption of a feminist perspective into familiar thought patterns is so unexpectedly incongruous that it forces recognition of what has been missing in the discourse of the classical American pragmatists. Furthermore, the similarities and differences are significant enough to require a revision of the pragmatist canon. Maureen L. Egan, for instance, argues that Charlotte Perkins Gilman, the author of the opening quotation, should also be included in the canon of classical

American philosophers, citing as common ground her pragmatism, her "search for a scientific explanation of culture and thought, and an evolutionary starting point for philosophy."[2] Jane S. Upin also includes Gilman as "part of our pragmatist legacy because her concerns, her insights and especially her method, converge with those of her contemporary, John Dewey," even taking pragmatism beyond his instrumentalism "by carrying out its environmentalist projects to a level beyond her male contemporaries."[3]

Gilman's contributions to feminism have for decades been recognized by feminists working in the field of literature. Her short story, "The Yellow Wallpaper," is routinely reproduced in Women's Studies texts and collections of feminist literature, and some of her other works of fiction, such as *Herland,* are also well known.[4] But her more theoretical writings have not received from philosophers the attention they deserve, despite the fact that she considered herself to be a philosopher and despite the fact that in her own day she was widely recognized as a major theorist and social commentator.[5] She was best known for a nonfiction work, *Women and Economics,* which was translated into many languages.[6] In her autobiography Gilman called herself a philosopher rather than a reformer, comparing herself to Socrates, who is remembered as a philosopher, not a soldier, although he went to war when Athens needed him. She summarizes her social philosophy: "My business was to find out what ailed society, and how most easily and naturally to improve it."[7]

Like John Dewey, the central figure of American pragmatists, Gilman argues that growth, not combat, is the major process and highest value of life and that the Social Darwinist exaltation of competition is seriously mistaken. Unlike Dewey, however, she attributes the theoretical appeal to competition as determinative of life and as a basic constituent of morality to "the universal masculine error" of assuming that what is true of males is true of life in general.[8] The recovery of Gilman's obviously feminist version of pragmatism provides an opening for recognizing others whose lives and works have not survived in the public records of academically based philosophy. Who else besides Gilman has been overlooked by the gatekeepers of serious academic philosophy? And do these exclusions help to explain why the absence was not even noted or its effects questioned by so many generations of women philosophers?

The first three sections of this chapter explain my preliminary efforts to identify women philosophers who wrote from a pragmatist perspective and who influenced, or were influenced by, the canonically recognized founders of classical American philosophy. The first section is therapeutic in that it not only explains the difficulties encountered in trying to identify pragmatist women philosophers, but it also tries to account for my own former perception that women were either absent from the original formulations of pragmatism or their work was peripheral and irrelevant to the really important and exciting philosophical issues. The second section provides both confirming and disconfirming evidence for my guiding hypothesis that if there were early women pragmatists, they must have developed feminist analyses of their experiences. According to William Gavin all "*re*-covery" of experience by philosophers such as William James is necessarily incomplete because in its inevitable selectivity "it is also a covering up, a re-*covery*." [9] In the third section I find, instead, that I cannot recover the lives and pragmatist positions of Elsie Ripley Clapp and Lucy Sprague Mitchell, the first two women I discovered, without trying to uncover why they were covered over in the first place.

The last two sections explore the consequences of recovering the lives and works of the first women students of classical American philosophy. The first elements of a specifically pragmatist feminism are developed in section 4 from what this early generation of women philosophers found empowering. The reasons for their disappearance from the history of philosophy are given in section 5, along with the specific factors that led some women to develop a pragmatist feminism while others did not. It is hoped that recovering the specificities of their exclusion and of the choices they made can aid in recognizing the generic traits found in contemporary situations that can be appropriated or rejected to achieve more desirable outcomes.

In this chapter I will concentrate on those who, unlike Gilman and Jane Addams, are seldom, if ever, mentioned in books on American philosophy. This recovery will make explicit by concrete example the usually hidden mechanisms of academic exclusion and marginalization. The recovery of their work is guided by the intention to discover the extent to which their writings are specifically feminist or even demonstrate a particularly feminine angle of vision. Only by further research extending my initial analysis of their writings will it be possible to determine the extent to which they revisioned pragmatism from a special angle of vision derived from their experiences as women of their time, place, social class, and race, as well as the extent to which these experiences led to or were informed by feminist insights. I hope that this recovery of a tradition of women pragmatists will enrich contemporary formulations of feminist pragmatism and pragmatist feminism, which have so far been lacking a historically concrete context in the discipline of philosophy. Moreover, I hope that bringing back late nineteenth- and early twentieth-century women philosophers into the contemporary conversation will encourage a revision of what constitutes classical American philosophy.

1. THE PROBLEM OF RECOVERY

According to Max H. Fisch, "most American philosophers have been amateurs; that is, they have been something else in the first place and philosophers in the second place." [10] This recognition, by no means usual in histories of philosophy, should have made it easier to acknowledge women's contributions to philosophy in America, but it has not. Until very recently, women, even more than men, have had to forge careers for themselves outside academia, since higher education was largely closed to them. This fact makes it particularly difficult to identify and recover women philosophers, since the designation *philosopher* has been—at least from the turn of the century—almost exclusively an academic one. The usual way to be recognized as a contemporary philosopher is through certification authorized by professors whose students in turn become professors. In order to count, anyone lacking the generational continuity such institutional affiliation provides must be repeatedly cited and discussed by those who are academic philosophers, thus being kept in mind as a thinker worthy of regard by each new generation of students. But with few exceptions, until very recent times women and minority groups have been absent from both professional positions in higher education and from citations by those who were in such positions. [11] Until the post-World War II civil-rights and feminist movements, they were not even conspicuously absent.

Since American pragmatism is a historically specific movement, the most obvious place to begin looking for women pragmatist philosophers is within the immediate vicinity of the recognized pragmatists. The classical American pragmatists are generally held to be Charles Sanders Peirce, William James, Josiah Royce, John Dewey, and George Herbert Mead. [12] The second generation of philosophical pragmatists, those who explicated the classical American pragmatists and continued developing the tradition further, those who produced the first comprehensive commentaries and contributed to *festschrifts,* were—not surprisingly—the students of the first generation. If one counts only those who are systematically studied, who appear on multiple reading lists, and who are given credit for defining the subject, one sees that they are all men. They include Herbert W. Schneider, Max H. Fisch, Ralph Barton Perry, Horace M. Kallen, and Sidney Hook. The first place to look for women who would be conventionally recognized as pragmatists, therefore, is obviously among the students of the classical American pragmatists, although not among their historically recognized professional disciples. Given the widespread prejudice until very recently against women assuming leadership positions in coeducational institutions, the sexism of philosophy departments in general, and of the elite schools in particular, it seems unlikely that the first generation had any women colleagues in their departments of philosophy, although they did sometimes have women students.[13]

Jane Addams is an obvious exception, being an equal both as an established professional with, and not a student of, the first generation pragmatists, and as making original (albeit mostly unacknowledged) contributions to the initial formulation of pragmatism.[14] But her works are never reproduced in such collections as Morton White's *Documents in the History of American Philosophy: From Jonathan Edwards to John Dewey* (1972), which includes no selections from women philosophers, American or otherwise.[15] Canon formation results from such selectivity. It is assumed that the sixteen philosophers included are more worthy of inclusion than those left out, whatever the specific criteria. The status of George Ripley and Theodore Parker is raised, for instance, by their being included as transcendentalists along with Ralph Waldo Emerson and Samuel Taylor Coleridge. Margaret Fuller is not included, thereby diminishing her intellectual reputation. Jane Addams is also absent, although she is now recognized as "a social theorist of major proportions."[16]

Mary Jo Deegan has argued powerfully for restoring Addams to her rightful place as a founding mother of the Chicago School of sociology. By piecing together the pragmatists' network of mutual influences, she also lays the groundwork for claiming Addams as one of the first-generation originators of philosophical pragmatism.[17] And Lynn D. Gordon details the close cooperation of reform-minded women and men during the first decades of the University of Chicago, which was founded in 1890 at the beginning of the Progressive Era.[18] Among them were women administrators and faculty, such as Alice Freeman Palmer, Marion Talbot, and Sophonisba Breckinridge; the women of Hull House, including Florence Kelley, Julia Lathrop, Alice Hamilton, and Ellen Gates Starr, in addition to Addams; and the reform-minded male faculty, especially Dewey, Thorstein Veblen, W. I. Thomas, James R. Angell, and Mead. Deegan makes the startling assertion that it is out of the "collegial contacts and intellectual exchanges" of Dewey and Mead with Addams and other residents of Hull House that "Chicago pragmatism was born. . . . They wanted to combine scientific and objective observation with ethical and moral values to generate a just and liberated society."[19]

Deegan's assertion sounds excessive only against the backdrop of the virtually total silencing of women in the long history of philosophy, which is a particular instance of a wider neglect. Ellen Fitzpatrick also reports that "very little attention has been given to the university-trained women who helped construct and carry out the Progressive agenda."[20] Since there are no women acknowledged in the canon of American pragmatists, how could one be a major figure, even a founding member? In the patriarchal records, philosophers relegate Addams to sociology, while sociologists relegate her to amateur reformism, at best to the status of a social worker. Her intellectual contributions are thereby erased from the histories and definitive works through which new members are inaugurated into the academic disciplines of philosophy and sociology.

Although Dewey acknowledged Addams's impact on his thinking, this influence was not followed up in standard philosophy texts on pragmatism (*LW* 5:421). In 1935, for instance, Dewey dedicated *Liberalism and Social Action* "To the Memory of Jane Addams." The book is now out of print, and the dedication has disappeared from the current critical edition (*LW* 11). Philosophers can claim as a mitigating circumstance the fact that Addams identified herself as a sociologist, rather than as a philosopher. She is undeniably a pragmatist, however, and pragmatism, like feminism, cannot be confined to any one discipline. She is an exemplary case of how pragmatism, like feminism, internally disrupts artificial and counterproductive disciplinary boundaries.

2. PRELIMINARY FINDINGS

My original hunch was that the first women who studied classical American philosophy would use it to analyze their own experiences as women and would develop a pragmatist version of feminism. It seems obvious that a philosophical perspective based on the importance of praxis, one that explicitly develops the relation of experience to theory, would encourage women to use their own experiences to develop pragmatist theories of women's oppression and a pragmatist philosophy responsive to women's interests. But neither of the first two women I investigated, Elsie Ripley Clapp and Lucy Sprague Mitchell, seemed particularly interested in women's issues, at least not to the extent of making them a focus of their theoretical work. This finding was consistent with what I already knew about Mary Whiton Calkins, who studied with James, Royce, and Hugo Münsterberg in the early 1890s at Harvard and who was the first woman to become president of both the American Psychological Association (1905) and the American Philosophical Association (1918).[21]

The name of Christine Ladd-Franklin has at least survived in footnotes in histories of American philosophy. I at first assumed that she fitted into this pattern of lack of interest in women's issues since her pioneering work was in color vision, logic, and mathematics, areas somewhat removed from feminist concern. She was a member of Charles Sanders Peirce's first class at Johns Hopkins and completed all the requirements for a Ph.D. in mathematics and logic by 1882. She was not awarded the degree because she was a woman, but unlike Harvard's continued refusal to recognize its earlier women graduates retroactively, Johns Hopkins belatedly conferred a doctoral degree on Ladd-Franklin in 1926. Since the only references to her in standard works of philosophy concerned her work in logic, usually insofar as it illuminated Peirce's work, it was a pleasant surprise to discover recently that she also wrote on a wide range of social issues, including the treatment of women.[22]

An equally belated discovery is that Jessie Taft, under the direction of Mead at the University of Chicago, wrote a doctoral dissertation in 1913 on "The Woman Movement from the Point of View of Social Consciousness."[23] This may be the first philosophy dissertation written on a feminist issue. According to Rosalind Rosenberg, "Of all the efforts made at that time to describe the feminine character and the woman's movement, Taft's dissertation was particularly insightful."[24] Taft received a fellowship to attend the University of Chicago and studied both philosophy and sociology from 1909 to 1913.[25] I initially concluded that she was an exception to the emerging pattern of indifference to feminism by the women who studied with male academic pragmatists. But at least her work with Mead, James H. Tufts, and other socially-minded faculty provided evidence that, given the right conditions, pragmatist philosophical openness to experience, social reconstruction, and pluralism can empower women to articulate feminist theory.

More evidence confirming my initial hypothesis keeps appearing. While researching Calkins, for example, I discovered Ethel Puffer (Howes), who, together with Calkins, was offered a Radcliffe doctorate in 1902. This was in lieu of the Harvard Ph.D. that she had earned in 1898. Unlike Calkins, she accepted it.[26] In 1937 she blissfully recalled her graduate studies with James, Royce, Münsterberg, George Santayana, and George Herbert Palmer during "the golden age" of the Harvard philosophy department.[27] Again unlike Calkins, Howes was a feminist, both in her writings and in her activities.[28] A decade and a half after Taft's analysis of the woman movement, she wrote "The Meaning of Progress in the Woman Movement" for a special issue of *Annals of the American Academy of Political and Social Science* on "Women in the Modern World." Earlier, in 1923, she wrote a yearlong series of articles in *Woman's Home Companion* that acknowledged the drudgery of women's lives and the need for them to work together on their common problems. Beyond that, she gave hands-on advice on starting laundry, kitchen, and nursery cooperatives.[29]

It is against this recently rediscovered background of a more vigorous tradition of pragmatist feminism that my initial findings about Clapp and Mitchell are presented.

3. TWO WHO DISAPPEARED

I have only begun exploring in detail the lives and writings of two women, heretofore unknown to me despite my area of specialization in classical American philosophy—Elsie Ripley Clapp and Lucy Sprague Mitchell. Clapp was an innovator in progressive education, and Mitchell was a pioneer in both higher education for women and early childhood education. Both kept in touch with large networks of women friends, colleagues, and activists, and tracing these connections promises to lead to other discoveries.[30]

Elsie Ripley Clapp.
Clapp (1882–1965) earned a B.A. in English at Barnard College (1908) and an M.A. in philosophy at Columbia University (1909), where she also took all the required courses for doctorates in both English and philosophy but never completed either degree.[31] She took no less than fourteen courses from Dewey at Columbia University and Teachers College from 1907 to 1912, and she was his graduate assistant for twelve courses between 1911 and 1927.

Why I did not even suspect Clapp's existence becomes clearer on rereading such introductions to Dewey's work as the one written by Sidney Ratner and Jules Altman for *John Dewey and Arthur F. Bentley: A Philosophical Correspondence, 1932–1951,* which traces the mutual influences between Dewey and his colleagues and students. While recounting Dewey's many accomplishments at Columbia University from 1904 through the 1930s, Ratner and Altman report that he took part in "a vigorous, varied, and imaginative philosophical group." They mention briefly his colleagues and their accomplishments and single out for praise his best students: "Sidney Hook, Joseph Ratner, Herbert Schneider, John H. Randall, Jr., Ernest Nagel, and Irwin Edman, brilliant graduate students of Dewey's in the 1910's or 1920's, soon established themselves as thinkers in their own right and contributed to Dewey's development of his system by their suggestions, essays, and books."[32] From the listing of elite male students, one would not guess that Dewey had any women graduate students, still less a teaching assistant who collaborated with him for many years. In *The Philosophy of John Dewey,* which inaugurated the prestigious Library of Living Philosophers series, Dewey's daughter Jane, who edited material he supplied, gives the same impression in her biographical chapter.[33]

All his life Dewey developed his ideas in interaction with philosophic co-workers, and he frequently acknowledged their collaboration. Jane M. Dewey reports her father as saying that except for "his movement from idealism to his naturalistic and pragmatic experimentalism personal contacts had, on the whole, more influence in directing his thought than the books he read." In the same 1939 biography John especially mentioned his wife, Alice Chipman Dewey, and Ella Flagg Young, the District Superintendent of City Schools in Chicago and the first woman president of the National Educational Association, as the greatest influences on him in educational matters during his Chicago years. He also singled out Jane Addams and other close friends at Hull House as particularly important, though their influence is tellingly characterized as "deriving from residence in Chicago rather than from his professional position." Still, John attributed "much of his enthusiasm of his support of every cause that enlarged the freedom of activity of women to his knowledge of the character and intelligence of his wife, of Ella Flagg Young, and of Jane Addams." [34]

But how did Dewey recognize this influence at the time? The first volume of *The Middle Works* brings together all the revised editions of *The School and Society*, which relay Dewey's educational philosophy as it developed out of his association with the Laboratory School, started in Chicago in 1896. In the Author's Note to the 1900 printing Dewey acknowledges that the school was a joint undertaking and mentions that "the clear and experienced intelligence of my wife is wrought everywhere into its texture." He also says that "the wisdom, tact, and devotion of its instructors have brought about a transformation of its original amorphous plans into articulate form and substance with life and movement of their own" (*MW* 1:4). But neither in the note nor in the text of the book are the teachers' names given—nor is his wife's, for that matter.

Even chapter 4, the most detailed description of the founding and the day-to-day organization of the Laboratory School, does not mention by name anyone who was involved, despite the fact that Dewey goes out of his way to deny that the school simply developed ideas he already had:

> It has been popularly assumed that I am the author of these ready-made ideas and principles which were to go into execution. I take this opportunity to say that the educational conduct of the school, as well as its administration, the selection of subject-matter, and the working out of the course of study, as well as actual instruction of children have been almost entirely in the hands of the teachers of the school; and that there has been a gradual development of the educational principles and methods involved, not a fixed equipment. (*MW* 1:58)

Thereafter, Dewey uses the pronoun, *we*, whether reporting on the teaching or the administrative aspects of the school, thus appropriating the women's contributions and taking on the role of authoritative interpreter or theorist. He spoke truer than he realized when he said that "our ideal has been, and continues to be, that of the best form of family life," since he reproduces the dynamics of the patriarchal family in which all contribute their talents, but the male head of the family assumes the roles of public representative and intellectual delegate (*MW* 1:65).

If Alice Chapman Dewey, Ella Flagg Young, and Jane Addams are indeed among the teachers, administrators, and colleagues whose ideas were worked out in the Laboratory School, which, in turn, was the experiential basis underlying Dewey's first expression of his educational philosophy, neither their names nor those of the other teachers were judged sufficiently important to bring to the notice of the readers of *The School and Society*. Dewey thus manages both to acknowledge them as influencing his ideas and yet obscure this very influence. The problem is not just that women are not often referred to by name but that their contributions are not taken with the same seriousness as those of other philosophers whose ideas are discussed in detail. Dewey does specifically acknowledge his indebtedness to Ella Flagg Young, but he does so only by references in footnotes and prefaces, rather than by analyzing or discussing her contributions. Moreover, his acknowledgments often appear in addresses published in obscure or popular journals, rather than in his major works.[35]

The problem of influence is, as Deegan points out in regard to Addams and Dewey, that "Addams's influence on his social thought has appeared primarily in books written about her and not in books written about him."[36] Christopher Lasch says in *The Social Thought of Jane Addams*, "It is difficult to say whether Dewey influenced Jane Addams or Jane Addams influenced Dewey. They influenced each other and generously acknowledged their mutual obligation."[37] And Katherine Camp Mayhew and Anna Camp Edwards open their book, *The Dewey School*, with an introduction by Dewey, quote extensively from him, and even include two pictures of him. In marked contrast to Dewey's reticence about naming his women collaborators, they include a two-page appendix listing all the teachers and assistants in the Laboratory School.

Given such explicit, even effusive, acknowledgments as those in Mayhew's and Edwards's books and Dewey's contrasting gratitude to what remain virtually anonymous women co-workers in his own books, it is not surprising readers assume that all the meaningful intellectual influence went from him to them and not the other way around. Despite Dewey's explicit acknowledgments that the school "inspired and defined the ideas" of his educational philosophy and that the teachers and not he gradually developed the educational principles, it should now be obvious that the way the acknowledgments were actually made would tend to obscure for contemporaries as well as posterity the intellectual contributions to pragmatism of pioneering women in the field (*MW* 1:3–4 and 58). In the introduction to volume 1 of *The Middle Works,* which includes *The School and Society* and other educational writings at the midpoint of Dewey's tenure at the University of Chicago, Joe R. Burnett mentioned only such male intellectual influences on Dewey's thought as Royce, Hegel, Plato, Wilhelm Wundt, G. Stanley Hall, James, Hugo Münsterberg, Peirce, Rousseau, and Pestalozzi. He thus continued a tradition of constructing intellectual lineages through "the fathers" and totally ignored even the intellectual contributions of women whom Dewey at the time specifically acknowledged as central.[38]

Following this pattern of effusive acknowledgment in the private sphere and virtual silence in scholarly publications, I first discovered Clapp's existence in private correspondence in the Dewey archives at Southern Illinois University. In a letter of September 2, 1911, Dewey thanked her both for a particular conversation and for written communications which helped him connect some of the chief issues in philosophy with difficulties in everyday life.[39] He added, "So great is my indebtedness, that it makes me apprehensive—not, I hope, that I am so mean as to be reluctant to being under obligation, but that such a generous exploitation of your ideas as is likely to result if and when I publish the outcome, seems to go beyond the limit." Not that he wanted her to stop on that account. He continued, "At the same time, I want to hold you to your word about further communication."

Dewey enclosed an early draft of a paper analyzing the topics of repetition, or reflex, and desire in experience. He remarked again on how much her criticism had helped him and acknowledged, "The fact is I am of those who get clamped up in writing, without I can get the response of others." After mentioning that he had written about 8,000 words of his textbook on the philosophy of education, he playfully warned her that if she encouraged it enough she would be in danger of getting at least parts of it sent to her. He closed by saying that he would write again after letting what she had already written "soak in," although from what he had already seen, she had said "about all there is to say on these points."

In a pattern already noted, Dewey publicly acknowledged Clapp's contributions to *Democracy and Education,* the book on which he was working from 1911 to its publication in 1916. But the acknowledgment occurs in the preface, written in August, 1915, where he gives "hearty acknowledgments" to three persons, among them "Miss Elsie Ripley Clapp for many criticisms and suggestions" (*MW* 9:3). None of the three appear in the index, however, and this reference to Clapp is also left out of the cumulative index to the collected works. The one reference to her in the index refers to the foreword Dewey wrote for her book, *Community Schools in Action,* in which he says that reading her book recalled "many stimulating conversations with its author" as well as "a most enjoyable visit" to Arthurdale.[40]

It is clear from their letters that Clapp helped Dewey with the content of the courses in which she assisted and not just in grading papers or teaching sections. He often thought through whatever was puzzling him at the moment in his classes, and these reflections would appear in his next book. In a letter setting up an appointment with her before the start of one semester, for instance, he asked Clapp to arrive early so that he could get her suggestions and reflections since the course was still "in a dim and inchoate state." He sent along his early attempts to work out such problems as the "inner-outer distinction" and how to relate literature to philosophy in general. He often thanked her for specific ideas relating to problems he was working out, such as her ideas regarding "the mind in the world—the world's mind—fine art."[41]

Dewey is quite specific about Clapp's substantive contributions in a letter of October 10, 1911, concerning one of the two courses in which she was assisting, Philosophy 104: Analysis of Experience, and Philosophy 105: Theories of Experience. "I really think it is quite unfair to you that Mrs. Sait should explain the course to you, even if it is funny. It makes me feel all the more that I should have printed in big letters on the blackboard this, that the other idea is Miss Clapp's."[42] Unfortunately, Dewey never spelled out publicly precisely which ideas Clapp contributed or how she helped to refine his ideas. Again, the problem is that Clapp's contributions are either acknowledged privately or else appear in her books, not in his. Or, when they are acknowledged, as in the preface to *Democracy and Education,* the acknowledgment is so vague and so further diluted by his acknowledging all the students he ever taught that we are left with the impression that her contributions were neither extensive nor of any particular importance.

Clapp helped found and was the principal or director of two experimental schools, the Roger Clark Ballard Memorial School in Jefferson County, Kentucky, from 1929 to 1934, and the Arthurdale School and Community Activities in Arthurdale, West Virginia, from 1934 to 1936. She was also the editor of *Progressive Education* from 1937 to 39. The Arthurdale community was a resettlement project for unemployed miners on land purchased from the federal government. Eleanor Roosevelt was the instigator and moving force behind the project, which she envisioned as a model community that could serve as a laboratory for others.[43] She interviewed Clapp for the position of principal and personally raised money to pay her salary. She also helped to establish a National Advisory Committee that included John Dewey and Lucy Sprague Mitchell, and she brought in Jessie Stanton, who was Mitchell's colleague at the

Bankstreet Nursery School in New York, to set up the nursery school. There were many such collaborative networks of women and men among the socially active pragmatists. They provided as many opportunities for the women's ideas and experimental findings to influence the male pragmatists as vice versa.

Clapp's pioneering work in developing progressive education in rural communities is set forth in her first book, *Community Schools in Action* (1939).[44] Her second book, *The Use of Resources in Education* (1952), develops a case for utilizing the whole community as an educational resource. The title reflects Dewey's rejection of the practice of elites imposing solutions on communities and his development of the principle that theories ought to arise out of an understanding of the possibilities and limitations of concrete, historically specific situations. He argued that "available resources suggest both the things to attempt, the objects to strive for, and the ways of doing. The passage or transition that constitutes the present is always from *something that is there.* All intelligent direction and control of the transition take account of this something" (LW 5:364).

Inspired by Dewey's idea that schools in rural districts have a unique opportunity to function socially, Clapp first undertook work at Ballard Memorial School in Kentucky.[45] Here she saw a chance to turn an abstract idea into reality. Speaking of her staff as well as herself, she says that their idea of a community school arose "partly from a longing that education really function in people's lives, and partly from a growing feeling about America, and an interest in using its cultures and resources and its regional differences. With us it needed the experiences of work in a rural community to quicken our understanding of the school as a social institution that John Dewey had expressed forty years before." *Community Schools in Action* opens with an acknowledgment of Dewey's contribution: "Although he is in no way responsible for what was done, everything that we have learned from our experiences in this attempt we learned in a special sense from him." [46]

But there is another reason why Clapp's first position was that of an administrator in rural education. Dewey retired from active teaching at Teachers College in 1927, and Clapp was still teaching with him in the Winter session of 1926–27. She wrote in her private notes: "The greatest honor of my life was the fact that, on his retirement, Dr. Dewey named me as his successor for the courses in Education which he had been giving at Teachers College. I was not appointed." [47]

Lucy Sprague Mitchell.
Lucy Sprague Mitchell uniquely bridges both the circle of Cambridge pragmatists and the University of Chicago-Columbia University school of

pragmatism. As a student at Radcliffe College (which was the Harvard Annex until 1894) from 1896 to 1900, she took courses from the Harvard luminaries James, Royce, George Santayana, Münsterberg, and George Herbert Palmer.[48] Mitchell was the only Radcliffe graduate in her class to receive honors in Philosophy. She not only lived with the Palmers, but Alice Freeman Palmer made it possible for Mitchell to matriculate at Radcliffe, and she soon became a role model for Lucy. Alice was the second president of Wellesley College—a brilliant one by all accounts—and later a visiting Dean of Women at the University of Chicago from 1892 to 1895. It was in Chicago that Mitchell first met her as a visitor in her parents' house.

Mitchell had met Dewey and his wife, Alice, who were frequent houseguests in Chicago, before she left home to study with the Harvard philosophy professors at Radcliffe. She soon read everything that Dewey had written. He became a lifelong friend and intellectual resource. Later, in 1913, Mitchell attended Dewey's and Edward Thorndike's lectures on education at Teachers College, Columbia University, for two terms. There she heard the key ideas of what Dewey published in 1916 as *Democracy in Education*. Mitchell's biographer, Joyce Antler, says the positions of Dewey that had a lasting influence on Mitchell's educational practice were "education as growth, a continuous 'reconstruction or reorganization of experience'; an emphasis on 'continuity' rather than the traditional 'dualisms' between subject matter and method, intellect and emotion, theory and practice; and the principle of education as a 'social function,' promoting the ideal of a 'truly shared or associated life.' "[49]

Unlike Clapp, Mitchell had no desire to pursue further studies in philosophy or to teach it. While still a student she tried on the role of philosophy professor. She reports on her plan to test James's theory that behavior produces emotions by behaving like each of her prestigious professors in turn to see if she would feel the way they did. She walked breezily like James, letting her mind and speech fly off at tangents; she tried being remote and acting slightly superior as Santayana did; in imitation of Münsterberg she "looked at people as physiological specimens with reflexes and receptors for impressions," and she imitated Royce by pretending "her head was so large she could scarcely hold it up" and sitting "with massive shoulders hunched and unseeing eye and contemplated the problem of evil."[50] Since she lived in such close proximity to George Palmer, she did not dare imitate him, but she does mention that he felt he was the power behind the throne of Harvard University.

It is clear from Mitchell's humorous characterizations of the Harvard philosophy professors that she could identify neither with their sense of self nor with their philosophical outlook. Instead, Alice Freeman Palmer, whom she describes as "enchanting," was clearly her role model. She had been a pioneering college president at an elite women's college, and she persuaded other women to take up administrative careers; but her style of influencing others behind the scenes clearly differed from that of her ambitious husband. She had many social obligations and was on innumerable committees yet found time to go on shopping sprees to cheer up Lucy Mitchell, self-described as a worn-out student. Alice Palmer was a woman of strong beliefs and effective action, yet "was personal without being mawkish or sentimental." Clearly, here were behavior and feelings that inspired Mitchell and with which she could identify. What especially appealed to her, what none of her male professors could offer, was a way for a woman to successfully combine home and career at a time when most middle- and upper-class women could only aspire to one or the other. In Mitchell's words, "She loved life—her profession and her home."[51]

Like her role model, Mitchell became an administrator and a mentor—the first Dean of Women at the University of California at Berkeley. In making the move to Berkeley in 1903, she was excited by the prospect of "a job which had no tradition but had to be created."[52] To legitimate her presence on campus, she asked to be made a faculty member in addition to serving as dean. Significantly, she chose English, not philosophy, as her home department. Although her pioneering work for women was much praised, she never really felt comfortable without a post baccalaureate degree among the status-conscious professors at Berkeley, nor did she feel she had found her true vocation. Her decision was no doubt affected by the pervasive sexism she experienced on campus. But her cool reception could not be attributed solely to her lack of a higher degree. She noticed that the only other woman on the faculty, Jessica Blanche Peixotto, who had a Ph.D. and was equal in training and intelligence to her male colleagues, was treated similarly simply because she was a woman.[53]

Although Mitchell did not view herself as "an aggressive feminist," she felt that her decision to accept a position for which she did not think she was adequately prepared was justified as "a significant step ahead for women as a sex." She had encountered frustrations before, but had not been able to analyze their source in a pervasive sexism before her consciousness was raised by the blatantness of the sexism experienced at Berkeley. In her autobiography she wrote: "It came as a shock when I realized that most of the faculty thought of women frankly as inferior beings. The older men were solidly opposed to having any women on the faculty. Any woman who, intellectually, could hold such a position must be a freak and 'unwomanly.'" Of course, such attitudes were also widespread at Harvard, but Mitchell reported that she had not personally encountered them in her own teachers, who "were outstanding scholars who repeated their courses [at Radcliffe] at great personal sacrifice just *because* they believed in women and wished them to have a chance." Royce had even encouraged her to earn a Ph.D. in philosophy and to go into college teaching. Furthermore, she testified that "no one who had lived with Alice Freeman Palmer could believe that an intellectual career must make a woman unwomanly—or unfeminine, either."[54]

After many years of searching for her true vocation, Mitchell settled on early childhood education and teacher training because, like Dewey, she felt that "public education is the most constructive attack on social problems, for it deals with children and the future. It requires endless research concerning children and what they need to make them grow wholesomely. It requires experimentation in curriculum for children and in teacher education. It requires an understanding of our culture. It is the synthesis of all my interests, all my hopes for humanity."[55] Her interests after Berkeley converged in her founding the Bureau of Educational Experiments, later called the Bank Street College of Education.

Antler points to the important connection of experience to theory in Mitchell's life: "Because of Lucy Mitchell's exceptional openness to experience, the personal markers of her life help to illuminate larger cultural patterns regarding the situation of women. By her explicit references to the events of her own life as sources of her developing intellectual and professional ideas, she provides a vital link between individual experience and changes in the social order."[56]

Mitchell, who had been raised in a strict Victorian patriarchal household, struggled all her life to overcome the sense of inferiority that defined her femaleness. On the intellectual level she rejected the domineering authority typical of patriarchal masculinity, but it was not easy to do so emotionally. For many years she refused to marry Wesley Clair Mitchell, largely because marriage and children almost inevitably meant the end of a professional career for her generation of white women.[57] She herself had spent much of her youth caring day and night for a sick and irascible father. In an extraordinary exchange of prenuptial letters she repeatedly raised obstacles to married life, and Wesley repeatedly reassured her that he cherished her autonomous life as much as she did. But even while testing his resolve not to submerge her fragile sense of self in the excessive demands of a form of family life from which she was just escaping, she admitted at one point that she nonetheless missed in him a certain "virility" or power to dominate that she still associated with masculinity. After marrying him she characterized her husband as "a new kind of experience to me. He had not a trace of the masculine infallibility which had afflicted the older men who had influenced my life."[58]

Dewey had been instrumental in freeing Mitchell from Victorian patriarchal control. She says that before meeting him, she "had never before questioned Father's attitude toward children and education." Unlike the marriages with which she was acquainted, all of which to varying degrees conformed to the oppressive Victorian model, Dewey first gave her a glimpse of a positive alternative to authoritarian patterns of education, one which she was to develop further over the course of her professional life. She said that Dewey had given her her first conception of experimental education and that "it was in large measure his influence that determined [her] interests and choice of a profession in later years." But Mitchell had already begun to feel guilty about her privileged social status and wealth as a result of visits to Hull House. Even before meeting Dewey she testified to having "fallen under the spell of Jane Addams . . . a spell which never lost its hold" on her. Addams, she said, "became for me a symbol of the 'real' world—a world of work and of people that I longed to reach but could not." [59]

Since women were, with few exceptions, excluded from philosophy professorships in men's and coeducational colleges in the last half of the nineteenth century through the first half of the twentieth, the pragmatist justification of the authority of experience over that of elitist texts must have been especially empowering. No women were included in the canon of philosophers. The implicit philosophical linkage of rationality with masculinity served to justify cultural prejudices, while the pragmatist realignment of rationality with praxis provided a means of subverting such prejudice. In view of the standard philosophical practice of citing what are considered to be the best models of rational thinking in support of one's own position, Mitchell's habitual recourse to experience as the source of her insights is a radical departure. Classical American philosophy provided a justification for doing so, but the inevitableness of turning to experience when written texts either distort or ignore important aspects of women's lives is primarily a function of the circumstances of women's marginalization. Despite their openness to experience, the actual context of pragmatist analyses still reflected a male-oriented perspective, and this seems to have played a part in Mitchell's rejection of philosophy as a profession. She felt that her undergraduate philosophy courses offered little that was directly relevant to her experiences as a woman. Years later, in 1956, she told an audience of Radcliffe alumnae that "never once was the word mother or child mentioned" during her four years at college. [60]

While still a dean at Berkeley, Mitchell often cared for a friend's child, Polly Miller, who died at the age of four. She traced her interest in early education to her relationship with Polly, with whom she first glimpsed how small children think and talk and how they are dominated by muscular and sensory experiences. Her devoted care soon expanded to include observations and notes on Polly's interests and language. Mitchell subverts the authoritarian, hierarchical model of influence when she calls Polly her "first great child teacher." [61] It is noteworthy that Dewey's pragmatist philosophy of education only became truly meaningful to her when her interest in children's patterns of development was awakened in an intimate relationship.

4. THE FIRST GENERATIONS' REVISIONING OF PRAGMATISM

Two aspects of pragmatist philosophy were found especially empowering for the first generation of women students. The thesis that theory arises directly from and is accountable to experience allowed them to trust their own experiences even when those experiences ran counter to accepted dogma. They were thus able to claim as sources of genuine knowledge those of their insights that had been dismissed throughout their education as merely deviant opinions or untrustworthy female sentiments. For pragmatists, however, experience is not simply uncritically reproduced; it is interrogated as to its value for a richer, fuller, more expansive life. Therefore, the second pragmatist principle, deriving from the process character of reality, is the definition of knowledge as the outcome of experimentation according to ends-in-view. Both themes are understood as socially and contextually based. Experience and experimental understanding dynamically interact with tradition and community to bring about an altered state of affairs thought to be more valuable.

The pragmatist notion of experiment and hypothesis verification should not be confused with the detached, value-free positivist notion that eventually replaced it. Lucy Mitchell, for instance, praised Harriet Johnson, her closest friend, co-worker, and mentor, for her rare imagination and avoidance of stereotyped thinking. Mitchell characterized Johnson as combining two traits not usually found together: "She was thoroughly scientific, always pushing for evidence, always open-minded, experimental, always re-examining her own practices in the light of new evidence. Yet she was humanly warm with children, full of delight at their ways, humorous and playful with them, a true companion as well as a profound student of little children." [62]

Pragmatist experimentation is transactive, changing both the investigator and the object of investigation. The model is not the lone heroic inventor like Thomas Edison, but a community of investigators, whether of individual sciences, like biology, or more dynamic, holistic communities like the settlement houses and community-based educational settings. Social reform was not supposed to be imposed on passive, needy communities by intellectual, economic, and political elites, but to arise out of the community's own experiences, guided by intelligent reflection, projection, enactment, and revision based on actual outcomes. Pragmatist theory is continuous with, and arises out of, experience. It rejects the standpoint of the neutral observer as both epistemologically bankrupt and morally pernicious.

Education, for Dewey, is not restricted to the classroom; it "includes all the influences that go to form the attitudes and dispositions (of desire as well as of belief), which constitute dominant habits of mind and character" (*LW* 11:42). Education, therefore, has the potential to bring about the most deep-rooted and far-ranging changes in society, outstripping that of violent revolution, which leaves old habits, such as sexism and racism, unchanged. Dewey says, for instance, that the task of breaking down the barriers that isolate the proletariat "is impossible of achievement by any revolution that stops short of affecting the imagination and emotions" (*LW* 10:346). He credited Jane Addams and Hull House with sharpening and deepening his "faith in democracy as a guiding force in education," citing her conviction "that democracy is a way of life, the truly moral and human way of life, not a political institutional device." [63]

Clearly, education cannot fulfill its potential if it continues to be thought of as transferring a body of information from one generation to another or as limited to the exchange of ideas. Dewey denied that education could fulfill its task by simply working on the minds of people without also engaging in actions effecting actual institutional change. "The idea that dispositions and attitudes can be altered by merely 'moral' means conceived of as something that goes on wholly inside of persons is itself one of the old patterns that has to be changed. Thought, desire and purpose exist in a constant give and take of interaction with environing conditions," which is not to deny that "resolute thought is the first step" (*LW* 11:44–45).

Dewey's educational theory exposed the deleterious effects of the artificial boundaries that isolated the school from its environing community. Women pragmatists took his argument one step further by adopting the radical position that scholars ought to be or become members of communities plagued by the problems their theories are supposed to solve. They uniquely integrated their professional and personal lives, deliberately putting themselves in experimental situations for the purpose of answering their own needs along with those of others. [64] Their experiments were experiments in community living as well as in community problem solving. Dewey points out, for instance, that "one of Miss Addams' main convictions was that the associations formed through Hull House were as important for those from homes more privileged in economic status and cultural opportunities as for the poorer residents of the district around the House." [65] Alice Hamilton, who lived at Hull

House from 1898 to 1919 and operated a well-baby clinic there while also teaching at Women's Medical College of Northwestern University, explained that life at Hull House "satisfied every longing, for companionship, for the excitement of new experiences, for constant intellectual stimulation, and for the sense of being caught up in a big movement which enlisted my enthusiastic loyalty." [66]

Addams, Clapp, and Mitchell literally created their own environments by developing and living in innovative educational communities as a means to radical social change. Beginning in 1889 Jane Addams, Ellen Gates Starr, Julia Lathrup, Edith Abbott, and other women residents of Hull House lived, ate, and worked together in a neighborhood of "the poor and disenfranchised, communicating with them across class, sex, religious, and ethnic divisions. . . . They wrote together, formed organizations together, and campaigned as a united force." Although their "team approach to problem solving and social research was Mead's idea of a 'working hypothesis,'" the integrative, holistic instantiation of theory and practice at Hull House was a unique accomplishment and unacknowledged contribution of women to pragmatist philosophy. They rendered concrete and successfully tested Dewey's steps to problem solving in *How We Think* (1910), *Democracy and Education* (1916), and *Logic: The Theory of Inquiry* (1939): "They would suspect that a certain problem existed, gather data documenting that such a problem did exist, form a policy for social action based on this factual evidence, and then lobby political and community forces to alleviate or eliminate the problem." [67]

Did they learn this logical method from Dewey, or did he learn it from them? According to pragmatist theory, the question misconstrues the dynamically interactive character of influence. This pragmatist attitude is evident in Clapp's summary of what she and her staff had learned at Arthurdale, that "changes in living and learning are not produced by imparting information about different conditions or by gathering statistical data about what exists, but by creating by people, with people, for people." [68] Intellectual influence goes both ways. In the preface to *How We Think,* for instance, John credits his wife, Alice, not only with inspiring the ideas in the book but with working them through concretely by embodying and testing them in practice through her work in the Laboratory School. He also acknowledges "indebtedness to the intelligence and sympathy of those who cooperated as teachers and supervisors in the conduct of that school, and especially to Mrs. Ella Flagg Young" (*MW* 6:179).

For female students of the classical American philosophers in the late nineteenth and early twentieth century, as for male students, vague aspirations for curing the ills of their society took on the definite structure of experimental projects. [69] But the enthusiasm and persistence with which women embraced the experimental method outside the confines of the scientific laboratory testifies to the special appeal it had for them as women.[70] Dewey credits Young with naming the school set up under his supervision at the University of Chicago. The Laboratory School was "a place for activity . . . inclusive of all fundamental human values," where leading hypotheses were developed that, through application, could lead to new understanding.[71] This experimental method gave women a powerful tool for escaping the constraints and prejudices of tradition. Their projects did not have to be justified by appeal to established principles already acknowledged in the old order, since they were bringing about a new reality which could only be evaluated in terms of the new values it instantiated.

Lucy's husband was also a student of Dewey, but Wesley decided on a career in economics.[72] Lucy's explanation of the nature of Wesley's debt to Dewey reveals a nonpatriarchal pattern of influence, one which women who were working their way out of repressive Victorian models found congenial. She says that Wesley,

> like so many others, absorbed Dewey's thinking and applied it to his own science in his own way. It has always seemed to me that Dewey's greatest contribution lies in the striking way his influence permeated many fields of thought rather than in his "followers," who have been lesser folk than he. Robin [Wesley] was in no sense a follower of Dewey. But Dewey stimulated him to new and independent thinking about economics.[73]

Dewey's philosophy, like James's and Royce's before him, explicitly empowered his students to throw off discipleship and the dead weight of tradition and to trust their own experiences as they sought to create a better world.

5. WHY THEY WERE LOST

It seemed clear that women pragmatist philosophers were excluded from the history of American philosophy primarily because they were excluded from the faculties of philosophy departments and were seldom, if ever, acknowledged in professional journals or books. Jane Dewey, for instance, listed as students who influenced her father only those men who "became members of the faculties of Columbia and neighboring institutions."[74] Even scholarly publications and brilliant careers in education could not keep the names of women pragmatists alive in philosophical records, reflecting both the exaggerated disciplinary boundaries that accompanied the professionalizing of philosophy and the low status of disciplines like education, whose efforts were directed toward children and whose members included large numbers of women. Deegan explains the parallel development of a dual system of sex-segregated labor in the professionalizing of sociology. "Male sociologists were expected to be abstract thinkers" and "academic positions were to be held by men who were institutionally encouraged to become professors. Women sociologists were expected to work in 'women's' sociological institutions," such as social settlements and women's colleges.[75]

Jessie Taft's lack of visibility in philosophic circles, like Clapp's and Mitchell's, stemmed from her postgraduate career. Despite graduating *magna cum laude* from the University of Chicago, she could not find an academic position.[76] After two short-lived positions as assistant superintendent of the New York State Reformatory for Women and director of the Mental Hygiene Committee of the State Charities Aid Association of New York, for ten long years she succeeded in obtaining only the marginalized faculty status of a part-time instructor in extension courses in psychology at the University of Pennsylvania. Yet she continued writing and emerged as a social work leader, having developed an original theoretical framework that combined both Mead's social philosophy and Otto Rank's psychology. In 1934, twenty-one years after completing her doctorate, she was hired by the School of Social Work at the University of Pennsylvania and eventually became director of the school.

In the early years of the University of Chicago, Dewey and Mead, along with other activists among the newly emergent discipline of social science, forged a bridge between academic departments and community-based institutions "through their work with women students and their ideological support of women's equality."[77] Dewey's and Mead's support of women as individuals and as professionals is well documented and frequently attested to by the women who benefited from such mentoring. It was not unusual for women who worked with Mead and Dewey to cite their active public support and personal encouragement to pursue professional careers as creating bonds that often lasted a lifetime and that contrasted sharply with obstacles placed in their way by other men in positions of power and influence. Myrtle B. McGraw, a pioneer in experimental psychology who, as a poor teenager from a rural area, corresponded with Dewey for years before eventually attending Columbia University, stated that "John Dewey's influence over my personal, intellectual, and career development was so extensive, intensive, and profound that it is absurd to mention it in a couple of sentences in a manuscript."[78] And as late as 1948 Dewey wrote many letters to the John Dewey Society for the Study of Education and Culture urging them to award Clapp a writing grant for *The Use of Resources in Education*.[79] He even agreed to write an introduction to the book, when that was made a condition of the grant, and he wrote again to the society expressing his appreciation for their decision to fund Clapp.

But despite the male pragmatists' theoretical integration of theory and practice and despite their practical support of women and women's rights, there still remained in classical American philosophy an unacknowledged residue of the sexist association of theory (and therefore higher education) with men and of practice (and therefore of precollegiate and nontraditional education) with women. It is equally important to recognize that they did not explicitly argue for the commonly held belief in the gendered nature of theory and practice. In fact, Dewey alluded to the negative effects of such hierarchical rankings when he complained that philosophers, as opposed to teachers, were ignoring the best summary of his philosophy to date because it was expounded in a book on education: "Although a book called *Democracy and Education* was for many years that in which my philosophy, such as it is, was most fully expounded, I do not know that philosophic critics, as distinct from teachers, have ever had recourse to it" (*LW* 5:156).

This complaint could illustrate an unrecognized sexist residue to the extent that it implies that recognition by philosophers is more important than recognition by mostly women teachers, but it could equally well be interpreted as simply recognizing an unfortunate state of affairs, one which Dewey himself was trying to overcome by presenting his philosophical views as educational theory. Lending support to this latter interpretation is the fact that in *Democracy and Education* Dewey explicitly criticized this very association of women with practical life and men with rational life (*MW* 9:261–69). But lending support to the existence of unexamined sexist assumptions in Dewey himself is the manner in which he recognized women's influence, that is, in introductions and footnotes, in general rather than by actually engaging the ideas of women in theoretical discussions in the body of the text, and in confining his allusions to women scholars to educational writings rather than philosophical publications. Such unrecognized assumptions do not make Dewey a sexist nor do they override his explicit rejections of sexism when he consciously reflects and deliberately acts on the issue, but only illustrate how deeply embedded such attitudes can be and how difficult they are to root out. It is no wonder that women, who also internalize such conflicting cultural messages, experience difficulty in trying to negotiate their way through the minefields of a patriarchally defined social order which conceals its masculinist value-orientation.

Good intentions and even solidarity with women in their struggles for equality are unfortunately not sufficient to dismantle deeply ingrained sexual stereotypes in the absence of such explicit and ongoing critiques of the sources and consequences of sexism as is found in Gilman's exposure of our androcentric culture. The absence of such an explicit and sustained criticism of sexism in academic pragmatism accounts for its unwitting reproduction of the hierarchical priority of theory over practice in regard to women's roles and experiences, despite the repudiation of any such division in theory. It is also worth noting that, in the absence of such explicit analyses of sexism, the women students of the early pragmatists often attributed the difficulties in their career paths to personal differences rather than to sexist attitudes, and thus did not develop an explicitly pragmatist feminism.

Myrtle B. McGraw recounts several episodes from the thirties that "could have been interpreted as reflecting a bias against women in psychology," including the failure of psychology textbooks to cite her work despite its centrality to one of the major controversies at the time concerning maturation versus learning. But she says that she "never interpreted the rejection of the textbook writers as indicating a position against women in psychology. Instead I thought of it as a rejection of my methodology of studying overt behavior development in infants." On some level she did seem to recognize the unacknowledged sexism, as evidenced by remarks she still remembered years later, such as "She's a nice young woman sentimental about babies, but she's no scientist," and her recollection that she "didn't let them upset me too much." The support of a small but significant group of scholars was crucially important to her ability to continue trusting her insights, despite such negative evaluations by the profession at large. She took comfort from the fact that "my interpretation of process, the interconnection of forces and systems, and the synthesis of multiple forces and systems in neuromotor development had the endorsement of Dewey, Tilney, and Frank."[80]

Although none of the original male classical American philosophers incorporated reflections on women's oppression into their own philosophical theories, Dewey and Mead encouraged women to overcome the restrictions society placed on them. Explicitly theoretical criticisms of sexist ideology were developed by women like Gilman, Marion Talbot, and Addams, who were independent scholars or colleagues of the male pragmatists, and by women like Ladd-Franklin, Puffer (Howes) and Taft who were their students.[81] They reflected on their own experiences and appropriated whatever theoretical positions illuminated these experiences and enabled them to overcome obstacles. But none of them ever held a tenured position in a department of philosophy, nor were their writings on women quoted by academic philosophers. Mary Whiton Calkins, who taught philosophy at Wellesley College, dissociated herself from feminism.[82]

One factor that seems to distinguish women who developed a pragmatist feminism from those who did not was their participation in a lively women's culture, particularly of social activists.[83] McGraw worked outside academia in an all-male laboratory, while the first generation of women at Hull House and the University of Chicago, such as Taft, were part of lively women's networks. What Taft had and many other women philosophy students apparently did not, was such a supportive network and a knowledge of explicit criticisms of sexism.[84] That Mead and Tufts validated the subject matter of her dissertation was certainly important, but so was her ability to cite Gilman and Edith Abbott (a University of Chicago graduate), along with other critics of sexism.[85]

Another factor seems to be the extent to which research on the situation of women could be an explicit field of study integrated into academic work. The emphasis in philosophy on theoretical analysis of issues already determined by centuries of canonically sanctioned philosophers made it particularly recalcitrant to the explicit development of feminist theory until recently. Pragmatism as it was developed at the University of Chicago consciously sought to break with this pattern of subservience to the classics. The interdisciplinary character and the political and social orientation of Chicago pragmatism, combined with an active women's network joining the socially conscious faculty with the needs of the city and the activities of Hull House, made it particularly hospitable to research on women.

Calkins and Puffer (Howes) provide an interesting basis for comparison, since they were both pioneering women scholars in the all-male world of Harvard graduate studies in philosophy/psychology. Puffer went on to an active feminist life; Calkins did not.[86] Calkins never married, although she insisted that motherhood was a woman's true vocation, and she is the only woman student of the classical American philosophers known to me to have obtained a tenured college faculty position in philosophy (and psychology). Puffer's marriage to Benjamin Howes in 1908 frustrated her professional aspirations, and she eventually began to write on "the persistent vicious alternative' confronting women: 'marriage *or* career—full personal life versus the way of achievement.' " Although Howes never obtained a full-time position in her profession, she remained politically active after the birth of her two children, working for the suffrage movement and the war effort. She received a three-year grant in 1925 to set up and direct an institute for the Coordination of Women's Interests at Smith College to explore practical ways of combining marriage and motherhood with professional work.[87] Developing a cooperative nursery school and food service was only one of many projects she initiated.

The grant was not renewed, partly because of its emphasis on applied research rather than theory and partly because the institute was not integrated into the Smith College curriculum because of faculty opposition to what they conceived as diluting literal education with vocationalism. This traditional academic tendency to value theory over practice and to isolate the liberal arts from political and social issues would explain why some women who studied with the classical American philosophers, like Calkins, did not develop an explicitly feminist pragmatism. But pragmatism itself undermined these valuations and exclusions, which explains why, given the right conditions, women like Howes did begin to develop a feminist-oriented pragmatism.

Clapp and Mitchell do not seem to have developed a pragmatist version of feminism; instead, they seem to have developed feminine—perhaps even incipiently feminist— versions of pragmatism by deliberately bringing politically informed points of view as women to their work in education. Mitchell, for instance, worried that illustrative sketches in a book on elementary education that she edited showed boys causing trouble more often than girls, and attributed this imbalance to actual differences in classroom behavior. She went on to comment that how far this behavioral difference reflects "different cultural pressures to which they have been subjected is an intriguing question that has never been satisfactorily explored, so far as we know."[88] She also hastens to add that not only troublemakers have problems: "Girls have no fewer troubles, no less acute needs than boys."

Clapp and Mitchell were not retreating to a women's sphere, but deliberately chose childhood education as a way of radically reorienting the social and political goals of the nation by developing new habits of thought and action before old prejudices were hardened. Unlike today's model of institutionalized education, which is literally confined within the four walls of buildings, their experimental models of childhood education were fully integrated into the life of the community. Rather than focusing on women's issues as such, they seemed to want to build on women's sense of themselves as full citizens—a legacy of the exhausting struggles for the franchise—to develop a new model of cooperative responsibility for social change. I agree with Antler that "the histories of women such as Lucy Sprague Mitchell reveal feminism not as theory but as a hard-fought life struggle."[89]

Including women philosophers such as Gilman and Addams among those who count as classical American philosophers will revise and enrich that heritage. Their explicit denunciation of sexism contributes a dimension missing in our definition of what counts as pragmatist philosophy. We also need to study the lives and writings of women like Taft, Howes, and Ladd-Franklin to understand why even an explicitly emancipatory philosophy like pragmatism and the activism on behalf of women's causes by Dewey and Mead were not sufficient to generate and preserve an explicitly feminist version of pragmatism.

Some early women pragmatists, like Clapp, were pushed out of an academic career in philosophy. Others, like Mitchell, left voluntarily in order to pursue careers more relevant to their interests. Still others, like

Taft, involuntarily left the academy and struggled for many years before achieving academic success in the allied fields of psychology, social work, and clinical sociology.[90] All three moves were a direct result of the masculinist perspective that dominated both the traditional subject matter of philosophy and the attitudes of most philosophy professors. Mitchell later reflected, though, whether she could "have stuck it out . . . if [she] had become a teacher of metaphysics."[91] And she seems to allude to this conflation of philosophy with masculinity when she continues: "And if I had, *what* would I be like now?" It is also clear from the instances I have so far turned up that some of the women students of the founding pragmatists had begun revisioning pragmatism out of their own experiences, frustrations, and aspirations as women. Logically, the next step would be to recover and study their writings in order to revise the history of pragmatism and thereby contribute to the continuous reconstruction of pragmatist philosophy as well as to developing an explicitly pragmatist feminism.

A few fledgling steps in this direction are taken in the next two chapters. A set of conditions conducive to developing a pragmatist feminism and for feminist insights influencing pragmatism came together around the turn of the century at the University of Chicago. Aspects of this early coalescence, as well as some of the countervailing forces that led to its untimely demise, are discussed in chapter 4. One of the earliest and most influential sources of Dewey's striking rejection of a long tradition of isolated individualism that grounds so many epistemological and metaphysical theories as well as ethical, social, and political ones is his involvement with early childhood education. His original transformation of the Hegelian emphasis on relations into a pragmatist model of social intelligence is mediated through educational theories and practices in which women play a dominant role. I argue the importance of Dewey's educational theory for interpreting his pragmatism in chapter 5, where I also argue that a feminist perspective requires some transformations of that theory.

Four

Acknowledging Mutual Influences:
The Chicago Years

In 1908, during the summer break from their high school teaching, Jessie Taft, twenty-six years old, and Virginia Robinson, twenty-five, began studying philosophy at the University of Chicago. Robinson wrote to a former classmate: "Pragmatism is in the air and everybody starts with it as a basis. I do not know how I shall escape the influence."[1] Indeed, not only did the earliest generations of women who studied philosophy in colleges and universities not escape the influence of pragmatism, but the most exciting and profitable years for both coincided. Although Dewey had already left Chicago for Columbia University in 1904, the department he had assembled was still active in pragmatist and feminist research.[2] The coincidence was both fortuitous and codependent, and the fortunes of pragmatism as an academic discipline and women's presence in graduate schools of philosophy, psychology, and the social sciences— insofar as their growing numbers encouraged research on women and issues important to women—waxed and waned together.

Rosalind Rosenberg astutely charts the mutual influences as she uncovers the "roots of modern feminism" in *Beyond Separate Spheres.* In their lifetime the women who studied with the first generation of pragmatist philosophers uneasily bridged the earlier women's movement, which valorized women's superior selflessness, purity, and fitness to reform society because of their maternal instincts and "the values of individualism, egalitarianism, scientific objectivity, and careerism that characterized the scholarly outlook in the emerging American university."[3] Noting that "after 1920 it became increasingly difficult to reconcile reform with science," the first generations of college-educated career women, with their new faith in the power of scientific research to break down old prejudices, were increasingly alienated from reformers united by a common sense of purpose, largely derived from their Victorian idealization of womanhood.

Daniel J. Wilson also uses the 1920s as the watershed decade after which philosophy had shifted "to a professional, specialized academic discipline," ripe for the scientism of the logical positivism of the 1930s.[4] The growing emphasis on logic and epistemology as value-free endeavors gradually displaced pragmatist emphasis on such themes as the interdependence of the humanistic, social, and biological research programs; the continuity of organism and environment, feelings and thoughts, facts and values; and the goal of philosophy as a community-based search for solutions to common problems.

1. THE PROGRESSIVE ERA: RESEARCH AND REFORM

For a brief period philosophy, psychology, education, and the social sciences defined their goals as reconstruction of the cultural, social, and political order for the purpose of empowering all members of society to take their places as participants in a democratic process.[5] During the same progressive era predominantly women's institutions such as the Hull House settlement, led by Jane Addams; experimental schools such as the Community School at Arthurdale, led by Elsie Ripley Clapp with the support of Eleanor Roosevelt; and the Bank Street School of Teacher Training, led by Lucy Sprague Mitchell joined their sense of mission as women with their newly acquired professional skills. The pragmatist position that values do and should guide scientific and philosophic projects supported women's beliefs that as women they had something special to contribute to the public as well as the private sphere.

Although it seems obvious that the issues of women's nature and place in society have only begun to be integrated into many academic disciplines in the last few decades of this century, there was actually a brief period at the beginning of this century when excitement over the direction the disciplines were taking coincided with excitement over new research on and by women, research that not coincidentally included race.[6] According to Rosalind Rosenberg, the University of Chicago at the turn of the century was in a unique position to challenge conventional notions about women because only it could lay claim to three supporting conditions: "coeducation, innovative research, and committed feminists." As she goes on to demonstrate, however, the moving force on the side of academia was the pragmatist, interdisciplinary philosophy department and the surprising fact that in 1900 women outnumbered men in the departments of philosophy (which included psychology and pedagogy), history, sociology, Greek, Latin, the modern languages, and English.[7]

John Dewey was head of a vital multidisciplinary department, and its members also interacted with many of the other departments, even jointly directing graduate students. According to Darnell Rucker, the Chicago School was unusual in its emphasis on community—both as means and end—and its concern with cooperation to address the most pressing needs of the time. "Philosophy had to look to psychology, sociology, economics, education, religion, etc., for the content of its own value problems, just as it had to count on those disciplines maintaining a connection with it. The key to the entire operation, of course, was a set of conditions conducive to the willingness of the men concerned to listen to what their colleagues in other departments were saying."[8]

Many women who enrolled in philosophy did so in order to become teachers, other to study psychology. The fact that philosophy was so closely integrated with pedagogy and psychology helps account for the large numbers of women in philosophy, but they could only pursue iconoclastic research on women if, in addition to their numbers, they were encouraged to do so. Once again, an unusual set of circumstances helps account for this encouragement by their philosophy professors. All four faculty members, George Herbert Mead, James Rowland Angell, James Hayden Tufts, and Dewey were interested in reconciling their religious commitments, which included belief in the power of individuals to define their own destinies, with the ideas of modern science, particularly in response to the growing conviction that human beings were wholly determined by their empirical circumstances. Their concerns led them to challenge the increasingly dominant mechanistic and individualistic interpretations of Darwinian evolutionary theory and to incorporate organism and environment interaction into their developmental philosophies and psychologies while still defending genuine choice. They did so by demonstrating the social basis of human development. They could therefore undermine traditional theories of mind/body dualism and show the importance of the actual physical and social context to any theorizing about the human condition without reducing higher brain functions and intelligence to their underlying physiological and empirical conditions.

Angell, Mead, and Dewey were also similar in that, even before they arrived in Chicago, they were positively influenced by educated, socially conscious women to welcome women's expanding roles in society. Mead's mother had been president of Mount Holyoke College, and Angell, Mead, and Dewey all married university graduates who were actively involved in community affairs and outspoken in their beliefs in women's equality. Marion Watrous Angell, Helen Castle Mead, and Alice Chipman Dewey are all credited with intellectually liberating their initially more conservative husbands, particularly with regard to women's strengths and rights, egalitarianism in regard to class and race, and skepticism in regard to religion.[9] Rosenberg says that "married to exceptionally well-educated women who were all involved in the community activities of their day, these young philosopher-psychologists tended to accept and encourage talent among their women students to a degree unusual for that time."[10]

The career of Helen Thompson (Woolley) illustrates all too clearly the negative effects on women and theories of women's emancipation in the shift from a pragmatist to a positivist conception of science and philosophy and from an integrated interdisciplinary approach to academic specialization. Whereas Wilson develops the negative consequences for philosophy of increased specialization and professionalization, Rosenberg shows how claims that the feminization of higher education was threatening the masculine nature of intellectual life were deliberately used as an incentive to speed up both specialization and professionalization and stem the growing influx of women into higher education.[11]

In 1898, working with Angell, Thompson began her dissertation on the mental differences between men and women.[12] She found in her literature search on sex differences covering the previous twenty-five years the assumption that women were more mediocre, emotional, and irrational than men, due to basic physiological differences between the sexes, and because of their different metabolisms, the belief that women were better fitted for family life and social activity and men for lives of science and commerce. She believed that these formalistic, rigid, deductive analyses contributed to the many current inconsistencies and contradictions about the nature and extent of sex differences and that it would take careful experimental investigation to determine actual differences. In her own motor, perceptual, and sensation testing of fifty Chicago undergraduates Thompson found only random slight patterns of sex-based differences. She agreed with Mary Calkins's conclusions about her tests in "association"; namely, that whatever differences there were in thought patterns, they were not innate or physiological but were due to different experiences.[13]

As extreme differences between men's and women's behavior and attitudes lessened in proportion to their coeducational experiences, those who supported conventional gender roles feared that each sex was losing its distinctive psychological traits and complementary contributions to the welfare of society. But the women carrying out the new research were elated by this evidence that differences thought to be insurmountable because biologically based were actually amenable to circumstances. When some differences nevertheless remained, Thompson did not assume they must be evidence of innate gender-based differences, but "applied the functionalist argument that mind shaped experience even as it was being shaped, and that to study women at a specific point in history was to miss the transitional nature of their psychological development." [14]

Thompson's attitude and experiments thus provided evidence of the emancipatory power of science for women, evidence which could have bolstered Dewey's own liberatory view of science had he thought to incorporate, or even refer to, her findings in his own writings. Unfortunately, these feminist gains were obscured by simply continuing the conventional masculinist bias in language, as in such Deweyan locutions as "instead of enslaving man to a fixed and finished structure, the progress of science has been accompanied at every step by an expansion of man's practical freedom, enabling him to use natural energies as agencies, first liberating his aims and then providing him with means for realizing them" (*LW* 15: 238). An opportunity was thus lost for pointing out that women and blacks were among the first to grasp the emancipatory potential of science and to recognize, as well, how often it was used instead to give pseudorespectability to ancient prejudices by those opposed to expanding the practical freedom of either women or minorities.

Thompson was awarded the Ph.D. degree *summa cum laude*. Both Dewey and Angell thought her 1900 thesis the best ever written in the department, and William Isaac Thomas praised it as the most important contribution to the field of sex differences, one which also had obvious implications for race. [15] James B. Watson, who graduated *magna cum laude* two years later, admitted to jealousy of her success, but in a pattern all too frequent for generations of educated women, his own professional success immediately outstripped hers. His later fame, which stemmed from his rejection of functionalism for behaviorism, is a further indication of the direction psychology took as it left behind its pragmatist roots.

After graduating and traveling and studying for a year abroad on a fellowship, Helen Thompson accepted a position at Mount Holyoke. A year later she married Paul Woolley, which effectively ended her academic career because of the widespread prejudice against married women professionals. Despite the lack of academic support, having to move many times with her husband, and taking care of her children, she nonetheless distinguished herself as a child development specialist, reformer, and suffrage leader. She had turned down an offer to teach at the University of Chicago after graduation because her adviser, Angell, pointed out the difficulty of her continuing with her research as long as the administration applied a double standard in promoting instructors. Female instructors were requested to supervise women's residence halls and were expected to be "good hostesses and surrogate mothers" rather than good scholars. [16] Just a couple of years earlier, W. E. B. Du Bois was similarly discouraged by William James from seeking a position teaching philosophy because there was "not much chance for anyone earning a living as a philosopher." [17] He did not need to add that the chances approached zero for blacks and other minorities who aspired to careers in white institutions of higher learning.

Rosenberg notes that more than most women of her generation and educational level, "Helen Thompson Woolley succeeded in wedding her interest in science to a commitment to social reform. While other women social scientists, especially those who remained in academe, were beginning to retreat from the field of reform because they thought that its claims too often compromised the objectivity of science and woman's place within it, Woolley saw no reason why science should not guide reform nor why reform should not direct the use of science." [18] Because her family obligations precluded an academic career, Woolley retained the pragmatist view of science that she had learned in the department of philosophy, psychology, and pedagogy at the University of Chicago, whereas other women who continued in academia, who entered it later, or who were never introduced to pragmatist theory in the first place, were forced to come to terms with the new scientific ideology of positivism. In ignorance of the devastating pragmatist arguments against the newly ascendant positivistic scientific orthodoxy, they were forced to choose between value-guided research and reductionist science, reform-mindedness and the new codes of professionalism, social engagement in solving the pressing problems of the day and a cultivated stance of neutrality.

Nowhere was the relation of social science to reform more strongly urged and more extensively developed by Dewey than in his philosophy of education. In his article, "The Relation of Theory to Practice in Education," he acknowledges his indebtedness to Ella Flagg Young's book, *Scientific Method in Education,* for the noteworthy development of the conception that "scientific method is the method of mind itself" (*MW* 3: 263). What this means is explicated more clearly in Mayhew's and Edwards's book, *The Dewey School.* Besides the two features mentioned earlier of the value-ladenness of science and hypotheses as leading ideas, teachers are said to be like laboratory workers in that they must be acquainted with past accomplishments without being enslaved to them and must employ "the best skills that have been worked out by the coöperative efforts of human beings." [19]

Sidney Ratner and Jules Altman point out that Dewey attributed to Young and to his wife Alice the greatest influence on his educational theories and activities during the period 1894–1904. [20] But despite the fact that Young and Alice Dewey were credited with providing the greatest influence on John Dewey's educational theories in his Chicago period, and education with being the epitome of his philosophy, the precise nature of their contributions is not mentioned. Since Dewey is said to have hammered out his logical and cosmological theories as a member of "a gifted philosophical group" composed of Mead, Tufts, Moore, and Angell—all men and all faculty members at the University of Chicago—it would be reasonable for the reader to assume that, whatever the women's contributions were, they were not philosophical. Moreover, the male professors are described as active collaborators: "chief stimulus," "co-explorer," "most able champion," while Young and Alice Dewey are passively credited, at secondhand, as in "Dewey attributed to . . . ," so the editors do not even join in the evaluation, thus further weakening the women's importance and distancing their connection to philosophy.

2. JANE ADDAMS, HULL HOUSE, AND JOHN DEWEY

In *The American Evasion of Philosophy* Cornel West continues a venerable tradition of tracing influence "through the fathers" when he not only begins his interpretation of pragmatism by invoking Emerson, but also continues to see his influence at every important juncture. West defends his starting point as appropriate because of his own emphasis on the political and moral side of American pragmatism. Emerson invokes a mythic self, larger than life, as representing the content and character of America. But the political and moral power that West finds emblematic is godlike. According to Emerson, " 'the only sin is limitation,' i.e., constraints on power." Emerson extols conquest and deeply distrusts the masses. His vision "promotes separateness over against solidarity, detachment over against association, and individual intuition over against collective action." In his deliberately provocative account of Emerson, West wants to break with a scholarly tradition of giving him the benefit of the doubt.[21] But he does not break with the tradition of male intellectual genealogies.

A different lineage can be constructed, for John Dewey at least, one that recognizes the influence of hitherto ignored women and emphasizes a very different relation to power. Even before moving to Chicago Dewey had visited Hull House and soon became fast friends with Jane Addams and the first generation of activist women residents.[22] He became a member of the Hull House Board of Trustees when it incorporated in 1895 and extolled the Hull House model of interactive educational practices. In 1898 he wrote to Addams that he was glad to have his mistaken ideas corrected by his visit to Hull House and conversations with her before he "began to talk on social psychology as otherwise I should have made a mess of it. This is rather a suspicious conversion, but it's only a beginning." It was the beginning of a lifelong interest in learning from the successes and failures of the Hull House community in their efforts to transform the city and from their reflections and writings.[23]

Rosenberg says that "for Dewey, Hull House was a laboratory and an example of what he was trying to accomplish in education."[24] But Hull House was not so much an example of Dewey's theory of education, as it was already exemplary of what Dewey sought to theorize. Early on, he clearly develops the impact of Hull House on his educational theory in "The School as Social Centre" (*MW* 2: 80–93). And much later, on the occasion of the fortieth anniversary of Hull House, he emphasized an aspect of the settlement house that was central to his own vision of democracy: "In these days of criticism of democracy as a political institution, Miss Addams has reminded us that democracy is not a form but a way of living together and working together."[25]

Compare Emerson's mythic view of America's unbounded power, his distrust of the masses, and his praise of individualistic detachment, with Jane Addams's legacy of exhaustive service, empowerment of the immigrant poor, and cooperative problem solving. A resident of the settlement house made the following observation about the 1906 or 1907 Hull House ambience:

> In other groups where social idealism brings its practitioners very liberal funds, high prestige, and flattering publicity, the will-to-rule is likely to be stimulated, which in a hysterical period like the present leads to intrigue and politics and ends in the will-to-war. But this irony never confronted Hull-House, where there was little prestige or publicity and no pay. The House not only recruited strong characters, it was excited about them.[26]

Lois Rudnick argues that in writing *Twenty Years at Hull-House* Addams deliberately set out to reshape the Anglo-American male success myth by creating "a paradigm of national character and culture that is predominantly female and includes previously excluded racial and ethnic groups."[27] By recovering and emphasizing the contributions of Addams and other women with whom Dewey interacted in Chicago to the original formulations of pragmatism, a very different exegesis of pragmatism emerges, one no less justified than West's by its emphasis on its political and moral side. But it inverts Emerson's vision, stressing solidarity over separateness, association instead of detachment, and collective action as the arbiter of individual intuition.

Although Addams and Dewey acknowledged their influence on each other, the failure of philosophers to follow up this connection leaves the impression that the influence was one-sided. The presumption is that Dewey influenced Jane Addams. One must go outside standard philosophical literature to find evidence of reciprocity. As if to establish her own credentials, Jane Addams identifies what she calls "a bit of premature pragmatism" in a speech she gave while still in college. She is refer-ring to her rejection of the meaning of justice as either a mere emotion or as a goal only to be achieved by heroes in a far future millennium. Instead, she argued that actual justice is the result of a trained intelli-gence and broadened sympathies toward every individual man and woman we meet. It is not merely a grandiose abstract concept but a prac-tical, day-to-day affair of small steps. The one quotation from Dewey that Addams includes in *Twenty Years at Hull-House* is his definition of educa-tion as "a continuing reconstruction of experience," a phrase which per-fectly expresses her own educational philosophy.[28]

In remarks made in response to speeches given at a celebration in honor of his seventieth birthday Dewey pointed out that Jane Addams too modestly credited him with what she herself accomplished and learned at Hull House.[29] Among the many things he learned from her was to tear away prejudice and convention in order to fully share in "the more unfamiliar and alien ranges of the possibilities of human life and experience" (*LW* 5: 421). He then admonishes the younger students of philosophy in the audience to seek happiness by broadening their "in-tellectual curiosity and sympathy in all the concerns of life," which is the very lesson he had just attributed to Addams (*LW* 5: 422).

He most often praises her "intelligent pacifism," which is not con-tent with simple resistance to war but which stresses the need for "a wider life of coordinated activity" among peoples (MW 10: 266). In a foreword to Addams's 1922 book, *Peace and Bread,* written by Dewey on the occasion of its republication in 1945, he gives as the key to her phi-losophy her statement that "social advance depends as much upon the process through which it is secured as upon the result itself" (*LW* 15: 195). Given Dewey's own moral instrumentalism, it is no surprise that he also finds the means-ends continuum central to Addams's philosophical position. He applauds her refusal to depend on the exaggerated nation-alistic and power politics among nations to guarantee peace, and he em-phasizes that her proposals not only cut across nationalistic lines but also across the barriers of race and class to appeal for the development of people-to-people international organizations. She sought to build on the fact that real cooperation was possible among the diverse immigrant populations in the Hull House neighborhood and looked for ways to extend the mechanisms of cooperation back to their mutually hostile countries of origin.

Like Dewey, Addams relied on democracy, both as process and insti-tution, "to replace coercion by the full consent of the governed, to edu-cate and strengthen the free will of the people through the use of demo-cratic institutions."[30] Moreover, since her peace proposals are grounded in a solid experience of the past successes of humane organizations, they should be judged to be at least as realistic, if not more so, than traditional appeals to political and legal force. Addams always insisted that settlement workers and others who worked for social change received as much as they gave to those with whom they worked. This deep and abiding faith in the common people grounded her faith in democracy. She saw her role not as deciding what is right for others, but as a trustee of their interests. She sought to replace the leadership ideal of the righteousness of "the great man" with that of "fellowship."

Besides these explicit acknowledgments by Dewey of the importance of Addams for philosophic thinking and of her influence on him, many aspects of Addams's thought develop and expand on pragmatist themes in original ways. Her perspectivism and her pluralism were concretely grounded. She was more explicit than the male pragmatists about the value of the insights of women and of disadvantaged ethnic groups. In *Twenty Years at Hull-House* she reports that she was joined as chair of the federation of a hundred women's organizations by working women who sought the franchise "in order to secure for their workshops the most rudimentary sanitation and the consideration which the vote alone obtains for the working man; by federations of mothers who were interested in clean milk and the extension of kindergartens; by property-owning women, who had been powerless to protest against unjust taxation; by organizations of professional women, of university students, and of collegiate alumnae.[31] A Hull House resident reported that "one feels in her presence that to be an 'other' is itself a title to her recognition. . . . She has included Turks, Greeks, Soviet, Reactionary. . . . She has asked for no passports nor installed an Ellis Island." Another resident, Alice Hamilton, said that "Hull-House was American because it was international, and because it perceived that the nationalism of each immigrant was a treasure, a talent, which gave him a special value for the United States."[32]

Although Alice Hamilton was a professor at Women's Medical College of Northwestern University, she chose to live at Hull House from 1898 to 1919, when she left to become the first woman professor at Harvard Medical School. She undertook a reverse commute from the inner city to her work in suburban Evanston because life at Hull House "satisfied every longing, for companionship, for the excitement of new experiences, for constant intellectual stimulation, and for the sense of being caught up in a big movement which enlisted my enthusiastic loyalty." A scientist dedicated to improving people's condition, she invented the field of industrial medicine. In her autobiography she also reveals how the Hull House residents uniquely joined the pragmatist theses of learning from experience, perspectival views of knowledge, and antielitism into a democratic, multicultural ethos:

Life in a settlement does several things to you. Among others, it teaches you that education and culture have little to do with real wisdom, the wisdom that comes from life experience. You can never, thereafter, hear people speak of the "masses," the "ignorant voters," without feeling that if it were up to you whether you would trust the fate of the country to "the classes" or to "the masses," you would decide for the latter. But it also makes you distrust the sharp division which young radicals are always making between "proletariat" and "petty bourgeoisie." (Why always "petty"? Is the *haute bourgeoisie* more enlightened than the *petite*?) [33]

For Dewey, too, drawing on Hull House as his "working model" for the school as social center, schools should not simply engage in formal discussions and argumentation, which by themselves can breed misunderstanding and deepen prejudice but should be a means "of bringing people together, of doing away with the barriers of caste, or class, or race, or type of experience that keep people from real communion with each other" (*MW* 2: 91). Like the women of Hull House, who were both part of the elite and marginalized by their status as women, W. E. B. Du Bois, part of the black elite and even more marginalized by racial prejudice, expresses the same pragmatist criticism of elitism and makes the same call for inclusivity:

Again, what is this theory of benevolent guardianship for women, for the masses, for Negroes—for "lesser breeds without the law"? It is simply the old cry of privilege, the old assumption that there are those in the world who know better what is best for others than those others know themselves, and who can be trusted to do this best. [34]

Because they lived on such intimate terms with the problems generated by political corruption, poverty, and ignorance, the Hull House residents did not sentimentalize democracy. As Hamilton says, "In settlement life it is impossible not to see how deep and fundamental are the inequalities in our democratic country." [35] These realizations developed over time, as their experiences working with impoverished immigrants brought about significant revisions of the uplifting, elitist moral platitudes commonly taught to respectable, white, middle- and upper-class women. An eighty-year retrospective captures the interplay of personality and event that contributed to "Jane Addams' great experiment in social welfare." Founded by Addams and Ellen Gates Starr in 1889, it was later acknowledged that though "impractical and patronizing aspects of the settlement program remained," the arrival of Florence Kelley, Alzina Stevens, and Julia Lathrop in the first decade of its existence "helped push the settlement toward research and reform, but the depression of 1893 and the suffering it created also shocked the residents to action." [36]

Addams credited Julia Lathrop with helping her realize that she should not set the agenda for Hull House but instead should meet the needs of the neighborhood. Florence Kelley, a Cornell graduate who received a law degree in 1894 from Northwestern and a socialist who believed in "the necessity of applying the power of the *state* to prevent the modern industrial system from destroying its own workers, particularly women and children," was responsible more than anyone else for making Hull House a center of social research and "a center for reform, rather than a place to study art and hear lectures on Emerson and Brook Farm." [37]

Jane Addams's insistence that reciprocity ought to characterize the relationship between social worker and client, teacher and student, and her testimony that she daily learned as much from the poor among whom she chose to live as she taught them, were neither a priori deductions from moral principles nor idle platitudes, but conclusions reached from reflections on her experience. She consciously tested her own beliefs in her interactions with others and discarded or revised them as needed. She brought with her to Hull House a profound respect for the Other in her or his uniqueness, for example, but throughout *Twenty Years in Hull-House* she reveals how the concrete specificity of her interactions helped her recognize the class and ethnic prejudices informing her good intentions while at the same time providing the means for developing an authentic appreciation of and a more knowledgeable response to a lived diversity that could not have been predicted beforehand.

John C. Farrell finds yet another influence transforming Addams's originally religious and aristocratic motives in founding the Hull House settlement in "John Dewey's emphasis on experiment, experience, and democracy." [38] But he also pointed out that Addams adopted "Dewey's pragmatic ideas and vocabulary" only after a series of jarring experiences prepared the way. The severe depression of 1893–1894 called into question the efficacy of charity work; her service on a citizen's arbitration board failed to mediate the Pullman strike and led her to compare the motives of the labor movement and Pullman in developing a model company town; and three unsuccessful campaigns to unseat corrupt aldermen in the Hull House ward led her to reject top-down patrician political reform. She adopted pragmatism because it provided a means not just of understanding experience but of transforming it.

These three themes of experiment, experience, and democracy recur in the writings of women and men who identified themselves with pragmatism. According to pragmatist theory, experience, even when personal, is always also social; it is a developmental process that can be nurtured, frustrated, succumbed to, or redirected. This insight was as empowering for early feminists as it was for later ones who rediscovered the political dimensions of personal experiences through the practice of consciousness raising. Reflection arises in response to problematic situations, and thinking is a powerful means of bringing about morally responsible social change. Having demolished traditional claims to dogmatic certainty or privileged perspectives, pragmatists argue that experimentation is the intellectual appropriation of experience most likely to undermine prejudice and direct actions to justifiable outcomes, justifiable both epistemologically and morally.

Although pragmatists deny that any person or group can claim privileged insight into the being of things, they also show that each person's perspective is unique and irreplaceable. Until each person's perspective on a situation that includes her or him is heard and acknowledged, the complexity of the situation cannot be grasped, and possibly relevant insights may be lost. Claims about what ought to be done based on the truth of any given situation can therefore be justified only in practice. This means that not only should the projected results of acting on such beliefs be evaluated by all those affected but also the actual results themselves. Since effects can be long-term as well as immediate, confirmation is in principle ongoing and subject to revision. Social democracy, as extended from a theory of political governance to a practice of organized life, is thus conceived as a means for guaranteeing the dignity and freedom of persons by its structural incorporation of the widest possible inclusiveness and participation in determining the conditions for our existence. According to Anne Phillips in *Engendering Democracy,* the more recent women's movement also "drew on its concern with forms of organization and inter-personal relations to develop a radically participatory notion of democracy, and this was applied not only to women's groups but to every aspect of political life."[39]

3. ELLA FLAGG YOUNG AND JOHN DEWEY

Ella Flagg Young was both a student and a colleague of Dewey. But when she first enrolled in 1895 in Dewey's seminar at the University of Chicago, she was already a mature woman of fifty returning to school after years of teaching and while she was still an administrator in the public schools. After four years of taking Dewey's afternoon seminars on logic, ethics, metaphysics, and Hegel's philosophy, Young resigned as district superintendent of schools in Chicago and studied philosophy and psychology for a year. Following her resignation, President Harper had offered her a full professorship in the department of pedagogy, but Young insisted on earning a doctoral degree before accepting his offer because she did not hold even a bachelor's degree, having only finished Chicago Normal School. She joined Dewey's department in 1899 and wrote a dissertation on "Isolation in the School," for which she received her doctorate in 1900.[40] In the same year John Dewey appointed her the general supervisor of the Laboratory School and the following year Alice Dewey as principal.[41] Young resigned from the department in 1904 when Dewey left the University in protest. Even though she was asked by Harper to continue in the department of education, she chose not to work under the changed conditions.[42]

Throughout the years of course work and later for five years as a colleague Young shared her experiences as an elementary school teacher and public school administrator with Dewey, and she drew on his pragmatist theories to express her insights. John T. McManis reports that "the courses of Mr. Dewey and Mrs. Young in the University were developed so as to complement each other, and students in the department felt the force of these two great minds coming at problems from distinctly different points of view yet developing a common underlying philosophy of the subject."[43] They also collaborated on six monographs published in the series *Contributions to Education,* each writing three of them.[44]

In a letter published in 1916 Dewey tried to explain what each contributed to the other. Young's influence on his thinking was, he wrote, so continuous and detailed that he had difficulty separating out single ideas, but what he especially learned from her was "the translation of philosophic conceptions into their empirical equivalents." Time and again, it was only after Young explained back to him what his ideas meant to her that he himself grasped their import. Ironically, Young often felt that Dewey had meant to say what she herself had just realized. Countering such self-deprecation, Dewey gave three examples of how her original interpretations and applications of his theories went beyond his own understanding.[45]

Dewey acknowledges that Young acquired from him a theoretical grounding for her educational practices and support for her experimental belief in and respect for the intellectual integrity of her students. But he also says that in his logical theory he had not realized, until she emphasized it, the extent to which freedom meant just such a respect for the inquiring or reflective processes of individuals. Second, he was impressed by Young's keen sense of the way that the interactions of persons with one another influences their mental habits. As a teacher, she was acutely aware of the subtle but pervasive ways she influenced her students, so that the "give and take" of the interaction entered into the conscious conditions supporting further intellectual development.[46] Finally, his association with Young drove home to him how all psychology that was not simply physiological was social.[47]

Young, for her part, was acquiring from Dewey a specific philosophical viewpoint and terminology that helped her clarify and express her experience. Dewey suggests that gaining this intellectual self-assurance led her to overestimate the specific content of his contribution. In a remark both psychologically insightful and characteristically self-effacing, Dewey explains: "That is, she gave me credit for seeing all the bearings and implication[s] which *she* with her experience and outlook got out what I said." As a student, she tested theory in terms of experience, not the moribund experience inhabiting philosophical discourse but experience as it would be transformed in practice. "She had by temperament and training the gist of a concrete empirical pragmatism with reference to philosophical conceptions before the doctrine was ever formulated in print." Dewey was greatly impressed with the range of Young's experiences and with the fact that as she got older she not only retained an openness and flexibility of mind but cultivated them to an extraordinary degree.[48]

There was only one other person, also a woman—unnamed, but presumably Jane Addams—whom Dewey thought could with such penetrating insight reflect on her experiences and turn them into meanings and guidelines for future use. And Dewey says that only Roosevelt's knowledge of politics could compare with Young's knowledge of educational matters, though Young's was more reflective. Dewey gives Young his highest praise when he says that her practices were in perfect harmony with her belief in the life of the mind and the freedom of interaction between teacher and student.[49]

Besides the value of direct intellectual exchanges with Young, Dewey also praises her administrative contributions. In a review of *School and Society in Chicago* by George S. Counts, which examined the tumultuous political and social history of the Chicago public schools, Dewey focuses on the contrasting educational philosophies of two superintendents, Young and William McAndrew.[50] Young's policies had the sympathies of the Federation of Labor, while the Association of Commerce supported McAndrew. McAndrew, unlike Young, tried to enforce reform from the top down, rather than engaging the active cooperation of the teachers. Among the many conflicting interests clashing over the direction the schools should take, Dewey contrasts the efforts of business interests to control the school system with "the conscientious endeavor of women's organizations at educational improvement." He nonetheless points out that these women's organizations were themselves handicapped because of their exclusive membership in one class. He could have added race.[51] Dewey recommends Counts's book because it examines the social setting of a school system in a large, industrialized city, and he holds that no intellectual proposals for reform will get anywhere unless they view events in relation to their background and social setting. It is the very specificity of the analysis that will lead to an understanding of trends in school systems similarly situated.

Dewey chides Counts for failing to uncover in Young's superintendency her governing ideal of always taking teachers into active partnership in developing the schools in which they worked. He points out that Counts was mistaken in attributing to himself and Colonel Parker this policy, which in fact "was the matured fruit of [Young's] own personal experience as she moved from classroom teacher to administrator." Again Dewey insists that "as far as personal indebtedness is concerned, the ideas came to me from her and not *vice versa.*" He castigates Counts for not stressing enough the fact that when Superintendent McAndrew abolished the Teacher's Councils, which were initiated by labor and wiped out by business interests, he struck at this comprehensive policy of Ella Flagg Young's.

4. TWO UNHAPPY ENDINGS FOR WOMEN AT THE UNIVERSITY OF CHICAGO

Two major crises Dewey had to cope with at the University of Chicago involved education and women. The first was a battle over segregating women students in 1902 after they had already been part of a coeducational environment since the founding of the university in 1892. The second related to the autonomy of the governance, educational philosophy, and community involvement of the Laboratory School after it was formally integrated into the university. This crisis was precipitated by the dismissal of Alice Chipman Dewey as principal. In both cases the moves were initiated by President William Rainey Harper.

By 1902 the enrollment of women had grown from 40 percent of the undergraduate student body to more than half.[52] Harper feared that admitting women on equal terms with men, a practice first instituted out of economic concerns, would end by feminizing the university, discourage men from attending, and prevent the university from becoming a prestigious research institution. He therefore proposed segregating women undergraduates. Dewey, along with Angell, Mead, and a minority of the senior faculty members, signed a petition protesting the move to segregate women. He also wrote a strong letter to Harper defending the value of coeducation. But despite the fact that segregation was opposed by every woman faculty member and despite the fact that the dean of women, Marion Talbot, provided evidence that demonstrated the academic success of women undergraduates in a coeducational environment, the faculty voted to impose segregation by gender. Although this decision was never fully carried out in practice, the proposal did reflect widespread prejudices toward women among many male faculty members and administrators, and women's enrollment in and contributions to the university steadily declined in the following decades. Dewey's defense of coeducation in an article published in *Ladies' Home Journal* a few years later takes on added significance when read in light of this earlier incident and his positive experiences with women faculty and students.[53]

In response to the second crisis, Dewey surprised just about everyone by abruptly resigning from the university over the treatment of the Laboratory School shortly after it had been incorporated, along with the Chicago Institute, the Parker School, the Chicago Manual Training School, and the South Side Academy, into the University of Chicago's School of Education. This second episode has come down to us as a rather murky affair, one best passed over as quickly as possible. West's 1989 account is fairly straightforward and upbeat. He says that "in 1904 Dewey's school came to an end after a series of mergers and the subtle dismissal of Dewey's wife from its principalship by University of Chicago president William Rainey Harper. Dewey immediately resigned from the university." Without commenting further on the cause of the resignation or on its implications, West calls our attention to the happy ending: "Luckily, Columbia University moved quickly and financed a new chair in philosophy for him. And the luck was American pragmatism's too, for it was in New York City, and maybe it had to be there, that Dewey emerged as a world-historical figure."[54]

Twenty-five years earlier, Ratner and Altman had written that Dewey had resigned as director of the School of Education and as professor of philosophy because he came into sharp conflict with Harper, "especially on a moot point concerning Mrs. Dewey's tenure as school principal."[55] Again, no motivation other than a vaguely administrative one is supplied, and Mrs. Dewey's tenure is designated a "moot point."

Robert B. Westbrook delves more deeply into the politics of the situation in his 1991 account.[56] He says that the merger elicited fierce opposition from the teachers already in the School of Education, who feared losing their jobs, and from Wilbert Jackson, a supporter of Colonel Parker who had been opposing Dewey since 1901. They particularly objected to Alice Dewey's serving as principal of the new school because of her outspoken opposition to the Parker school and her willingness to fire incompetent teachers. Harper agreed to terminating Alice Dewey after a year to stave off threatened resignations from many of the opposing faculty, but he did not make this arrangement clear to either of the Deweys. Westbrook deplores the fact that "the documents that remain from this train of events make it appear that Dewey resigned simply because his wife lost her job" and quotes from a letter to Harper by Dewey complaining that Harper was trying to embarrass him by making the resignation seem a fit of pique over his wife when there were also long-standing disagreements involved.

The worst innuendos are found in James Miller's review of West-brook's book. After quoting Dewey's 1898 statement about education as "the fundamental method of social progress and reform," Miller comments: "Not for the last time, Dewey's lofty hopes fell short in practice. In 1905, he left Chicago under acrimonious circumstances, accused of nepotism and academic empire-building after he appointed his wife principal of the lab school." [57]

In 1936 Mayhew and Edwards differ from Miller. Far from being a calculated move to consolidate power, Dewey's resignation, they say, "was quite as unpremeditated on his part as it was unexpected to his associates." They report that in 1903 "Mr. Dewey accepted the directorship of the School of Education with his understanding that the regular teaching and administrative staff of the Laboratory School was to be taken over by the School of Education and was to continue in office indefinitely." But early in the spring of 1904 he was informed that no such promise had been made.[58]

Robert M. Crunden questions the accuracy of both Mayhew and Edwards's report and John's own recollections, saying that *The Dewey School* "is full of problems as a source, since material from thirty years later is often mixed with contemporary data, and the Dewey version of events does not always correspond to contemporary documents, especially those about his resignation." [59]

Since what had struck me from the first about the affair was the fact that John Dewey resigned after his wife was dismissed as principal, I was somewhat surprised to find that none of the accounts explored the implications for women of the fact that a prominent philosopher had taken such an unprecedented step. Robert L. McCaul is no exception, but in 1961 he gave the most thorough and detailed explanation of what happened, based on an examination of the documents in the archives of the University of Chicago, and he does provide sufficient evidence to allow one to make an independent judgment.[60] His motivation is to investigate two legends in educational circles as to "why [John] Dewey left the University of Chicago." The first places the blame on Harper for making promises about the Dewey schoolteachers behind the back of John, who then honorably resigns even though he has no other academic position, and the second blames Alice because she cannot get along with the teachers, who rebel, forcing Harper to ask her to resign, and she then puts pressure on her husband to resign as well. Instead of these simplistic scenarios, McCaul sees the affair as the result of the different personalities and administrative styles of "two great men," who both made critical mistakes in a series of complex decisions and events.[61]

Alice, who also taught English, was first given a one-year appointment as principal of the Laboratory School by John in 1901. When John learned that Harper was surprised by Alice's appointment because both the budget and personnel appointments had been submitted to the University Trustees without prior consultation, he apologized for the oversight. Harper had no desire for any readjustments. In that school year, the Chicago Institute and its Parker Elementary School became the School of Education at the University of Chicago and thus the University acquired a second elementary school. Both schools fiercely guarded their independence. After Francis Wayland Parker's death March 2, 1902, however, John was found acceptable by both faculties and was appointed director of the School of Education in addition to being head of the renamed Department of Education. Wilber S. Jackman, who was Parker's righthand man and who had already clashed with John, was also a candidate, but he was instead appointed dean of the School of Education.

The two elementary schools continued to operate independently in the 1902–1903 academic year, although under John's directorship. The newly named University Elementary School had only an acting principal (Zonia Baber) and Alice was still principal of the Laboratory School. Confusion understandably arose among parents and applicants about having two elementary schools within one University structure, and the faculties of the two schools looked on each other with some suspicion. When John proposed combining the two schools for 1903–1904—a move originally advocated by Harper in 1901—and named Alice as principal, Jackman wrote a letter in May, 1903, to Harper, complaining that John favored the Laboratory School over the University Elementary School. After listing five specific complaints he suggested, in McCaul's words, that "a good man ought to be made principal of the [combined] University Elementary School, a man who would exercise a strong and reasonable influence and be a neutral figure around whom all factions could group themselves. It would be seriously detrimental to the school if a person with divided allegiances were appointed or if the position were made 'a family affair as has been proposed.'"[62]

John indicated that he would have to dismiss some of the University Elementary teachers as a result of the merger. The teachers and its institute trustees feared that Alice would be only too happy to implement his educational theories and proposals for dismissal and prevailed upon Harper to accept the merger on condition that Alice not be appointed. John, feeling his authority threatened, refused the condition. As a compromise Harper extended job guarantees to the teachers and agreed to a one-year contract for Alice as principal.

Harper wrote John in February of 1904 to remind him that "the appointment of the present principal of the Elementary School was contrary to the best opinion of the Committee and the Trustees; not, of course, from the point of view of the person involved, but on the ground of the principle which I have discussed with you at least two or three times." The principle involved, which "remains fixed," concerns "the employment of a wife of a professor in an administrative or definite position in the university." Concerning this principle, "the experience of the past in other institutions, as well as in our own, is absolutely convincing." He also hopes that "arrangements for the present year will appear to you and Mrs. Dewey to have met all the demands that were involved in the complication of last spring." [63] McCaul points out that although the letter implies that Alice is not to be reappointed principal for 1904–1905, it is not explicitly stated. He also points out that Harper appeals to a principle [of nepotism] and not to any professional or personal failings on Alice's part. In fact, although no documents exist in the University of Chicago archives revealing how Alice got along with her teachers, there is evidence that John and Jackman still clashed over many issues, including their respective administrative spheres, and that there were budgetary disagreements with Harper. [64]

John left on March 13 for a series of lectures in New York. Harper met with Alice on March 27, telling her that he and John had understood a year earlier that it would be her "pleasure to withdraw from the principalship at some time not fixed, but presumably within the year covered by the appointment." The news apparently came as a great shock to her, for John "was to claim that he had not understood that her appointment as principal of the University Elementary School was to be for no more than one year." [65] Within ten days of the interview both John and Alice had submitted their resignations from the School of Education, and a few days later John also resigned as professor of philosophy.

Harper did not want to lose John. He consulted with two groups of advisers, who split over the nepotism issue. John's closest friends, George Herbert Mead and James Rowland Angell, advocated retaining Alice, while Harry Pratt Judson, dean of the College of Arts, Literature, and Science, and Albion Small, professor of sociology, recommended that she not be reappointed. Mead "stressed the fact that Mrs. Dewey played a very 'prominent' part in Dewey's research work." Angell, for his part, emphasized the importance of keeping John, who should therefore "be permitted to appoint a principal of his own choosing for no less than three years, and that Jackman be replaced as dean of the School of Education by someone agreeable to Dewey." Moreover, Angell thought that Harper should apologize to Alice. Judson also recognized the administrative difficulties that John was laboring under and thought that he should be allowed to dismiss members of the staff and reconstruct it according to his views, with the lone exception of Alice, because "the relation of husband and wife in such a position cannot fail to cause embarrassments, depriving each of liberty essential to successful work." He proposed that "Mrs. Dewey should retire from an official position which must mean friction and which must hamper Mr. Dewey's larger usefulness." In fact, he thought that John was imperiling his educational experiment by making an untenable demand for Alice's retention.[66]

Although Harper met several times with John to dissuade him from resigning, he did not agree to Alice's retaining her position as principal. He thanked both of them for their contributions to the university and apologized to Alice for assuming in their March 27 conference that she knew about the temporary nature of her appointment and had agreed to it. He submitted their resignations to the board of trustees on May 2, the same day that Columbia announced John's appointment. John's final expression of disagreement with Harper over the affair is given in a letter written to Harper on May 10 and quoted in full:

> As you are aware, the construction you put by statement and by implications of context upon my resignation in your letters of April 30th do not represent my own reasons for resigning—a point upon which I am presumably the better informed.
>
> In presenting my resignation to the board of trustees, and in recommending its acceptance, I request you to make it clear to the board that the question of the alleged failure to reappoint Mrs. Dewey as Principal of the Elementary School is in no sense the cause of my resignation, and that this question had never been discussed between us till after our resignations were in your hands. Your willingness to embarrass and hamper my work as Director by making use of the fact that Mrs. Dewey is principal is but one incident in the history of years.[67]

From my perspective Dewey's resignation appears to be one of the earliest principled protests against the use of administrative appeals to nepotism as an excuse for discriminating against women. The University of Chicago, in fact, continued to invoke the specter of nepotism as a way of denying women equal access to academic positions and promotions well into the second half of the twentieth century. In his letter to Harper, Dewey resisted the characterization of his resignation as a private affair, that of a husband defending his wife, and instead directed attention to the issues of governance involved and the struggle over the integrity of the Laboratory School's educational vision.[68] In fact, in response to Max Eastman's prodding many years later, John puts Alice's firing at the center of the incident because "she was the sole channel through which Dewey's ideas could naturally get down into action. She was too deeply bound up with bringing them down to be eased out as incidental to a

'Dewey School.' Dewey surmised, besides, that his other trained teachers would be eased out in the same sly fashion." [69] By refusing Harper's appeal to the separation of the private and the public spheres as a way to diffuse his protest and retain him as a faculty member, Dewey contributed to dismantling the use of the ideology of separate spheres for women and men as a way of keeping women in (or returning them to) the private sphere. Alice, to be sure, was his wife, but she was neither fired merely on that account, nor was her firing protested on that account. Both actions stemmed from her public office, and her relationship to her husband should not have been used as a smokescreen to disguise the issues involved. In calling for Alice's resignation, various factions were actually striking at John's educational and administrative policies.

Continued reports of the mysterious circumstances surrounding his resignation stem from the fact that—apart from his dramatic gesture—Dewey did not publicly state the reasons for his resignation.[70] They also suggest a climate of prejudice in which Harper's invocation of nepotism found ready acceptance. To compound the problem, some documents crucial to determining the exact reasons for the dual resignations are missing, such as John's and Alice's letters of resignation.[71] And in his letter of May 10 to Harper John even goes out of his way to deny that Alice's forced resignation was the cause of his own. But it is clear from McCaul's article that even if there were long-standing disputes involved that finally led to their resignations, the principle appealed to by all those giving reasons for asking Alice to resign was that she should not be employed by the university if her husband was. In not acquiescing to this condition, John did in fact implicitly protest the principle on which it was based. But only Mead reportedly spoke at the time to the issue of Alice's intellectual contributions and what the university would lose in forcing her to resign.

McCaul's "case study in administrative relationships" highlights the tragedy of "two good men" whose misfortunes were brought on by institutional circumstance and errors of judgment. McCaul does not mention that the resignations effectively ended Alice's professional career. He lists among Harper's errors the fact that he should have acted sooner to dismiss Alice, either in 1901 or in 1903, instead of waiting until 1904 "to invoke the principle that husband and wife should not hold line administrative posts." He never questions a principle that reduces a woman's career to being an adjunct of her husband's and that regards it as being dispensable. Although he upholds the principle that administrators should strive to implement their ideas and appoint subordinates of their own choosing, he nonetheless faults John for "an unfortunate tendency to lean on some of the women who surrounded him" and "his willingness to let Mrs. Dewey and Mrs. Young speak for him and fend for him in administrative affairs."[72] It never occurs to him that the reputation and careers of two good women are also at stake.

John's smooth transition to Columbia University muted the controversy before it had properly been aired and, in any case, still left Alice without a professional position. The repercussions for her were devastating. She never got over the shabby and unjust treatment of what she took to be her husband's great ideas and her own intense involvement in bringing them to fruition. Along with the death of a son that followed almost immediately, the deprivation of any outlet for her social zeal and leadership skills changed her once exuberant personality into a resentful, bitter one. No wonder it turns out that Alice wanted John to make a public statement at the time, "but [John] Dewey decided to swallow his chagrin, and so everybody else, for some thirty-five years, remained sitting decorously on the lid."[73]

John apparently regretted the decision in hindsight and blamed it on a failure of nerve: "Mrs. Dewey always said I made a mistake not to publish the whole thing when it happened. She had more nerve and courage than I have."[74] But the harm was already done, both personally and publicly. At the very time when women were first struggling for acceptance as educational leaders, both as teachers and administrators, an opportunity was lost for raising the issue of nepotism as a tool for discriminating against them. Once again, the failure of philosophers to reflect seriously on such issues as nepotism rules and to speak out clearly and unambiguously about their injustice can be seen as contributing to the persistence of appeals to nepotism to discriminate against women in hiring, tenure, and promotion well into the twentieth century.

Five

Educational Experiments in Cooperation

Thanks to new perspectives raised by feminist theorizing, philosophers may at last be ready to take the theory and practice of education—especially concerning the growth and development of infants and young children—with sufficient seriousness to recognize its centrality to Dewey's reflections and its importance as an essential interpretive key to his writings. His early educational writings can unlock a whole range of meanings that would otherwise be distorted by confusing them with deceptively similar but distinctly different usages of terms taken from other philosophical traditions.[1] The first section of this chapter demonstrates the importance for pragmatist philosophy of Dewey's educational theory of the transactive relationships that characterize individuals and communities. His replacement of the isolated ego of epistemological models with a pragmatist model of social intelligence is shown in the second section to owe much to his choice of parent-child interactions as a model of learning. The shortcomings of even this promising model, in turn, become apparent when feminist concerns are raised in the third section. In thus concluding with suggestions for changes that are required to re-vision Dewey's connection of intimate relationships with a transactive model of social intelligence in order to eliminate traces of sexist and racist assumptions, I once again return to the puzzle of why the early efforts of women pragmatists did not coalesce into a uniquely pragmatist feminist theory.

1. MAKING THE FACT OF ASSOCIATION ITSELF AN ISSUE

We heard in chapter 3 Dewey's complaint that philosophers did not take his 1916 book, *Democracy and Education*, seriously enough as the most complete explanation of his philosophy at the time. He gives as the probable reason for this neglect the fact that philosophers did not think any rational person would seriously consider "education as the supreme human interest in which, moreover, other problems, cosmological, moral, logical, come to a head" (*MW* 9:ix, n. 1).[2] As Dewey recognized in other essays, it was not irrelevant that while women were in the majority in teaching and in schools of education, male professors dominated departments of philosophy.[3] In the preface to *Democracy and Education*, Dewey specifically acknowledges the extensive criticisms and suggestions of Elsie Ripley Clapp, as well as those of two male faculty members of Teachers College of Columbia University. It is unlikely that his colleagues in the philosophy department of Columbia University would be inclined to acknowledge the influence of educators or of educational issues in the higher reaches of abstract philosophical reflection.[4]

Although Dewey made his complaint in 1936, contemporary philosophers such as Richard Rorty still neglect this important source. As a result, in his aptly titled article, "The Priority of Democracy to Philosophy," Rorty says that although Dewey believed that "a conception of the self that makes the community constitutive of the self does comport well with liberal democracy," it is not of any great significance. According to the Deweyan view Rorty attributes to John Rawls, no such discipline as philosophical anthropology is required to understand democracy, but only history and sociology. Questions about the point of human existence or the meaning of human life can be reserved for the private sphere. In short, Dewey's assertion of communal and public disenchantment "neither presupposes nor supports a theory of the self." Finally, according to Rorty, Thomas Jefferson's and Dewey's idea of America as an experiment means that "social institutions *can* be viewed as experiments in cooperation rather than as attempts to embody a universal and ahistorical order," but presumably they do not have to be.[5]

The view of liberal democracy that Rorty attributes to Dewey cannot be reconciled with Dewey's commitment to social democracy in *Democracy and Education*. In it Dewey develops his understanding of democracy from the point of view of the social development of the self in what can fairly be described as a historically and developmentally informed philosophical anthropology.[6] He deliberately subverts the essentialism of Enlightenment models of human nature that have been thoroughly criticized in late twentieth-century postmodernist philosophies, but without discarding a recognition of those concrete relationships that reveal a common humanity. In *Human Nature and Conduct* Dewey says that a morality based on his reconstruction of human nature "would find the nature and activities of one person coterminous with those of other human beings, and therefore links ethics with the study of history, sociology, law and economics" (*MW* 14:11). He often develops a pragmatist theory of human nature from the concrete perspective of lived experience, situating persons in "some 'social' context and functional relationship—parent, citizen, employer, wage-earner, farmer, merchant, teacher" to undercut the exaggerated individualism of classical liberal theory and to diagnose the social and political ills that result from separating the individual and social traits of human beings.

Dewey's position is similar to that of Judith W. Kay when she asserts that "successful coalitions and political action require a substantial concept of common humanity grounded in an explicit notion of human nature." Her suggestion that political practice should generate and improve "working hypotheses about human nature that do not regard it as either biological determinant or ahistorical essence" but serve to "guide the emancipatory labor of dismantling internalized oppression."[7] Not only is the meaning of life central to his explanation of human growth and development, but in making his case by seamlessly joining childrearing practices with formally educational ones, Dewey deliberately subverts the public/private split.[8] Dewey's philosophical positions presuppose a very specific theory of the self and community, one which he developed in many of his writings. I agree with Rorty that for Dewey social institutions are better understood as experiments in cooperation rather than as embodying some timeless order, but I would go even further by stating that Dewey viewed human development as requiring cooperation. I would also add that by reflecting on two of the specific historical orders that Dewey originally drew on, namely, his experiences of and experiments with early childhood education and the Hull House settlement, a more philosophically promising understanding of experiments in cooperation can be developed than by limiting discourse to political theories of liberal democracy.

Dewey's theory of education is constructed from the point of view of a democratic society and deconstructs theories of knowing and morality arising from earlier social arrangements that continue to obstruct the democratic ideal. Seeking, as always, to situate theory historically, it "connects the growth of democracy with the development of the experimental method in the sciences, evolutionary ideas in the biological sciences, and the industrial reorganization" taking place in society (*MW* 9:3). This approach also broadly informs his other writings, as *The Quest for Certitude* and *Reconstruction in Philosophy* make clear.[9] But the book begins, not with issues of abstract scientific or economic theory, as one might assume from Dewey's statement of his goal, but with reflections on life as a self-renewing process, continually readapting to an ever-changing environment. Although Dewey drew on the biological sciences, he early appropriated conceptions of experimental method and evolutionary ideas and transformed them into powerful conceptual tools for reconstructing philosophical methods and outlook.[10] For humans, for instance, he points out that life includes social, cultural, institutional, and recreational activities as aspects of the environment, and Dewey uses "the word, 'experience' in the same pregnant sense" of such a "continuity through renewal" (*MW* 9:5).

Helen Longino's characterization of her feminist view of scientific knowledge and reasoning in *Science as Social Knowledge* has some striking similarities to Dewey's. She calls it a modest empiricism which assumes that "what we can know is what we can experience." Such oppositional science can transform mainstream science only by changing the social relations of the context in which science is done. Rejecting the presumption that truth is monolithic, we can still rank theories as to their acceptability, "in particular their worthiness as bases for collective action to solve common problems." Other things being equal, inclusive communities are taken to be better guides than exclusive ones. "It is better not as measured against some independently accessible reality but better as measured against the cognitive needs of a genuinely democratic community. This suggests that the problem of developing a new science is the problem of creating a new social and political reality."[11] But such a "successor science" as Longino is calling for was already developed in remarkable detail in the "predecessor" theory of pragmatism.

Dewey argues that society cannot exist without the transmission of the hopes, opinions, beliefs, and values of one generation to the next, an ongoing communication of ideas and practices that is not static, but involves "the constant reweaving of the social fabric" (*MW* 9:6). Persons, then, live in community, not as isolated individuals. But such natural communities can also aspire to a higher form of genuine community insofar as, through communication, its members become cognizant of a common end and so interested in achieving it that they regulate their specific activities in view of it. Only a few communities achieve such consensus by communication, however. The vast majority are instead composed of unequal, hierarchical relationships in which individuals are used to get results "without the emotional and intellectual disposition and consent of those used" (*MW* 9:8).

Communication is educative because in formulating my experience for another, I must get outside it—seeing it as the Other would see it and connect it with the experiences of the Other—if I want to get it in a form she could sympathetically understand. To express this interactive character of understanding, Dewey frequently modifies the words *understanding* and *intelligence* in such phrases as *cooperative understanding, social intelligence,* or *sympathetic understanding.* Because imaginative apprehension of the point of view of the other is required for intelligently communicating one's own experiences, "all communication is like art." We learn from each other merely by living together, but genuine education takes place only insofar as the worth of social institutions, economic, domestic, political, legal, and religious, are measured for their effects in enlarging and improving experience (*MW*9:9).

Dewey connects his analysis of the social nature of the human condition with educating children because when one does so, the fact of association itself becomes an issue and gains in importance. Since the goal of education is to enable new members to share in a common life, those involved are acutely aware of whether the children's and young people's abilities and powers are being formed in such a way as to enable them to do so. When formal education fails to explicitly connect "the acquiring of information and cf technical intellectual skill" with "the formation of a social disposition," then it can only produce "egoistic specialists." To the extent that societies value institutions for their distinctly human effect, that is, for their effect upon conscious experience, then to that extent they have learned the lesson "largely through dealings with the young" (*MW*9:10, 12). Using his criteria, we can conclude that a society like ours, which does not value its children enough to provide a genuine education for all of them, is not likely to hold its other institutions to standard of human development. Likewise, a philosophical profession that does not incorporate into its reflections the perspectives of those who interact with and care for children is unlikely to value or to focus research on the fact and nature of association in all its variety and diversity.

Since intentional education, as opposed to unreflective learning through membership in a group or groups, is "a fostering, a nurturing, a cultivating process," it includes "attention to the conditions of growth." Human growth takes place within a social environment, and since we are connected to others, we cannot act without taking the actions of others into account. Even "thinking and feeling that have to do with action in association with others is as much a social mode of behavior as is the most overt cooperative or hostile act" (*MW*9:14–16).

In the United States, composed of different groups with different customs, "the intermingling in the school of youth of different races, differing religions, and unlike customs creates for all a new and broader environment." In passing from one social environment to another, from the family to the street, to the store, to the religious association, the young person encounters different codes and antagonistic pulls, and consequently different emotional reactions. These antagonistic demands pose the danger of splitting her into conflicting judgmental and emotional compartments and impose on the school the need for a steadying and integrating mission (*MW*9:25–26).

2. SOCIAL INTELLIGENCE AND INTERDEPENDENCE

In expanding on the meaning of social environment, Dewey criticizes the two common tendencies—to exaggerate either the moral importance of direct personal approval or disapproval or to exaggerate the intellectual content arising from contact with a purely physical environment. Although Virginia Held distances herself from a reductivist empiricism, her understanding of experience ignores its social dimension. She distinguishes sharply between perception and action on the basis of a positivistic realist notion of perception that is inadequate to support her sense of testing in the moral realm. She still treats perception as passive and moral choice as singularly active: "In the case of perception, we ought to let the world impose its truth on our observations; we ought to be passive recipients of the impressions leading us to consider observation statements as true or false. In the case of action and of approval, we ought to shape the world actively in accordance with our choices. We ought to be active rather than passive beings."[12] Even though she acknowledges, with italicized emphasis, that *action is as much a part of experience as is perception,* her psychological assumptions ignore the active aspect of perception and the physical components of choice.

According to Dewey, any direct personal influence involves a physical intermediary environment, such as frowns, smiles, and rebukes. The false psychology of learning the quality of things through sense impressions, which are then associated into ideas, ignores the fact that meaning arises from use, not from mere impact. To have an idea of a thing means to be able to foresee the probable consequences of its action on us or of ours on it. Knowledge, learning, require a social medium. It is through observation of and participation in the ways that others use things, the instrumentalities through which they accomplish their ends, that the young learn most effectively (*MW* 9:33–35).

Education assumes three special forms: direction, control, and guidance. Guidance "best conveys the idea of assisting through cooperation the natural capacities of the individuals guided; control conveys rather the notion of an energy brought to bear from without and meeting some resistance from the one controlled; direction is a more neutral term and suggests the fact that the active tendencies of those directed are led in a certain continuous course, instead of dispersing aimlessly." (*MW* 9:28). Significantly, while Dewey's examples for deficient modes of control include that of shutting a man up in a penitentiary to make him penitent and the empiricist theory of sense knowledge, his primary example for control in the sense of guidance is that of the interaction of mother and daughter:

Even if the mother never told her daughter to help her, or never rebuked her for not helping, the child would be subjected to direction in her activities by the mere fact that she was engaged, along with the parent, in the household life. Imitation, emulation, the need of working together, enforce control.

If the mother hands the child something needed, the latter must reach the thing in order to get it. Where there is giving there must be taking. . . . Multiply such an instance by the thousand details of daily intercourse, and one has a picture of the most permanent and enduring method of giving direction to the activities of the young. (*MW* 9:33)

Despite an unquestioning acceptance of women's special role in the domestic sphere and in nurturing children, Dewey undercuts the devaluation of women's experiences in the home by refusing to restrict the value of domestic activity to its contributions to the private sphere. As is usual with him, the force of his example extends far beyond the insights gained through typically women-dominated perspectives of everyday life, primary education, and developmental psychology by being linked to theories of knowledge, ethics, and the basic sociality of human beings in their person-environment interactions. His example not only illuminates the principle that "participating in a joint activity [is] the chief way of forming disposition" but also the central pragmatist principle that meaning involves the *use of things* (*MW* 9:33).

Mere responsive adjustment to physical stimulus is not the same as acquiring meaning, which involves intentional responsive activities. Such activities, with ends-in-view, require social interactions. Human intelligence is therefore irreducibly social. Social intelligence is developed through the shared activities of communities in which each person refers what she or he is doing to what the other is doing. Language, too, is "a case of this joint reference of our own action and that of another to a common situation." Ideally, communities should build on these learning processes to encourage each person to deliberately view the consequences of her or his own acts as having a bearing on what others are doing and should take into account the consequences of their behavior on her or himself (*MW* 9:35, 37).

Dewey illustrates the process of learning by contrasting different methods controlling children. A child forced to sit by physical pressure instantiates merely a responsive adjustment that may lead to automatic responses but no true learning, while leading a child to respond in a certain way by having her adopt an end-in-view relies on intelligent guidance. Once again, Dewey then explicitly relates what is learned in the process of educating children to theories of knowledge: "To have an *idea* of a thing is thus not just to get certain sensations from it. It is to be able to respond to the thing in view of its place in an inclusive scheme of action; it is to foresee the drift and probable consequence of the action of the thing upon us and of our action on it."

Just as important as the relevance of the social nature of intelligence to theories of knowledge is the manner by which Dewey demonstrates the way that values are also implicit in the community-based nature of human development. Since meaning is acquired in the first place by intentionally pursuing ends-in-view and reflecting on the outcomes of such environmental interaction, an interaction that includes other persons as well as the physical environment, why not build on this insight? We can do this by developing the awareness that our actions affect others and theirs affect ours in ways that can be helpful or harmful to the well-being of each as members of a community. The next step is to take account of the consequences of our behavior and that of others in order to intentionally foster a community in which everyone flourishes. In this context, Dewey once again interjects: "Take one more example of a less imaginary kind. An infant is hungry, and cries while food is prepared in his presence . . ." (*MW* 9:36). He then proceeds to theorize on the assumption that such intimate parent-child interactions can be valuable models of the responsible acquisition of meaning.

They are not the only models, of course. Dewey avoids privileging paternalistic situations where one person is more competent and knowledgeable in relation to a less mature person by consistently exploring the reciprocity even in such unequal relationships. But he also uses other models that emphasize an equality of relationship, such as friendship. In *Individualism Old and New* he says: "I often wonder what meaning is given to the term 'society' by those who oppose it to the intimacies of personal intercourse, such as those of friendship." He contrasts the "cooperative consensus" required for institutional organizations to be socially responsible with the artificially induced uniformity of thought and sentiment that results from deliberate manipulations to induce conformity.[13]

In thus consistently linking knowledge and values, Dewey shows how values can arise and can be inculcated through thoughtful reflection on the conditions of human development. This is done by first recognizing and then appreciating aspects of this process, devising ways to raise to consciousness in all members of society these connections of self with others, and developing means to bring them about. Held, by contrast, drives an artificial wedge between moral experience and empirical experience, emphasizing that moral theories are normative, not empirical. She thinks that "critics of naturalism in ethics have provided arguments that I here take to be sufficient to require avoidance of the subsumption of ethics under science."[14] But these arguments do not begin to respond to either pragmatist naturalism or its understanding of science. According to Ralph Ross, "the pragmatic naturalism from which Dewey criticized was far more developed by 1912 than naturalism would be by most others as late as the 1930s." Believing that human beings were "as natural as stones, trees, and stars, [Dewey] had pressed on to reveal the characteristically human as natural, and thus included mind, consciousness, values, and ends in nature."[15] The values in the naturalistic ethics of pragmatists are not *found* in nature; they are intelligent appropriations of some natural processes as more desirable than others. These judgments are tested for the adequacy of the means chosen to the ends desired and subsequently evaluated as to whether the ends actually attainable are still desirable after they have been concretely realized. Individual insight and imaginative forecasting are required components of valuations, but so are the social context and community testing and evaluation. Held rightly rejects causal accounts of explanation and epistemologies dominated by a model of picturing the world because they deal inadequately with women's experiences and with women's oppression and the means required for liberation. But I believe that pragmatism fulfills the conditions she demands in an alternative model of experience that she thinks has not yet been developed in philosophy—one that instead incorporates empathetic understanding in explanatory accounts, that theorizes on the basis of human relationships, that is intrinsically liberatory, and that attends to cultural interpretations and realms of the imagination.[16]

Unlike many postmodernists, pragmatists believe that mind always involves social control, which can therefore never be bad in itself, though a worse rather than a better means of control can be employed and though control can be used for bad ends. Minds are not disembodied spirits or merely the imagined accompaniment of firing neurons. Instead, they are "the organized habits of intelligent response . . . acquired by putting things to use in connections with the way other persons use things. The control is inescapable; it saturates disposition." The primary example once again is how a child learns through language and through observing that other persons use physical objects such as chairs and money in certain ways. When a child sees a proffered hand and extends her own to shake it, for example, she is learning a habit of intelligent response that is "the deepest and most pervasive mode of social control" (*MW* 9:37–38). But given the history of social control in the sense of social engineering and brute force, and in light of such noncoercive examples and Dewey's own distinctions between direction, control, and guidance, it would be better to drop the misleading phrase, *social control,* in contemporary appropriations of pragmatism. Misconceptions can be avoided by substituting *social guidance* or *social direction* for *social control* in pragmatist reflections on the inherent sociality of mind.

Dewey relates the future of societies with the care they give in educating their young. In chapter 4 of *Democracy and Education* he develops with great acuity the social interplay of young children who are "marvelously endowed with *power* to enlist the cooperative attention of others" and grownups persons, few of whom "retain all of the flexible and sensitive ability of children to vibrate sympathetically with the attitudes and doings of those about them." Continuing to develop a point of view that seeks to empower children, Dewey defines immaturity as a condition of growth, which is therefore characterized not as an absence but as the ability to develop. It encapsulates the premier human ability—"the ability to learn from experience; the power to retain from one experience something which is of avail in coping with the difficulties of a later situation." He labels as a facile social response the frequently heard criticism that children are egotistically self-centered, attributing the judgment to the propensity an adult often exhibits, namely, to be so absorbed in his own affairs that he thinks children are unreasonably engrossed in *their* own affairs (*MW* 9:48–49).

From this perspective of child-adult interaction, Dewey develops a powerful criticism of the model of the isolated individual that underlies both liberal theory and capitalism, thus anticipating what is more extensively developed in *Individualism Old and New, The Public and its Problems,* and *Liberalism and Social Action*.[17] He says that "from a social standpoint, dependence denotes a power rather than a weakness; it involves interdependence." The danger in overemphasizing personal independence as the epitome of adulthood is that it leads to decreasing the social capacity of the individual. Self-reliance, in making a person more self-sufficient, can lead to aloofness and indifference: "It often makes an individual so insensitive in his relations to others as to develop an illusion of being really able to stand and act alone—an unnamed form of insanity which is responsible for a large part of the remediable suffering of the world" (*MW* 9:49). Later, in his classic *Experience and Nature* Dewey again reemphasized the madness caused by the disconnectedness of modern life and the need to recover sanity by reconnecting ourselves with others (*LW* 1:224).

The power, already mentioned, of carrying over from a prior experience factors that modify subsequent experiences is the capacity to acquire habits. "A habit means an ability to use natural conditions as means to ends." Walking, talking, playing the piano secure direction of the environment and not just of the body. Education does more than develop habits that adjust individuals to environment; it seeks actively to utilize the means necessary for achieving the ends desired. Habits involve "formation of intellectual and emotional disposition as well as an increase in ease, economy and efficiency of action." It involves inclination, active preference, and choice. Educational habits are intellectual dispositions: "there are habits of judging and reasoning as truly as of handling a tool, painting a picture, or conducting an experiment." Without these aspects of intelligence, habits are reduced to mere routine and "degenerate into ways of action to which we are enslaved (*MW* 9:51–54).

In his thoroughgoing naturalism, Dewey enunciates one of his fundamental propositions: "Since in reality there is nothing to which growth is relative save more growth, there is nothing to which education is subordinate save more education" (*MW* 9:56). But it must be stressed that for human beings growth includes intelligent direction and emotional development. Education is not passive, but dynamically empowers persons to transform their physical and social environment. "The educational process is one of continual reorganizing, reconstructing, transforming" (*MW* 9:54, 82).

The pragmatist understanding of the social nature of intelligence so integrates what in the contemporary discipline of philosophy has been sundered into epistemology, metaphysics, ethics, science, the social and political, and aesthetics, that it problematizes the practice of treating these topics as compartmentalized academic subjects. Its criticism of the fundamental dualisms that characterize so much of philosophical thinking means that we can no longer isolate questions of knowledge from questions of value, nor psychology from sociology, nor investigations of the physical world from the cultural context in which they take place. It opens up an expanding universe for reflective interaction. Instead of disguising itself as one discipline among others, with a distinctive body of knowledge, philosophy has to own up to its unique critical and integrative mission.

Dewey thought that as women moved increasingly into the public sphere they would have a special contribution to make to the intellectual criticism of compartmentalized thinking and to the further exploration of the social dimension of intelligence that had been so neglected in philosophy. In 1930 he confidently predicted that "the growing freedom of women can hardly have any other outcome than the production of more realistic and more human morals." In thus framing the issue of women's contributions to morality in terms of realism and common humanity rather than of sentiment and separate spheres, he was no doubt influenced as much by the social and political successes of active networks of women during the Progressive era and after as by women's greater sensitivity to the reality of relations, given their long apprenticeship in the domestic sphere. If many of his writings use as a paradigm an emancipated form of family life in which relations are reciprocal, in these passages the realities of associated life on which he thinks women will draw incorporates a feminist critique of the conventional forms of sexuality and marriage. He says that "present ideas of love, marriage, and the family are almost exclusively masculine constructions. Like all idealizations of human interests that express a dominantly one-sided experience, they are romantic in theory and prosaic in operation." Such sentimental idealizations only exacerbate the inequities of a conventionally-based legal system. It is this mixture of sentimentality and legalism that he thinks has obscured the realities of the relationships among men, women, and children and that he expects will be undermined as women increasingly free themselves from its constraints. This feminist understanding of morality would exhibit both a new freedom and a new severity: "For it will be enforced by the realities of associated life as they are disclosed to careful and systematic inquiry, and not by a combination of convention and an exhausted legal system with sentimentality." 18

3. RECLAIMING THE ROLE OF SOCRATIC MIDWIFE

Dewey's reevaluation of the domestic sphere as a significant although not an exclusive model of the educational process provides a basis for calling into question traditional views of philosophy and a means for radically reconstructing that process. Given the many positive features of Dewey's critically engaged educational theory, it is all the more important to begin examining it more closely from a feminist perspective. In his introduction to the unfortunately named book, *The Problems of Men* (*LW* 15, 1942–1948), for example, Dewey says that in a world full of insecurities, more alien than homelike, less amenable to grand system-building than to disintegration, philosophy may gain a role for itself by considering more closely why persons are so alienated from other persons. "It may turn to the projection of large or generous hypotheses which, if used as plans of action, will give intelligent direction to men [and women] in search for ways to make the world more one of worth and significance, more homelike, in fact. There is no phase of life, educational, economic, political, religious, in which inquiry may not aid in bringing to birth that world" which is yet unborn, the very "act of midwifery that was assigned to it by Socrates twenty-five hundred years ago" (*LW* 15:169).

Dewey's facility in drawing on the founding figure in Western philosophy to add support to his call for a pragmatist realignment of philosophy with contemporary problems stemmed from the principle that "the past is a great resource for the imagination; it adds a new dimension to life, but on condition that it be seen as the past *of* the present, and not as another and disconnected world" (*MW* 9:82). Dewey's women students would resonate to his view that education should liberate the young from an outgrown past, not recapitulate it. But he followed up this principle with the statement that "the social environment of the young is constituted by the presence and action of the habits of thinking and feeling of civilized men" (*MW* 9:79). Indeed, these habits were so ingrained that Dewey did not notice the absurdity of imagining that children's social environment is constituted exclusively, or even primarily, of men, civilized or not.

Pointing out the use of male forms of pronouns and of *man/men* for *human* is not just the anachronistic nitpicking of dogmatic feminists. If the past is the past of the present, then it is imperative to see what insights it can offer to issues of pressing contemporary concern. A critical task for feminists is to uncover the mechanisms by which women are excluded, ignored, belittled, discriminated against, or even battered and killed, as well as explaining how such practices can persist for so long. Whereas James's statement that the use of higher education is to allow us to recognize a good man when we see him is consistent with his support of the public man/private woman tradition, the fact that Dewey often explicitly includes women and revalues women's experiences in his writings makes his reversion to androcentric terms more troubling and calls for explanation. Given his lifelong commitment to radical social change, it is unlikely that he is deliberately extending some of the parameters in which women and men are coequals, only to exclude women from others. More likely, he is unwittingly instantiating the persistence of habitual ways of seeing, thinking, speaking, and writing that he, more than anyone else, recognized and systematically analyzed. The fact that he often included women on an equal basis demonstrates that habits can be intentionally transformed; that he did not do so all the time also shows the limits of transformation, given the hold of habits formed under different conditions.

Not only is the passage of time, with its new experiences, needed for the intelligent transformation Dewey attributes to habits as dynamic processes, but such changes must be both motivated and significant. W. E. B. Du Bois recounts the years it took for him—first, teaching at Wilberforce, an African Methodist School in southern Ohio, then studying blacks in Philadelphia for the University of Pennsylvania, and finally serving as professor at Atlanta University—to become sufficiently conscious of the structures that oppressed blacks. He reports that he developed from being their captious critic, to their cold and scientific investigator, to hot and indignant defense when, in a few short years at Atlanta, "I saw the race-hatred of whites as I had never dreamed of it before,—naked and unashamed!" [19] It takes the concretely different experiences of women, of sexual orientation, of class division, of ethnicity and race to lead to different theoretical interests and value judgments. These differences can then feed back to those not so affected in the first place to open up new ways of seeing, valuing, and acting.

Use of metaphors of being at home in the world or alienated from it can mean very different things to women like Gilman, Puffer, and Mitchell, for whom the home was an environment that alienated them from responsible participation in the public sphere and thwarted their full intellectual and emotional development. For women domestics working in upper-class homes who were drawn from recent immigrant populations—an earlier stream of white women from Europe and later of black women from the South—the home evoked still other multiple and conflicting emotions and thoughts. Patricia Hill Collins joins with other black women intellectuals in deconstructing "the image of Black women as contented mammies by challenging traditional [white] views of Black women domestics." [20] We can only guess what images "homelike" evoked for lesbians like Harriet Johnson and Harriet Forbes, who set up housekeeping in a homophobic world. [21] What is merely an unexamined metaphor for Dewey was for these women an often ambivalent, sometimes even excruciating, experience that led them to reflect, critically analyze, and write letters, articles, and books on the subject.

In their own liberation from a past that frequently ignored, if it did not directly oppress women, did some of his students silently add *women* to such statements, just as I have added "[and women]" to a quote above? Were there women who were actually midwives or who had used the services of a midwife among the students exhorted to be a philosophical midwife to a world yet unborn? Were there women who actually and not just figuratively gave birth? Did they consciously raise these dissonant experiences as material for reflection, or did they, like Lucy Sprague Mitchell of an earlier generation at Harvard, argue in their student papers against philosophical claims that did not cohere with their experiences, without being about to explicitly relate their disagreements to issues of gender? We know that students such as Helen Thompson (Woolley) debunked psychological literature purporting to demonstrate women's exaggerated emotionality and intellectual inferiority. We know, too, that her dissertation on sex differences was highly praised by Dewey.

I would not expect Dewey to raise the issues that many of the women pragmatists did. That is not the point. If he were to have had the same insights on all issues, there would be no intellectual need to include women in the discipline of philosophy, although there would still be moral grounds for doing so. What I do expect of any responsible person is that she or he be responsive to those differently situated, be willing to learn from them, to take them seriously even in disagreement, and to work with them to alleviate injustice. Not only have most of the pragmatists under consideration done so most of the time, often in exemplary ways, but pragmatist theory gives good reasons for doing so. In light of this, it is worth pondering why the feminist issues raised did not develop further or remain part of pragmatist discourse and, therefore, of the discipline of philosophy.

Apparently two different streams of criticism appeared side by side: the criticisms of traditional views and practices of gender hierarchy and male privilege by such women as Gilman, Puffer, Woolley, Taft, and Addams, and the criticisms of traditional, hierarchical dualisms such as mind/body, knowledge/feeling, reality/appearance, individual/social, and fact/value by both the academically-based male pragmatists and women feminists. Although the influences went both ways, since the male Chicago pragmatists in particular supported women's rights in practice and incorporated many of their women colleagues' and students' insights into their own writings, they did not develop or incorporate a specific criticism of sexism. Some of the women pragmatists, on the other hand, did use pragmatist theory to develop their feminist theories of gender. And some, like Gilman and Addams, developed their own versions of pragmatism as well as of feminism.

In hindsight, one may speculate that the very support of the male pragmatists discouraged some women from a more radical analysis of pragmatist writings. Since so much in those same writings encouraged and supported their own feminist analyses—in sharp contrast to the prolixity of misogynistic scholarship, opinion, and practices emanating from academia—they may not even have noticed any failings. In a pattern repeated in the Civil Rights era of the 1960s and 1970s, it is also likely that the close collaboration of women and men reformers during the Progressive era and extending into the period of the New Deal led the women to focus at first on what were considered broader social issues and to neglect specific issues of sexism. In any case, the gains made by the pragmatist theory and practice of the transformative power of education were lost to later generations of students in the School of Education at the University of Chicago when Charles Hubbard Judd took it over five years after Dewey and Ella Flagg Young resigned. According to Ellen Condliffe Laggemann, "Judd believed there should also be differences of gender—teachers should be female, researchers, male; and differences in levels of education—teachers should not be required to pursue graduate training, researchers should possess the Ph.D." Judd gathered around him many male colleagues supportive of his views. "There were, by conviction, no women," and this group "became well-known in the so-called 'scientific movement in education.'"[22] By contrast, the women pragmatists used pragmatist philosophy for their own ends, and the male pragmatists encouraged them to do so. The disparity of institutional power between the male professors of prestigious educational institutions and the women's precarious academic positions and presence in alternative institutions such as Hull House, joined with the hostility of the larger culture to any changes in women's status, must also have played a role.

Since both the men and the women pragmatist philosophers held that theory arises from experience and is answerable to liberating experience from oppressive practices, both might have believed that women were the most appropriate generators of new theory on sexism and that, anyway, the ultimate goal was to change society and institutions, not necessarily theories. It seems that the women working most closely with the male pragmatists were more interested in disproving notions about the inferiority of women and in improving women's actual situation than with designating the situation as oppressive or theorizing about the causes of women's problems in the culture and practice of misogyny. The male pragmatists cannot be blamed for not incorporating a theory of women's oppression into their writings if the women pragmatists who did incorporate women's issues into their analyses did not themselves develop a specifically feminist theory of oppression.

Gilman, who did explicitly and frequently analyze the androcentric nature of the culture around her, was least in contact with other pragmatists. Jesse Taft's judgment in her dissertation that Gilman was too shrill a man hater provides a clue that the academically-influenced women pragmatists generally did not take the depth and intensity of prejudice against women seriously enough to develop a radically feminist theory. It is likely that Taft is expressing a view commonly held by her male pragmatist professors, who apparently supported women's rights without concurring in more radical analyses of the causes of women's oppression. In a letter to the belligerently antifeminist writer, Scudder Klyce, Dewey distinguishes between "professional feminists" and women who use their experiences to convict men of being "essentially hogs." He criticizes Klyce for not agreeing with the women who accuse men of being hogs [male chauvinist pigs?] on the grounds that men think that their work is the most important thing in the world and, by implication, devalue all the other facets of life. And in another letter to Klyce he concurs that it is quite natural to be disgusted with part of Gilman's work—though he goes on to defend her plea for the economic independence of women.[23]

One male pragmatist did develop a more radical critique of sexism. While joining in common cause with white feminists, his analysis of the conjoined effects of racism and sexism from the standpoint of their impact on black women enabled him to analyze the nature of oppression more effectively. Nellie Y. McKay points out the distinctiveness of the radical feminist position developed by W. E. B. Du Bois, who called for black women's "economic and work independence, and for their individual right to choose or reject motherhood." It is "the damnation of women," he writes that "only at the sacrifice of intelligence and the chance to do their best work can the majority of modern women bear children," and he warns that "the future woman must have a life work and economic independence. She must have knowledge. She must have the right of motherhood at her own discretion (*Darkwater,* 164)." [24]

Du Bois argues that when all women—black, brown, yellow, and white—are valued only as virgins or mothers, then both mothers and virgins are degraded.[25] It is intolerable to bifurcate women's sexuality into that of either prostitute or nun. Having argued for the right to the full development of women's powers of intellect, economic independence, motherhood, and sexuality, he then uses the concrete circumstances of black women, whose relations to marriage, family, and children were tried to the utmost under the crushing weight of slavery, to develop a feminist theory of emancipation. In doing so, he demonstrates the limitations of evocations of family life and educational development that do not take into consideration the conjoint operations of racism with sexism. The attitudes toward and treatment of women slaves by their white masters and the strength with which black women surmounted the degradations of slavery reveal the shortcomings of theories of women's nature derived largely from the perspective of a white middle-class world. Du Bois not only draws on a different view of family life as lived in Africa, but he brings to the reader's attention a long line of courageous, virtuous, and intelligent black women, from lesser-known figures such as "Mum Bett" and Mary Still, to better-known ones such as Harriet Tubman, Sojourner Truth, and Phillis Wheatley.

Starting from the point of view of the situation of black women, whose beauty is often denigrated in comparison with a dominant model of white beauty, Du Bois both pluralizes ideals of beauty by praising the specific physical qualities of black women and undermines the reduction of women's worth to their appearance by holding them instead to standards of accomplishment.[26] He thus avoids falling into either trap—dismissing questions of appearance as irrelevant to women's emancipation or mystifying women's special relationship to nature and the body. And he points out that in a world where over half the black women work outside the home as compared to a fifth of the white women, and where black women can more readily find work, although at very low wages, than can black men, whose wages are also below average—in such a world the movement to return women to the home to allow more work and higher pay for men is not economically feasible. Du Bois goes even further and argues that women's economic freedom is good in itself and they should not in justice be forced back into the domestic sphere and be limited to a few, unskilled jobs. The advantages of Du Bois's perspective for a pragmatist feminist analysis are most evident when it is realized that of all the pragmatists Du Bois alone argues that the three most important modern causes are those of race, peace, and women's emancipation and that the conscious combination of two of the issues in the persons of black women will have revolutionary consequences for the thought and action of the whole country.

I think that it makes sense, therefore, to see the contemporary project of explicitly raising gender and racial issues in regard to pragmatism as a second stage of a historically developing feminist pragmatist consciousness, one that draws on the earlier stages in order to go beyond them.[27] The first stage, though promising, was ultimately sidetracked not only because so few women could surmount the hurdles set up to keep them out of positions of authority in academia as well as other institutions but because they did not carry their own analyses of women's oppressive situation far enough. Others who did more explicitly develop feminist theory, such as Gilman, Addams, and Puffer Howes, worked outside universities, and their feminist analyses either never became part of philosophy in the first place, or when they did, in the writings of women pragmatists, were ignored when these women left the university. As a result, their fledgling analyses of sexism never became a part of the ongoing debates in philosophy, psychology, education, sociology, and their early versions of a pragmatist feminism were lost to succeeding generations.

I can now add to my account of why so few pragmatists for many decades past were feminists. As we saw in chapter 3, the first generations of women pragmatists did not inspire others to develop their feminist insights further because their exclusion from tenured positions at leading institutions meant that they literally had no students. It does not follow that they did not have followers who carried on a feminist tradition— we know they did—but only that these activities took place outside colleges, universities, and professional academic organizations.[28] Second, those predominantly male philosophy students and the few women students of pragmatists who came along later seemed to think that they were already beyond the stage of feminist criticism because in their pluralism they addressed all forms of oppression and found it regressive to favor any one of them, including feminism, which perhaps seemed to them both shrill and dogmatic. These beliefs stem from the incomplete incorporation of feminist theory into the pragmatist theory of the founding generations and the loss of what was there. Rather than being beyond feminist insights, the last few generations were too often blind to evidences of sexism that were all around them and did not in any case think there was anything of theoretical significance to be learned from feminism. In this matter they were often less open than were Dewey, Mead, Du Bois, and some other founding pragmatists to women's contributions as women.

In the absence of an explicit and thorough feminist theory of gender, with all its ramifications, piecemeal reforms will not sum themselves up into the liberation of women or of society from its prejudices toward women. Until very recently the even more complete absence of women of color from the ranks of academic philosophers has had the same predictable result of covering over the prejudices toward and the struggles of racial and ethnic minorities occasioned by the absence of explicit theoretical formulations of the effects of the conjunction of racism, sexism, and classism. Without such explicit theoretical analyses women will also not be empowered as pragmatists to develop areas of research of particular interest to them, nor will such forums of pragmatist exchange as conferences, journals, and books welcome such new topics nor reconstructions of traditional ones. A broad theory of oppression and of pluralism is helpful but not sufficient. As pragmatists should be the first to recognize, only concrete analyses can provide satisfactory or worthwhile outcomes. And the absence of such members of the larger community as significant numbers of women in all their cultural, class, ethnic, racial, sexual, and theoretical diversity in philosophical forums means that their points of view are not being incorporated into the ongoing reconstruction of philosophy and that any conclusions being reached are correspondingly partial and distorted. For pragmatists, it should be an epistemological as well as an ethical issue and evidence of a flawed methodological procedure that relevant groups of people are simply missing in philosophy and that many diverse and challenging perspectives are marginalized or absent.[29]

2

Liberating Theory

Six

The Feminine-Mystical Threat
to Masculine-Scientific Order

In his obituary of 1910 John Dewey commemorated William James by praising "his intellectual vitality, his openness of mind, his freedom from cant, his sympathetic insight into what other people were thinking of, his frank honesty, his spirit of adventure into the unknown" (*MW* 6:96). In one respect, however, his sympathetic insight failed him, and that is in regard to women, whom he consistently viewed from a masculinist, or ideologically patriarchal angle of vision; that is, one which equates humanness with maleness and believes that women's proper role is to serve men's interests.[1] As a result of this devaluation of women, their experiences are distorted when they are not ignored outright, and customary and institutional barriers to women's emancipation are not challenged.

James's explicit support of the ideology of separate spheres, which restricts women to the privacy of the home and reserves the public sphere for men, mires him in sentimentality rather than in the sympathetic understanding so characteristic of his interactions with others whose way of life differs dramatically from his own. Insofar as he believed that women's nature predisposed them to higher moral standards, his views about women resemble those of his contemporary, Jane Addams, as well as those of Carol Gilligan and Nel Noddings in their more recent versions of an ethics of care.[2] The cultural feminism of Addams, however, a woman whom he greatly admired, differs from James's espousal of the ideology of separate spheres because she explicitly attacks men's injustices to women and argues that women should not let their responsibilities in the home prevent their active participation in society.[3]

There are at least three reasons why the topic of James's relations with women is only now being raised in a philosophic context. First, women have historically been excluded from full participation in philosophical discourse, particularly in institutions of higher learning, which were only fully opened to women well into the twentieth century.[4] And only late in the second half of this century have women been admitted in any significant numbers as professors of philosophy in coeducational institutions, which, along with all-male colleges and universities, have largely determined the proper subject matter of philosophical reflection, standard texts, and canonical philosophers. But these historical exclusions alone cannot account for the fact that this essay is only now being written. Absences do not make themselves felt unless someone is already aware of a presence that can be missed.[5]

The second reason for my writing this essay is that feminist theory has made us more aware that culture has been largely androcentric, as Charlotte Perkins Gilman wrote in 1914 in *The Man-Made World; or, Our Androcentric Culture.* She pointed out that not only has history been written largely by men about male accomplishments, but they have monopolized mental, mechanical, and social developments. The loss of an important part of my own philosophical heritage is illustrated in the fact that I became aware of feminist theory through a French work, Simone de Beauvoir's *The Second Sex,* at least a decade before realizing that Gilman had already written about women's oppression some thirty-five years earlier than Beauvoir. Androcentric cultures suppress or marginalize not only gynocentric views, such as Gilman's, but also any perspectives that reflect different centers of interest or principles of organization. This second reason helps account for why merely including women as philosophers is not sufficient to recognize sexist discourse, although it can help.[6]

After many years of scholarly engagement with James's philosophy, it is only recently that I have become aware of his pervasive sexism. How could it have escaped my notice for so long if it is so pervasive?[7] Philosophy teachers engaged in helping students uncover hidden assumptions know that what is most familiar is often most difficult to recognize and hold up for reflective appraisal. As Naomi Sheman points out, learning to do philosophy successfully means disciplining our own personal, idiosyncratic voices and engaging in the great questions deemed philosophically important.[8] The third reason, therefore, for not acknowledging even the small amount of sexism that one has recognized is that one must be sufficiently empowered to change the conversation, to make central what was marginalized, and to convince oneself as well as the profession at large that one's own interests are philosophically significant. As long as philosophy is understood as a quest for universal truth or is restricted to a predetermined set of topics, propositions, or texts, appeals to any particular cultural, gender, or racial perspectives are judged to be at best misguided and at worst to sanction bias.[9]

Moreover, James's philosophy and his way of expressing it was such an oasis from the conventional subject matter and method of philosophy, providing as it did such a powerful means of dismantling so many philosophical roadblocks and opening up promising new directions, that his own limitations in regard to women did not seem worth pursuing. So for many years I assumed that James's occasionally disparaging remarks about women were irrelevant to his philosophical perspective, which, after all, is pluralistic and antihegemonic. I simply ignored or skipped over them, much as Virginia Woolf did in her enjoyment of great literature.[10] This was easy to do, since the marginalizing of women in James's thought is reflected in the fact that his direct references to women are incidental to the main subjects under discussion. Substantial references are found in early, more obscure works and are not reprinted in his better-known books, and the references in his major works are either in footnotes or serve merely as examples of a larger point. They also occur more often in such sections as the physiological parts of his psychology, which are of less immediate interest to philosophers and are often not even read.

Like Woolf, I found that it was only by deliberately focusing on this issue that its dimensions have become more apparent and therefore more discouraging, since I have generally held that James's sympathy with the downtrodden and his vital pluralism shielded him from the more harmful forms of sexism. At a time when women were excluded from Harvard University, for instance, he was among the first Harvard professors to participate in the founding of the Harvard Annex, which later became Radcliffe College, by agreeing to teach women students. That I was wrong about the extent of James's sexist assumptions shows just how difficult they are to acknowledge and reject. It seems that sexism can very well coexist not only with individually cordial relations with women but also with philosophical perspectives that systematically affirm difference.[11] Inevitably, as women and those from other underrepresented groups move from the periphery to the center of philosophical discourse, our hitherto marginalized interests will increasingly become focal ones. As they do so, philosophy will approach more closely James's definition of it as "the habit of always seeing an alternative, of not taking the usual for granted, of making conventionalities fluid again, of imagining foreign states of mind" (*EPH*, 4). And in seeing "the familiar as if it were strange, and the strange as if it were familiar," it has the power to break up "our caked prejudices" (*SPP*, 11).

But why should the absence of women affect the subject matter of philosophy, which is often claimed to be a purely rational discourse or which claims to reflect on the human condition as such? James himself unwittingly provided the answer when he stated that "every human being of the slightest mental originality . . . is peculiarly sensitive to evidence that bears in some one direction. It is utterly hopeless to try to exorcize such sensitiveness by calling it the disturbing subjective factor, and branding it as the root of all evil. . . . Pretend what we may, the whole man within us is at work when we form our philosophical opinions. Intellect, will, taste, and passion co-operate just as they do in practical affairs" (*PM*, 77). It is not surprising that women would be more sensitive than his male readers to how James portrays women. Not just the whole man, but the whole woman within us participates philosophically and responds emotionally as well as intellectually to what especially pertains to her. For James this perspectival character of our perceptions enhances rather than distorts our understanding of reality, and therefore it should be encouraged in philosophical reflection, not rejected as a merely subjective distortion of presumptively unbiased analysis.

In this chapter I will examine James's relations with and attitudes toward women to demonstrate that his belief in separate spheres for women and men reflects the patriarchal ideology that only men are fully human, that is, fully rational, and reflects as well the Victorian sentimentalizing of this ideology, which holds that women are more emotional than men and thus the proper bearers of a morality based on care.[12] Not only are both attitudes detrimental to the full development of women's being-in-the-world, but they also subtly distort and undercut central positions of James. Since he argues that our feelings, attitudes, and beliefs inform our reflections, the feminist practice of "reading as a woman," that is, differently than the author intended, should not be judged as an invalid interpretive approach by other pragmatists. According to Nancy Tuana, the difference of such a reading consists in the overt rejection of "the process of definition of women in Western culture as not male, as Other." In regard to James, I show that what Tuana argues is a consequence of reading as a woman, namely, "the realization that some of the central categories of philosophy must be transformed in order to include woman and the variety of women's experiences."[13]

But although James's writings are among the least feminist of all the classical American philosophers (a distinction shared with Peirce and Santayana), they are also arguably the most conventionally feminine. Images of fluidity and merging abound; boundaries are permeable; and nuances usually lost in focusing on an object are recalled in his appeal to the fringes and horizons of knowing.[14] He develops a metaphysics of relations and an epistemology based on sympathetic concrete observation. His ethics requires responsive sensibility to the inner life and worth of others. Religion is defined through intensity of experience and not dogmatic formulas, and feeling is defended as intrinsic to cognition and the development of rationality. Morris Grossman writes: "The 'feminine' in James—the chthonic, the liquid, the vague, the inconstant, the chaotic—almost destroy him. . . . The 'embrace' of the feminine—the acceptance of the vague, the inchoate, the irresolute, the liquid, the emotive—saves him. . . . William also accomplishes a feminine embrace of chaos in favor of nature, abundance, inventiveness, fecundity and superfluidity." [15]

Perhaps it is the very prominence of this feminine side of himself that led James to emphasize manliness, the Promethean self, and the Goethe-like resolution to continually strive against overwhelming odds. However it affected his own life, his writings demonstrate an unresolved, creative tension between feminine and masculine desires and values. Both attraction to the feminine side of experience and assertions of masculinity pervade his published and unpublished writings, but are not themselves analyzed or challenged. His philosophy is so at odds with the masculine character ascribed to Western philosophy by many feminists, yet not yet free of sexist stereotyping, that it is particularly important to explore just how his sexism affects his appropriation of the feminine. Only then can a feminist radical empiricism be developed in recognition of the strengths, ambiguities, and distortions of the feminine inscribed in the text.

1. SENTIMENTAL IDEALS

Since James was a Victorian, after all, what does it matter that he shared the typical attitudes of his time toward women? It matters because his attitudes were not simply a reflection of his times but were deliberately adopted. Not all Victorian men succumbed to contemporary stereotypes of women. John Stuart Mill, for example, who wrote *The Subjection of Women,* did not, nor did Lester F. Ward, to whom Charlotte Perkins Gilman dedicated *The Man-Made World.* Furthermore, many nineteenth-century women, such as Ida B. Wells, Frances Wright, Margaret Fuller, Angelina and Sarah Grimké, Elizabeth Cady Stanton, Susan B. Anthony, and Sojourner Truth wrote and spoke against the stereotype and for emancipated womanhood. James was aware of at least some of this agitation on the part of women, and he even responded to Mill's analysis of women's subjection.

In fact, the one and only time James publicly wrote about the burgeoning women's movement, he uncharacteristically stepped back from an unknown he did not want to contemplate. In an unsigned review article written in 1869 while he was still a student, he supported Horace Bushnell's more reactionary book, *Women's Suffrage,* against John Stuart Mill's more revolutionary book, *The Subjection of Women.*[16] Bushnell's thesis is that the status of women ought to be improved by freer access to education and occupations, but they should not be allowed to participate in any form of governing. This limited view of women's education sheds light on James's later support of it. James agrees with Bushnell's reason for such a restriction, namely that women's nature is naturally subordinate. He actually believes that "the universal sense of mankind" confirms such subordination in women as an ideal (*ECR*, 247). But though he accepts Bushnell's basic premise, he disagrees with all of his supporting arguments and thinks that Bushnell does not specify the real cause of such clashes between the sexes as the fight for women's suffrage.

Although James thinks that Bushnell's style is too pompous and his utterances hollow, he nonetheless agrees with his sexist view of women, and although he praises Mill's clean, forcible rhetoric, which he says shoots straight to the target, he nonetheless rejects his contention that women should be emancipated. This uncharacteristic disagreement with Mill, to whom he later dedicated *Pragmatism*, saying that he "first learned the pragmatic openness of mind" from him, a man whom he would like "to picture as our leader were he alive to-day," is further evidence of the operation of prejudice rather than of James's usual, pragmatic openness.

James superficially criticizes Mill as quibbling over whether women have a fixed nature or not, since Mill argues that there are no fixed natural differences between men and women, only differences of education, and yet calls women's present condition unnatural. But in context Mill makes is clear that the Victorian exaggeration of differences between the sexes is not based on nature, as is claimed by those who want to preserve male privilege, but on socialization, and is only in this sense unnatural. James takes "the woman question" to be a practical one, by which he means that conservatives and reformers target for praise or for dispraise the same actual conditions of women, such as the restriction of women to the home and the failure to provide career opportunities for single women. He especially objects to Mill's attack on "the accepted sentimental ideal of the personal intercourse of man and wife," since James naively or chauvinistically believes that, by contrast with the situation in Europe, legal abuses are obsolete in America, where men do not express their superiority in brutality toward women nor do they object to their wives's occupying public roles (*ECR*, 251).

James likens what he calls "a hidden premise" in Mill's reasoning to a projectile whose explosive force propels it forward. He plainly fears the explosive effects of Mill's attack on the sentimentalizing of the Victorian family structure in which men rule and women serve. Mill argues, for instance, that what passes for a school of sympathy and tenderness in the family is more often an idealized selfishness, in which men's interests and self-worship condones a morality of submission for women and children. Mill advocates that a morality of justice, in which two human beings live together in equality, with leading and following reciprocally shared, ought to supplant the present state of marital affairs in which the husband is the absolute master. James responds that Mill is confusing friendship with love and that his advocacy of reciprocal superiority threatens "the conception of a wife as a possession" (*ECR*, 253). Although it is obvious that men's status is enhanced by their power to virtually own women, James never questions why women should welcome being treated as objects.

James defends the ideal of the representative American male, who craves dependency in his wife.[17] Since men struggle in the cruel public world of work and suffer from having their weaknesses exposed, they long for the security of the home where they will not be criticized and where their egos will be built up. Men's ideal of security and repose requires that he be the woman's mediator with the external world. Unlike Mill, James never inquires what women desire nor seeks to understand their needs or perspectives since he assumes, contrary to Mill, that he already knows "the true mental characteristics of women" (*ECR*, 251).[18] He contends that "mere mutual respect, and sympathy in some end" are weak ties in marriage compared to "that flattering interplay of instincts," egotism on his part and self-sacrifice on hers (*ECR*, 254). James fears the "extremely revolutionary import" of Mill's substitution of friendship for love as the basis for marriage, since friendship requires the equality of the sexes, while love requires that women be subordinate to men.

After examining this same 1869 review in 1986, Gerald E. Myers did not find any evidence of sexism. As I do in the opening paragraph of this chapter, he asks whether James's universally recognized tolerance, generosity, and goodwill went beyond mere tolerance to embrace a morally conscientious attitude towards women and concludes that "his ethics of individualism did not falter in its application to women." [19] He points out that James was highly sarcastic in his review of Bushnell and that he pilloried his redundant, careless, vulgar style. This assessment is accurate as far as it goes, but Myers does not notice that although James rebuts Bushnell's arguments, he does not challenge his basic positions. Bushnell argues against women holding public office or exercising the suffrage on the grounds of their feminine nature, which is naturally subject and meant to yield to evil rather than combat it with violence. Rather than finding this position morally repulsive, as Myers thinks, James at this point says, "So far, so good" (*ECR*, 247). He continues by saying that as long as Bushnell attributes these attitudes to "inexplicable sentiment" and holds them as ideals, "he remains in a strong position."

What James objects to are the reasons Bushnell gives in support of his dogmatic assertions about woman's nature and his view that being subjected to the will of another is a higher moral state than taking responsibility for one's own actions. James says that Bushnell's arguments are canceled out because he appeals to purely ascetic principles rather than to ones of justice. Myers defends his interpretation of James's non-sexist attitudes by giving the pertinent quotation: "Modern civilization, rightly or wrongly, is bent on developing itself along the lines of justice, and any defense of woman's position on ascetic principles will fall with little weight on the public ear." [20] But whatever James means by justice, it does not entail equality between women and men. In his arguments against Mill in the second half of the review, James quotes Bushnell to illustrate the horrors that follow when a woman no longer idolizes or idealizes her husband, insists on being his partner instead of his subordinate, and even refuses to accept his name. James once again objects to Bushnell's dogmatic assertion of what is a priori natural, but then goes on to appeal to less dogmatic minds that basically support Bushnell's contentions. These "other sceptics" object that, unlike the mutual sympathy which characterizes friendship, the sympathy between husband and wife should be hierarchical, and "the most thorough equality" between them is possible only within the restricted sphere that includes purely personal interests within the family and "the minor practical matters of life" (*ECR*, 254).

Myers points out that James had earlier mocked Bushnell's fears that women will lose their particular beauty and grace in assuming public roles. Bushnell cannot logically maintain the utterly radical difference of women's nature from men's, he says, and then be terrified that a few outward changes will fundamentally alter it. James gives so many examples of the silliness of Bushnell's characterization of women's simpering nature and men's thundering masculinity that it is easy to overlook the fact that he is intent on debunking Bushnell's arguments and ridiculing his style, but not necessarily his fundamental assertions. If Bushnell's ravings were allowed to stand without criticism, their obvious fallaciousness would weaken the moral grounds for subordinating women to men, grounds James wants to shore up by supplying the facts that will reveal just where "the true *puncta dolorosa* of the disorder lie" (*ECR*, 250).

In James's review of Mill's *Subjection of Women*, we have seen how he characterized the disorder being introduced into the conventional relations between the sexes by such new ideals as absolute equality between women and men, justice, and personal independence. Myers defends James's sentimental and self-serving rejection of Mill's arguments for women's emancipation. He prints a long passage in which James reiterates the theme of female subjection in marriage, proclaiming that "the wife his heart more or less subtly craves is at bottom a dependent being" and, after explaining the masculine ideal as including absolute validation in the private world of marriage, asks rhetorically whether the elements of security and repose essential to this ideal are "easily attainable without some feeling of dependence on the woman's side." [21] Myers says nothing about the one-sidedness of an ideal according to which men need to dominate women. Instead, without comment, he glosses James as appealing to "the *mutual* dependence in love," (emphasis added), as what will take modern marriage beyond friendship. He cautions against throwing custom overboard, since, according to James, custom represents the experimentation of centuries in coming to a moral equilibrium which should curb the arrogance of a self-assertion that challenges whatever it does not like.

By arguing only for the benefits that marriage brings to men and completely ignoring their negative impact on women, James's sentimentalizing of the patriarchal status quo uncritically espouses the very argument from custom that Mill so clearly demolishes in *The Subjection of Women*. The fact that after more than a century Myers can still find the appeal to custom convincing sadly demonstrates that Mill was right in attacking this source of women's subordination. James fails to rebut Mill's central claim that the principle separating modern liberal societies from earlier tyrannies is that conduct alone, and not the accidents of birth, such as sex, or of status, such as slave and citizen, should determine morality and politics. James concludes his review by advocating that everyone read Mill's essay, which will convert many who are skeptical or indifferent but will also strengthen those whose conservatism leads them to resist "the democratic flood which is sweeping us along" (*ECR,* 255). James wonders whether his own espousal of special moral ties that vary with circumstances or Mill's "passion for absolute equality, 'justice,' and personal independence" signals the future progress of evolution (*ECR,* 255–6).

In 1908, nearly forty years later, James repeats the view that women's role is to serve men. In a footnote in *The Meaning of Truth* James tried to correct a mistake he had made in *Pragmatism* when he asserted that "God" and "Matter" could be considered as synonyms, so long as no differences in practice could be deducible from the two conceptions.[22] In retracting this support for a godless universe, he developed an analogous case of an "automatic sweetheart," meaning a soulless body indistinguishable from a real maiden. The point of the comparison is that both God and maidens, though perceptually indistinguishable from their doubles, would not be accepted as equivalent to them. In the case of automatic sweethearts, even if they could perform all their functions perfectly, they could not perform the supreme female function, namely, to sympathetically reaffirm the importance and moral worth of their men. James argues in his imaginary anticipation of "The Stepford Wives" that the switch would not work pragmatically because what men's egos crave above all things is "inward sympathy and recognition, love and admiration," and the satisfaction of these needs requires belief that they are bestowed by a conscious being.

In this passage women are defined not only in relation to men but as fulfilling very definite needs of men. No reciprocity is implied or even logically possible because James is supposedly describing women's essential role as women. He gives as the curiously limited "feminine offices" of "a spiritually animated maiden" those of "laughing, talking, blushing, nursing us." A woman cannot even read the footnote logically; to do so in my analysis, for instance, I have had to substitute the term *men* for the original formulations, which include, besides "nursing *us*," "*our* egoism" (emphasis added). Once this masculine-centered perspective is recognized, then the gender restrictions of the phrases used in the analogous case of a godless universe a few lines later can also be recognized. James refers to "the chief call for a God on modern men's part" and "the craving of our ego" felt by "most men." Men apparently need women and God for the same reason.

James unquestionably assumes that women were created to fulfill men's deepest needs. They are quite literally God's surrogates on earth. And with a shudder I realize that it must follow that something of the absoluteness of God's love and sympathy is expected from women: never wavering, never withholding, never resenting. Justifications for self-regarding behavior that would be acceptable, even morally praiseworthy in men, would therefore be considered selfish, a moral fault, in women. Both women and men become morally worthy insofar as they live a full, human life. But for men this includes developing one's talents, while for women it means helping men develop their talents.

In an essay commemorating the eccentric individualist, Thomas Davidson, James mentions that a few independent women were among Davidson's faithful friends who attended his cultural summer school in the Adirondacks (*ECR*, 90). He condescendingly remarks that "naturally a man who is willing, as he was, to be a prophet, always finds some women who are willing to be disciples" (*ECR*, 96). The women's emotional attachments are emphasized by James's characterizing the women as warming themselves at the fire of Davidson's soul. He reports that Davidson, however, did not treat the women with exaggerated courtesy, but instead "told them truths without accommodation." Apparently surprised that Davidson did not seek to accommodate women's supposed sensibilities, but criticized them as sharply as if they were men, James remarks, after giving a few examples of such brusqueness: "Seldom, strange to say, did the recipients of these deliverances seem to resent them." The strangeness resides in the fact that the women students reacted as male students would, instead of according to Victorian stereotypes of frail femininity.

2. MASCULINE BRAINS AND FEMININE INTUITION

In his earliest essay on mental development (1878) James draws out the profound consequences of Darwin's theory for our understanding of human rationality as emergent rather than as a static property.[23] His explanation of "our concrete acts of reasoning" in "Brute and Human Intellect" introduces the fundamental Jamesian thesis of the distinctively human ability to extract from the phenomenal totality just that particular character that will best serve our purposes (*EPS*, 1–37). He explicitly rejects the interpretation of the mind as a passive mirror and emphasizes the creativity of human consciousness in determining the world of experience. The active rather than passive determination of the objects of consciousness supports feminist epistemological theories about the ways that our presuppositions influence reality, and his explanation of how reasoning by analogy links poetic with analytic thinking could be usefully appropriated for feminist aesthetics.

Reasoning is contrasted with narrative, descriptive, or contemplative thinking. Contemplative thinking utilizes "association by contiguity," which is the "procession through the mind of groups of images of concrete things, persons, places and events" mainly "derived from our actual experience of the order of things in the real outward world" (*EPS*, 2). It can also be expressed in revery, or "association by similarity," which more randomly joins images. Both are thinking through concrete whole representations, but contiguous associations are more common in dry, prosaic, and literal minds, while association by similarity is found more often in poetic and witty persons.

Reasoning differs from contemplation in that it abstracts from the relations in actual experiences and instead joins partial characteristics embedded in a totality of various items of thought. In rational judgment the connecting links are made explicit and the relation of the consequent to the antecedent is more evident than when they are related as undifferentiated wholes. Knowledge, which is initially vague, becomes ever more discriminating as various aspects of a complex whole get dissociated from the mass. Ever more nuanced distinctions can be made, and reasoning ability is measured by the power of dissociating hitherto unrecognized characteristics. This creative spontaneity is elicited by our practical and aesthetic interests, the "irreducible ultimate factors" in the growth of knowledge (*EPS*, 16). Experience is not equivalent to a predetermined outward order because "without selective interest, experience is an utter chaos" (*EPS*, 19). Unlike other animals, humans have the ability to break up the literal sequences of the order of things and imaginatively rearrange them. This dissociation of varied characteristics from a total phenomenon, as well as the ability to associate aspects not immediately perceived as connected, most clearly distinguishes human reasoning from nonhuman organization of experience.

The reasoning by analogy that distinguishes human thinking characterizes both poetic and analytic, or scientific, thinking, which differ in that the analytic thinker can explain the ground of the analogy, whereas the poet prefers to let the analogy resonate without discursive explanation. Neither is intellectually inferior to the other, although James prefers the splendor of poetic leaps of connection to the dry, plodding connections made in ratiocination. But after reaffirming the lack of superiority of the analytic mind to the intuitional one in any absolute way, he says that it is still true that the analytic mind *represents* the higher stage. To support this view he constructs a series of hierarchies, such as that philosophical reasoning by abstraction is a later stage historically than that of "savages," who can associate by analogy without knowing why the two cases are similar. The example he gives is that of Dr. Livingstone arguing with a "Negro conjurer." The savage state is to the civilized one as the uneducated to the educated, which he illustrates by contrasting an Irish girl with a male, educated friend.[24] He thus easily conflates savagery, Africans, the Irish, women, and ignorance.

Finally, man's most essential characteristic is said to be his ability to negate all fixed modes, to break up the received order into elements and combine them anew (*EPS,* 36). Man is preeminently human because he is an educable animal, not one who settles problems instinctively. But some humans are more educable than others. Italians, for instance, are not only said to be more instinctual and Germans more rational, but they will remain so despite education. An identical difference is said to exist between women and men. Women's likes and dislikes are set early in life, and their character is fully developed at twenty. A young boy of the same age is less developed and is awkward compared to the young woman. But this absence of a fixed character, of unfinished brain development, "is the very condition which ensures that it shall ultimately become so much more efficient than the woman's" (*EPS,* 37). The "masculine brain" can more flexibly determine classifactory schemes and deal with new complexities than can "the feminine method of direct intuition." No matter how admirable feminine intuition performs within its limits, competing with masculine rationality remains a vain hope.

"Brute and Human Intellect," which begins with the continuity of nonhuman and human, of primitive and developed, of contemplative and rational thinking, of feeling and intellect, and of art and science, ends with making a new hierarchy of them. It is true that James's sympathies are more often with the devalued terms of emotion, embeddedness in a holistic experience, contemplation, and poetry than with the more commonly valued terms of reason, abstraction, analysis, and science. He speaks, for instance, of "admiration at the *gracefulness* of the primitive human mind" and "disgust at the *narrowness* of modern interpreters" (*EPS*, 3). He even denies that the analytic mind represents a higher intellectual stage and the intuitive mind a stage of arrested development (*EPS*, 30). But his ethnic, class, and gender prejudices distort his pluralistic and developmental model. The equation of humanness with his own ethnocentric maleness effectively renders women and other races, nationalities, and classes as less than fully human. In these crucial areas he could not "break across in unaccustomed places," and he thus fell short of instantiating his own criterion for the distinctively human.

3. JAMES'S ETHICS OF CARE

James believes that the ability to sympathetically enter into the life-worlds of other persons is an asset, a positive ability, certainly not a negative one.[25] He argues that this precious natural ability of women not only can but ought to be learned by men, since it is an ability necessary to the proper moral development of everyone. Therefore, what is natural in women should become a learned moral habit in men. His ethics of care anticipates a similar version first elaborated by Carol Gilligan and further developed by others, such as Barbara Houston, Jane Roland Martin, Nel Noddings, and Mary Brabeck.[26] James, along with these feminists, believes that care and concern for others play a much greater role, perhaps even a dominant one, in women's ethical judgments, in contrast with men's moral reasoning, which emphasizes justice. They argue that ethics should be redefined to make caring a central moral issue.

Both current versions of an ethics of care and James's earlier version strike me as problematic.[27] The first difficulty with James's analysis, one which is also true of recent versions, is that he takes this sympathy to be a natural endowment of women. Since they do not have to strive for it, it does not seem something for which they should receive moral credit.[28] James says in *Principles of Psychology*, "If there is anything intolerable (especially to the heart of a woman), it is to do nothing when a loved one is sick or in pain. To do anything is a relief. Accordingly, whatever remedy may be suggested is a spark on inflammable soil. The mind makes its spring towards action on that cue, sends for that remedy, and for a day at least believes the danger past" (*PP*,II, 939).[29] Rather than in their exercise of sympathy, women's highest moral worth for James consists in their willingness to serve others uncomplainingly.[30] Such morally praiseworthy selfless service is facilitated by women's natural sympathy and empathetic ability to enter into lives other than their own.

There is no need, however, to attribute to sex-linked natural characteristics any systematic differences found in women's and men's differing approaches to moral reasoning. Not only women but any disadvantaged group whose well-being depends on the goodwill of others quickly learns to interpret nonverbal cues of the dominant group as a basic mechanism of survival. This learned ability comes to be seen as natural because it is so pervasive in women and so foreign to men who are able to ignore the interests of others because of their power to control them directly. Being the perceptive psychologist that he is, James is acquainted with these phenomenal facts, but he does not use them to rethink his appeals to innate gender differences. He says that "the impulse to conceal is more apt to be provoked by superiors than by equals or inferiors" (*PP*,II, 1050). The examples he gives of this hierarchy of concealment are boys toward their parents and servants toward their masters, including male and female servants, who must be hypocritical, given the unequal power relationships, since "servants see more of their masters' characters than masters of servants'."

That James does not draw a feminist conclusion from these insights is especially striking since Mill uses a very similar argument in *The Subjection of Women* to show why men cannot know how much women suffer under their oppressive rule—despite the fact that men live with women as wives, mothers, and daughters. They must wait until women tell them how their behavior is viewed "from below." And women are unlikely to disclose either minor annoyances or any mental or physical abuses they may suffer in the home as long as the complaints must be directed to the very person who, both by custom and by law, exercises nearly unlimited control over them. Since he reviewed Mill's book, we know that James was familiar with this line of argument. It is therefore even less defensible that he simply dismissed it, especially in light of the fact that he himself cited independent corroborating evidence of the psychological state in question.

James's belief that men are naturally belligerent and women naturally nurturant led him to systematically distinguish male from female virtue.[31] Heroism is first of all a male virtue, but since it is thus a preeminently human one, women can also share in it—but only according to their separate nature.[32] James says that "wars, of course, and shipwrecks, are the great revealers of what men and women are able to do and bear" (*ERM*, 134). And he gives as "the most genuinely saintly person" he has ever known a friend of his who was suffering from breast cancer and who, despite her considerable pain, continued to help others cheerfully (*ERM*, 143). Heroism always includes an active resistance to overwhelming odds, but men's heroism is described as taking place in the public sphere and women's in the private sphere. Furthermore, men's heroism is aggressively active, affecting whole civilizations, while women's is somehow passively active, primarily affecting only their immediate family and friends.

Women's heroism is categorized as "chronic" in comparison to men's "acuter proofs of human nature's reserves of power" (*ERM*, 152–53). James's "humbler examples" of women's sustained moral heroism include the cases of "illness nursed by wife or mother" and of "exemplary housewives," whereas masculine heroes include a man who survived a coal mine explosion and kept thirteen other men alive until they could be excavated twenty days later, and an army officer who carried on attacks despite sickness and appalling injuries. Female heroism is characterized by "sustained endurance" and selfless service of others, while male heroism is characterized as taking command over and disciplining others. Moreover, women are also expected to remain cheerful despite exhaustion, while it is all right for men to prop up their courage by taking brandy! Men's opportunities expand in heroic action, women's remain constrained; women can only be the "humble heroines of family life" while men are said to take on "new position(s) of responsibility" (*ERM*, 153).

4. THE MATERNAL JOYS OF A CAT (*PP*,II, 1055)

James's chapter on instinct in *Principles* is a veritable compendium of traditional sexist beliefs about the differing natures of women and men. Already at the nonhuman animal level, females and males are said to exhibit strikingly different instinctual behaviors. Females invariably either actively exhibit maternal instincts or are the passive objects of sexual love. Even the language James uses in examples of maternal instincts is condescending to the point of sarcasm. He says, for instance, that the hen "submit[s] herself to the tedium of incubating such a fearfully uninteresting set of objects as a nestful of eggs"; the broody hen would think it monstrous that every creature would not also find a nestful of eggs "the utterly fascinating and precious and never-to-be-too-much-sat-upon object which it is to her"; and "what a voluptuous thrill may not shake a fly, when she at last discovers the one particular leaf, or carrion, or bit of dung, that out of all the world can stimulate her ovipositor to its discharge?" (*PP*,II, 1007–8). Examples of sexual receptivity include "To the lion it is the lioness which is made to be loved; to the bear, the she-bear" and "bees follow their queen . . . because . . . the odor or the aspect of their queen is manifestly agreeable to the bees—that is why they love her so" (*PP*,II, 1008).

Male animals exhibit a wider range of behaviors, ones invariably active rather than passive: "The cat runs after the mouse, runs or shows fight before the dog, avoids falling from walls and trees, shuns fire and water, etc."; "a hungry lion starts to *seek* prey . . .; he begins to *stalk* it . . .; he *springs* upon it . . .; he proceeds to *tear* and *devour* it"; and a Scotch terrier made "a very elaborate pretense of burying things . . . he scratched the carpet . . . dropped the object from his mouth . . . , and then scratched all about it." (*PP*,II, 1005, 1006, 1019).

The nature of these sex-linked instincts would be a mere curiosity were it not for the principle that James uses in selecting them; namely, that "we can only interpret the instincts of brutes by what we know of instincts in ourselves" (*PP*,II, 1007). But women are not part of the seemingly gender-neutral collective pronouns just used: *we* and *our*. The perspective adopted is not that of humanity, but of male humans, as all of James's quotations make clear. Note the masculine gender of the word *our* in the following sentences: "The possession of homes and wives of our own makes us strangely insensible to the charms of those of other people. . . . The original impulse which got us homes, wives, dietaries, and friends at all, seems to exhaust itself in its first achievements" (*PP*,II, 1015). Since I cannot possess wives, he cannot be speaking to me, and yet he is describing human characteristics. He also gives the following definition of "The Empirical Self" or *me:* "*In its widest possible sense,* however, *a man's Self is the sum total of all that he CAN call his,* not only his body and his psychic powers, but his clothes and his house, his wife and children, his ancestors and friends, his reputation and works, his lands and horses, and yacht and bank-account" (*PP*,I, 279). Even the widest sense of self is not only gender bound but class bound.

Since James is best known for his arguments against determinism and for subjectively spontaneous creativity, these residues of belief in a fixed nature when it comes to gender are the more surprising. Female animals and women are assumed to be naturally caring and sympathetic; male animals and men are naturally pugnacious and violent. Sympathy, especially between mother and child, is given as an example of a primitive human instinct: "Danger to the child blindly and instantaneously stimulates the mother to actions of alarm or defense" (*PP*,II, 1029). Hunting and pugnacious instincts, such as is exhibited in "the cruelty of collections of men hounding each other on to bait and torture a victim," characterize men's instinctive nature (*PP*,II, 1030). The sympathetic instincts are not entirely lacking in men, but can easily be overpowered by their more dominant instincts of hunting and cruelty. Nor are women entirely devoid of pugnacity. They are even said to get angry oftener than men, "but their anger is inhibited by fear and other principles of their nature from expressing itself in blows" (*PP*,II, 1033). Exactly what women have to fear from men is not explored.

As these examples show, men tend to see women from their own perspective, and therefore women's potentiality is reduced to the two most important roles they play in men's lives—as mothers and wives. The question is never raised as to how women view their own lives. Just as the two instincts of maternity and sexuality are preeminent in James's descriptions of female animals, they are taken to be definitive of female humans. James asks, "Why does the maiden interest the youth so that everything about her seems more important and significant than anything else in the world?" He answers, "Nothing more can be said than that these are human ways . . ." and "The common man can only say ". . . *of course* we love the maiden, that beautiful soul clad in that perfect form, so palpably and flagrantly made from all eternity to be loved!" (*PP*,II, 1007, 1008). Woman as the object of desire is traditionally inseparable from unbridled passion, and James duly notes this danger for men: "The sexual passion expires after a protracted reign," and therefore habits of sexual restraint acquired in youth will tell in maturity: "Exposure to bad company then makes him a loose liver all his days; chastity kept at first makes the same easy later on" (*PP*,II, 1021).[33]

Although men are urged to keep their instincts under proper control, women are urged to wallow in them, as long as the wallowing is directed to men's well-being. James quotes at length G. H. Schneider's "lively description" about maternal instincts. Female cats are said to exhibit the instincts of "higher animal-mothers": "The maternal joys of a cat, for example, are not to be disguised. With an expression of infinite comfort she stretches out her fore-legs to offer her teats to her children." (*PP*,II, 1055). This quotation occurs in a passage extolling human motherhood because it causes a woman to turn away from exclusive interest in herself as a vain object of men's attention and to center her world instead on her child.

James adds to the passage from "the worthy Schneider" that "the passionate devotion of a mother—ill herself, perhaps—to a sick or dying child is perhaps the most simply beautiful moral spectacle that human life affords. Contemning every danger, triumphing over every difficulty, outlasting all fatigue, woman's love is here invincibly superior to anything that man can show" (*PP*,II, 1056). Women receive the highest praise when they fulfill to excess their natural function of taking care of others. But there are indications that not all women see themselves primarily as mothers. Schneider remarks that "Thus, at least, it is in all unspoiled, naturally-bred mothers, who, alas! seem to be growing rarer; and thus it is with all higher animal-mothers" (*PP*,II, 1056).

The valued human characteristics that James describes are the same as the characteristics ascribed to males. Women are defined as differing from men in specific ways and therefore differing from the human as such. When James says he is "leaving lower animals aside, and turning to human instincts," he reviews the stages of human life: the child, who plays; the youth, who engages in bodily exercises and enjoys "friendship and love, nature, travel and adventure, science and philosophy"; and the man, who exhibits "ambition and policy, acquisitiveness, responsibility to others, and the selfish zest of the battle of life" (*PP,*II, 1020). These life stages are then explored further, beginning with examples drawn exclusively from boys and continuing with *we, us, men.* In delineating the special human instincts of locomotion, vocalization, and imitation James again gives extended examples of children, who are in every case boys (*PP,*II, 1022–28). Women and "savages" do show up in some of the categories of human behavior patterns, such as those of human shyness, modesty, shame, sexual love, and parental love. James's ideal of the wife / mother who selflessly wears herself out serving the male sex is strikingly illustrated in a letter he sent to his wife from Vienna.[34] After having arranged for a year's leave from Harvard, he was touring Europe while she stayed at home in Cambridge to take care of their two little boys. He wrote her in 1882:

> Dear, perhaps the deepest impression I've got since I've been in Germany is that made on me by the indefatigable beavers of old wrinkled peasant women, striding like men through the streets, dragging their carts or lugging their baskets, minding their business, seeming to notice nothing, in the stream of luxury and vice, but belonging far away, to something better and purer. Their poor, old, ravaged and stiffened faces, their poor old bodies dried up with ceaseless toil, their patient souls make me weep. "They are our conscripts." They are the venerable ones whom we should reverence. All the mystery of womanhood seems incarnated in their ugly being—the Mothers! the Mothers! Ye are all one! Yes, Alice, dear, what I love in you is only what these blessed creatures have; and I'm glad and proud when I think of my own dear Mother with tears running down my face, to know that she is one with these.[35]

When James recalled this earlier impression in *Talks to Teachers* (1889), he did not explicitly link women with motherhood and unremitting labor (*TT,* 155). Instead he invoked the unremitting labor of peasant women and set the incident in a context that emphasized class and ethnicity rather than gender (*TT,* 154–63). It is given as one of the examples of the heroism of the laboring classes, whose patient endurance of backbreaking work is said to be as worthy of public monuments as are the deeds of those traditionally honored, such as generals and poets. Romantic idealism is blamed for blinding us to the heroism of everyday life, and it will continue to do so as long as we look at life "with the eyes of a remote spectator" (*TT,* 154). In a passage reminiscent of Walt Whitman, James testifies to undergoing a conversion experience on a train speeding toward Buffalo, when he says he noticed the daily heroism of the laboring classes (including Italian and Hungarian subway workers) "on freight-trains, on the decks of vessels, in cattle-yards and mines, on lumber rafts . . . and a wave of sympathy greater than anything I had ever before felt with the common life of common men began to fill my soul."

The passages are taken from one of the last three chapters of *Talks to Teachers*, which are separately listed under the heading of "Talks to Students." From the way James identifies those in our midst who are usually ignored and with whom "we" are being asked to sympathize, it is obvious that the authorial *we*, which encompasses both author and student, is middle- or upper-class, a member of a privileged ethnic group, educated, professional, and male. James is not only acknowledging a debt to those whose sacrifices make his privileged life possible, but also drawing the attention of his students to the heroic sufferings of the laboring classes, so that they will sympathize with, rather than despise, them. But there is no corresponding call to overthrow or even question the hierarchical relations that separate them.

James fears Tolstoy's "leveling philosophy" because phenomenal differences are not superficial but are the very relations that constitute personal identity (*TT*, 157–67). Nonetheless, he believes that humanity progresses by means of great prophets who preach "the religion of democracy," and thus nudge the world toward more humane relationships. But although he thinks that society should progress toward "some newer and better equilibrium," including the redistribution of wealth, true nobleness resides for him in the realm of ideals and high-mindedness, joined with "manly virtue." James's goal, finally, is not to question or undo the advantages accruing from unequal relationships, but only, *sub specie aeternitatis*, to develop a willingness "to live and let live." Such conclusions could seem desirable only from the point of view of one who was already on the favored side of the hierarchies: rich and poor, educated and uneducated, ethnic privilege and ethnic devaluation, professional and laborer, male and female. "Sympathy, insight, and good will" can indeed lead to "tolerance, reverence, and love for others" without shifting one iota the continued privilege on one side and disadvantage on the other.

Since in the original letter from which the later passage selectively quotes, laboring-class women are emblematic of all mothers and wives, that is, of women as such, then the distinctions of class, ethnicity, and education do not change women's status in the same way they change men's. Relegated to the private realm and to a distancing otherness does not leave women anything to hope for in democracy's slow progress to a new and better equilibrium. Rich or poor, black or white, educated or uneducated, women remain men's conscripts, alien lives "bent on duty, envying nothing, humble-hearted, remote" (*TT*, 155).[36]

5. MOTHER NATURE

James reproduces without criticism the ancient mythology that equates women and nature. He says that though idealists and empiricists use different analogies in their disputes with one another, as human beings they share the same essential interests. "Both are loyal to the world that bears them; neither wishes to spoil it; neither wishes to regard it as an insane incoherence; both want to keep it as a universe of some kind; and their differences are all secondary to this deep agreement" (*PU*, 10–11). We should subordinate such minor differences "in view of the fact that, whether we be empiricists or rationalists, we are, ourselves, parts of the universe and share the same one deep concern in its destinies. We crave alike to feel more truly at home with it, and to contribute our mite to its amelioration" (*PU*, 11). James is sure that his audience will not find his empiricist spirit "matricidal," since he is "as good a son as any rationalist among you to our common mother" (*PU*, 11).

His discourse echoes Emerson, who in his treatise *Nature* chides those idealists who ungratefully attack temporal nature in their longing for eternal, absolute spirit. Emerson says, "I have no hostility to nature, but a child's love to it. I expand and live in the warm day like corn and melons. Let us speak her fair. I do not wish to fling stones at my beautiful mother, nor soil my gentle nest." [37] This mother-child imagery seems benign and certainly close to recent ecological ethics and ecofeminism. The problem remains that the relation of man to nature reproduces a patriarchal interpretation of the relation of man to woman. The language of an absolute, brute dominance by which man tames nature has been mitigated into stewardship, to be sure, but the hierarchical relations are unchanged and nontransferable, since it would still be perceived as unnatural for nature to overpower spirit as for woman to be the guardian of man.

Emerson continues, "I only wish to indicate the true position of nature in regard to man, wherein to establish man all right education tends; as the ground which to obtain is the object of human life, that is, of man's connection with nature." The slippage from man to human to man is not simply an example of a generic usage of the word *man*. The man addressed as human is the male sex, as is more explicitly seen toward the end of "Nature." He illustrates his insight that "the mark of wisdom is to see the miraculous in the common" by a series of questions, including: "What is a day? . . . What is summer? What is woman? What is a child?" Woman is to man both common and mysterious. Both speaker and the audience addressed are men, as Emerson continues: "You also are a man." One's vocation as a man, as spirit, is to transform the rest of nature, which includes women and other men, through thought and action: "Man and woman and their social life, poverty, labor, sleep, fear, fortune, are known to you. . . . Know then that the world exists for you." [38]

James, too, slips easily into this equation of mankind with the male sex: "When we use a common noun, such as *man,* in a universal sense, as signifying all possible men, we are fully aware of this intention on our part, and distinguish it carefully from our intention when we mean a certain group of men, or a solitary individual before us" (*PP,*I, 248). Even generically, *man* means *men,* which usage can be distinguished from particular groups of men or even a single man, but which is not meant to distinguish a universal sense of mankind as distinguished from the male sex as such. Thus, the use of the term *man,* which is superficially gender neutral, is once again shown in actual usage to apply predominantly, even exclusively, to the male sex.

6. THE FEMININE MYSTICAL OR MAGICAL

James criticizes the scientific ideal "of a closed and completed system of truth" according to which what does not fit is thought to be absurd (*WB,* 222). He argues instead that the growth of knowledge depends on recognizing and taking seriously the exceptions and irregularities that challenge the rules. But nothing has been received with more contempt by scientists than mystical phenomena. "We college-bred gentry," he says, ignore those outside "the stream of cosmopolitan culture" and dismiss even prolific authors "whose names are never heard of in *our* circle" (*WB,* 223). James includes himself with tongue in cheek, since he is trying to rehabilitate psychical research, in which he is immensely interested and about which he is surely knowledgeable. He satirizes the snobbery and accompanying gatekeeping of his academic colleagues by pointing out that much of the world ignores the restrictive canons of science: "It always gives us a little shock to find this mass of human beings not only living and ignoring us and all our gods, but actually reading and writing and cogitating without ever a thought of our canons and authorities" (*WB,* 223). The "gentle reader" he addresses is certainly male because he is characterized as not caring for those who read such popular Victorian reading material for women as *Waverley* and the *Fireside Companion.*

James warns male gatekeepers that no one perspective, even the scientific, can encompass the totality of truth. He argues from his position of pluralistic perspectivism that "something escapes the best of us—not accidentally, but systematically and because we have a twist" (*WB,* 224). He finally explicitly identifies the rational, scientific perspective as male: "The scientific-academic mind and the feminine-mystical mind shy from each other's facts, just as they fly from each other's temper and spirit"

(*WB*, 224). And he argues that different perspectives disclose different facts, so that a man's world and a woman's world are not identical: "Facts are there only for those who have a mental affinity with them."

James's intention is to undercut the prejudices of scientific positivism by rehabilitating the feminine-mystical as a legitimate perspective that reveals aspects of reality not accessible to normal scientific procedures. All the founding members of the Society for Psychical Research were "gentlemen." Many—perhaps most—of their subjects were women. This is not surprising since men's view of women as Other, as closer to and emblematic of nature, the untamed, the irrational, the wilderness, would make them appear to be ideal witches or psychics, more in touch with the mysterious unknown than rational man.[39] James speaks of "a mother-sea" and a "psychic sea," that is, a sea of consciousness to which our puny, finite consciousnesses will one day return. The mother-sea "leaks-in" through the interstices of everyday life despite efforts to block it out.

James longs to return to the primal mother-sea, which he envisions as encompassing the finite, visible world of human experience, just as the atmosphere blankets and provides life-giving oxygen to the planet. He says in "The Confidences of a 'Psychical Researcher'" (1909) that his experiences have led him to "one fixed conclusion," namely, "that we with our lives are like islands in the sea, or like trees in the forest," which "may whisper to each other with their leaves. . . . But the trees also commingle their roots in the darkness underground, and the islands also hang together through the ocean's bottom. Just so there is a continuum of cosmic consciousness, against which our individuality builds but accidental fences, and into which our several minds plunge as into a mother-sea or reservoir" (*EPP,* 374). He suggests that "our ordinary human experience, on its material as well as on its mental side, would appear to be only an extract from the larger psycho-physical world" (*EPR,* 374–75).

The intellect misguidedly thinks of the world "as existing in a clean and regular shape." Instead, James multiplies examples of the messy, concrete world we live in. He dips into abnormal psychology to tell us "of oddities and eccentricities, of grotesqueries and masqueradings, incoherent, fitful, personal," so unsatisfactory to the "cut and dried classifications" of the medical and psychological minds of professionals.[40] We know that rationality and science are male domains for James and that untamed nature is female. Thus, when he says that "everything here is so lawless and individualized that it is chaos come again," he is referring to both physical nature and women. He continues by saying that most professionals "don't wish a *wild* world. . . . They are perfectly willing to let such exceptions go unnoticed and unrecorded." Facts can be noticed and accommodated in science only insofar as they can be made to fit an orderly pattern. But James believes that all great advances in science break the accepted order. In defending the wilderness against the inroads of science, he also celebrates women, who are associated with otherness, with disorderliness not tamed by men's rational order.

James can thus be read as arguing for pluralism, since he seems to be valuing different perspectives equally for their irreducibly distinct disclosures of reality. But this benign interpretation only works up to a point. Unfortunately, his characterization of these differences as male and female leads him to undermine the consistency of his perspectivism, which is infected and distorted by his belief that women are essentially different from men and naturally subordinate to them. The implicit denigration in the hierarchical subordination of women to men is extreme and undermines a genuine pluralism of creative difference by assuming a primal, predetermined one. Since creative spontaneity is for James the defining characteristic of the human, women's reduction to a predetermined nature can only dehumanize us. The oppressive hierarchy which is believed to properly characterize the subordination of women to men likewise characterizes the relation of male-defined rationality to a nature defined as feminine. Once the feminine-mystical facts have been

indisputably ascertained and admitted, the academic and critical minds are by far the best fitted ones to interpret and discuss them—for surely to pass from mystical to scientific speculations is like passing from lunacy to sanity; but on the other hand if there is anything which human history demonstrates, it is the extreme slowness with which the ordinary academic and critical mind acknowledges facts to exist which present themselves as wild facts, with no stall or pigeon-hole, or as facts which threaten to break up the accepted system. (*WB*, 224)

Male-defined rationality thus has for its primary task the control and forcible restriction within bounds of the unbridled, irrational female element in nature and society.

James is profoundly ambivalent about the sexual dualisms men have read into nature and the human appropriation of the world.[41] On the one hand, he supports the symbolic order in which the masculine scientific mind ought to interpret the feminine-mystical.[42] On the other hand, he wants to protect the wilderness of mysticism and psychic experiences from being explained away by scientific rationality.[43] The same ambivalence that mysticism introduces is found in regard to saintliness because both place a higher value on qualities traditionally associated with the feminine. Because of his failure to criticize the conflation of humanity with masculinity, James finds himself struggling to defend saintliness as an ideal that embodies feminine values while countering his own fears that it emasculates men.

He does not quarrel with the "ancestral evolution [that] has made us all potential warriors" and the military discipline that roots out excessive tenderness in regard to one's own person but only with developing them into extremes that can turn us into "monster[s] of insensibility" (*VRE,* 291).[44] He also fears the opposite tendency, which is manifest in the material wealth and luxury of the age and which makes for "effeminacy and unmanliness." His strategy is to argue for "a renovated and revised ascetic [religious] discipline" to replace the traditional military discipline of war, which is "too savage, too cruel, too barbarous" to serve as an appropriate "bulwark against effeminacy" (*VRE,* 292). If the great appeal of his proposal for a "moral equivalent of war" is that it develops a moral ideal of the strenuous life that does not need to go about "crushing weaker peoples" in order to avoid becoming like women, then the denigration of women is being woven into the very fabric of morality.

James's defense of saintliness against Friedrich Nietzsche's scorn is profoundly ambiguous and convoluted because James shares with him the equation of heroism and leadership with masculinity and the saintly qualities of sympathetic service, purity, and patience with femininity (*VRE,* 294–97). "The overpowering man of prey" excites "thrills of wonder veiled in terror," while women and saints embody "the mystery of gentleness in beauty" (*VRE,* 295–29). James concludes that "both aggressiveness and non-resistance are needful" and argues against any "one intrinsically ideal type of human character" (*VRE,* 297). He ultimately favors the saint as "abstractly a higher type of man than the 'strong man,'" but in concrete situations he admits that saints are liable to appear rather "insignificant and contemptible" (*VRE,* 298).

James labors mightily to show that saints are indeed greater and more appropriate heroes for the complexities of modern civilization than are "the strong men of this world," who easily degenerate into "bullies, robbers, and swindlers," but his struggles to do so all stem from his acceptance of the very masculinist view that he is trying to overcome. Although he includes such women as Agnes Jones, Margaret Hallahan, and Dora Pattison among the saints, he reminds us that "we must not forget" that "in discussing saintliness, we ask if it be an ideal type of manhood" (*VRE,* 298–99).[45] That it is an idealizing of womanhood is taken for granted. Since he strongly valued women as Other in their subordinate complementarity to men, he seems to be struggling with himself as well as with a masculinized culture in generating convincing arguments as to why men should find saintliness to be an ideal of manhood. His courage failed him, however, at the task of rethinking and rejecting the continuing masculinizing of rationality as the source of the distortion and disorientation.

Acknowledgment of the fact of women's full humanity and rationality would necessarily "break up the accepted system" of male domination, and James could not relinquish the privileges that accrued to him under the old system. Just as men and women are assigned separate spheres, so are facts and theories conceptually hierarchized into dominant and submissive. "In psychology, physiology, and medicine, wherever a debate between the mystics and the scientifics has been once for all decided, it is the mystics who have usually proved to be right about the *facts*, while the scientifics had the better of it in respect to the theories" (*WB*, 224). James says that he has been forced to recognize that mystics have access to "certain kinds of phenomenal experience," but he soothes the unacknowledged but obvious male anxiety over the "wildness" of the facts disclosed through female perspectives by assuring his male colleagues that philosophers can successfully deal with the repugnant mystical style of philosophizing by "reflecting upon them in academic-scientific ways" (*WB*, 224). In other words, men can legitimately appropriate women's insights by transforming them into masculinized rational discourse.[46]

The woman-as-nature analogy carries over into James's assessment of the nature of women's rationality. Nature speaks out of women; they do not have to pursue nature by use of a logical method. Since they are the objects of a masculine search for knowledge, they cannot themselves be striving for what they supposedly already are. As with moral sympathy, women cannot be credited with striving for and conquering truth, a state that they simply inhabit. In a brief, one-paragraph review praising Jane Addams's *The Spirit of Youth and the City Streets*, James points out how all its details flow from her central insight or persuasion. But analysis fails him: "Of *how* they flow I can give no account, for the *wholeness* of Miss Addams' embrace of life is her own secret. She simply *inhabits reality*, and everything she says necessarily expresses its nature. She *can't help writing truth*."

Admittedly, this is highest praise from James, who all his life tried to reach through rational means the wholeness exhibited in a mystical oneness with reality.[47] But it also strips women of their dignity as human beings, that is, those whose greatest suffering and greatest triumphs alike come from the struggle to organize the Walpurgis-like chaos of life into a finally satisfactory harmony. If women are the reward of the struggle or the oasis of escape from the burdensome duties of public life, they cannot themselves be engaged in the struggle as partners.[48] The bitter effect of such a marginalized existence restricted to the private sphere is poignantly illustrated in the life of William's brilliant sister, Alice, who was sickly all her life with one of those mysterious Victorian "wasting" ill-nesses with no diagnosed name, but which included mental depression.[49] She wrote to William: "I think the difficulty is my inability to assume the receptive attitude, that cardinal virtue is women, the absence of which has always made me so uncharming to & uncharmed by the male sex."[50] Unlike her mother, Alice was self-assertive; but, like her, she could imag-ine no acceptable, ladylike career outside of marriage to absorb her en-ergies. One may speculate whether it was her invalidism or her indomi-table personality, a Jamesian family characteristic that served her two famous brothers well, that accounted for her "sour spinsterhood," as she herself called it, and her wasted talents.[51]

7. MASCULINE VIEW OF CREATIVITY

In a 1907 interview with the *New York Times* James explained the core of his philosophy in gendered terms. He boldly claimed that "mind *engen-ders* truth *upon* reality." Rather than simply copying a reality complete in itself, "the *use* of most of our thinking is to help us to *change* the world." Adopting this perspective frees us "to use our theoretical as well as our practical faculties . . . to get the world into a better shape, and all with a good conscience. The only restriction is that the world resists some lines of attack on our part and opens herself to others, so that we must go on with the grain of her willingness."[52] James thus unselfconsciously paints a picture of the philosopher as a predatory male, one whose attacks are sometimes resisted, sometimes welcomed by a world/woman who liter-ally "opens herself to others." Just how big a grain of willingness is needed to justify such an attack, undertaken, "with a good conscience"? The fact that such passages have begun to be criticized only recently by feminists shows how easy it is to internalize the masculinist perspective that permeates traditional learned discourse.[53]

Late in life James is repeating, and thus reinforcing, a masculinist insemination view of how truths are forced upon the world. He had al-ready linked engendering to a submerged rape metaphor in *Pragmatism*, where he explained the creativity of our cognitive as well as our active life in a grammatical trope asserting that we make real additions to the subject as well as the predicate part of reality. He continued: "The world stands really malleable, waiting to receive its final touches at our hand. Like the kingdom of heaven, it suffers violence willingly. Man *engenders* truths upon it" (*PM*, 123). From the later reappropriation, we know that in this passage he is also thinking of the world as a *she*, not an *it*.

The explicit recognition of this masculinist perspective makes plau-sible the textual development from seeing the world as malleable, as re-ceptive to further touches "at 'our' hand" (which certainly cannot be referring to my woman's "hand") to a willing suffering of violence. No woman who suffers violence at the hands of another would call her participation willing. I in no way imply that philosophers who quote these and similar passages are consciously responding to the submerged rape metaphor, but rather to the largely unrecognized, because so familiar, heroic masculine perspective.[54] It is surely worth reflecting on the fact that women as well as men have been educated to take for granted a masculinist perspective of rationality, one which celebrates violence as a paradigm of knowledge. It takes a genuine paradigm shift, such as feminist theory introduces, to even recognize the hidden sexist assumptions operative in normal discourse.

But James does not simply take over from the tradition such an extreme masculinizing of rationality. And this fact helps account for the continuing attractiveness of his philosophy for both women and men. Characteristically he resists such hegemonic moves by strongly rejecting appeals to rationality as the forced imposition of received truths, as is evident in his defense of psychical research. He knows that "dingy little mediumistic facts" would not impress Huxleyan, that is, scientific minds, but he goes on to criticize the reductionism of the increasingly positivist view of the science of his time. He argues that science advances "by the little rebellious exceptions to the science of the present" (*EPR*, 375). Feminists, both women and men, can identify with these rebellious refusals that James provides but was unable to carry through to a liberating conclusion for women.

In "The Sentiment of Rationality," published in *The Will to Believe*, James struggled with "the unsatisfactoriness of all our speculations" (*WB*, 61). But they are unsatisfactory for a different reason for women who, as the objects rather than the subjects of the speculation, are not included in the possessive case *our*. I will try to make visible this exclusion by engaging in a brief, rebellious dialogue with James's text, one that his own attitude invites. In an extended passage (*WB*, 61) James sharply criticized the one-sided intellectualist drive toward theoretic simplification, which can retain a semblance of multiplicity only by invoking an "empirical sand-heap world." But "the practical man" is said to despise such an "empty barrenness," which mocks genuine diversity and fails to identify the essence of this or that concrete thing. How much more does "the practical woman" experience the empty barrenness of so many philosophical classifications that ignore the concrete specificity of her life?

James continues: "We are thus led to the conclusion that the simple classification of things is, on the one hand, the best possible theoretic philosophy, but is, on the other, a most miserable and inadequate substitute for the fulness of the truth."

The simple classifications of things as advanced by canonical philosophers most miserably and inadequately substitute for the insights of unrepresented groups and individuals, which is why there is currently pressure to expand both the diversity of philosophers and the subject matter of philosophy.[55] The fullness of the truth would have to include women's and minorities' experiences and varying perspectives.

"It is a monstrous abridgment of life, which, like all abridgments is got by the absolute loss and casting out of real matter."

The lives of women and minorities are abridged more than the lives of James and his sex, class, and race, and their loss is often absolute.

"This is why so few human beings truly care for philosophy."

Especially, I might add, minorities and women, whose numbers in philosophy are far below those in other liberal arts disciplines.

"The particular determinations which she [philosophy] ignores are the real matter exciting needs, quite as potent and authoritative as hers."

Yes, how much of women's lives and experiences have been ignored in philosophical reflection? How much resistance still remains to incorporating noncanonical texts by minorities and women into the philosophy curriculum?

"What does the moral enthusiast care for philosophical ethics? Or the artist for classical aesthetics?"

Or what do women care for a philosophy that stubbornly ignores or denigrates their lives and intellectual contributions?

Ironically, James may have seen women as marginal to the business of philosophers, but part of him desperately wanted to be on the margin with them. His fascination with the misfits of society and his belief that they—like instances of ecological diversity in nature—are an irreplaceable resource for the renewal of society surely account for the poignancy of his reflections and the passion with which he challenges philosophical business as usual. In warning Harvard University against stamping "a single hard and fast type of character upon her children," James insisted that "our undisciplinables are our proudest product."[56] His own ambivalence toward the socially defined masculine role and his attraction to the feminine opens a rebellious space which feminists can enlarge and reclaim.

8. CONTINUED INFLUENCE

Mary Whiton Calkins, Ethel Puffer Howes, Jane Addams, and other women students and friends have testified to James's friendly support for their intellectual endeavors, a support that was especially noteworthy at a time when so many academic doors were closed to them. But James's influence on women's education extended beyond the small number of women students that he taught during his lifetime, and, as we have seen, the beneficial nature of his written texts for women is more ambiguous. An excerpt from "Ethical and Pedagogical Importance of the Principle of Habit," taken from *Psychology: Briefer Course*, 132–38, turns up in 1925, for instance, in a small work intended as a handbook for young women just entering college.[57] Both his stature and the perceived relevance of his views for women are evident in the fact that the selection is the only posthumous one included. *The Freshman Girl: A Guide to College Life* is a collection of essays written by administrators, professors, and one dancing instructor, for the purpose of easing the transition from high school to college.[57] It is plain why the excerpt from James is included, since it encourages the growth of good habits in young people. It both motivates by emphasizing that habits largely determine character, and it gives practical advice on how to "make our nervous system our ally instead of our enemy."

But it also exemplifies the ambivalence created in women trying to understand their own role in life as college-educated women when they learn that role through male-defined texts and authors. For one thing, the youths addressed in the selection are upper-class gentlemen, destined for such "arduous careers" as those of doctors, ministers, and counselors-at-law. For another, activity itself is explicitly conveyed as prototypically male. The sentimentalist and dreamer are called contemptible types of human character because they wallow in "a weltering sea of sensibility and emotion," never undertaking a single "manly concrete deed."[58] Just as disturbing as the sexism is the racism and classism of the beliefs expressed. James praises habit, for instance, as the great conservator of the status quo of society because it discourages class warfare, prevents the lower classes from deserting the drudgery of hard labor, and "keeps different social strata from mixing."

James's criticism of those who praise the Good in abstract terms, but never act to carry it out in the messy particulars of everyday life, would scarcely be energizing for young women too often sententiously preached at and then denied any practical outlets for their zeal. His example of Rousseau arousing mothers to follow Nature by nursing their babies themselves and then sending all his own children away to a foundling hospital aptly characterizes the hypocrisy too often encountered. So does the example of a Russian lady weeping at a play while her coachman freezes to death. But then James goes on to label excessive novel reading, theatergoing, and indulgence in music as similarly "monstrous."

By selectively reading the essay as a call to action, young women could be and probably were encouraged to become responsible for their own actions on a larger, non-domestic stage. But the message is embedded in a pervasive sexism that could also inculcate ambivalence about the propriety of such an active role for themselves. It is directly addressed to male youths, and all the positive images are masculine ones, while many of the negative examples are taken from activities typical for women of that time. James even seems to go out of his way to criticize an emphasis on feeling that he usually defended in other contexts.

But the most misogynist remarks would not even be recognized at the time and so could affect the earlier readers only insofar as the attitude they express is conveyed as a pervasive background belief. They are to be found in James's readily recognizable class-based distinction between the habits of character that are set by twenty years of age and those set by thirty. By the age of twenty, he says, a person's personal habits, such as vocalization, gesture, and body language, are fixed. He illustrates this claim by saying that if a man is not born and bred a gentleman, the habits acquired after twenty will always betray his lower-class origins. The next plateau is the age of thirty, by which time a man's intellectual and professional habits are formed. The period between twenty and thirty is a crucial one because habits cannot be changed once one is set in a career path. It is even said to be a good thing that our character is set like plaster by thirty years of age because it is this factor that keeps the different social strata from mixing.

The ages of twenty and thirty are not picked at random. Recall that in an earlier article, "Brute and Human Intellect," James had said that a young woman of twenty knows how to act with alacrity in any circumstances in which she may be placed because her likes and dislikes are already formed and her opinions will not change much throughout life. "Her character is, in fact, finished in its essentials" (*EPS*, 37). A boy of twenty, by contrast, is still developing. With this knowledge we can see in hindsight how inappropriate it was to include the article on habit in a guide for "freshman girls" unless the intent was to encourage them to develop personal, but not professional, habits and to polish their skills but not their minds. The demeaning remarks about women at the end of the article on "Brute and Human Intellect" were later included in Chapter 22 on reasoning in *Principles* (see *EPS*, 393). James even added a footnote explicitly limiting women's abilities to the domestic sphere and emphasizing their lower position (along with "savages and boors") on the cultural scale (*PP*, II, 991, n. 25). These passages were most likely as little known to the editors of the 1925 book as they were noted by later pragmatists. But as with so many beliefs about women whose origins are now scarcely recoverable, the pervasive background of James's sexism colors and subtly biases less explicit texts. They will continue to do so until they are brought fully into consciousness and critically examined.

9. CONCLUSION

Although James is well known for his pluralism and emphasis on novelty, which challenge the accepted order of things, his romantic notion of women as Other leads to a glaring failure to challenge sexist stereotypes. Women's nature and role in society remain uncriticized and therefore unreconstructed. The association of men with reason and women with nature is so much a part of our culture that the uncharacteristic sexism of Dewey's remark in the following sentence in which he praises James can pass unnoticed, even by women: "America will justify herself as long as she breeds those like William James; men who are thinkers and thinkers who are men" (*MW* 6:96).

The association over the centuries of women with breeding and men with thinking has been challenged by many feminists, who have argued that the linking of rationality with maleness has distorted explanations of rationality as well as unfairly endowed masculinity with superior human qualities.[59] It is worth while to trace James's view of women because only by identifying the extent to which his sexism informs his philosophical analyses can we be empowered to reject the insidious because unrecognized embeddedness of misogyny in supposedly neutral analyses. Not only do we acquire one more bit of evidence for the maleness of Western philosophical conceptions of reason, but it becomes clearer how difficult it is to uproot sexist beliefs if they can infect even such an acute critic of hegemonic rationality as William James.

Since I have argued that James's philosophy exhibits many attributes traditionally associated with femininity and thus escapes many of the criticisms of feminists about the extreme masculinizing of philosophical thinking, his own severe circumscription of the nature and role of women presents an interpretive challenge. How can James both value and devalue the feminine, both use and abuse feminine style? My analysis has sought to show that valuing a femininity constructed within a patriarchal order of race, class, gender, and heterosexual privilege unacceptably narrows the possibilities of both women and men and distorts the multitude and variety of women's perspectives on the world. Only when James's own interpretive horizon of patriarchal values is recognized and rejected are we free to appropriate the subversive feminine that is also part of his text.

Seven

Who Experiences?
Genderizing Pluralistic Experiences

In *Incidents in the Life of a Slave Girl Written by Herself,* Harriet A. Jacobs wrote: "I have My dear friend—Striven faithfully to give a true and just account of my own life in Slavery . . . not to tell you what I have heard but what I have seen—and what I have suffered—and if there is any sympathy to give—let it be given to the thousands—of Slave Mothers that are still in bondage . . . let it plead for their helpless children." Jacobs, a freed fugitive slave, appealed to the authority of experience as she described to her friend, Amy Post, the manuscript about her life in slavery on which she was working: "I must write just what I have lived and witnessed myself."[1] In witnessing to her own suffering she was not asking sympathy for herself; she was urging action on behalf of those who continued to suffer, unheard and unknown.

It is not surprising that marginalized persons and members of subjugated groups should appeal to their own experiences and the right to interpret them because their lives and accomplishments are systematically ignored or distorted by those who have the power to make their experiences and history central to, and preserved by, a given culture. So important is the need to assert one's existence and perspective as the first step to redressing wrongs that many feminists, such as Carolyn Whitbeck, regard "feminist philosophy as primarily concerned with the construction and development of concepts and models adequate for the articulation of women's experiences and women's practices."[2]

Simply appealing to experience is problematic on many levels, however, which is why both feminists and pragmatists continue to develop theories of experience as well as theories out of experience. Catherine Petroski, in her review of Francine du Plessix Gray's book, *Soviet Women,* for example, says that "because her subject is women and their roles in society, Gray's approach can be described as feminist.[3] This assertion reflects a typical conflation of women's experiences and feminism by those who are not familiar with the theoretical or ideological bases of feminism. The connection does not seem quite so mistaken, however, as Petroski continues, "And the questions she asks Soviet women are the questions women of the late 20th Century are being asked everywhere: What most concerns you? What are your particular values and how are these perhaps different from the standard values of the society?" Contrary to Petroski's assertion, women are not being thus interrogated "everywhere." It is feminists who first stridently pointed out to a public largely unwilling to hear it that women, women's experiences, and women's values have been ignored, trivialized, or persecuted throughout history. And it is feminists who keep asking these questions and who consciously and deliberately seek to answer them.

This connection becomes obvious, given Petroski's list of the familiar women's issues that Soviet women address: "abortion, equal rights, equal pay for equal work, child care, personal fulfillment, the nature of the family." These are certainly issues that any woman might list, but the actual formulation of them has been brought into public discussion through feminist efforts. Although it is true that women's experiences and feminist explanations of these experiences are two different things, they are nonetheless closely related.

On the other hand, postmodernist feminists such as Denise Riley question the possibility of an experience that is specifically women's, as when she deconstructs the category *woman* in "*Am I That Name?*."[4] She examines the ambivalent attitudes toward the designation *woman* that feminists have exhibited over the centuries. The recurring difficulty is that the more women are differentiated as women, the less they embody the characteristics of humanity.[5] The instability of the designation *woman* is particularly problematic for political organization and emancipatory campaigns, since "to be named as a woman can be the precondition for some kinds of solidarity." The indeterminacy of *women* means that "while it's impossible to thoroughly be a woman, it's also impossible never to be one."[6] Irresolution about the issue is magnified in debates over women's experience.

Riley does not simplistically solve the problems she raises, since she expects that feminism will continue to oscillate between asserting and refusing the category *women*. She takes her stand "on a territory of pragmatism," arguing that "it is compatible to suggest that 'women' don't exist—while maintaining a politics of 'as if they existed'—since the world behaves as if they unambiguously did." Though she is using *pragmatism* in its conventional sense and not referring to the philosophical tradition of pragmatism, her further explanation is remarkably consistent with pragmatist philosophy: "And the less that 'women workers' can be believed to have a fixed nature, as distinct from neglected needs because of their domestic responsibilities, the more it will be arguable that only for some purposes can they be distinguished from all workers. Feminism can then join battle over which these purposes are to be."[7]

John Dewey, like Whitbeck, defends the primacy and ultimacy of concrete experience, understood as the process "of continuous and cumulative interaction of an organic self with the world."[8] Like Riley, he rejects fixed natures, replacing them with explanations of relative stabilities within the flux of experience that have developed over time. What has traditionally been called a nature is a way of effectively organizing experience to answer our needs, intentions, and purposes. Therefore, the traits of experience, whether of women's, of a subgroup of women, or of some other designated group, cannot just be read off from nature but must be reconstructed within a historical process with which we are continuous. We are not contemplatively detached from experience, but are ourselves formed within it as "desiring, striving, thinking, feeling creature(s)."[9]

Feminism and pragmatism, along with other dissident voices within a broad multicultural spectrum, thus share a common ground that strongly demarcates them from the logocentrism of much of mainstream philosophy. Because of the epistemological turn in philosophy, apprenticeship in the profession has often meant indoctrination into what Dewey called "the great intellectualist fallacy."[10] By this he means the subordination of all assertions to knowledge claims by the reduction of experience to its explicitly cognitive dimension and the consequent denigration of "everyday qualitative experience, practical, esthetic, moral." Anything that cannot be reduced to the properties of the objects of knowledge is disparaged as subjective and merely phenomenal. Dewey counters this move by pointing out the merely instrumental and abstract character of the objects of reflective knowledge when they are isolated from the situations in which they arise. By demonstrating the centrality of experience to philosophical analysis, he also demonstrates that the recent explorations of how experiences vary by ethnicity, gender, class, sexual orientation, and so forth, should be at the center, not the periphery, of philosophical discourse.

Because of "the indispensability of context for thinking," Dewey often warned of the negative effects of the epistemological eclipse of experience.[11] Both objective idealists and realists, for instance, rely on a Humean notion of experience, which they profoundly distrust. For the objective idealist "experience dwindles down to the narrowest sensible content of presentation."[12] The realist contrasts "our meagre flickering awareness of objects and the extensive and enduring world of *actually* known objects as proof of the independence of the object of knowledge from momentary awareness." Both stand "upon the ground of the limited and subjective character of experience" (*MW* 6:81). They conclude, therefore, that experience cannot be an ultimate criterion because it leads to subjectivist philosophy, since experience itself is subjective.

But if this is so, Dewey asks, to what does realism itself appeal? What is the relation, not between the concept of valid knowledge and the concept of experience, but between what exists as valid knowledge and what exists as empirical events? In order to distinguish a case of valid knowledge from that of the bare presence to objects we must nonetheless appeal to the conditions and consequences in experience. "Intellectualistic philosophers, rationalists and sensationalists alike, set to work to find some mark inhering in a valid object which would guarantee its validity" (*MW* 6:83). Clearness, universality, simplicity, and brute irreducible givenness have all been candidates, but they have all proven inadequate. In trying to affix to the object some special sign that witnesses its freedom from its own subjective influence, such believers in both genuine scientific knowing and in the subjectivity of experience act "as if suspected beef-packers substituted for the government inspection label a certificate that the meat was sound because they had done nothing to it—except produce it" (*MW* 6:82–83).

Meaning, for Dewey, does not refer to a self-referential series of symbols but to grasping the relationship that constitute the structure of an experience (*LW* 10:51). Previous recognition of webs of relationships enhances the ability to translate the perception of actions and their consequences into their explicit connections. In *Experience and Nature* communication is taken as central to language, not the expression of antecedent things or thoughts. Communication is "the establishment of cooperation in an activity in which there are partners, and in which the activity of each is modified and regulated by partnership." Meaning is not a psychic entity, but first of all a property of behavior and only secondarily of objects. "But the behavior of which it is a quality is a distinctive behavior; cooperative, in that response to another's act involves contemporaneous response to a thing as entering into the other's behavior" (*LW* 10:141).

In *Art as Experience* lived experience is explained as "the result of interaction between a live creature and some aspect of the world in which he lives" (*LW* 10:50). From the first, subjectivity and objectivity are not dualistic antagonists; they are reciprocal emphases in a transaction. Experience is organized dynamically, which means that it is characterized by temporality and growth. "There is inception, development, fulfillment" (*MW* 10:62).

This transactive character of experience is its most salient characteristic for pragmatists. Self and world, thought and action, are reciprocally related. According to Patricial Hill Collins, this transactive character of experience is also central to the standpoint of Black women: "This interdependence of thought and action suggests that changes in thinking may be accompanied by changed actions and that altered experiences may in turn stimulate a changed consciousness." The "Black women's standpoint rejects either/or dichotomous thinking that claims that *either* thought *or* concrete action is desirable." Instead it espouses "a both/and orientation that views thought and action as part of the same process." [13]

In this chapter I explore those aspects of Dewey's analysis of experience that seem particularly apt for enriching feminist explorations of women's experiences. These are (1) the identification and rejection of philosophical dualisms that have systematically distorted our understanding of everyday experience, (2) the thesis that ignoring the perspectival nature of experience is a source of oppression, (3) the development of standards of judgment and values from concrete experience, and (4) the role of feeling in experience. Throughout I interrogate Dewey's explanation of experience from the perspective of feminist analyses of women's oppression and of the negative effects of ignoring gender as a category of analysis. In the final section I suggest that the systematic identification and rejection of Dewey's neglect of sexism as a form of discrimination will begin to yield an analysis of actual existences and events capable of guiding those decisions about ends to strive for, goods to be obtained, and evils to be averted—decisions that both feminists and pragmatists seek.

1. LIFTING THE BURDEN OF TRADITION: ATTACK ON DUALISM

In *The Quest for Certainty* Dewey turns to history and anthropology in search of the origins of present-day beliefs, assumptions, and values. He strips away the veneer of pure rationality that is attributed to widely held attitudes by showing that they arose within definite human communities in answer to felt needs. He specifically wants to account for the hierarchical dualisms that have systematically distorted experience. The four in particular that must be rejected in order to clear the way for pragmatist philosophy turn out to be the same ones feminists have identified as oppressive: (1) the depreciation of doing and making and the overevaluation of pure thinking and reflection, (2) the contempt for bodies and matter and praise of spirit and immateriality, (3) the sharp division between practice and theory, and (4) the inferiority of changing things and events and the superiority of a fixed reality.

The criticism of dualism is also central to most varieties of feminist analysis.[14] Susan Sherwin, for instance, points out that most traditional philosophical methodologies accept dichotomous thinking that "forces ideals, persons, roles, and disciplines into rigid polarities. It reduces richness and complexity in the interest of logical neatness, and, in doing so, it distorts the truth." [15] Uncriticized dichotomies undergird patriarchy, which is sustained by power relations that both assume and construct unbridgeable differences between the sexes. A recent review applauds attempts to "move us beyond the oscillating dualism of sameness or difference" and "to articulate a new theoretical framework that sees gender as a social reality created through interactional processes. In [Candace] West and [Don H.] Zimmerman's classic formulation, we *do* gender rather than *have* gender." [16]

Dewey also argues that philosophers who denigrate doing and making and praise theory above practice are self-serving (*LW* 4:4). Although philosophers did not necessarily originate the dualistic thinking embedded in their cultures, they perpetuated it by first rationally formulating and then justifying it. The subordination of practice to theory originates far back in history, when physical work was onerous and done under the compulsion of necessity, and when intellectual work was associated with leisure. The least pleasant and more burdensome practical activity was forced on slaves, serfs, and women. The social dishonor attributed by those in power to the slave class and to women was extended to their work. Dewey asks why such attitudes to social castes and emotional revulsions should have been raised to dogma, since a class-based genealogy alone cannot explain why the body should be held in contempt in relation to spirit.

This is not just a historical question because the negative effects of these dualisms are still with us. Morals, for instance, have been understood as the province of an inner, personal attitude and not as "overt activity having consequences" in those areas in which action is manifested, such as industry, politics, and the fine arts (*LW* 4:5). Theories of knowledge and of mind also suffer from the separation of intellect from action. Dewey argues that the historical grounds for elevating knowledge above making and doing is the quest for certainty to overcome the perils which daily beset us in a hazardous world. We can change the world directly through "the complicated arts of associated living," such as building shelters and weaving garments (*LW* 4:3). Alternatively, we can try to coerce unpredictable forces by ritual, sacrifice, and supplication. In earlier times the security that could be obtained by an individual or a community through overtly changing environing conditions was inadequate to overcome the dangers encountered. Recourse to religious or rational absolutes was therefore more comforting.

Certain traits of practical activity account for this preference. A brief comparison with the absolute standards of rational thinking can bring them out. Practical activity involves individualized and unique situations, which undergo change, while rational categories are universals, and rationality privileges invariant necessity. In contrast to Platonic Forms, Aristotelian essences, and Cartesian clear and distinct ideas, overt action involves risk because eventual success is never entirely in our control. Since unforeseeable conditions can always thwart us, our intent alone cannot bring about a successful outcome, but we can unerringly assert the Kantian categorical imperative. If the perilousness of existence has tended to evoke a corresponding search for security, including intellectual stability, then one can understand why the absolute predictability of abstract principles comes to be more highly valued than the relative predictability of even the best understood practice. But this separation of theory from practice, of truth from the messy details of experience, of absolute good from particular, limited goods has had dire consequences.

Our understanding of knowledge and value must undergo a radical change. Once values are connected with the problem of intelligent action, then we can investigate what must be done in order to make objects of value more secure. Traditionally, philosophers obtained cognitive certification, whether through intuition or a process of reasoning, by seeking to identify an antecedently existing, immutable truth and goodness (*LW* 4:35). This understanding of knowledge as disclosure of a reality independent of the knowing process perpetuates the vain search for values subsistent in the properties of Being apart from human action.

All the ways that human individuals experience things, whether through love, desire, fear or need, are real modes of experience, not reducible to cognitive judgments. But until these emotional and practical realities are grasped intellectually, they remain fragmentary, inconsistent, and subject to forces beyond our control. We need a new way of dealing with these experiences, one which does not simply reduce them to cognitive objects. Dewey proposes examining the relations and interactions with one another of the widest range of experienced objects. This will yield a new kind of experienced object, no more or less real than unintellectualized experiences of objects, "but more significant, and less overwhelming and oppressive" (*LW* 4:175). The monopoly of more specialized forms of knowing can be broken by turning to the ways that welfare mothers, artists, students, daughters, and untold persons in everyday life manage to solve problems and thereby extract knowledge from their daily concerns. Dewey advocates that philosophers cease trying to formulate general theories which seek to settle for all time the nature of truth, knowledge, and value.[17] Instead, we should find out "how authentic beliefs about existence as they currently exist can operate fruitfully and efficaciously in connection with the practical problems that are urgent in actual life" (*LW* 4:36).

Although Dewey recognized and criticized the dominating dualisms bequeathed to us by Plato and Aristotle and reemphasized in medieval scholasticism, he did not recognize that the hierarchy of the public realms appropriated by men in classical and medieval times also rested on a gender hierarchy. His language reveals a male bias even as he exposes a bias of classical philosophy when he contrasts the philosophical valorizing of the ideal and eternal over "the world in which men act and live, the world we experience perceptibly and practically" (*LW* 4:15). Since Being is the privileged term in traditional philosophy, which takes "the disclosure of the Real in itself" as the goal of knowledge, the industrial and fine arts, as well as morals and politics, are relegated to the inferior region because they are subject to change and therefore "infected with *non*-being" (*LW* 4:14–15).

The distinctive characteristic of practical activity is its uncertainty. Traditional thinking seduces us to desire a Being that is fixed and immutable, rather than trusting to actions that cannot guarantee more than a precarious probability. The "quest for complete certainty can be fulfilled in pure knowing alone," since "according to traditional classic doctrine, 'mind' is complete and self-sufficient in itself" (*LW* 4:7). We have to break away from the burden of tradition in order to realize that present experience does not leave us at the mercy of physical forces over which we have no control. Dewey then uses the generic form *man* to argue that despite the new perils that his machinery has involved him in, man nevertheless has learned to play with danger and reject "the routine of a too sheltered life" (*LW* 4:7). But the maleness of the supposedly generic *man* can become visible by reflecting on the fact that the mention of shelter immediately calls up the image of women. Dewey applauds "the enormous change taking place in the position of women" as an example of "a change of attitude toward the value of protection as an end in itself" (*LW* 4:7–8).

The subtheme of women/protection is introduced to illuminate the larger theme of humans/protection to help us realize that the security sought in earlier times is no longer such a driving force in human behavior because so many dangers have been mitigated in the modern world. As an example of how far we have learned to bring under control the dangers to which humans have been exposed for eons, Dewey points to the fact that even women themselves no longer seek protection. He may have been thinking of the fact that by 1929 many feminist reformers advocated the repeal of special protection laws for women, arguing that they simply added another barrier to women's full and equal access to the labor market. Since other feminist reformers had worked long and hard to put the special protection laws on the books in the first place in order to ameliorate the terrible working conditions for women and children, this reversal of perspective in such a short time would be likely to provoke controversy, then as well as now.

The idea that it is women who originally sought protection and not men who enforced subordination and developed social attitudes hostile to women is surely a masculinist view. Dewey says that if "contemporary western man" would throw off the old beliefs about knowledge and action, he would be confident that he could achieve security through the use of his own powers (*LW* 4:8). Would contemporary western woman be so confident? Perhaps, but only if the burden of beliefs and actions oppressing women were also thrown off. The reason women cannot be so straightforwardly included in the seemingly inclusive *we* of the text resides in the differing relations of women and men to the structures of power, a relation that Dewey sometimes seems to recognize, but not to the extent of developing a sustained explanation for it nor for its being overcome. Insofar as women are systematically discriminated against in their access to the power needed to overcome the dangers that they encounter, dangers that are not primarily those of brute physical forces, then they cannot be subsumed under a general critique of the classical glorification of theory over practice.

When *women* is substituted for *men* in the text, a very different reading emerges, one that enhances rather than diminishes the original criticism that links privileged control with a metaphysics of Being. How would the world in which *women* act and live be perceptually and practically experienced? What happens when work in the home is "infected with *non*-being" and excluded from philosophical consideration? It becomes apparent that the classical Greek philosophers could place their own contemplative rationality at the tip of the pyramid of valued human activity because they were privileged not only by class and race, but also be gender. Dewey was able to recognize and denounce classism and racism in philosophical analysis, partly because of the discontinuities of the modern world of science and liberal democracy from the ancient one. But philosophy itself continued to be a traditional part of men's lived world, a fact that helped obscure the sexism of its unquestioned masculinist point of view. By bringing in women's experiences, pragmatist philosophy would move closer to its goal of undermining pernicious dualisms and generating reflections that operate efficaciously in connection with the practical problems of everyday life.

2. EXPERIENCE *IS* REALITY

Taking over James's characterization of experience as a double-barreled word, Dewey says that "like its congeners, life and history, [experience] includes *what* men do and suffer, *what* they strive for, love, believe and endure, and also *how* men act and are acted upon, the ways in which they do and suffer, desire and enjoy, see, believe, imagine—in short, processes of *experiencing*" (*LW* 1:18). Dewey spoke more accurately than he knew when he defined experiencing as what men do, feel, value, and imagine. Historically, men have had disproportionate power to inscribe their point of view on the world.

Given the exaggeration of gender differences in most organizations of society, it would be expected that women's experiences will differ in various ways from men's, and certainly women's access to dominant structures of power has been severely restricted in most societies at most periods of history. Dewey most likely did not realize that he was privileging a masculine perspective, since he did not do so in his political activities, but his gendered discourse nonetheless testifies to a male bias. Since he was also alert to hidden forms of oppression, this bias does not vitiate what he says, but disappears once it is exposed. If anything, it provides unintended—and therefore even more forceful—evidence for his claim that our experiences influence our perspectives and value judgments.

What he said can be appropriated by feminists to good effect. By taking the integrated unity of what is experienced and the concretely embodied way of experiencing as the starting point of philosophic thought, Dewey avoided the extremes of materialism and idealism, and he provided a means of legitimating women's special angles of vision and their tendency to theorize on the basis of our experiences. The concrete specificity of Dewey's explanation of experience stands in stark contrast to the practice of philosophy as sterile argumentation and symbol manipulation. He says, for instance, that "*experience* denotes the planted field, the sowed seeds, the reaped harvests, the changes of night and day, spring and autumn, wet and dry, heat and cold, that are observed, feared, longed for; it also denotes the one who plants and reaps, who works and rejoices, hopes, fears, plans, invokes magic or chemistry to aid him, who is downcast or triumphant" (*LW* 1:18). The *him* can be replaced by *her* without distortion or gender privilege, which is not true of most male-biased theoretical discourse.

Long before the current wave of poststructuralism, Dewey argued that "our analysis shows that the *ways* in which we believe and expect have a tremendous effect upon *what* we believe and expect" (*LW* 1:23). Following Hegel and anticipating Foucault, he showed how our inherited beliefs and institutions continue to influence our perceptions, that is, how historicity is constitutive of our peculiarly human interactions with nature. "We learn, in short, that qualities which we attribute to objects ought to be imputed to our own ways of experiencing them, and that these in turn are due to the force of intercourse and custom." Moreover, he argues that "this discovery marks an emancipation; it purifies and remakes the objects of our direct or primary experience."

As far back in history as we have records of women's denunciation of their situation, we have evidence that women have recognized the emancipatory potential of the discovery of the effect of preconception on reality. When once we realize that what we take to be straightforwardly matters of fact are actually active transformations of experience that include socially transmitted preconceptions, then we can dispute historically widespread claims that women's perceived inferiority is due to a fact of nature and is therefore unalterable. Even facts can be questioned.

Not only presuppositions, but social, political, economic, and psychological practices contribute to the facticity of facts. There is no way to strip away all subjective factors and just reductively identify the facts that remain. So-called subjective factors help constitute the objectivity of the facts. Therefore, it is not irrelevant to respond to a cited statistic about the different mathematical ability of boys and girls by asking for the underlying cultural expectations and political agenda which helped constitute the experimental procedure. Expectations, values, and beliefs are already part of any experimental situation. By drawing our attention to them, feminists and pragmatists are not politicizing an otherwise neutral, objective field; they are seeking to disclose the full complexity of the actual situation. It is pernicious to deny minority groups and women the means to develop the intellectual skills needed to function successfully in a highly technological society just because such denial does not leave the victims intact; the assumption of lesser ability contributes to bringing about as an actual result what was initially merely a preconception.[18]

But some feminist theorists presuppose that it is possible to expose the misogynist biases of explanations that perpetuate distorted views of reality and replace these with objective claims that transparently capture reality as it really is, apart from any presuppositions or value orientation. They think that anyone could just look and see that the feminist explanation is the one true one. According to William James as well as Dewey, this belief in a univocally true transcription of reality, which is the possession of any one group or theoretical stance, is itself one of the bases for many oppressive practices over the centuries.

That one has good intentions in pointing out what reality really is does not lessen the oppressive results of the belief. It is the belief itself that one has a privileged access to reality that does the harm. If I am simply right about reality, for instance, in some absolute way, and if you oppose my claim with a different one, then it follows that you are necessarily wrong. This accounts for the confrontational basis of so many academic disputes and wider social ones. The stronger the belief in one's own integrity, the greater the confrontation.

That reality is always as much a function of one's angle of vision and lived experience as it is of what is available to be experienced has been dramatically enacted over the years in challenges to feminist theory from within. African-American feminists charge white feminists with racism; lesbian feminists charge heterosexual feminists with homophobia, and third-world feminists charge first-world feminists with colonialism.[19] The early feminist agenda of speaking out on behalf of women has been challenged as leading to distortion by those who want to speak in their own voice about their own experiences. This phenomenon could simply be interpreted as an initially false theoretical position being challenged by the true one. The earlier theories were homophobic, sexist, and racist, and the new ones replacing them are not. But this does not adequately describe the complexity of the dynamics. Earlier feminists conscientiously argued against oppression as they saw it. But their angle of vision was necessarily partial. They recognized some aspects of the situation, but not all. This does not show that their original position was false, only that it was finite, incomplete, and in principle capable of revision when new experiences and reflective interpretations became available. These were quickly supplied by women who felt that their experiences were not being accurately described.

In the sixties and seventies, through consciousness-raising sessions and critical reflections on personal experience, it became possible to recognize, name, and criticize the web of social, cultural, and political structures within which experiences took on the particular oppressive dimensions they did. The very homogeneity of the white middle-class experiences being expressed generated a sense of sisterhood and conviction that their political analyses truly named, and provided a remedy for, the felt oppression. It soon became evident, though, that not everyone had the same experiences or shared the same values. It took different perspectives to recognize the hidden biases that had not been detected. And these challenges were often put forth as themselves complete and the final word. Some lesbians, for instance, accused heterosexual feminists as not only perpetuating homophobia, but as being fundamentally flawed in their way of life. They said that these misguided sisters could not be totally emancipated until they gave up their sexual orientation and became completely woman-identified.

The finite partiality of lesbian experiences allowed lesbians to recognize the one-sided nature of heterosexual experiences, but not of their own, just as the one-sided nature of the heterosexual experiences had blinded heterosexuals to their homophobia. If one looks at the complex dynamics of the sometimes confrontational dialogues over the years, it is obvious that the wrong position was not simply replaced by the right one but that gradually each modified her initial stance as she assimilated different ways of naming the contested experiences. The quality of the experiences themselves changed as beliefs changed, and beliefs changed in response to new experiences.

How, then, can we appeal to experience as a bulwark against the ideological distortions which we have absorbed merely by growing up as a member of a particular community? Dewey's philosophy is a major achievement precisely because it combines explanations of the perspectival character of our grasp of reality, which is active and transformative, with analyses of the ways in which we can legitimately distinguish merely subjective from warrantably objective claims about reality. Dewey denies that the unavoidably subjective element in our active dealings with the world makes it impossible to determine objectively genuine aspects of any given situation. He also denies that there is an infinite regress or infinite plurality of interpretations of experience, just as he denies that there is one, hegemonically definitive transcription of reality.

We cannot grasp Dewey's accomplishment unless we realize that he rejects the privatization of experience that has come to be taken for granted. The recognition of the contributing influence of personal attitudes and their consequences, which was liberating in actual life, had pernicious results in philosophy (*LW* 1:24–26). When philosophy took the subject matter of psychology to be the interior or subjective response to objective reality, then experience was reduced to the act of experiencing, and experience to the single aspect of perceiving (*LW* 1:11). Dewey asserted instead "the primacy and ultimacy" of the material of ordinary experience (*LW* 1:24). Experience is primary in uncontrolled form, and it is ultimate as regulated, given significance through "the methods and results of reflective experience." In rejecting the subjectification of primary experience, Dewey provides arguments for acknowledging the reality of the material conditions, the objectivity, of women's experience. But in distinguishing between the experiences with which we begin and those that are the result of directed inquiry, he also develops a method for correcting misconceptions or less valuable interpretations about the nature of particular experiences and thus avoids relativizing them.

Pragmatist analysis of the difference between experience as origin and as the outcome of reflection, a reflection directed by the intention to change situations so as to facilitate emancipation, can be usefully applied to many feminist research projects. A case in point is found in *Engendered Lives* by Ellyn Kaschak, in which she explains the psychological development of women and men from a perspective which recognizes that "the most notable aspect of current gender arrangements is that the masculine always defines the feminine by naming, containing, engulfing, invading, and evaluating it. The feminine is never permitted to stand alone or to subsume the masculine." [20] This regulative perspective has emerged from reflections on primary experience but is not identical with it. As Judith Lewis Herman points out in her review of *Engendered Lives*, it is easy to achieve this basic insight in the abstract, less easy to sustain it in the particular, as Kashak does. According to Herman, Kashak is interested in the " 'lived and ordinary experiences of women,' which she invites us to examine, as if for the first time, with newly opened eyes."[21] By "making visible the hidden effects of gender in ordinary life" Kashak helps liberate women to "learn to see with their own eyes, from their own point of view."

The lived experiences of the women subjects are already being interpreted by them through whatever cultural perspectives are available. But their interpretations cannot be assumed to merely reflect more global, more repressive, views; they also contest or individually appropriate them. Kashak brings a feminist perspective to her reflections and thus liberates aspects of the original experiences that otherwise would not have been so explicitly recognized or articulated. The primary experience and the emergent experience are not identical, but they are dynamically related. As George Herbert Mead argues, in the process by which we develop as persons, we first adopt the point of view of the generalized other, of culture and society, as a prerequisite to developing our own, more individualized perspectives. In the process, beliefs and attitudes shape our insights whether we are self-consciously aware of them or not. But the ongoing process of constructing our self-identity by putting ourselves in the place of the Other and then reacting to the perception Others would have of us allows for a range of possible responses, from abject conformity to sharp revolt.[22] Therefore, it makes sense both to say that as women we already see the world from a woman's perspective and that we must learn to see from the point of view of women.

Harriet Jacobs's slave narrative, already mentioned, is a case in point. Ironically, it was later challenged as inauthentic because of its traditional forms and genteel style. But Jacobs wrote in the language of her time and place, sometimes straightforwardly and sometimes using the language of Garrisonian abolitionism. When writing of her sexual life, for example, she spoke as a respectable nineteenth-century woman, with omissions and circumlocutions. Lacking a more appropriate model, "she used the style of the seduction novel."[23] But how else do we communicate our own unique experiences except by encasing them in words and styles developed independently by others for other purposes? We not only communicate using borrowed feathers, but we feel and judge our experiences by borrowed standards. Jacobs had to overcome intense feelings of shame about her sexual life outside of marriage before she could bear to expose it to a hostile public by writing about it for publication. In doing so, however, she was empowered to give a new meaning to her life by questioning whether the sexual standards imposed on free women were relevant to women held in slavery. She had to confront the sexual ideology of white patriarchy in order to expose white racism.

According to feminist theory, the initial perspective of most women would be—to a greater or lesser degree—that of a womanhood as defined within a culture which devalues women and femininity and privileges men and masculinity. Moreover, a woman may or may not self-consciously think as a woman or identify her femaleness as a condition she shares with all women. Nor is there any reason to believe that one's gender identity leads one to assert any politically relevant salient characteristics as inhering in one's gender or as arising from membership in a class. Unlike an initial or inherent perspective, only an emergent perspective could consciously identify the oppressive horizon within which many women come to self-consciousness. Such a recognition incorporates a sense of oneself as a woman who has learned from other feminists many of the ramifications of what it means to become a woman within a particular milieu and what it takes to make choices rather than unwittingly confirm choices already made.

Another layer of complexity arises in moving from reflections on one's own experience to that of others. It is difficult to negotiate the terrain between simply imposing my perspectives, my theories, on the lived or ordinary experiences of others, sympathetically hearing their expressions and interpretations of their own lives, and developing emergent meanings out of the interaction of theories of the gendered nature of experience and reexaminations of one's experiences in light of such engendering. Moreover, gender is not the only salient characteristic as multiple identities reflecting such relations as ethnicity and class are simultaneously negotiated or ignored. As Patricia Hill Collins points out, "Black women's concrete experiences as members of specific race, class, and gender groups as well as our concrete historical situations necessarily play significant roles in our perspectives on the world. No standpoint is neutral because no individual or group exists unembedded in the world. Knowledge is gained not by solitary individuals but by Black women as socially constituted members of a group." [24]

3. LIFE-EXPERIENCES

Pragmatist philosophy begins with life-experience, which consists of both doings and undergoings (*LW* 10:9, 50–53). Experience is not just naively undergone; it is overlaid and saturated not only with previous philosophical interpretations but also with past beliefs, values, and classifications. Since the origins and validity of these earlier interpretations are for the most part lost, they differ little from prejudices. But whether they are taken as the incorporated results of past reflection or as prejudices, they are welded onto genuinely firsthand experiences and can be a source of enlightenment when reflected upon. They distort present experience just to the extent that they are not detected. "Clarification and emancipation follow when they are detected and cast out; and one great object of philosophy is to accomplish this task" (*LW* 1:40).

Dewey moves back and forth between labeling earlier interpretations of experience, which continue to influence our understanding of present events, as sources of enrichment or causes of distortion. Consequently, it sometimes seems that the reflective effort to identify them should properly issue in deliberate recovery, and then again, in rejection and emancipation. This ambiguity is deliberate because we ought to reflect, continually and critically, on these inheritances. Some will be found to be enhancements of present experience and others to be distorting and counterproductive. Which is which cannot simply be decided hegemonically by a privileged elite or tradition, nor can it be determined beforehand by purely rational analysis. Dewey calls his critically empirical philosophy "a kind of intellectual disrobing" because of the importance of holding up for inspection the beliefs and values we assimilate by virtue of belonging to a culture (*LW* 1:40). "But intelligent furthering of culture demands that we take some of them off, that we inspect them critically to see what they are made of and what wearing them does to us."

Dewey calls the discriminative judgment by which we decide to continue or reject aspects of our culture the cultivation of a naïveté of eye, ear, and thought. But this is not a return to an original innocence, rather it is a genuine grasp of experience acquired through a discipline of severe thought. In fact, traditional philosophy has failed the ordinary person by denigrating just such a concern for everyday experiences. The authoritarian arrogance of much philosophizing has given the impression that only those few who have access to the classical thinkers of the past are qualified to judge what is important and what not. The denigration of ordinary experience and praise of pure thought or rational analysis for its own sake is one of the greatest failings of traditional philosophy precisely because it denies to nonspecialists the authority of their own experiences. By focusing almost exclusively on classical texts or papers given at professional meetings or articles published in professional journals, philosophers "have denied that common experience is capable of developing from within itself methods which will secure direction for itself and will create inherent standards of judgment and value" (*LW* 1: 41). An avowed pragmatist goal, therefore, is to create and promote respect for concrete human experience and its potentialities.[25]

"*Whose* experience?" feminists want to know.[26] Not only have classi-

cal texts and elite professional discourse characterized traditional philosophizing, but male reflections and experiences have been exclusively
privileged. Dewey explicitly raises the issue of "*Whose* experience?" as a
criticism, but only in order to deny its relevance (*LW* 1:178–81). His
intention in doing so is a good one—to undercut the subjectivity traditionally ascribed to experience as a basis for excluding it from the abstractly rational deliberations of philosophers. However, good intentions
do not override the harm done by not taking the objection more seriously. Unlike Dewey, I cannot ignore the source of experienced claims
because, from my point of view as a member of a marginalized group,
the male-centered angle of vision of supposedly generalized experiential
claims is both obvious and oppressive. I grant the validity of Dewey's rejection of the subjectification of experience, since women's experiential
perspectives have consistently been dismissed by philosophers as being
merely subjective. But defenses of the objective character of experience
can be made without denying that gender, as well as race, class, sexual
orientation, and many other distinctions contribute to its objectivity, and
therefore it is not only appropriate but imperative to question whose
experience is being used as a paradigm for explication.

My objection, therefore, is not meant to undercut Dewey's explanation that experience is dependent on the objectively physical and social
structures of natural events. "It has its own objective and definitive
traits," which are describable without reference to a self, if by self is
meant the isolated individual in the privacy of consciousness (*LW* 1:
179). Moreover, selves are specifiable, definable events within experience and not occurrences outside, underneath, or beside experience, as
they are traditionally held to be in the pernicious dualisms of spirit and
matter, mind and body.

Dewey argues that for some purposes and consequences, it is imperative to recognize and acknowledge personal ownership. The self can
be objectified, just as other objects like trees and planets are discriminated as aspects of experience. "To say in a significant way, '*I* think, believe, desire' . . . is to accept and affirm a responsibility and to put forth
a claim" (*LW* 1:179–80). It signifies the self as an organizing center,
who accepts future benefits and liabilities as the consequences of one's
deliberate actions, rather than crediting them to nature, family, church,
or state. "Existentially speaking, a human individual is distinctive opacity
of bias and preference conjoined with plasticity and permeability of
needs and likings. One trait tends to isolation, discreteness; the other
trait to connection, continuity. This ambivalent character is rooted in
nature" (*LW* 1:186). For certain purposes we can distinguish what pertains more to the subject and what more to the object. Dualisms are ob-
jectionable when they convert dynamic principles of formulation and

interpretation into antithetical absolutes. "Sociability, communication are just as immediate traits of the concrete individual as is the privacy of the closet of consciousness" (*LW* 1:187).

In the second chapter of *Experience and Nature* Dewey suggests that philosophers ought to draw more on the findings of anthropology because they were not isolated from culture in the way that psychology was. Anthropology can provide a safeguard against the myopia of provincially universalizing what is true of one's own limited experience. Philosophy should not simply adopt an anthropological view of culture, however, "but in a different context and by a different method, it has the task of analytic dismemberment and synthetic reconstruction of experience" (*LW* 1:42). Among the traits of experience derived from such cultural phenomena as recurrences of plague, famine, wars, and disease are its precariousness, unpredictableness, and hazardousness. Our emotional responses reflect this environment. Emotions are not in the first place private, subjective events, but are revelatory of situations in which we find ourselves. Women and men fear because they exist "in a fearful, an awful world. The *world* is precarious and perilous" (*LW* 1:43–44). While security in the past was sought in myth and magic, today it is more often sought through science, which changes the world to make it more conformable to our needs. Rain dances have been replaced by irrigation, for instance, and tuberculosis controlled through penicillin. But the drive to have "the stability of meaning prevail over the instability of events" is so much a part of human intelligence that it is imagined to reside as a property of things rather than of art (*LW* 1:49). This renders effort useless and makes the accidental well-being of a class seem natural rather than the result of the toil of another class. Classical, orthodox philosophy privileges a metaphysics of Being, of stability and universality, and it denigrates becoming. It seeks control through meaning and sidesteps the painful work of regulating actual events to render uncertain conditions more stable.

Nature is both relatively stable and relatively contingent (*LW* 1:56). To valorize only stability as real falsifies experience. The unstable equilibrium of the hazardous and the stable both sets problems for us and makes possible the movement toward a resolution. Because we desire change and satisfaction, its instantiation can be recognized as an accomplishment, judged good, and asserted as a value. Ideals are also features of experience because as imaginative anticipations of a more desirable future state of affairs they are an "appropriate phase of indeterminate events moving toward eventualities that are now but possibilities" (*LW* 1: 57). The dualistic thinking of traditional metaphysics has sharply distinguished thought from its objects and characterized as real Being only what is consistent, rational, certain; and it has relegated contingency, ambiguity, and process to phenomenal status. Pragmatically empirical philosophy points, instead, to "the contextual situation in which thinking occurs" (*LW* 1:61). Beginning with an actually problematic situation, "it perceives that thinking is a continuous process of temporal reorganization within one and the same world of experienced things," not the bridging of a chasm between reality and appearance or between abstractly rational thought and qualitatively immediate sensations. Uncertain situations are empirically concrete; they are not just puzzles proposed and solved within an isolated intellect.

"Every existence is an event," not a predetermined essential nature (*LW* 1:63). Consequently, "the conjunction of problematic and determinate characters in nature renders every existence, as well as every idea and human act, an experiment in fact, even though not in design." By recognizing the experimental character of everyday experience, pragmatism has developed a theory that has the potential to empower those whose class, ethnicity, gender, or sexual orientation have not been privileged in the cultural setup. "To be intelligently experimental is but to be conscious of this intersection of natural conditions so as to profit by it instead of being at its mercy" (*LW* 1:63). Dorothy E. Smith captures this pragmatist sense of the experimental character of everyday experience in a book aptly titled *The Everyday World as Problematic: A Feminist Sociology:* "If we begin where people are actually located in that independently existing world outside texts, we begin in the particularities of an actual everyday world. As a first step in entering that standpoint into a textually mediated discourse, we constitute the everyday world as our problematic." [27]

One of the most striking features of human experience, Dewey says, is direct enjoyment, as found in feasting, ornamentation, dance, and festivities of all kinds. Luxuries and embellishments transform the everyday even at the subsistence level, so that those living in hovels nonetheless build and decorate temples of worship and adorn their bodies, even if clothing is scarce. Useful labor is transformed by ritual and ceremony: "Men make a game of their fishing and hunting, and turn to the periodic and disciplinary labor of agriculture only when inferiors, women and slaves, cannot be had to do the work" (*LW* 1:69). This examples passes without comment or criticism from Dewey, who is too intent on demonstrating the connection of the consummatory phase of the direct appreciative enjoyment of things with instrumental, laborious productivity.

Not until the end of the chapter does he remind us that "to point out something as a fact is not the same thing as to commend or eulogize the fact" (*LW* 1:97). He criticizes the class structure that permitted a privileged elite to engage in purely intellectual activity without the need to make a living. The ultimate contradiction for the philosophical tradition is that though it praised thought as universal and necessary and the culminating good of nature, it did not bother to condemn the restriction of its exercise to a small and exclusive class, and therefore did nothing to extend it to those not privileged by birth or by economic or civil status.

Obviously, why women were taken to be inferiors is not an issue that interests Dewey to the extent that class does, nor does he seem aware of the male-centered view uncritically expressed. He does continually criticize and seek to overturn the class-based nature of traditional philosophizing, pointing out its dependency on slave labor, but he does not similarly reject its gender bias. His arguments for the objectivity of experience can be supported without agreeing that the question of whose experience it is should not be raised. We can only realize the full emancipatory potential of the pragmatist analysis of experience by bringing in those whose experiences have been excluded in the past.

The concrete specificity of the anthropology Dewey drew on, like the conceptual frameworks and practices of sociology according to Smith, developed without taking into account the standpoint of women as "an 'embodied' subject located in a particular actual local historical setting."[28] In contrast, feminist sociologists, along with feminist investigators generally, "start, as we must, with women's experience (for what other resource do we have?); the available concepts and frameworks do not work because they have already posited a subject situated outside a local and actual experience, a particularized knowledge of the world."

4. FEELING AS A QUALITY OF LIFE-FORMS

Pragmatist explanations of the relation between self and world, experience and knowledge, theory and praxis deny the strict separation of emotions and intellect that feminists frequently criticize as a masculinist distortion pervasive in the Western tradition of philosophy. In Dewey's transactive model of experience, feelings and intellect are continuous, although distinguishable for certain purposes. Needs, efforts to satisfy needs, and satisfactions distinguish living from nonliving things (*LW* 1: 194). When the activity of need-demand-satisfaction acquires certain additional abilities to secure the interactive support of needs from the environment, the subsequent organization is psychophysical. The perpetuation of patterned activities as an aspect of organizing capacities serves as the basis of sensitivity. Selective bias in interactions with environing conditions serves to perpetuate both the organism and the whole of which it is a part. Sensitivity is thus always making distinctions. On a more complex level of organization, biases becomes interests, and satisfaction of needs is reflectively determined to be values, rather than simply mere satiation.

Dewey's use of the term *organism* instead of *person* or *body* is deliberate. He speaks of the "organism in its entirety" (*LW* 10:64) and "the whole of the live creature" (*LW* 10:87). This usage emphasizes the post-Darwinian awareness of human continuity with other animals and recognizes that we are not embodied minds but interactive organisms with many ways of taking in the world and responding to it.[29] The mind/body split is an inherited dualistic classification, which makes such a rigid distinction between body and mind that it becomes impossible to figure out how they are related, or else pits each against the other in an adversarial relationship. Both feminists and pragmatists have pointed out at great length the oppressive consequences of this split. It is difficult to retain one side of the dualism, the body, without its ghostly double distorting what is meant by body, embodiedness, or lived body. By contrast, we experience organic transactions within situations, and we are aware that this process does not leave either pole of the transaction unchanged.

Our inherited philosophical vocabulary, which sharply distinguishes mind and body, impedes a more organic, emergent view of human beings. Dewey invents the term "*body-mind*" to designate "what actually takes place when a living body is implicated in situations of discourse, communication, and participation. In the hyphenated phrase *body-mind, body* designates the continued and conserved, the registered and cumulative operation of factors continuous with the rest of nature, inanimate as well as animate; while *mind* designates the characters and consequences that are differential, indicative of features that emerge when *body* is engaged in a wider, more complex and interdependent situation" (*LW* 1:217). In chapter 7 of *Experience and Nature,* titled "Nature, Life and Body-Mind," he explains that sensitivity and interests are realized as feelings, which can be sharp and intense or vague and diffuse, as in massive uneasiness or comfortableness. "Activities are differentiated into the preparatory, or anticipatory, and the fulfilling of consummatory" (*LW* 1: 197). Anticipation of food or sex or danger is suffused with the tone of the consummated activity. This capacity to anticipate an outcome is actualized in feeling. Feelings, therefore, are not simply private, internal events, but a valuable "susceptibility to the useful and harmful in surroundings," a premonition of eventual lived consequences.

When the consummated satisfactions or disappointments accrue, they reinforce the anticipatory activities, including feelings. The experience is no longer haphazard, but becomes an integrated accumulation. "Comfort or discomfort, fatigue or exhilaration, implicitly sum up a history, and thereby unwittingly provide a means whereby (when other conditions become present) the past can be unravelled and made explicit" (*LW* 1:197). Although feelings themselves are relatively undifferentiated, they have the capacity to take on innumerable distinctions. As they are refined, they can vary more and more in quality, intensity, and duration.

Feelings are thus related to environing conditions and interactive outcomes. They *have* these connections, though not necessarily mentally, as an explicit grasp of meaning. When feelings are meaningful as well as experienced, then mind has emerged. In an intricate but succinct summing up, Dewey adroitly manages to avoid dualistic explanations while retaining the complexity of human organisms. "As life is a character of events in a peculiar condition of organization, and 'feeling' is a quality of life-forms marked by complexly mobile and discriminating responses, so 'mind' is an added property assumed by a feeling creature, when it reaches that organized interaction with other living creatures which is language, communication" (*LW* 1:198). Feelings become suffused with meaning as they serve to objectively discriminate external things and relate past and future episodes. They recall and foretell. As language develops, pains, pleasures, colors, and odors acquire the capacity to objectify the immediate traits of things. Qualities do not essentially reside in organisms or in things but emerge in interactions with each other. But for purposes of control they may be treated as if located in one or the other. Psychologists, for instance, have traditionally treated women hysterics for their symptoms, thus substantializing the subjective pole and privatizing it, rather than taking the hysteric behavior as a quality of their interactions with their human and material surroundings. The latter would make it possible to objectively identify the hysteria as a process whose roots, and therefore cure, are deeply entangled in an objectively identifiable situation.

Sensory qualities do not identify themselves. They exist as the indispensable means of any noetic function, but must be transformed through a system of signs. When a particular feeling of listlessness is identified as a response to repeated beatings, for instance, then attention is directed to a particular, objective interaction, and it becomes possible to change the conditions that are bringing it about. Qualities just merge into the general situation until, through communication, as shared meanings to social consequences, they acquire objective distinctiveness (*LW* 1:199). When the same listlessness is interpreted by society as inappropriate behavior for a wife or partner, and the woman internalizes this explanation, then she is likely to cooperate in therapies designed to change her behavior rather than her surroundings, including the actions of her batterer.

Feelings inhere neither in matter nor in mind but are qualitative aspects of a particular field of interacting events. A battered woman feeling badly enough to seek help can be aided or obstructed in the identification of the objective interactions defining her situation, depending on the meanings projected onto the events by others. It cannot be assumed that the woman already has an explicit understanding of the full reality of her situation, which is why she can be caught in a series of inappropriate responses. Neither can it be assumed that neutral observers, such as social work professionals or law enforcement officials, have a privileged access to the truth of her situation. Interactive communication is required for a progressively better understanding of each particular abusive situation. But the battered woman has one advantage no one else has. She knows how she feels and what she observes, and these can be articulated ever more accurately as meaningful connections begin to be appropriately named.

5. EXPERIENCE IS EMOTIONAL [30]

Dewey's explanation of how feelings permeate situations provides a powerful alternative model to the traditional relegating of emotion to a purely private, subjective realm. Emotion is objective as well as subjective because it is "something called out *by* objects, physical and personal; it is response *to* an objective situation. . . . Emotion is an indication of intimate participation, in a more or less excited way in some scene of nature or life; it is, so to speak, an attitude or disposition which is a function of objective things" (*LW* 1:292).

In "The Man of Reason" Genevieve Lloyd points out that Descartes ushers in modern philosophy by sharply distinguishing sensuousness from thought. "The search for the 'clear and distinct,' the separating out of the emotional, the sensuous, the imaginative, now makes possible polarizations of previously existing contrasts—intellect versus the emotions; reason versus imagination; mind versus matter." Lloyd warns against a repudiation of reason that simply embraces the devalued term: "Critics of reason too easily fall into a sterile repudiation of the rational, a vacuous affirmation of the importance or superiority of feeling or imagination." [31] She appeals to Henri Bergson's intuition and Robert Pirsig's *Zen and the Art of Motorcycle Maintenance* to overcome the sterile dichotomy of the classical and romantic styles. But the most thoroughgoing critique of the ideal of disembodied reason, one that explores the cognitive dimension of feeling without abandoning intelligence, can be found in pragmatism.

According to Dewey, any significant experience is a unity of practical, emotional, and intellectual qualities (*LW* 10:61). The emotional phase pervades and unifies the others. Experiences are intellectual simply because they have meaning, and they are practical in the sense that organisms interact with surrounding objects and events. On reflection, these aspects can be distinguished. Since one aspect may dominate the others, an experience can be accurately described as primarily intellectual or aesthetic, but to substantialize these distinctions distorts the original unity of the experience and ignores the influence of the subordinate aspects.

Emotions are objective because "the perceived object or scene is emotionally pervaded throughout" (*LW* 10:59). Only in pathological conditions are they private. Emotions belong to selves, but selves who have grown beyond merely reflexive reactions to a concern for objects and their outcomes. The emotion then becomes part of an inclusive and enduring situation (*LW* 10:49). Experiences are fraught with anticipation as the initiating phase moves toward fulfillment through a series of varied incidents. Dewey gives as an example the experience of an employer interviewing a potential employee. The character of the applicant is filtered through the emotional reactions of the employer, who imaginatively projects the applicant into the job situation. "The presence and behavior of the applicant either harmonize with his own attitudes and desires or they conflict and jar" (*LW* 10:50). These inherently aesthetic factors are said to enter into the settlement of every situation and carry it forward to a decisive conclusion.

What is remarkable about this example from a feminist perspective is the consequences that follow from Dewey's explicit assumption that both employer and employee are male. The opportunity is lost to use the example to demonstrate how prejudice operates toward those different from ourselves in gender, ethnicity, or class. Dewey has developed a powerful analytic tool for demonstrating how the varied intensities of the employer's emotionally pervaded preconceptions and anticipations are just as much part of the objective situation as is the discussion of salary ranges. But he uses the example only to demonstrate the objectivity of emotions. Feminist analyses of the ways that sexism disadvantages women job applicants would not only strengthen, rather than diminish, this objectivity, but would also extend the analysis into an instrument of concrete social change. The generality of Dewey's analysis would gain by this specificity and his usual connection of description with reconstruction would be rendered more explicit.

Experience is not just the interaction of a live creature with some aspect of the world in which she lives; the interaction takes place according to a pattern or structure. What is undergone becomes the basis of anticipation and directed action. The relation between an action and its consequences can be misperceived, and the meaning of the experience consequently distorted, when the perception of the relations between undergoing and doing is limited. Limitations can be on the side of doing or of undergoing, which Dewey elaborates as excessive action or excessive receptivity. His explanation can be transformed into a critique of stereotypical gender relations by reworking the two limitations as descriptions of what happens when women's options are distorted through an excess of receptivity, or undergoing, and when men's are distorted by an excess of doing or lust for action.

The lust for action leaves many men, in the hectic pace of modern life, severely impoverished in their experiences. The dispersal of attention leads to experiences that are not carried through to fulfillment and thus are not reflectively appropriated to enrich the next experience. The quantity rather than the quality of actions becomes decisive. Worst of all, "resistance is treated as an obstruction to be beaten down, not as an invitation to reflection" (*LW* 10:51). When the resistance comes from the women in men's lives, Dewey's statement about being beaten down takes on an ominousness beyond any that he imagined at the time.

But excessive receptivity can also prevent experiences from maturing. When women either prize mere undergoing for its own sake or when they are forced into immobility by constricting circumstances or deliberate hostility, they cannot derive from their experiences the fullness of meaning. There must be some balance between doing and undergoing in order to apprehend their interrelations in a way of thinking that is one of the most exacting tasks of intellectual labor. Women and others isolated in domestic or impoverished ghettos are artificially cut off from the full realization of their possibilities for action because their own experiences are so severely limited. They may come to see themselves only as helpless victims without the possibility of initiating needed changes. "Some decisive action is needed in order to establish contact with the realities of the world and in order that impressions may be so related to facts that their value is tested and organized" (*LW* 10:52). The terror of the experience of an abusive husband or partner can distort the magnitude of his power to control his partner's life to such an extent that she cannot even imagine which actions she can initiate in her own behalf that might be effective.

Perception is not passive. It is "an act of reconstructive doing . . . for to perceive, a beholder must *create* [her] own experience" (*LW* 10:59–60).[32] For an experience to be maximally intelligible, it must be lived through without excessive limitations on the undergoing and the doing. Successful anticipation of outcomes means that the relations structuring any given situation are sufficiently grasped to direct the fulfillment congruently with one's own intentions. Imaginative anticipation links receptivity with intentional outcome. "What is done and what is undergone are thus reciprocally, cumulatively, and continuously instrumental to each other" (*LW* 10:57).

Impulsion is the initial stage of a complete experience that calls the whole self into play (*LW* 10:64). When obstacles are encountered, the living creature becomes aware of its own intentions because it has to convert the obstacle into a favoring agency if it is to continue. Growth would be limited if the environing conditions, social and physical, were either always congenial or always hostile. An environment that is always congenial would stifle thoughtfulness because we would not need to give an account of objects to ourselves. Awareness would not be awakened, since objects would not be emotionally encountered as obstacles to be surmounted and consciously appropriated. Instead, they would simply be undergone.

On the other hand, an environment that was "always hostile would irritate and destroy" (*LW* 10:65). Oppositions that are arbitrary and extraneous block rather than promote growth. Arbitrary obstacles are those that bear no intrinsic relation to the ongoing process, as when women are excluded from positions of responsibility and authority merely because they are women. "Mere opposition that completely thwarts, creates irritation and rage," rather than intelligent action (*LW* 10:65–66).

The level of resistance that leads to growth, then, is one that is intrinsically related to what it obstructs. Awareness requires that there be obstacles that need surmounting. We need resistance to grow, to generate curiosity and solicitous care. Resistance converts "direct forward action into re-flection" and transforms energy into thoughtful action (*LW* 10: 66). Past experiences of obstacles successfully overcome, when thoughtfully re-created rather than just repeated, provide the basis for generating meaning.

Dewey's explanation of the role that obstacles play in meaningful experiences needs feminist criticism to keep a reader from misunderstanding it. He moves too quickly from a discussion of excessively hostile environments to a discussion of diminished forms of resistance. This move allows him to develop a positive philosophy of growth, and this investigation of the developmental nature of human intelligence and the emergence of values from reflectively appropriated experience can be usefully appropriated by feminist theorists. But it is overly optimistic to the extent that it does not recognize, expose, and suggest means for overcoming the excessively hostile environments that are all too often the lived experience of oppressed persons and groups.

It is possible to reconstruct from a feminist perspective Dewey's explanation of how mere activity is converted into an act of expression when it encounters genuine means rather than a smooth passage or blind obstructions. Dewey says that expression is thwarted when "storms of passion . . . break through barriers and . . . sweep away whatever intervenes between a person and something he would destroy" (*LW* 10:67). He ignores the fact that such rage may objectively change the situation.

because he only wants to deny that mere emotionality constitutes expression for aesthetic theory. When we realize that the object a man is most likely to destroy or harm in a fit of passion is a woman, then drawing such a trivial consequence is disconcerting, to say the least. The extreme situation that Dewey uses as a means to make his point is never identified as one of oppression. Doing so explicitly makes possible a very different interpretation of the text.

Dewey points out, for instance, that when spectators say that a man they observe losing his temper is expressing his dominant character, they are mistaking a mere fit of passion for something constitutive of the person. But why is this a mistake? Dewey uses the example of the cry or simile of an infant, which expresses something *to* a mother, but he observes that this is not necessarily something expressed *by* the baby. The mother indeed recognizes that the something that has been expressed enlightens the situation, but the child is directly engaged in some action and is not necessarily, or even possibly, deliberately trying to express something to a caretaker. Mere discharge of inner agitation in a laugh or a cry should be distinguished from self-expression, which involves an active shaping of objective conditions. "What is sometimes called an act of self-expression might better be termed one of self-exposure; it discloses character—or lack of character—to others." (*LW* 10:68).

But Dewey's example of an inarticulate child unfairly biases the explanation. A man's destructiveness in a fit of passion is not expressiveness in any eulogistic sense, but it is nonetheless intentionally motivated and does objectively change the situation. Enraged men do not always, or even often, pick a victim at random. Even random attacks on strangers are often selected in advance as to sex, race, and perceived vulnerability, if nothing else. Dewey is right in arguing that such fits of passion are not conducive to growth, but this is not due to the expressiveness failing to work on a medium (*LW* 10:69), but because the aim of the expression is intentionally destructive. On Dewey's own transactive model of experience, enraged action destroys both the victim and the victimizer, although not in the same way or to the same extent. Without analyzing the corresponding dark side of experience, the bright side cannot be properly appreciated.

Finally, what happens when the passage on expressiveness is read within a situation of oppression in which the angry person is taken to be a woman? Again, her expression of rage can genuinely change the situation. As was said in regard to the angry man, such an outburst may not be the occasion for growth but instead may issue only in exhaustion, frustration, and repetition of the interactions that led to the outburst in the first place. Oppressed women are thus doubly victimized, first in the conditions of day-to-day life, and second, in the obstacles that numb their sensibilities and prevent them from abandoning their habitual patterns of behavior to effectively appropriate the aspects of the situation that will lead to a fulfilling consummation. On the other hand, being able to express rage may be a genuine precondition for growth when every other outlet is blocked. This possibility would be worth exploring further.

Dewey is right in questioning those who witness only the moment or aftermath of a woman's storm of passion and then judge that she is revealing her innermost character—that of an emotionally overwrought, bitter woman. In giving way to a fit of passion, the victimized woman is revealing something of the dynamics of the situation in which she may well feel trapped. Unlike the infant, the woman's expression of emotion can be an intentional cry for help, one which, in fact, signals an initial breakthrough from an excessively receptive to an active appropriation of experience. New meaning can then be given to Dewey's insight that "opposition that completely thwarts, creates irritation and rage. But resistance that calls out thought generates curiosity and solicitous care, and, when it is overcome and utilized, eventuates in elation" (*LW* 10: 65–66).

The ideal, of course, is still to engage in experiences that reach their full consummation through converting mere impulsion into more rich and gracious human intercourse. An intentional expression of welcome converts smiles and hugs into an "organic means of communicating delight upon meeting a valued friend" (*LW* 10:69). Even friendship is not without obstacles, but they should call forth reflection and solicitous care rather than sheer frustration (*LW* 10:66). Such positive Deweyan examples should not be lost sight of when we are pointing out less satisfactory transactions because they provide a model both of ends worth striving for and the means that can be reflectively acquired and acted on to bring them about.

6. THE VIEW FROM THE FRINGE

For all his sensitivity to different angles of vision, Dewey does not finally recognize how much his philosophic perspective derives its strength from the fact that it is a view from a privileged center. He comes so close to the realization, and even provides the philosophic resources for doing so, that the fact that he does not gives added weight to his own claim that there is something authoritative about experience that cannot be had any other way. He deliberately and consciously subverts the hegemony of privileged centers, and the means by which he does so can still be appropriated to good effect. He recognizes, for instance, that "if the ruling and the oppressed elements in a population, if those who wish to maintain the *status quo* and those concerned to make changes, had, when they became articulate, the same philosophy, one might well be skeptical of its intellectual integrity."[33] Nonetheless, he himself is not a member of any group whose experience has been systematically distorted and therefore has not developed a sensitivity to some specific limitations of his own experiential understanding. Pragmatist feminists can profitably criticize, incorporate, and develop Deweyan pragmatism further, just as socialist feminists have moved on from Marxism, but first it is important to see just what is missing.

In *Experience and Nature* Dewey says that "it is natural to men to take that which is of chief value to them at the time as *the* real" (*EN* 1:25). Dewey takes *men* as a generic term for *human*. His intention in doing so is benign, but the consequences are not. Compare Dewey's statement with a superficially similar one from Simone de Beauvoir, where by *men* she means males as distinguished from females: "Representation of the world, like the world itself, is the work of men; they describe it from their own point of view, which they confuse with absolute truth."[34] Oddly enough, Beauvoir and Dewey are making substantially the same point— that what we take to be objectively given reality is actually filtered through our presuppositions and values. Given a different perspective we would literally be experiencing a different reality. They are also making the point that we are usually blind to this intersubjective character of the constitution of reality and that its realization is the first step to liberating ourselves from the pernicious effects that follow from not doing so.

The consequences of not recognizing his own gender bias is apparent in Dewey's subsequent remark that "in ordinary experience this fact does no particular harm." It does no harm in everyday experience because it is easily compensated for by simply turning to other practical experiences exhibiting other interests. The harm comes from reflective disciplines like philosophy, which are deliberately removed from everyday experience and therefore encounter no corrective influence from contraindicating events. This indictment of modern philosophy for substituting categorical analysis for reflections on concrete experience is well taken, but not the claim about the self-corrective nature of ordinary experience. At the very least, some qualifications about how it is corrective have to be introduced.

Elizabeth Cady Stanton, in a speech before the New York legislature in 1860, pointed out precisely what harm is caused in everyday life by men's conflating what they value with what is real. She said that "man, the sculpture, has carved out his ideal. . . . He has made a woman that from his low stand-point looks fair and beautiful, a being without rights, or hopes, or fears but in him—neither noble, virtuous, nor independent. . . . We have bowed down and worshiped in woman, beauty, grace, the exquisite proportions, . . . her delicacy, refinement, and silent helplessness—all well when she is viewed simply as an object of sight." [35] She contrasts this type of womanhood carved by man, with "our type of womanhood," namely, "the women who are called masculine, who are brave, courageous, self-reliant and independent, . . . they who have taken their gauge of womanhood from their own native strength and dignity—they who have learned for themselves the will of God concerning them." Stanton is not just pointing out women's disadvantages relative to men in nineteenth-century America. She also identifies its source in the masculinist angle of vision and suggests how this perspective can be contested when she refers to those "who have learned for themselves." The reasons she gives for this disparity can still be usefully applied in our own century.

Stanton points to the *deliberate* maiming of women to make them appear lesser—to themselves as well as to men. Such distortion of women's experiences is motivated by the drive to gain, consolidate, or extend power. This strategy works best when some noble motivation is explicitly claimed. For one thing, this renders plausible the accusation that those pointing out the implicit motivation hidden under the explicit one are inventing ill will where none exists. There are many ways to explain situations, depending on the aim in doing so. The same situation can be described neutrally, that is, as a slice of life, as if causes were too diffuse to identify. The causes can also be described in moral or psychoanalytic terms, so that the larger structural or institutional web in which they are embedded is ignored. For instance, it is reported that a husband shoots his wife because he has been drinking or because he is jealous, as though this were an isolated incident, totally explainable in terms of the man's moral shortcomings or pathology.

In order to bring out the full dimensions of the social structures which contribute to such behavior patterns, the incident can instead be related to many others very similar to it. The facts that assaults against women by men occur much more frequently than those of women against men and that less violence against women is perpetrated by strangers than by intimates are seldom mentioned as relevant to the incident. Many newspapers and magazines follow this policy of isolationist, know-nothing reportage. This false neutrality is defended as keeping editorializing off the news pages. But it obscures relevant causal factors, ignores aspects of the situation which have to be understood in order to bring about effective changes, and neutralizes critics by making their obviously politicized rhetoric appear by contrast to seem shrill, self-serving, and ideological.

Those on the sidelines who do not have an immediate stake in the particular incident being reported are often attracted to calm recitals of facts rather than to seemingly shrill rebuttals by feminists who point out connections that are being ignored or distorted. This preference reinforces our sense of ourselves as rational beings, considering objectively the facts of the case. Since every single significant improvement in women's situation—from property rights, access to education, divorce, and birth control, to enfranchisement and legally protected sexual orientation—has been controversial, bitterly contested, and won only after many years of struggle, we can begin to perceive one source of the otherwise puzzling phenomenon of women actively opposing their own betterment. Isolated incidents of men pathologically or evilly assaulting individual women do not sum themselves up into an indictment of marriage as an institution or of patterns of behavior and expectations in a particular society. When more immediate and acceptable explanations are available, more far-ranging and radical ones appear less plausible.

Geneva Overholser's adoption of a feminist perspective in the *Des Moines Register,* of which she was editor, illustrates how the rejection of a falsely neutral perspective can provide not only a fuller understanding of events, rather than a lesser or distorted account, but also one which is perceived as both plausible and fair. Her newspaper won a Pulitzer Prize in 1991 for a graphic story on rape. In reporting the story *Newsweek* credited Overholser with fashioning "what may be the most feminist daily in America," by which it meant one which proves "that so-called women's issues can be important to every reader." [36] Acknowledging that the *Register* formerly reflected the interests of its mostly male editors, *Newsweek* remarked that "Overholser has not so much altered the paper as added to it. Topics such as day care, sexual harassment, and the safety of contraceptives receive prominent, thoughtful coverage. Reporters and editors have come to view routine stories through new prisms: last week a homicide account noted that five other Des Moines women had died in recent domestic assaults."

Philosophical analyses of the objectivity of experience that ignore the central role of power among the complex motivations that structure our perceptions of the world are themselves part of the problem of discrimination against women that feminists address. In other words, self-proclaimed neutral analyses, whether put forward by philosophical realists or by feminists, are actually biased in a way that is eventually harmful to women and other oppressed groups. The radical political agendas of feminists are better served by radical analyses of the relation of self to world.

7. CONCLUSION

Dewey stands out, even within the pragmatist tradition, for attacking the supposed neutrality of our perceptions of reality. He analyzes the com-

plex ways our perceptions are enmeshed in past beliefs, current anticipations, and values. I have interrogated his analyses of how our experiences interactively construct reality from the point of view of a feminist
critique of the structures of women's oppression. This interrogation is
consistent with Dewey's contention that we are interested in purposefully
managing the traits of experience so that we can avoid being victimized
by inherited structures and develop ones more conducive to growth. Reflection is not a luxury reserved to a leisure class, but "exists to guide
choice and effort" (*LW* 1:67). Only through thoughtful observation and
experiment can the frail and transient goods we experience be substan-
tiated, secured, and extended. But since observations are always from a
particular perspective and the good outcomes desired are relative to concretely experienced needs, it follows that feminist angles of vision will
extend Dewey's insights in new and unexpected ways. We've seen that he
even predicted such an outcome (*MW* 11:45).

Dewey empowers individuals to trust their own experiences as a litmus test of theoretical explanations. Philosophical theories have long
served to repress and distort women's experiences because, like Plato's
Forms, they have provided Procrustean beds on which women had to fit
at the pain of seeming irrational. Dewey's emancipatory move reverses
this priority by making theory answer to practice. This does not mean
just repeating what we already know or do. It can include strikingly different interpretations and actions and even the unmasking of our own
misconceptions. One relevant criterion is that theory ought to clarify
rather than distort our lived-through experiences; another is that theory
ought to facilitate valuable transformations of everyday experience: "A
first-rate test of the value of any philosophy which is offered us: Does
it end in conclusions which, when they are referred back to ordinary
life-experiences and their predicaments, render them more significant,
more luminous to us, and make our dealings with them more fruitful?
Or does it terminate in rendering the things of ordinary experience
more opaque than they were before, and in depriving them of having
in 'reality' even the significance they had previously seemed to have?"
(*LW* 1:18).[37]

Eight

What's Wrong with Instrumental Reasoning? Realizing the Emancipatory Potential of Science

Although Jürgen Habermas was not the first to criticize merely instrumental reasoning because it neglected the central moral issue of which ends ought to be pursued for the merely technological question of how to achieve predetermined ends, he has raised the issue once again in regard to our postindustrial society. Because of the growing success of positivistic scientism, Dewey was forced to defend his radically different version of instrumentalism from similar accusations. He did so, for instance, in "Liberating the Social Scientist" (1947):

> By one of those curious distortions so over-frequent in philosophical discussions, my use of the word "instrumental" in previous writings has been often represented and criticized as if it signified that "knowing" must be limited to some *predetermined specific* end. What I have said, time and again, is precisely to the opposite effect. It is that *scientific* knowing is the only *general* way in our possession of getting free from customary ends and of opening up vistas of new and freer ends (*LW* 15: 228, n. 2).

We have seen in earlier chapters how the separation of desirable ends from the means of their attainment is a legacy of a pre-Darwinian ontology, one that sharply distinguishes mind and body and ignores the historicity and fallibility of human understanding. By assuming, according to John Lachs, "an essential incompatibility between ends-in-themselves and means, between ultimate value and utility[,] [p]hilosophers since Aristotle have . . . maintained that whatever aims at some goal beyond itself cannot also carry intrinsic worth. Astoundingly, no one challenged this idea until the twentieth century. Much in Hegel hinted at its wrongheadedness. But Dewey was the first to bring it into question and to develop an alternative conception." [1]

174   In commenting on the "cartoonlike characteristics" of the position

set forth by Richard Rorty, Nancy Fraser admits that they "do not do justice to the complexities of the Romantic and pragmatic traditions." Even in its philosophy of science, pragmatism does not conform to the characteristics given, but they are worth reiterating because they so often pass for an accurate characterization of pragmatism itself. According to her caricature, because pragmatism is "goal-directed and purposive," it would care less for originality than for results:

> Problems solved, needs satisfied, well-being assured, these would be its emblems of value. For the Romantic's metaphorics of poetry and play, it would substitute a metaphorics of production and work . . . words would be tools and culture an outsize tool kit . . . history as a succession of social problems posed and social problems solved, a succession that is in fact a progression. Crediting progress to the account of common sense, technical competence and public-spiritedness, its ethos would be reformist and optimistic, its politics liberal and technocratic.[2]

In contrast to Rorty's neopragmatism, classical American pragmatism does not compartmentalize science and art, the practical and the creative, imagination and goal orientation, play and work, the public and the private. Far from believing in the social Darwinist myth of inevitable progress or in fragmented, piecemeal reform, pragmatism is emancipatory and radical in its reform efforts and, in Dewey's words, strongly rejects "*traditional* 'liberalism,' . . . based upon acceptance of an economic 'individualism'" that is now simply the "defense of one set of economic institutions" (*LW*15:231). Pragmatism also rejects the implied model of an essential separation of knowing from doing as a pernicious legacy of a class-based denigration of everyday needs and problem solving. Operational thinking challenges this very degradation of the physical and material as a lower type of value in contrast to the higher type of values found in disembodied ideals (*LW*4:203–28).

Dewey's choice of experimentalism as philosophical methodology logically follows from his interpretation of reason as "a natural function of an organism at a certain level of complexity of interaction with its surroundings; and science, ethics, and art alike are products and characteristics of that functioning."[3] He therefore opposed the epistemological turn that still dominates philosophy as a reactionary return to a pre-Darwinian psychological model. In "The Need for a Recovery of Philosophy" he argued against five features of epistemology-centered analysis: (1) reduction of experience to a "knowledge-affair," (2) knowledge understood as psychical event infected with subjectivity, (3) registration of what has taken place as the goal of knowledge, (4) acceptance of the isolated sense data of empiricist theory, and (5) treating thought and experience as antithetical. He argues instead (1) that experience is to be understood "as an affair of the intercourse of a living being with its physical and social environment," (2) that such experience suggests a genuinely objective world as entering into the actions and sufferings of persons and being modified through their responses, (3) that "experience in its vital form is experimental, an effort to change the given; . . . characterized by projection, (4) that experience is "pregnant with connexions," and, finally, (5) that experience "is full of inference." Instead of being primarily a knowledge-affair, "experiencing means living; and that living goes on in and because of an environing medium." In thus interacting with the natural and social environment, experience, as "a future implicated in the present," necessarily acquires a directive function, but one that is sensitive to the rich complexity of the specific affairs of everyday life (*MW* 10:6–10).[4]

Pragmatist instrumentalism is a logical outcome of the intellectual revolution sparked by reflections on Darwinian evolutionary theory. If human beings were situated within nature instead of transcending it, ends could no more be cavalierly divorced from the means necessary for their achievement, nor means from the values that inform them, than individuals could be understood apart from their relations to nature and society. The revolutionary import of this transactive instrumentalism for philosophical thinking in general and for feminist challenges to traditional beliefs in particular is developed in the first section of this chapter. Misunderstanding of the way that scientific understanding should inform all critical thinking is inevitable if the model of science itself is not revisioned from a pragmatist perspective. In the second section, I make a beginning toward showing the radical transformation of our understanding of intelligence that is required by recognizing the instrumental character of human understanding. For pragmatists, recognition of the experimental procedures by which indeterminate situations are transformed into known objects should lend support to cooperative behavior, criticism of inherited structures, and transformation of present possibilities into a better future. This nonpositivist understanding of rationality and science are seen to inform the emancipatory agendas of minorities and women.

Since the emancipatory potential of science can be realized only in the service of a future implicated in the present but not yet apparent, imagination plays a central role in experimental understanding. In the third section this role of imagining future possibilities links artistic creativity to scientific methodologies. These possibilities are distorted when the limitations of present understanding are not recognized. Alain Locke and W. E. B. Du Bois provide a needed corrective to the tendency of the classical pragmatists to recognize the positive contributions of diverse points of view by deepening and extending the pragmatist analysis of the lack of neutrality of scientific endeavors to include the effects of prejudice. Lastly, the fact that Dewey drew on the use of the experimental method in education and social work while Peirce drew on mathematics and the laboratory sciences may help account for their different versions of the pragmatist reconstruction of scientific method. In the fourth section, pragmatist experimentalism is explicated as it was developed at the Laboratory School as a cooperative venture between Dewey and the faculty and administrators and as a cooperative activity between Jane Addams and other Hull House settlement members and their neighborhood community.

1. THE VALUE OF SCIENCE FOR LIFE

For pragmatists, the publication of Charles Darwin's *Origin of Species* in 1859 was a watershed event, one that would forever change the way human beings understand their place in the universe. We have seen how Gilman used evolutionary theory primarily to explain how men exaggerated the maleness of human nature, practices, and institutions and overemphasized the biological femaleness of women, thus preventing them from developing their full human potential. For Peirce, James, Mead, and Dewey, Darwinian theory demonstrated the continuity of human beings with nature, and shifted interest from speculations about transcendence, permanence, necessity, invariance, and certitude to reflections on finitude, temporality, relativity, chance, and fallibility.

A central thesis of Dewey's philosophy is that the notion of the evolution of species, although originally an epochal event in the natural sciences, also embodied an intellectual revolt overturning two thousand years of philosophical beliefs about nature and knowledge. In a self-fulfilling prophecy, he says in "The Influence of Darwinism on Philosophy" that this revolt against the superiority of the fixed and final over change, of permanence over development, and of static perfection over gradual improvement "was bound to transform the logic of knowledge, and hence the treatment of morals, politics, and religion." But to understand the revolutionary nature of this change, it is necessary to understand how what the Greeks called *eidos* and the scholastics *species* dominated Western philosophy and influenced pre-Darwinian beliefs (*MW* 4: 3–4).

According to Aristotle, not only does the term *species* designate the formal activity that operates to regulate structure and function throughout a series, but earlier changes are regulated in view of a predetermined later event, or *telos*, a final, perfect end. When applied to knowledge, this central principle of nature meant that knowledge consisted in grasping a permanent end or essence hidden under the appearance of changes, thus denigrating the ordinary modes of perception and inference of the direct and practical experience of nature. Although the classic philosophy of nature and knowledge was already called into question by Galileo and Descartes, the new scientific method was not yet extended to human affairs because of the continued assumption of an unbridgeable disjunction between the inorganic world and the world of plants and animals as opposed to the ideal and moral life of the mind. "The influence of Darwin on philosophy resides in his having conquered the phenomena of life for the principle of transition, and thereby freed the new logic for application to mind and morals and life" ($MW_4:5-8$).

The Darwinian principle of natural selection by constant variation and differential reproductive success because of environmental conditions directly challenges the argument from design and a myriad of supporting assumptions about first or final ends determining the intelligibility of nature and informing the morality of fulfilling ultimate goals. In an evolutionary world, it no longer makes sense for philosophy to pursue ultimate goals and absolute origins "in order to explore specific values and the specific conditions that generate them." Dewey attributes three intellectual transformations to the Darwinian revolution, all of them crucial to understanding the feminist potential of pragmatism. In the first transformation the key word is *shifts*:

> Interest shifts from the wholesale essence back of special changes to the question of how special changes serve and defeat concrete purposes; shifts from an intelligence that shaped things once for all to the particular intelligences which things are even now shaping; shifts from an ultimate goal of good to the direct increments of justice and happiness that intelligent administration of existent conditions may beget and that present carelessness or stupidity will destroy or forego ($MW_4:9-11$).

Second, classic logic sets out to prove what transcendent qualities and values life must have in order to be rational, rather than consulting experience to recognize the actual evils it contains and the promised goods it fails to deliver. Such thinking by recourse to transcendent ideals cannot be refuted logically, but Dewey hopes it will fall into disuse because of its futility in solving the concrete problems of everyday life. "To improve our education, to ameliorate our manners, to advance our politics, we must have recourse to specific conditions of generation," not to ideal first or final principles.

And, third, by recognizing its own limitations, the Darwinian genetic and experimental logic introduces responsibility into the intellectual life. Since solutions cannot simply be deduced from ideal rational principles, they must be subjected to experimental tests to see how they work in practice and not just in theory. This recourse to specific conditions of value and specific consequences of ideas radically transforms the nature of philosophy. What Dewey predicts in 1909 that any philosophy cognizant of the implications of the Darwinian revolution must become, actually foretells his own radical reconstruction of logic in his 1938 *Logic, the Theory of Inquiry* (*LW* 12); namely, "a method of locating and interpreting the more serious of the conflicts that occur in life, and a method of projecting ways for dealing with them: a method of moral and political diagnosis and prognosis" (*MW* 4:12–13).[5]

These three intellectual transformations which Dewey derives from the Darwinian revolution also characterize the works of many contemporary feminist philosophers of science. Donna Harraway, for example, started out "by showing the radical historical specificity and so contestability, of *every* layer of the onion of scientific and technological constructions." But, along with Evelyn Fox Keller and Sandra Harding, she also remained "leery of a radical constructivism conjugated with semiology and narratology." She calls for a feminist account that is "*simultaneously* an account of radical historical contingency for all knowledge claims and knowing subjects . . . *and* a no-nonsense commitment to faithful accounts of a 'real' world, one that can be partially shared." As with pragmatist accounts of objectivity, for Harraway "feminist objectivity means quite simply *situated knowledges.*" It means rejecting the practice of science tied to militarism, capitalism, colonialism, and male supremacy. "Objectivity turns out to be about particular and specific embodiment and definitely not about the false vision promising transcendence of all limits and responsibility."[6]

Strange as it sounds, in view of the current widespread distrust of science especially among radical intellectuals and including many feminists, the earliest generations of women pragmatists were especially attracted to the pragmatist emphasis on scientific experimentation.[7] The reason is not hard to find, given Dewey's insistence on its emancipatory potential. As so often happens when women become aware that they are being oppressed by suffocating misogynistic beliefs, laws, and practices, women entering colleges and universities in the decades before and after the turn of the century had in some way to confront the contradiction involved in their pursuit of higher education within a prevailing social consensus of women's lesser intellectual abilities. Although some, perhaps many, must have been satisfied to demonstrate their individual worth or to subordinate their interests to the goals of the larger society, others welcomed a methodology that challenged traditional beliefs by providing a rational means of discrediting them.

When misogynistic traditions are asserted in learned discourse as expressions of truths, then counterassertions about women's intellectual abilities and moral worth or even isolated demonstrations of equality are less than convincing as rebuttals. How much more persuasive are the demonstrations available through the use of scientific method, defined by the pragmatists as "freedom from control by routine, prejudice, dogma, unexamined tradition, sheer self-interest" (*LW* 13:273). Just as important, the scientific temperament of questioning what is usually taken for granted can act as a midwife, delivering young women from vague feelings of dissatisfaction to concrete recognition of the discrimination they encounter. This is more likely to happen when science is taught as "the method of emancipating us from enslavement to customary ends, the ends established in the past" (*MW* 8:81).

Dewey's intriguing characterizations of science as "experience becoming rational" (*MW* 9:233) and "intelligence in action" and his repeated description of the scientific attitude and method as "the method of free and effective intelligence" (*LW* 13:279) connects up the otherwise formidable discipline of science with everyday life. To be sure, there are discontinuities as well as continuities between science and everyday experience. Whereas in ordinary life uncertainty is an irritant we usually seek to resolve speedily by any means, the scientific attitude maintains what is doubtful until what is causing it has received sustained attention. In fact, the warranted objectivity of science requires this "willingness to hold belief in suspense, ability to doubt until evidence is obtained; willingness to go where evidence points instead of putting first a personally preferred conclusion; ability to hold ideas in solution and use them as hypotheses to be tested instead of as dogmas to be asserted; and (possibly the most distinctive of all) enjoyment of new fields for inquiry and of new problems" (*LW* 13:166). Moreover, it was not the "physical or even quasi-mathematical form" (*MW* 3:5) of science that Dewey thought could revolutionize philosophy, but its technique, temper, and attitude. It was the turn away from purely rational deductive inference and dependence on canonical texts to addressing the urgent problems of modern life by employing "systematic methods of inquiry, which, when they are brought to bear on a range of facts, enable us to understand them better and to control them more intelligently, less haphazardly and with less routine" (*LW* 5:4).

This demystification of the often inaccessible realm of science and insistence that it be put at the service of the betterment of humanity and not just serve powerful economic interests and personal aggrandizement appealed to those traditionally deprived of scientific education. It did so by showing the continuity of scientific endeavors with everyday life and also the relevance of the scientific method for solving everyday problems and not just arcane scientific problems, thereby supplying a motivation for women and minorities to enter the typically white male domain of science. These possibilities not only motivated women to enter the emerging disciplines of psychology, pedagogy, and sociology, but also encouraged them to maneuver the subject matter toward issues that especially concerned women. Women had much greater difficulty entering or remaining in the male-dominated and male-identified profession of philosophy, which perhaps accounts for why feminist revisionings did not take hold there, despite the fact that pragmatic philosophy developed the theoretical basis for doing so in other disciplines.

Sophonisba Breckinridge and Edith Abbott were among the second generation of college women to receive their doctoral degrees in the early 1900s. They were more seriously committed to an ideal of professionalism than their predecessors, among them Jane Addams, Julia Lathrop, Florence Kelley, and Lillian Wald, who were still active at Hull House and whose continuing influence helped them obtain positions in 1908 of running the research department at the Chicago School of Civics and Philanthropy. According to Robyn Muncy, Edith Abbott underwent a dramatic conversion as she became involved with the Hull House community. She had earlier enthusiastically embraced the ideals of dispassionate professionalism and the neutrality of science and "saw herself as an economist whose research had no immediate political motive and who was not in special sympathy with America's reform movements." But having already been excluded from the highest positions in their fields of study because of the prejudices of male professionals who regarded women as sentimental do-gooders, Abbott and also Breckinridge still insisted on tying social reform to the most stringent scientific methodologies, rather than relying primarily on personal experiences and interactions. They "required their students to master statistics and the latest social research methods; to contribute to the expanding body of information on social legislation, social conditions, and reform experiments; to formulate recommendations for the change in the conditions they studied; and to become the prime movers in making those changes."[8]

Muncy finds Abbott's appeal to her own understanding of social work as scientific to be problematic, relating more to the prestige it enjoyed in the Progressive era than to any particular content or method, especially since it was marked by inconsistent characteristics and understandings. I think, though, that some, but not all, of the alleged inconsistencies may be due to a lack of understanding of the pragmatist philosophy of science. While it may be true that for some progressives, the "primary purpose" of the appeal to science "was to cloak their work in [its] authority," for pragmatists—feminist and nonfeminist alike—scientific attitudes and methodology were consciously goal-directed and reform-oriented, and any outcomes its use brought about could not be justified by authoritative appeal to a superior scientific expertise. By sympathetically attending to the concrete situation and what could actually be effected by concerned persons, pragmatist experimental methodology sought to replace both the palliative sentimentalism of charity work and the destructiveness of technocratic arrogance. It directly challenged the authority of mere expertise by deliberately seeking to involve those for whom the situation was problematic or disadvantageous in the first place. Abbott and Breckinridge thoroughly absorbed the pragmatist understanding of science as a human endeavor, which therefore always expresses interests, and they recognized that the most important issue was determining whose interests would be privileged. As members of the nation's leading educators in social work, they had the power to build into the structure of the profession itself their conviction that it should be directed to social reform and not simply to diagnosis or to merely palliative efforts. According to Abbott, "We [social workers] have other friends who are afraid we are not scientific because we wish not only to learn to diagnose the social evils with which society has to deal but we insist on going on to find out what ought to be done about them. But if trying to follow diagnosis by curative treatment is being unscientific then we must be content to be described in some other way."[9]

Unfortunately, although Breckinridge and Abbott "made the connection between research and activism central to their profession," their focus on being taken seriously as professionals caused them to reject the other essential component of a pragmatist feminist philosophy of science; namely, that it be undertaken "as a cooperative effort between the weak and the strong." Graham Taylor, the founder of the Chicago School of Civics and Philanthropy, believed, as did Dewey and Adams, that settlement workers gained whatever authority they had from their continuous interactions with those whom they hoped to help—this in contrast to Breckinridge and Abbott, whose research department spawned a more detached, statistical approach to social problems.[10] This failure to include the working-class immigrants in their scientific decision-making process and its implementation meant that for all their accomplishments—and they were many—Breckinridge and Abbott ultimately contributed to establishing a nonpragmatist, nonfeminist version of social science as they merged the Chicago School of Civics with the University of Chicago's School of Social Service Administration. Insofar as they linked social science research with public social service, they did continue part of the pragmatist/feminist tradition, but insofar as they repudiated the central norm of inclusive, consensual problem solving, they subverted it.

2. RECIPROCITY OF MEANS AND ENDS: SCIENCE AS A REVOLUTIONARY TRANSFORMING AGENT

A long-standing criticism of Dewey is that he was so enamored of science and so optimistic about the era of progress it would supposedly inaugurate that his philosophical embrace of the scientific attitude in pragmatism is compromised and ought to be rejected. Given the current fin de siècle suspicion of science, it is not surprising that this issue has already been raised in recent feminist reappropriation of pragmatism by Jane Upin, who nonetheless acknowledges that Dewey rejected the positivist notion of science as free of value and emotion and that he argued against accepting the dogmatic pronouncements of a philosophical or scientific elite who claim superior insight into the inner truth of things through their scientific method. But she is still troubled by what she takes to be his "(sometimes excessive) claims for science." She denies, for instance, Dewey's assertion that "if ever we are to be governed by intelligence . . . science must have something to say about *what* we do, and not merely about *how* we may do it most easily and economically" (*MW* 6:78–79).[11] She then quotes him in a more careful moment when he acknowledges that science cannot tell us what to do ethically: "Science both physical and psychological . . . will never tell us what to do ethically, nor just how to do it. But it will afford us insight into the conditions which control the formation of aims, and thus enable human effort to expend itself sanely, rationally and with assurance" (*MW* 1:150).

Actually, I think that this second quotation supports the earlier one and therefore should give us pause about just how carefully Dewey has to be read if the full force of the revolutionary import of his reconstruction of science is to be available for feminist analysis. He *is* asserting that science has something to say about what we do as surely as it does about the easiest and most economical means of achieving those ends, an instrumental function of science already freely acknowledged. Notice that in the second quotation Dewey denies that science can supply *either* the *what* or the *how*, ends or means, in the traditional sense of directly supplying a priori ends or in the simple application of a predelineated method that just blindly grinds out results. What it can do instead is to give us insight into the conditions by which aims are formed in the first place, and such knowledge can contribute to a more rational use of means to their attainment. The transfer of the experimental method from its technical setting to areas of broader human concern provides a powerful means of examining the actual effects of inherited beliefs and institutions on everyday life and of intelligently considering the concrete ways they must be modified to produce a more desirable outcome (*LW* 4:218).

It is a "sign of the paralysis of the imagination," according to Dewey, to attribute a malevolence to technology rather than to the uses to which it is put. Such a paralysis is, if anything, even further developed today. The problem, then as now, is that we have harnessed the power of technology "to the dollar rather than to the liberation and enrichment of human life." We have done so "because we have been content to stay within the bounds of traditional aims and values although we are in possession of a revolutionary transforming instrument" ($LW$5:87). Its revolutionary potential for transforming our thinking about our place in the world is even greater than its transformation of the material conditions of our lives, but unless technology is to be left in the hands of those whose sole aim is to advance their own fortunes, its potential for radically affecting our underlying aims must be unflinchingly explored. Scientific thinking has destroyed many traditional values. How can it also be "a potential creator of new values and ends"? ($LW$5:118).

Science, which is inseparable from technology or the instruments necessary for experimentation, can create new values through its demonstration of the connection of intelligence with action—not action of any sort, but directed action carried out to realize ends thought to be desirable. But the ends actually achievable as revealed through what is actually achieved are not predetermined; they are discoverable only after experimentation. Even the horrors perpetrated on humanity in the twentieth century by the use of technology demonstrate the inseparable connection of even the most arcane knowledge, such as physics and chemistry, with actual changes in the human condition. Philosophies that stubbornly ignore the connection between intelligence and action contribute to the deification of the present and of the power structures already in place. In "The Construction of Good" Dewey argues that a radical transformation of ethics is required by the scientific revolution, one which undercuts the assumed disjunction between mind and matter, between higher and lower values, between transcendental values and those emergent in everyday life. In doing so, he contributes to undermining the very dichotomy between spirit and body that has impacted so negatively on women ($LW$4:203–28).

We have seen in chapter 7 that for Dewey communication requires cooperation, and meaning is the property of behavior that is distinctively cooperative. He also explains in *Experience and Nature* ($LW$1, 1925) that because tools are things used as means to consequences, they have played a large role in the consolidation of meanings. Without transcendence or reference to what is absent, tools cannot even be tools; they are "relational, anticipatory, predictive." Tools, the concrete instantiation of means to consequences, "can originate and develop only in social groups made possible by language. Things become tools ceremonially and institutionally." In order for tools to be perpetuated, the relationship between them and their consequences must be recognized and shared. As with tools, this possibility of sharing gives meaning its generic or universal character; there is something in common "between speaker, hearer and the thing to which speech refers." Meaning is a method of action, and the application of some meaning to bring about changed conditions ceases only when things refuse to be so treated. "Meanings are rules for using and interpreting things; interpretation being always an imputation of potentiality for some consequence" (*LW* 1:146–47).

Anne Philips draws on the last twenty years of the women's movement to show that although "the emphasis on means as well as ends was not exclusive to feminism," the movement can nonetheless "legitimately claim to be its foremost practitioners." [12] And Helen Longino argues that the boundaries between observation and theory are not fixed and are best set in a communicative context. "Experience itself must be rethought as an interactive rather than a passive process." She echoes the position of Dewey and other pragmatists in pointing out that "our experience is a product of the interaction of our senses, our conceptual apparatus, and 'the world out there.' It is also a function of what aspects of 'the world out there' we choose or are directed by intellectual or other commitments to interact with." In line with James's theory of selective interest, she holds that "in giving coherence to our experience we by necessity select out some facts and ignore others" and that "the subject of experience, the individual, is a nexus of interpretation coming into existence at the boundary of nature and culture." [13]

In "The Need for a Recovery of Philosophy" (1917) Dewey criticizes the schematic formalism that characterizes so much philosophical discourse and argues for redirecting philosophy toward bringing "to consciousness America's own needs and its own implicit principle of successful action" (*MW* 10:47). Rather than simply reproducing what is imperfect and unjust in our concrete social environment, this means holding our actions to the criteria of what renders life more reasonable and what increases its value.[14] Dewey fights against both the epistemological claim that science merely reveals a ready-made order and the appropriation of science by a powerful, entrenched elite who use it as means to dominate others. Moreover, he sees the epistemological claim and the political fact as intimately related. He thus anticipates what Lynn Hankinson Nelson calls the central thesis underlying all feminist science criticism; namely, that the belief in the autonomy of science has pernicious consequences. Given our society and our science, "the myth of science's detachment and insulation from the social and political context of our larger community has . . . epistemological, social, moral, and political implications." [15]

To make Dewey's claims plausible it is necessary to understand the radical reconstruction of intelligence they presuppose. Intelligence is not a passive observer that registers the spectacle of nature by the expedient of distancing itself from its object; it emerges from within the midst of nature as a novel "revelation of the meaning of that transformation of past into future which is the reality of every present." Intelligence not only emerges in nature to guide and give significance to action; it brings imagination, novelty, and creativity to what the human organism undergoes in connection with our actions. Such intelligence is not simply an abstract faculty or a function of brain activity but "the sum-total of impulses, habits, emotions, records and discoveries which forecast what is desirable and undesirable in future possibilities, and which contrive ingeniously in behalf of imagined good" (*MW* 10:48).

To take as authoritative the inherited categories by which past intelligences have already organized experience not only denies the novelty of the ongoing transformations of the past into the future through which we live, but it blindly validates all those class, gender, racial, and sexual interests that have shaped those categories. Instead of sanctifying them or taking them for granted, philosophers ought to continually interrogate our inherited beliefs to discover their biases and to develop new beliefs that can contribute to bringing about a better state of affairs than the present with its deification of existing centers of power. One of the most succinct expressions of the role that Dewey assigns to intelligence pragmatically understood as a humanly evolved life function is his statement summing up what he has already said: that our salvation consists in "faith in the power of intelligence to imagine a future which is the projection of the desirable in the present, and to invent the instrumentalities of its realization" (*MW* 10:48).

Faith is invoked because we have no guarantees that the trust we place in our own intelligence will be justified, that our intelligent actions will in fact bring forth good rather than bad consequences. But having been cast adrift from any more than human understanding, in what else can we trust? Such faith is not a blank check; it seeks to avoid both the reification of the present power structures and the ungrounded speculation that characterizes so much of contemporary philosophy.

3. CHALLENGING THE BURDENS THAT OPPRESS, INDIRECTLY BY IMAGINATION AND DIRECTLY BY NAMING RACIAL PREJUDICE

In *Art as Experience* (*LW* 10, 1934), Dewey elaborates on his insight that "only imaginative vision elicits the possibilities that are interwoven within the texture of the actual." But now he says that "the first stirrings of dissatisfaction and the first intimations of a better future are always found in works of art" rather than in scientific practices. It is this very "impregnation" of the art being made in the present with values at odds with current beliefs that causes conservatives to reject it as "immoral and sordid" and to prefer the classic art of the past. Dewey contrasts aesthetic imagination with the practices of merely factual science, which in collecting statistics and charting its findings makes predictions that are little more than "past history reversed." In art a sense of possibilities not yet realized contrasts with actual conditions and thus puts them in question. By contrasting the present conditions with unrealized possibilities "we become aware of constrictions that hem us in and of burdens that oppress" (*LW* 10:348–49).

In clear contrast to the positivist's assumption of immaculate perception as a precondition for good science, Dewey holds that the function of good literary and other artistic criticism is to reeducate perception of works of art and thus encourage in us the difficult process "of learning to see and hear." This moral office of criticism can only indirectly guide individuals toward the enlarged and quickened experience that follows from making her or his own appraisal. The moral function of art itself is not simply to call forth emotional responses or preexistent subjective judgments of approval or condemnation. It is, instead, "to remove prejudice, do away with the scales that keep the eye from seeing, tear away the veils due to wont and custom, perfect the power to perceive" (*LW* 10:328). The prejudice from which art emancipates us is "the conception that objects have fixed and unalterable values" because values taken for granted are the result of conventional associations (*LW* 10:101).

William James also argued that natural history methodology and artistic vision were complementary, not antithetical, ways of understanding experience. Both required "inventiveness and sympathetic concrete observation" (*TT,* 16).[16] Like Dewey, James warned against the positivistic scientific turn in philosophy. In the first decade of the twentieth century, for example, he wrote to three students, commenting on their work and sharply criticizing the dialectics and logic-chopping that inevitably accompanied the emergence of graduate schools in philosophy, with their rite of passage, the doctoral dissertation.[17] The change in philosophical style from being concerned, reflective, and literary to being detached and technical was also due to the historical ascendancy of the philosophies of Bertrand Russell, G. E. Moore, and Alexius Meinong.

James was objecting to the new model of professionalism and scientism when he told the students that he expected philosophy to be advanced not by critically demolishing alternatives but by developing positive visions. His preference for positive construction over the argumentative style of "splendid philology" stems from his intention to bring about a paradigm shift rather than to labor at the mundane tasks of ordinary science working within an already established paradigm. He was more interested in why theories or visions were accepted and in how they provided the horizon within which the details could be elaborated than in tinkering with the constituent parts once a paradigm had been elaborated enough to encourage further research within its parameters.

James opposes the academic artificiality of dialectics to "the study of reality in its concreteness." [18] This positive work can be served by technical skill but will be subverted insofar as technique is developed for its own sake. He even accepted the dogmatic expressions of magnificent visions, as long as they exhibited rhetorical power. What counts is that philosophies be sufficiently developed and *lived* to provide enough evidence for judging their value for life. All philosophical visions are experiments put before the public to be socially judged. The criterion is satisfaction, not coherence, since every person—and therefore every philosophy—is incoherent. Satisfactions are comparative only: Does this philosophy or that one seem a more promising way to interact with concrete reality?

James thought that too many students of philosophy were being seduced by the new positivism to succumb to the disease of logic-chopping on the mistaken supposition that by multiplying subdivisions and articulations meaning would somehow emerge. But individual passages or propositions do not sum themselves up into a system; the center of vision must first be grasped by an act of imagination in order to understand how and whether all the parts cohere. James thought that Bertrand Russell's philosophical experiment ultimately failed because he viewed truth as utterly independent of the truth seeker. A noncooperating, will-less intellect cannot be a human one, operating in real life.

These informal remarks are backed up by James's sustained reconstruction of rationality as both theoretical and practical, first articulated in two articles on "The Sentiment of Rationality." [19] In the first of these essays, which are among his earliest expressions of pragmatism, the initial ground of rationality is said to be an aesthetic craving for simplicity or unity joined with its rival passion of clarity or distinguishing particulars. The primary interest of philosophers is in "reducing the manifold in thought to simple form" (*EPH,* 35). But this interest becomes diseased when pursued for its own sake, apart from practical interests. It is only part of a more encompassing interactive process of making oneself at home in the world. We are not thinking machines but are always already engaged in selectively taking in and responding to environing conditions, both physical and social. The development of a brain and nervous system functionally able to create symbolic systems freed from passive replication of immediate stimuli means that as humans we are co-responsible for the sort of world in which we choose to live.

Although technical virtuosity in symbol manipulation is a prized skill in the day-to-day business of philosophers, such skill has no point outside of its contribution to a way of life. And what makes one way of life preferable to another cannot be determined apart from value commitments. To make these commitments explicit, hold them up for review, and suggest appropriate courses of action is not peripheral but central to what makes philosophy. The intellect is built up of these practical interests which preperceive the world of experience and insure that knowledge of objects means learning how to behave with regard to them. Unless aesthetic rationality is guided by practical rationality, it will follow its own predilection for ever more minute distinctions and will engage in endless unproductive logic-chopping.

Alain Locke and W. E. B. Du Bois at midcentury, together with feminist philosophers of science at the end of the twentieth century, demonstrate the continued importance of such nonpositivist understandings of rationality and science as that of the pragmatists to the emancipatory agendas of minorities and women. By making explicit how background conditions and beliefs have a negative impact on those outside the various power elites, they show the practical harms that are exacerbated by assuming the neutrality of scientific endeavor. They also show the positive gains to be made by enlarging the relevant community of investigators and explicitly including divergent viewpoints.[20]

Longino argues that questioning the relevance of evidence presented in support of a hypothesis is not only crucial for the problem of objectivity but is the most promising aspect of scientific inquiry for feminist revisioning. The debate is not about data. It is about how data are interpreted, and it "amounts to questioning the background beliefs or assumptions in light of which states of affairs become evidence." Such pragmatist, contextual analyses expose the limits of purely empirical considerations in scientific inquiry. "As long as background beliefs can be articulated and subjected to criticism from the scientific community, they can be defended, modified, or abandoned in response to such criticism." Debates over the adoption of background assumptions are not arbitrary, even though "sociologically and historically, the molding of what counts as scientific knowledge is an activity requiring many participants." In line with the pragmatist emphasis on the role of the community in determinations of scientific objectivity, Longino argues that "objectivity, then, is a characteristic of a community's practice of science rather than of an individual's, and the practice of science is understood in a much broader sense than most discussions of the logic scientific method suggest." Longino suggests that feminists could engage in science by "(1) recognizing the ways in which the background assumptions of mainstream science facilitated certain conclusions and excluded others, and (2) deliberately using background assumptions appropriately at variance with those of mainstream science." This feminist or "oppositional science, is always local and respectful of some of the standards of a specific scientific community." [21]

It should be noted that Longino's book on the centrality of the social dimension of science is a striking example of reinventing the pragmatist criticism of reductionist accounts of science by developing its social basis. Likewise, Nelson's *Who Knows?* advocates a contemporary, nonpositivist version of empiricism that challenges the boundaries between science, metaphysics, methodology, epistemology, values, and politics, as a basis for feminist philosophy of science. Her reconciliation of "a sufficiently rich empiricism" with feminism entails rejecting its individualistic premises in the way that the pragmatists did.[22] A treatise could be written collating specific passages from both sides.[23] However, the time lost in having to reinvent this critique is more than made up for in the specificity and theoretical sophistication of their contemporary accounts and the cogency of their emphasis on its feminist implications. Although Hilary Putnam is the only pragmatist acknowledged in Longino's bibliography and although W. V. Quine is the focus of Nelson's book, it is not unlikely that various aspects of pragmatist positions have already been absorbed through the generations into the explanations on which they draw. What has suffered in the loss of a continuous pragmatist feminist tradition in departments of philosophy is the range and depth of its analyses, the need for which is now more urgent than ever. This loss is apparent in Longino's and Nelson's concluding remarks, which ask for the development of a philosophical position that was already explored in depth in pragmatism.

In 1942 Alain Locke sounded the alarm on the mainstream, positivist science that had continued to dominate in universities and institutions around the world, despite pragmatists' objections. He said that "with the broadened scientific perspective on human social history that has been achieved one might logically expect enlightened social understanding and intercultural appreciation and tolerance. But this has not been so." Instead, "people still read and write history from the chronic attitudes of cultural pride and prejudice, and sometimes deliberately, sometimes subconsciously, impose interpretations upon civilization that are steeped in cultural bias and partiality." Too much theorizing about culture and civilization "is mere rationalization of the claims and counterclaims of various national and racial groups seeking partisan vindication and glory. Special interests and asserted superiorities are thereby reinforced with justifications bearing the outward stamp of scientific objectivity and impartiality . . . and irrationality in social thinking grows apace." [24]

This exposure of the partiality of scientific research strikes a new note in pragmatist thinking. Although Dewey recognized and warned against the domination of the political and social realms by those privileged by wealth and class, it took the perspective of such blacks as Du Bois and Locke to expose the corruption of scientific thinking by racist prejudices. According to pragmatist theory as expressed by Locke, "it is insufficient, however, merely to expose the theoretical fallacies of racialism, which carry the blight of pseudo-science into history and social theory. The practical role of such fallacious doctrines must also be traced, since their deepest significance and explanation lies in their practical objectives and consequences." But the understanding that what is usually explicated under the benign characterization of "perspectives" often hides a will to dominate is a distinctive contribution of African-Americans to pragmatist theory. According to Locke, racialist doctrines incite group rivalry as a weapon "in the struggle for group power and dominance, and it is of the greatest importance to see and understand them in this light. Carefully analyzed, their major objectives are seen to be the justification of conflict and exploitation through the disparagement of other group cultures and the promotion of prestige and group morale through self-glorification and claims of superiority." [25]

In his last autobiography W. E. B. Du Bois explains how for decades he conducted scientific investigations into the plight of blacks and placed his hopes for a better social order in science and the scientific attitude. For thirteen years at Atlanta University he and other researchers published thousands of pages of scholarly studies on blacks in America, which received widespread recognition. [26] He hoped to receive further institutional and financial support for a comprehensive "study of the history of economic co-operation among Negroes," which would demonstrate their positive contributions. His hopes were based on his "firm belief that race prejudice was based on widespread ignorance." He believed that the truth gathered from careful investigations demonstrating that neither color nor race determined a person's abilities or worth would be sufficient to overcome such ignorance. Du Bois was, therefore, "infinitely disappointed" to realize that the work of the Atlanta conferences would not be supported. Such repeated experiences of prejudice within academic and scientific communities, as well as within governmental bureaucracies, led him to recognize how "colonial imperialism, based on the suppression of colored folk," would not finance or support such research "at a Negro college under Negro scholars." [27]

Without a direct attack on the principle of exploitation, namely, the capitalist exploitation of labor, scientific solutions were insufficient.

Nonetheless, even in the midst of his political organizing Du Bois never lost his belief that scientific investigations had a central role to play in the emancipation of blacks. But the science had to be pragmatist. He fought against the dominance of white leaders who would not let "educated Negro opinion in the United States . . . have the right and opportunity to guide the Negro group." Along with agitation against race prejudice, there was "still need of systematic, comprehensive study and measurement, bringing to bear the indispensable point of view and inner knowledge of Negroes themselves." Even the National Association for the Advancement of Colored People was not sufficiently democratic, and leaders gave in to the temptation to use their "limited knowledge and experience to push through decisions and compel action, instead of trusting the slower, muddled and hesitating development of mass action." All the matters dealt with by the NAACP called for "trained knowledge and expert advice and wide experience," but this would lead to tyranny without the democratic process which encourages "thoughtful cooperation." [28]

Among possible sources of error in theories of culture, according to Locke, is parochialism, which can be corrected by an enlarged perspective; "others are pseudo-scientific and need to be squared by wide-scale comparison with the fullest known facts." The subversion of scientific methodology can be attacked by demanding pragmatic pluralism of perspectives and cross-cultural comparisons. But the drive toward exploitation hidden under appeals to scientific objectivity must also be directly addressed: "Still others, most difficult of all, must be submitted to critical examination of their ulterior motives and the stark exposure of their partisan objectives." Only then can a sound view of human civilization be constructed. [29]

Despite his disparagement of the failure of the social sciences to root out racism, colonialism, and ethnocentrism, Locke goes on to say that "the history of civilization takes on new aspects from the viewpoint of a scientific tracing of culture and culture history." Not only does a different type of act stand out as historically important than would otherwise be the case, "but there is also a radical reversal of values," such as making "peoples and varieties of living more interesting than heroes and dynastic successions." In introducing and quoting Buell G. Gallagher in "American Caste and the Negro," Locke says:

> But in the present situation it is regarded as almost axiomatic that the "white man's floor is the Negro's ceiling," that certain symbols of superiority and inferiority should be maintained strictly, in order to preserve the status quo and keep the system intact, and that caste should obliterate

all class lines and all other distinctions to place "all Negroes below all whites."

Trivialities of social intercourse are exposed as conventionalities of symbols that encode relations of superiority and inferiority: "Thus the prescribed social etiquette assumes practical importance beyond its superficial ceremonial meaning, for it reinforces the majority policy of dominance as expressed more realistically in economic exploitation, disfranchisement, group intimidation and social ostracism." [30]

In Locke's opinion, European ethnocentrism is even more troubling than nationalism, though they share analogous tactics of dominance, such as overidealizing the values of one ethnic group and denigrating others. Although the United States is culturally an offshoot of Europe and thus shares in its exploitative social arrangements, its differences are also significant. Along with other pragmatists Locke thinks that some of the particularities that constitute the United States as a distinctive entity also offer some leverage for constructive change. It is, for instance, "one of the most polyglot and multi-racial nations on earth, and has relatively speedier assimilative processes and less historical antipathies than any of the great European nations having heavily mixed populations." The point is not to downplay the very real racism present but to assume responsibility for ending prejudice by drawing on the resources available: "As such this country has the unique opportunity of working out the adjustment of many national and ethnic groups under common institutions and democratic ideals." But "the immigrant, Orientals, the American Indian and the Negro" have not been allowed to participate in the majority democratic tradition. The acute minority problems of America are "challenging tests of the American tradition and its professions of equalitarianism." [31]

Science and technology will continue to be part of the problem rather than the solution to the extent that they are removed from the efforts Locke demands for undermining dominance and exploitation and for encouraging the widest range of ethnic and class participation. The transformative possibilities of a scientific attitude are maximized in the pragmatist understanding of experience as experimental and explains the importance pragmatists attach to education and to learning as an everyday affair of securing and averting consequences. A pragmatic intelligence is not only practical, it is also creative. Unless the vision and the imagination demanded of philosophy are carried out in action, it will modify nothing and hence resolve nothing. Pragmatists think that "intelligence frees action from a mechanically instrumental character" at the same time that it emphasizes that "intelligence is, indeed, instrumen-

tal *through* action to the determination of the qualities of future experience" and the enrichment of life. "Knowing is a human undertaking,
not an esthetic appreciation carried on by a refined class or a capitalistic
possession of a few learned specialists, whether men [or women] of science or of philosophy" (*MW* 10:45).

4. THE EXPERIMENTAL METHOD IN EDUCATION

The first turning point that Dewey gives as characterizing his intellectual
development in "From Absolutism to Experimentalism" is the great importance of the practice and theory of education, especially the education of the young.[32] It was his interest in education that enabled him to
"fuse," or bring together in a unified theory two other interests, "that in
psychology and in social institutions and social life." Secondly, he became increasingly "troubled by the intellectual scandal . . . involved
in the current (and traditional) dualism in the logical standpoint and
method between something called 'science' on the one hand and something called 'morals' on the other" (*LW* 5:156). Dewey attributes the
development of his instrumentalism to his efforts to develop an effective
method of inquiry, or logic, that applies without discontinuity to both.

The third major influence was William James's *Principles of Psychology*, published in 1890. Similar to the pleasant surprise of late twentieth-
century philosophers who rediscovered a rich strain of phenomenological description in *Principles*, but dissimilar in that it "acted as a ferment
to transform old beliefs" and thus entered into the very warp and woof
of his own thinking, Dewey found James's writings revolutionary.[33] Because James's inspiration was artistic and moral rather than reductively
scientific, "the distinctive factors of his general philosophic view, pluralism, novelty, freedom, individuality, are all connected with his feeling for
the qualities and traits of that which lives." The organism was not taken
structurally and hence statically, but from the point of view of life in action. James not only thoroughly discredited the old psychology of "sense
data," which so misguidedly influenced British philosophy, but he developed a new psychology in which thinking is organically connected to
the environment, thus linking "philosophy to the significant issues of actual experience." Instead of the "exaggerated anxiety about formal certainty" so characteristic of traditional philosophic thinking, James's psychology provides a means by which philosophy can once again focus on
"what is distinctively human" (*LW* 5:157–59).[34] According to Darnell
Rucker, Dewey's most distinctive contribution to the Chicago School was
in the field of logical theory. And according to Addison Webster Moore,
a member of the Chicago School who had studied logic with Dewey, what
is most distinctive about Dewey's logic is that he took the central insight

of pragmatist psychology—that all ideas are purposive—and carried its implications into logic, ethics, metaphysics, and theology. This radical move created the greatest philosophical opposition.[35]

Dewey calls the emphasis on the living organism James's "objective biological factor" or "biological approach," which should warn contemporary readers not to confuse it with what would be called a biological approach today. Just how different the two are is evident in what Dewey calls the fourth major influence on his philosophical development, namely that such an "objective biological approach . . . led straight to the perception of the importance of distinctive social categories, especially communication and participation." He calls for a major transformation of philosophizing by connecting its reflections with the social rather than the physical sciences. Thus, although Dewey's call for a philosophy "congruous with modern science" might superficially sound like what is already going on in dominant current modes of philosophy, he means by his call that philosophy should be "related to actual needs in education, morals, and religion" (*LW* 5 : 159).

Much of current philosophizing takes its cue, as does Peirce's, from the mathematical and physical sciences, whereas Dewey thinks that a great deal of our philosophizing has to be done all over again from the point of view of the social issues as raised in "anthropology, history, politics, economics, language and literature, social and abnormal psychology, and so on." Today I would say that feminist philosophy and multicultural studies, which draw on feminist and critical research going on in all these fields, come closest to realizing Dewey's "intellectual prophecy" that "the next synthetic movement in philosophy will emerge when the significance of the social sciences and arts has become an object of reflective attention in the same way that mathematical and physical sciences have been made the objects of thought in the past and when their full import is grasped" (*LW* 5 : 159).[36]

Education, as "a continuing reconstruction of experience in the light of past experience and present problems," is "not only a principal means of inculcating social awareness, but an instrument of social change."[37] According to Dewey, it should foster an open and inquiring attitude, and "should not be confined to making a choice among already formulated conflicting alternatives," but instead should offer "a field for genuine discoveries." But the experimental attitude is "the most difficult single condition to realize." Scientific method "substitutes detailed analyses for wholesale assertions, specific inquiries for temperamental convictions, small facts for opinions whose size is in precise ratio to their vagueness." It rejects totalizing views, the "theatrical oppositions of order and freedom, individualism and socialism, culture and utility, spontaneity and discipline, actuality and tradition."[38]

One way to get at the mutual influence of Dewey and the women who worked with him and to see what women valued in a pragmatist approach to science is to explain pragmatism as it was developed in the writings of these women. I will therefore explore the pragmatist notion of experimentation by first drawing on a few of the many ways it functions in the Dewey School of Mayhew and Edwards and then on Jane Addams's *Twenty Years at Hull-House*. Mayhew and Edwards's book is itself a collaborative effort with Dewey. Not only do Mayhew and Edwards ask Dewey to clarify his views on various aspects of his theory of education in relation to the school but Mayhew's chapter, "The Evolution of Mr. Dewey's Principles of Education," was published along with Dewey's "The Theory of the Chicago Experiment" as two appendices when the book had to be shortened for publication. This arrangement structurally emphasizes what is also demonstrated in the body of the book—on the one hand, the close connection of the origins and development of Dewey's thinking on experimentation with education and the women of the Laboratory School of the University of Chicago; and, on the other hand, the centrality of scientific experimentation to the theory and practice of education as developed by the teacher-administrators, most of whom were women.

In the preface, the school is described as "an early organized experiment in progressive education," which took place from 1896 to 1903 at the University of Chicago. Although under the direction of Dewey, from the very beginning it was a cooperative venture of parents, teachers, and educators. Neither the curriculum nor the methodology were ready-made, but they slowly evolved through joint experimental efforts. The main hypothesis was that life itself, especially in the sense of occupations and associations serving the needs of humanity, would be the basis of the educational experience. This includes the hypothesis that the freedom to express oneself in action is a necessary condition for growth, but an equally necessary condition for children is that this expression must be guided. Hypotheses must be tested, and in this case "the test of learning was the increasing ability of the child to meet new situations through habits of considered action which were even more social in character." It is reported that among the findings of the educational experiment as carried out is "that satisfaction and emotional stability accompany such growth." Throughout the book, Mayhew and Edwards also report when hypotheses do not work out in practice and have to be revised, and they note the disparity between high expectations and actual results.

Significantly, in the troubled times when the book was published (1936), the authors reaffirm their belief in the way that cooperation and experimentation were carried out in the Laboratory School more than thirty years earlier: "A type of education in which there is steady maintenance of coöperative processes and constant use of the scientific principle of objective testing of ideas through action and evaluating the results of such action for future planning, has significant implications for the world ferment of the day." [39] They still have faith in what they were trying to accomplish, despite the fact that the experiment was never allowed to come to fruition. The constant coupling of cooperation with experimentation, also found throughout Jane Addams's writings about Hull House, is a distinctive feature of pragmatist feminism. [40]

Later in the book, Edwards emphasizes the deliberate rejection of traditional approaches to teaching and administration by the parents, teachers, and administrators of the Laboratory School and the need to feel their way as they went along in their efforts to reinvent the school as a social institution. They sought to develop in individuals a method of growing, and they encouraged creative expression "that was social in its character and purpose. In such a school, coöperation must replace competition" as each strives to work together, rather than antagonistically, to search for a common end. The sense of empowerment that this emphasis on cooperative experimentation gave to elementary school teachers, mainly women, is evident throughout the book. In chapter 18, at the request of the authors, Dewey clarifies his theory of the school. In the course of doing so he argues that elementary-school teachers should have the same right and power as university professors to develop the subject matter of their teaching and to invent and use their own methods of instruction. He goes on to say that the experience of the teachers of the Laboratory School proves that their union of intellectual freedom and cooperation can develop the same "spirit prized in university teachers, and that is sometimes mistakenly supposed to be a monopoly of theirs." After this passage, Edwards comments, "This testing in practice of the educational theories set forth in its hypothesis made the teachers of the school also investigators. [41]

It was a tenet of the Laboratory School that children learn by doing. Mayhew comments on the method used to seamlessly join the everyday world of children to the world of science:

> Scientific method was the constantly used tool not alone in the science laboratories. By common consent it was the method at all times and in all situations where processes and activities were such that active investigation, testing out of guesses or theories, imagining possible results of this or that physical or social relation could be carried on. Systematized facts and knowledge (commonly called scientific) were also made available to the child. [42]

Mayhew testifies that Dewey sought to develop a working hypothesis of the controlling principle of physical and mental development from studying the growth of the newborn infant in the earliest stages immediately following birth. He criticized the reflex arc concept of sensation-idea-movement as too mechanical and argued instead for the unity of the act as a single concrete whole. Mayhew quotes Dewey: "Many intelligent parents, especially mothers, are repelled from the work of infant observations simply because there appears to be only a jumble of disconnected facts. . . . Moreover the individuality of the child is completely concealed in the uncontrolled accumulations of facts with resulting disjointed arrangements." [43]

Interpreting the data collected by compartmentalizing it into sensations, movements, ideas, and emotions distorts the continuity of function that connects earlier and later facts into a living unity. Dewey's working hypothesis is that "the unit is the act" as an organic whole. Sensation is just one element in the act, of which coordination or sensory motor adjustment is the fundamental fact. The laws of the earliest developing coordinations in infants are found to operate in more complex operations, leading to a conception of lifelong learning in which persons obtain "a wider command of body and environment as tools of thought." [44]

Mayhew points out that although Dewey's psychological theory was originally known as behaviorism, it was markedly different from the later version of behaviorism, in which the sensory-stimulus and motor response are regarded as distinct entities and which excludes conscious behavior, purposeful action, the conflict of ideas, and emotion as a form of conscious life. Dewey holds, by contrast, that "in a series of acts there is a continuing reconstitution whose meaning is interpreted as a revaluation of the present act in the light of the meaning of the past, out of which, and as a result of which there follows a recasting of the purpose of the act on the basis of which the decision to act again is made." [45]

Intelligence is included in activity, and human growth is more than merely physiological development. Mayhew develops Dewey's use of the principle of growth to analyze what constitutes a moral act and character. She gives the kernel of it as "*the moral act is the consciously completed act which expresses the unified self.*" She derives two working principles from his theory of education: that the child's inner self should be developed and that its development should be fostered in social relationships, but that neither can be considered apart from the other. The heart of Dewey's theory is "the belief in responsibility for consequences," for the constant recognition that we do not live in a physical environment alone, but also in a society of other persons. For clarification she quotes Mead: "In a moral act, the will, the idea, and the consequences are all placed inside of the act, and the act itself only within the larger activity of the individual in society." [46] In short, "a moral act is thus seen to be a social act."

Mayhew concludes: "Just as the organic circuit concept with its emphasis upon the reactive function of the act had organized psychological thinking, so, Mr. Dewey perceived, constructive cooperative activity was the organizing principle that would bring unity, order, and social concern into the chaos of educational practice."[47] But the importance of Dewey's early educational theory and practice extended even further. The four aspects that Dewey gave as marking his development of pragmatist philosophy, characterized as experimentalism, were already prominent in his years at the University of Chicago and, according to Joe R. Burnett, "found expression in day-by-day experiences at the Laboratory School as well as in the numerous writings on education."[48]

The other educational resource for experimentalism understood as constructive, cooperative activity was the Hull House settlement. The women of Hull House pioneered a pragmatist feminist approach to problem solving that put knowledge at the disposal of society's poorest and weakest members. Addams's *Twenty Years at Hull-House* chronicles the experiences through which she learned by sympathetically interacting with her neighbors to avoid the usual trap of those privileged by knowledge, status, and economic security—the trap of assuming a patronizing attitude. Among the varieties of the imposition of power of which she and other Hull House residents became particularly wary were the brute force used by capitalists, government at every level, and the police force, all these often exacerbated by the press on one side, and on the other the patronizing attitude of charity workers and of revolutionists imposing their ideological programs on the recalcitrant lower classes.[49]

These pragmatist feminists sought ways not only to put their recently acquired knowledge at the service of those less advantaged. They were also keenly aware of the failure of their own college studies to understand or provide means of effectively dealing with complex social problems. They came to respect, seek, and use as their touchstone the hardwon knowledge of the immigrant poor among whom they worked and the actual effects on them of their experimental efforts.[50] In the preface to *Twenty Years at Hull-House* Addams says that in her other writings during those twenty years she tried "to set forth a thesis supported by experience, whereas this volume endeavors to trace the experiences through which various conclusions were forced upon me."[51] She exemplifies the process of coming to understand by listening to those among whom she and the other residents worked, responding to their needs directly both by creating political and governmental institutions responsive to the needs of the community, by seeking ways to empower the immigrant poor to participate in the process themselves, and finally, by revising their own proposals and practices when they resulted in more rather than less suffering for those they were supposed to benefit.

The experimental method was literally one of learning from mistakes, and Addams points out repeatedly how her attitudes and proposals caused harms that could have been avoided had she listened more carefully to those she was supposedly helping. The effectiveness of the experiment was determined not by whether it met her original expectations but by whether it met those of the recipients. Their situation was either improved or it worsened, and the beneficiaries were either empowered to better their own condition or they were not. Addams also judged her own efforts by the extent to which they led her to develop better ways of involving the persons affected from the first formulation of the problem, to suggestions for solving it, to carrying it out, to assessing its impact.[52] She singles out those most in need: women working for long hours at hard manual labor for starvation wages and still having to care for young children; the sick, the unemployed, and workers striking against inhuman conditions without any economic or social resources; the elderly, who were often isolated by language and custom from their children and surroundings; and children and young people left to fend for themselves by overworked or abusive parents or condemned to the physical, mental, and economic abuses of underage labor.

Addams's experimental method was not just a piecemeal trial-and-error affair. It was the expression of a pragmatist feminist interpretive framework, one informed by her conscious intention to "retain and utilize past experiences"; to combine intellectual insight with "the moral perception which is always necessary for the discovery of new methods by which to minister to human needs"; to seek, no matter how wearisome the effort, "to secure the inner consent of all concerned," particularly "the sanction of those upon whom the present situation presses so harshly," rather than imposing top-down solutions; and to "put truth to 'the ultimate test of the conduct it dictates or inspires.'" This interpretive framework is summed up in a phrase frequently used by both women and men pragmatists: "sympathetic understanding." The practice of sympathetic understanding is reciprocity. Hull House was founded "on the theory that the dependence of classes on each other is reciprocal; and that as the social relation is essentially a reciprocal relation, it gives a form of expression that has peculiar value."[53]

This moral judgment that social relations ought not to be hierarchically determined but should be reciprocally worked out in conditions of free and effective participation is fundamental to the pragmatist/feminist position. It is based on the historical, psychological, biological, and cultural evidence of actual reciprocity in human and environmental relations. Dewey, for example, rejects and criticizes the elitist appeal to science and privileged expertise as justifying the intrusive bureaucratic control that some have blamed progressivism for fostering as it developed into the New Deal. Although Dewey sometimes expressed the need for "social control," Westbrook points out that he, "like many progressives, meant by the term only a generic 'capacity of a society to regulate itself according to desired principles and values' and he distinguished democratic social control from other forms of control."[54] In language reminiscent of Addams's chapter, "Charitable Effort" in *Democracy and Social Ethics*, Dewey says in his 1908 *Ethics*:

> The vice of the social leader, of the reformer, of the philanthropist and the specialist in every worthy cause of science, or art, or politics, is to seek ends which promote the social welfare in ways which fail to engage the active interest and cooperation of others. . . . Many a man, feeling himself justified by the social character of his ultimate aim (it may be economic, or educational, or political), is genuinely confused or exasperated by the increasing antagonism and resentment which he evokes, because he has not enlisted in his pursuit of the "common" end the freely cooperative activities of others. This cooperation must be the root principle of the morals of democracy.[55]

According to Dewey, "democracy is bound to be perverted in realization" when those who monopolize social power glorify instrumental reasoning by separating habit from thought, means from ends, practice from theory (*MW* 14:52). Something is dreadfully wrong with such merely instrumental reasoning masking its oppressive agenda behind protestations that means need not be scrutinized as long as agreement is reached on supposedly desirable ends. Pragmatism aims at tearing away this self-serving masquerade that those who merely carry out means are not responsible for the ends thereby attained by interpreting experience as art, that is, as the creative transaction of self and nature in which the instrumental and the final mutually inform each other. It demonstrates "the gratuitous falsity of notions that divide overt and executive activity from thought and feeling and thus separate mind and matter" (*LW* 1:293). Unless activities are simultaneously instrumental and consummatory, they partake of the alienated character of "much of our labors in home, factory, laboratory and study." It is the task of pragmatist feminism to rehabilitate the means-ends continuum of an instrumentalism cognizant both of the effect of means upon "the quality of human life and experience" and of the desirable in the present that inspires practical efforts toward its further realization (*LW* 1:271–72). Nothing is wrong with such instrumental reasoning that more such "intelligent remaking" cannot redress as long as "we understand operations of the self as the tool of tools, *the* means in all use of means" (*LW* 1:189).

$\mathcal{N}ine$

Who Cares?
Pluralizing Gendered Experiences

Beginning with *In a Different Voice: Psychological Theory and Women's Development*, Carol Gilligan is usually understood as making two claims of particular interest to those engaged in the area of moral development, but whose implications range far beyond any one disciplinary field.[1] The first is the empirical claim that women and men, as a matter of fact, differ in their approaches to moral reasoning, with women emphasizing care and men justice. The second is the value claim that since an ethics of care is at least equal to, and perhaps better than, an ethics based on fairness, moral theory, which has traditionally emphasized justice and ignored or trivialized caring relationships, ought to be restructured to take account of the importance of caring. The first claim is problematic in ways that the second is not. In exploring some of the different assumptions underlying the two claims and some of the consequences of acting on them I will be drawing on a reconstructed, feminist pragmatism to suggest an alternate approach to the first and a defense and expansion of the second.

Even if differences in moral reasoning between men and women turn out to be statistically significant, I have serious reservations about the value of research that reinforces the stereotypical association of care with women and justice with men, rather than investigating the constellation of factors which have given rise to this stereotype and its impact on women's and men's gender identity and social situation. Therefore, I will seek to show how associating these orientations primarily with situations and only secondarily with gender will lead to more worthwhile results than continued empirical research intended to demonstrate that women's moral reasoning differs in kind from men's. This is not an attempt to impose moral standards on an otherwise neutral scientific methodology but to point out some consequences for research programs of the realization that values and expectations are always already incorporated into empirical research. On the other hand, I think that there are good reasons to support the second claim that care as a primary ethical orientation has been devalued because of its association with women and that the dimension of care ought to be central to any system of moral reasoning worth supporting.

1. IDENTIFYING DIFFERENCES OF MORAL REASONING WITH GENDER

The empirical claim has not been satisfactorily demonstrated so far, but there is some evidence to suggest that certain aspects of moral reasoning show up more clearly in women's responses than in men's. Whatever future investigations in this area may reveal, it seems to me that any differences that are found to distinguish women's and men's responses can be better accounted for by identifying the common traits of the situations of those for whom care plays a larger role and distinguishing these from the traits found in the experiences of those who respond in terms of justice.

We now know enough about the different expectations of and behaviors toward infants and children insofar as their caretakers identify them as female or male, to realize how large a role socialization plays in the formation of one's sense of self as male or female. We also know that human individuals are not simply imprinted but that from at least birth on, if not before, they actively respond to and reject such environmental constraints in unique ways. Furthermore, clusters of traits assigned on the basis of sex have been found to reflect the negative evaluation of women compared to a positive evaluation of men. Therefore, we need not a value-neutral assignment of traits assumed to be male or female, but a critique of the ways in which certain personality and behavior traits have been differentially assigned to women and men in any given society.

Once it is realized that maleness and femaleness are both constructed in interaction between individuals and their social milieu, including their primary caretakers, then it is as misleading to try to identify traits as specifically female as it is to deny that similar socializing processes can produce similar "second natures" or patterns of behavior, including reasoning processes, in men. If some traits, such as particular patterns of reasoning, are found disproportionately in women, then what we have discovered is a successful set of circumstances for producing that trait. But because of the variability in the circumstances of growing up not only across cultures but within cultures as well, I would expect to find variability in the occurrence of the trait; that is, it will not be found in all women and it will be found in some men as well.[2]

But because of women's reproductive capacities and the delegation of early childhood care to them, as well as long-term care more generally, across a great variety of cultures, and because of the wide dissemination and acceptance of sex stereotyping and discrimination against women, I would also expect to find some divergences along gender lines. The exact distribution can only be empirically determined, provided such research findings are sensitive to a whole range of differently structured and multi-structured situations.

Once it is realized that the "naturalness" of sexual identification can no longer be maintained, then the rationale for attributing traits on the basis of sex would have to change radically. The questions we would need to ask about any such project also change. Instead of "What does this tell us about women?" "How would we respect this difference in deference to women's importance?" and "Why has not this undeniable difference been noticed before?" the more appropriate questions would include "What does this tell us about the way women are brought up and perceived?" "Has the inculcation of this trait differentially in women been generally beneficial or harmful to them and to society as a whole?" and "What expectations do we as researchers bring that allows this trait to emerge and what expectations prevented it from being apparent before?"

The claim that women differed significantly from men is welcome news for those feminists who valorize the feminine and argue that women's special way of being in the world has been both ignored and trivialized. But for feminists who are working for equal treatment it is seen as a misguided attempt to claim for women those very characteristics that have been traditionally attached to the female and that have provided justification for treating them as inferior. It is possible and desirable to be sensitive to both these concerns when examining Gilligan's work. Among the first questions that have been raised about her research is whether women actually do differ in the specific ways that she claims they do. The evidence is not yet all in, but most of it so far disproves Gilligan's claim of distinctive gender-based moralities, while keeping open the possibility that some differences correlated with gender nonetheless exist.[3]

But this empirical question as to the existence of gender-based differences cannot be raised, researched, or resolved outside of the context of expectations, beliefs, values, and practices of those formulating the question, of those responding to it, and of those interviewed. Consequently I do not expect that any empirical findings can determine whether women and men reason differently about moral situations just because they are women and men. This does not rule out the possibility that empirical research can validate or deny the claims that most, some, or all women differ from most, some, or all men in the way they arrive at moral decisions. Even if some such findings were made, we would still have to determine to what they were attributable in order to make the causal connection. And this could not be decided without recourse to certain more basic beliefs and values, such as whether one believes in biological or psychological determinism or psychosocial constructivism.

Since I think that specific modes of thinking and holding values arise from transactions within contexts, I would expect to find that insofar as women are found in situations that share some experiential features which differ systematically from men's, they would also be found to share insights into the generic traits of these experiences and develop values appropriate to such insights.[4] It is entirely plausible, for instance, that early childhood caretakers would develop different insights, method-ological approaches, and values than those who interact primarily with adults. There are also good reasons why subordinate groups and in-dividuals would tend to develop more sensitivity to the nuances of be-havior of those in power, as John Stuart Mill and William James already recognized, and as contemporary research has confirmed.[5] The more a woman's situation approximates a man's—in expectations, upbringing, opportunities, self-esteem, physical prowess—the more her and his in-sights and values would converge. Since gender is so strongly marked in our society, it is unlikely that women's and men's situations are ever iden-tical, and since so much of a culture is also shared, it is unlikely that women's and men's situations are totally different, but there would be varying degrees of sameness and difference. At one extreme, gender dif-ferences would be insignificant in comparison with other differences like talent, while at the other extreme gender differences would overwhelm and define all other differences. But most would fall somewhere in between.

The research of Muriel J. Bebeau and Mary Brabeck supports this expectation of similarity when women and men share similar contexts of profession and education: "Consistent with the literature we reviewed on gender differences in moral reasoning (component 2), women who were at the same educational level as their male counterparts did not give greater priority to issues of care, nor were there differences in the ability of males and females to integrate care and justice issues." They did find that women dental students exhibited "significantly greater sensitivity to the ethical issues contained in professional dilemmas than did their male colleagues," and they suggest that this gender difference may be due to another finding of researchers, namely "that women are socialized to be more empathic, altruistic and nurturing."[6]

Pragmatists reject biological reductionism and its psychological cor-ollaries and attribute gender differences, like all other interesting hu-man variations, to an individually creative response, including a genetic component, to patterns of culture, socialization, and belief structures; in short, to nurture interacting with nature to such an extent that we can only distinguish them functionally by adopting different methodologies and having different ends-in-view.[7] Insofar as it is shown that some women approach ethical questions differently from some men, we should be interested in asking what conditions bring this about and why some women do not exhibit this difference. What are the positive and negative outcomes of this difference? Are the positive values being recognized by the persons holding them and by others not holding them? If it is determined that these differences allow values to be expressed that have positive significance for other persons and in other situations, then the investigation into the conditions of their development will give us a basis for determining a strategy for disseminating these values. If it is determined that the same conditions also generate values that negatively impact on those holding them or on others, then what can be done to begin to eliminate this aspect of the conditions and the values?

These preliminary questions are being raised to break down the simplistic equation of women with care and nurturance and men with justice and autonomy. It is meant to decenter the gender issue and replace it with engendering. Since to be female or male is not to instantiate an unchangeable nature but to participate in an ongoing process of negotiating cultural expectations of femininity and masculinity, then what does it mean to investigate the factual basis for the claim that women's moral reasoning is different from men's? It means at least that a specific value component is being added to, or at least recognized in, the social construction of gender and its investigation. Empirical investigation does not just disclose facts of nature. Insofar as it is shown that this configuration of values is strongly tied to women's socialization, then two outcomes are predictable. One is that this cluster of values, including processes of moral reasoning which interpret and apply them, will be found to have suffered the same trivializing and devaluing as the oppressed group with which it is associated. The proper response would seem to be the reclamation and positive reevaluation of this cluster of values. The other is that these values will be found to have been inculcated in such a way as to have contributed to the subordination of the oppressed group, that is, women. The proper response to this finding would seem to be to root out of the cluster and its inculcation whatever has contributed to these negative outcomes.

2. AN ETHICS OF CARE

The value claim that informs Gilligan's research can best be defended by calling into question major assumptions that support traditional ethical systems. I will defend the claim that there is something about caring that ought to be central to value systems. The fact that women seem to realize this more than men must not be allowed to debase either the value or women. Not only women but any systematically oppressed group will experience the world differently from those not oppressed. And, conversely, the expectations and values of women privileged by race, class, heterosexuality, or other factors would likely reflect these factors in their assumption of gender. It can be expected both that there will be assimilation to the values of the dominant group or groups by those less privileged and that there will also be selective rejection of some of these values and substitution of other values and patterns of judgment. These differences are due to the dynamics of situations, including individual patterns of development, and not to women's supposed nature, and therefore particular values can be linked to specific interactive processes that can be investigated. Not all women experience the world identically as women, and the differences can be crucial. Likewise, patterns of oppression can be found that link sexism, racism, classism, and homophobia, which is not to deny that specific differences are also present and just as important to take into account.

Although dominant groups will generalize their experiences and values and dignify them as neutral, objective, and universal, they are no less partial and constrained by the conditions in which they were developed. The ability to universalize as a criterion of ethics or value systems should be unmasked for the drive for domination that it is. No woman must favor care over concerns such as equity or the redress of grievances, in order to fulfill some universalizable criterion of what constitutes feminist ethics. Universalizability should be replaced with a recognition of the diversity of values that have been developed to answer to different needs. It should be replaced with investigation into what is required for developing harmonious communities that nurture individual growth based on cooperation rather than co-optation. Caring is initially a value because someone holds it to be so, but to be continually reaffirmed as such and to be accepted by others, it must be judged by evaluating the outcomes that follow from holding it. Since these have historically been both negative and positive, the original understanding and practice of caring should be investigated and modified to bring out more strongly the beneficial aspects and to lessen the negative ones.

Not entirely because of the trivializing factor, women have also been disproportionately oppressed through their caring. We know from personal experience as well as historical hindsight the devastating effects of assigning care to women as a means of assuring that their labor, their goods, and their very persons will primarily benefit men and their institutions. As Simone de Beauvoir put it, "To identify Woman with Altruism is to guarantee to man absolute rights in her devotion, it is to impose on women a categorical imperative."[8] Some feminists have recently nonetheless linked care with women by claiming that women's nature as women so informs every aspect of their being that all women, merely by being born a woman, think, feel, act, work, and dream in gender-specific ways. This deliberate reduction of the social construction of gender to a natural process of hormones and blood can only exacerbate rather than lessen the negative effect of associating care with women, despite the best intentions of valorizing it.

A pragmatist feminist model assumes the social construction of gender, one which avoids the negative aspects of equating care with biological femaleness by emphasizing the contextual basis for the perceived differentiation rather than the gender basis.[9] This does not mean ignoring the specific ways in which women express caring as central to ethics nor ignoring the consequences of the societal assumption that women must define themselves as the caring sex. This reconstruction of the empirical claim that caring is uniquely linked to women also involves showing how, given women's situation, they often need to reject or modify their caring approach and develop other values such as autonomy or abstract justice. In situations where care is eclipsed by overemphasis on these other values, the opposite would be the case. Insofar as men are systematically socialized into overdeveloping autonomy and justice from a position of dominance, then these values are also necessarily distorted and have to be reconceptualized, revalued, and their practice modified.

What has been conceptualized according to essentialist models as care versus justice and relatedness versus autonomy, thus converting functions of reorganization into metaphysical realities, needs to be reconceptualized according to the pragmatist model that understands these distinctions not as "ideal objects" but as "patterns for use in the reorganization of the actual scene" (*MW* 14:39–40). Such distinctions as that of care versus justice are better understood on the model of Dewey's reconstruction of "objectivism-subjectivism," namely, as a "cooperative interaction of two distinguishable sets of conditions, so that knowledge of them *in their distinction* is required in order that their interaction may be brought under intentional guidance," but they are not isolated in practice, where "personal-social factors" intertwine.[10]

Much of the controversy over a "woman's morality" arises because of a misplaced faith in the possibility and desirability of an objective, neutral description of the world. Comtian positivism developed this myth of scientific neutrality just in time to infect the newly emerging science of experimental psychology. But the contemporary history and philosophy of science of Helen E. Longino, Bas Van Fraasen, Nancy Cartwright, Stephen Toulmin, Sandra Harding, Thomas Kuhn, and Paul

Feyerabend—not to mention the powerful critiques developed by their predecessors, Antoinette Brown Blackwell, Friedrich Nietzsche, Charlotte Perkins Gilman, William James, W. E. B. Du Bois, and John Dewey— have thoroughly disproved this assumption of a neutral descriptivism. Every description incorporates a particular "angle of vision" and value orientation. It would be odd if women's moral development, too, as women—and by this I mean insofar as they are socialized as women and/or encounter stereotypical responses to their gender—would not bear traces of this situatedness, to the same extent that men do.[11] Why is it so often assumed, in formulating an ideal morality against which actual moral development is measured, that it must be one which applies universally, that is, in this case, equally to women and men, in order for it to be exemplary? Why is it assumed that if a morality develops out of some women's unique experiences, then this restricted origin, as such, would invalidate it? This is a fallacy not only of false universalism in general, but specifically of the centuries-old habit of taking the categories that men have developed from their point of view as absolute, thus covering over their one-sidedness in male experience.

If it can be shown that no value claims can be universally applicable without distortion, self-deception, casuistry, or violence, then the fear that "women's" values may not apply equally to men is irrelevant. If it can be shown that all interpretations of experience, because they are value-laden, are partial and limited, then the fact that some values are demonstrably typical of some women's situations is no criticism of them. Furthermore, if patterns of moral development and systems of ethics that claim to be both gender neutral and universally applicable—that is, human—can be shown to be, in fact, male biased and situation bound, then a hypocritically impossible task is being imposed on educational theorists to prove that their woman-centered theories can also be neutral and universal according to a pattern that disguises its own partiality.

This should not be taken as an endorsement of any particular factual claim, by Gilligan, Nel Noddings, or others, that they have identified values which originate in women's differential development. What I have been advocating is a reconsideration of the context of investigation and discussion. The title of Gilligan's first book to raise the issue of women's distinctive moral development is *In a Different Voice*. This has been taken by her and others in this controversy to mean "in a *woman's* voice." Therefore, what voice is this different from? Why, a man's voice, of course. Simone de Beauvoir's characterization of woman as "the *second* sex" in her book of that title is meant to point out that insofar as woman has been taken to be other than man she has been understood as less than him; there has been no reciprocity between men and women "for man represents both the positive and the neutral, as is indicated by the common use of *man* to designate human beings in general; whereas woman represents only the negative, defined by limiting criteria." [12]

To be sure, Gilligan wants to encourage the reciprocity of men, men's interests, and men's values, with women, women's interests, and women's values. But as critics have already pointed out, this can not be done as long as women, as such, are devalued in comparison with the valued group, men. Even so, the answer cannot be that women's values are not essentially theirs but are also applicable to and teachable to men, so long as the criterion of acceptability is seemingly neutral; that is, a man would also find it valuable and so claim it as a moral enhancement, but surreptitiously male/rational. In other words, it is acceptable only on the terms already found to be congenial to another way of thinking, as, for example, in Kohlberg's stages of moral development or John Rawl's veil of ignorance. [13]

Ironically, I think it is only by decentering the genderizing of the caring-nurturant ethic that women can come out of the closet of patriarchal society and reclaim these values. Let us accept the claim that the care-nurturant ethics *is* "a different voice"—not *the* different voice, the Other standing in dialectical opposition to the same voice—the essential, the male—but one voice among many other different voices, not only of justice, but of liberation, of the greatest happiness, of the *Übermensch*, of "growth for the sake of growth." Feminists have taught us not only to distinguish between biological sex and socially constructed gender, but also between gender and individual persons. Rousseau's sexist remark that men are men only at times but women can never forget their sex has the intention of imprisoning women in their gendered roles and freeing men to think of themselves as limiting their maleness to a few occasions and assuming an expansive humanness on most other occasions. Consequently, they can think of themselves as making moral decisions strictly from a calculation of justice and not as a particularly male way of categorizing actions. That justice is a fundamental value may or may not be a particularly male perspective, but the consequence of simply assuming one's assessment to be neutral is to be empowered to dismiss criticisms arising from other perspectives as "interested" and "merely subjective."

One reason for some women's negative response to "a woman's morality" is surely a legitimate reaction to the predictably asymmetrical pattern that results. They would be forced to choose between a "woman's morality" and "morality," since few defenders of traditional moralities have ever claimed that they were "men's moralities," despite their creation by men and obvious encoding of their interests. This not only pits "woman's morality" as a part against the whole, but also as a partial and therefore distorted view against the impartial and therefore sovereign overview.

I would therefore advocate a plurality of voices, which instantiate values particularized as they develop out of specific contexts and are reflectively affirmed or denied. The origin of values neither legitimizes nor delegitimizes them. Only reflective affirmation, based on the congruency of the effects of holding them with the outcomes desired, can do that.[14] But their origins in some special angle of vision will contribute to their appeal to those similarly situated and will provide the concrete basis without which discussions of morals remains aridly casuistic. There may be a recognizable set of characteristics typical of women's values, just as there are of men's values, in societies which strongly mark gender, and these characteristics will vary independently not only among societies, but also among individual members of societies. Theories of moral development are interested in women and men, not "woman" and "man," and therefore care should be taken to distinguish in individual developmental sequences not only how far particular women and men converge with or diverge from societally-based gender stereotypes but, more important, the extent to which the association of some values with women has led to their devaluation, whether found in women or men.

It is not sufficiently emphasized that not only do some women recognize their own moral development in Gilligan's account and others do not, but also that some men likewise recognize themselves. Despite Freud's reductionism, not all values have their origins in our development of gender identity, but surely some of them do, just as, despite Marx's economic reductionism, not all values reflect the economic and social disparities of capitalism, but surely some of our values do. It would be much more profitable to study which developmental contexts lead to an emphasis on care and which to an emphasis on abstract principle, how one orientation or the other is fostered or discouraged, and what factors, including but not limited to gender, are part of these various contexts. The statement by Bebeau and Brabeck that "moral sensitivity is an ability that can be developed" and their suggestions for research projects are good examples of what I mean.[15] But we will continue to find what we expect to find in an unproductive way that will not resolve current disputes unless we recognize and explicitly discuss the purposes that guide our findings, chief among which is the determination of what we take to be the desired moral outcome, that is, our definition of moral maturity. The factual dispute over whether moral development can be differentiated by sex cannot be resolved profitably so long as we are not clear about what such a finding would mean in terms of the goals we take to be most desirable.

Gender is not just socially constructed, it is also individually assumed; and its boundaries can be much looser than we care to admit. By looking at gender as a process and not as an accomplished fact at some arbitrary stage of development, women and men are better served in their process of continuous assumption of gender by learning what the effects of assuming certain values has both on their sense of their gender and on their interaction with other aspects of self and world. Nurturance and caring have been linked to passivity and a lack of assertiveness as values particularly appropriate for women in certain contexts, such as those permeated by patriarchal value systems, but that does not establish either that they are necessarily linked together as values or that they are necessarily linked to women. Women in our society are both expected to be and perceived as being more nurturant than men and less assertive. If nurturance is good and submissiveness bad, it would seem reasonable to investigate not only what conditions develop such values in women, but also the relevant variants, such as which conditions generate the same combination of values in men, which generate nurturance but not submissiveness, which submissiveness but not nurturance. This would enable us to understand better which antecedent conditions are more favorable for desired outcomes and therefore provide reasonable guidelines for promoting them. By asking questions in terms of outcomes desired and not just insofar as they relate to a factual determination of existing conditions, a whole new range of possibilities emerges. This way of thinking avoids some of the problems associated with uncritically identifying care with women.

It is widely acknowledged that there are not just two versions of values, his and hers, but not so widely recognized that there are not just two easily identifiable genders.[16] What different cultures have selected as a suitable range of behaviors for males and females varies so widely that it is surprising we have not been more perplexed than we seem to be in assigning such a wide array to only two types. Another way to put this is to point out that of all the ways of thinking of ourselves that of identifying ourselves as male or female as our primary orientation toward the world is much less productive of outcomes desired than any number of other orientations, for example, as creative, as free, as persons, as curious, as hardworking, and so on. Just as we have outgrown thinking that our place in life is naturally determined by birth, so perhaps it is time to discard the belief in the natural assignment to one of two rigidly defined categories of gender. This cannot be successfully carried out, however, without first identifying and exposing the crippling effects of rigid gender assignments and rescuing those aspects of human behavior that we approve of but that have been unfairly limited by gender.

3. A JUST COMMUNITY APPROACH:
CONTEXTUALIST OR UNIVERSALIST?

If we link the notion of contexts which instantiate values with the understanding that each of us, singly and as members of groups, takes in the world according to our varied perspectives, we can then make of the limitations of our finitude an advantage rather than a detriment to our understanding of our relatedness within the world. Since what is apparent from one angle of vision is not necessarily available to other perspectives, we are dependent on each other's disclosures of reality. Most of us accept the scientific assumption that facts can validate or invalidate theories, but we are generally less aware of the extent to which our beliefs, expectations, and values permit or obscure the recognition of some facts rather than others. Women's unique angles of vision can therefore be affirmed, as well as the correlative need for the interaction of many such interpretations in order to compensate for the blind spots of any one.

The understanding of moral development as specifically women's or men's and as needing correction by reference to an ideally neutral and independently generated moral system of values can thus be recognized as being both inadequate to the multitude of overlapping contexts and the cause of much unnecessary confusion in the search for Platonic values that precede and exist independently of particular human contexts. Just as we have many contexts in which persons interact, with different describable features, so there are many ways to categorize them by taking our clue from the ends or purposes we have in mind; for example, insofar as they further some women's or men's nurturing relations with others or insofar as they lead to a just distribution of goods, offices, and services. Some, but not all, the features of contexts are unique, and one way of transcending the particularity of context is to identify desired outcomes. Every family is unique, yet also shares some goals in common. Moral judgments grow out of reflection on experience and the codification of such findings as beneficial or not. In this way features of a morality are developed that span more than one context, but not necessarily all contexts. The convergence toward principles of wider and wider extent is a project to be achieved, subject to constant reassessment, and not a preexistent given.

In contrast to the naturalism of this model of critical contextualism, Noddings wants to construct "a genuinely universal interpretation of culture," despite the fact that she links the companion concept of universalism, the "equity model," with the male perspective that equates humanness with maleness.[17] Ann Higgins also argues for a morality that is universal and necessary and not open to negotiation. She enunciates a feminist position that values cannot be relative "since feminism holds equality between the sexes as a universal, non-relative value and the elimination of social injustices due to one's gender as an absolute good." As the best way of eliminating injustice to women due to sexism she suggests the model of a "just community approach" to moral education. For it to work, "the rules and concerns of the programme" must "become personally felt and community-shared responsibilities of and to all members." This responsibility to the community is enacted through "the ideas of mutual respect and treating each other fairly." But "the just community programme's norms are cooperation and responsibility to the group." Moral growth occurs in this democratic setting through "stating an idea, listening to others agree or disagree with it, taking others' perspectives and considering their ideas, modifying one's own, restating it and listening again." [18] The only check on this respect for one's own opinions and those of others is that both the opinions and the way they are expressed help build a just community.

Higgins acknowledges the influence of Dewey on the just community approach to restructuring education, and she brings a welcome contemporary feminist outlook to the issues, an outlook too often ignored in earlier formulations. I would like to encourage the consideration of an even more radically democratic approach than the one she develops, however, since appeals to absolute goods and universal, nonrelative values make poor bedfellows with the democratic ideal and democratic processes as revisioned by pragmatists. Belief in absolute values and informed community approaches to problem solving represent two largely incompatible approaches to value formation that will sooner or later collide.

The ultimate norm in the community as proposed is the justness of the community being developed. But this presupposes someone knowing what a just community is. Since the students are portrayed as coming to this conclusion through the process itself and the teachers are responsible that the process be democratically fair, what ultimately prevails is the teacher's judgment, no matter that this is done in a noncoercive way. But the democratic process, as process, will work only if each person's perspective is genuinely respected as a contribution to the shape the community is taking. The strong peer group pressure in any such setting is toward conformity to group standards. The questions then arise: Whose norms? Whose community? If the values and norms of the group are already set and the teachers play a game with the students to get them to work out by trial and error what these are, then the democratic process is only a facade and does not differ from group indoctrination, such as that operative in Alcoholics Anonymous meetings, where all discussion and acting-out is directed to a predetermined goal. This goal is often discussed but never itself subject to veto or modification.

In sharp contrast, in the democratic process there is no king, no binding arbiter, no absolute values, goals, or procedures except those set by the group itself. What about the injunction to continue the process as process? This is an absolute value only relatively. It is binding only as long as the group continues to bind itself by it. The American Civil War is elegant testimony to the always possible move to refuse to be bound by that process. Thomas Jefferson drew the conclusion that if the people within the democratic process are genuinely responsible for the shape of their own political governance, then constant revolution cannot in principle be ruled out. But, as we know, in the Western democracies there is not continual anarchy, but considerable continuity. Higgins can argue that this stems from the adherence of members of the group to certain universal moral principles, such as the often-cited Bill of Rights. But this sidesteps the issues of how these moral imperatives came about in the first place, which ones are continued and expanded, which ones quietly dropped, and what they mean concretely. On each of these issues we can trace the actual democratic process of give and take, compromise, and impassioned plea that brought them about and continue to do so. If absolute values played any role, they did so only as tokens. Every side— and there were and are many more than two—claimed to be bound by eternal values. The only thing eternal about them is the eternal struggle to claim one's own insights to be the only true understanding of them.

The power of a democratic process that is genuinely followed is that it starts out by recognizing that no one has a monopoly on "eternal" values and then provides a means of developing a community that will work, despite the lack of common agreement and without resorting to coercion. What Oliver Wendell Holmes argued, and what most nineteenth-century jurists did not want to hear, is that there is no way to interpret law in a democratic society without creating new law, new precedent. To do otherwise is to shackle people to forms of justice developed in one historical period, with all the limitations this implies. Feminists have nothing to fear from abandoning a positivist understanding of values as eternal, since as one of the groups not present when these "eternal" values were first articulated and propagated, their well-being was not inscribed in them. The eternal truth that "all men are created equal" gave way after great struggle to the temporal truth that "former black male slaves are created (partially) equal," and, after even more struggles, to the truth—the exact moment when it became a value can be temporally located—that all women are (partially) equal. We still have not worked out what it means in practice for all persons to be equal. The appeal to any phrase which purports to state once and for all what this means theoretically—as though this can be done in isolation from practice—is a vain appeal to a wished-for certainty of a value not subject to further revision. To call any assertion the expression of an eternal truth or an eternal value rather than one that has been temporally determined is to devalue the creative thought, the blood, sweat, and tears that have made it—not found it to be—a value. Eternal values are supposedly self-evident and nonnegotiable, and we have yet to see any such values, judging by the proliferation of disputes and wars over disparate value claims.

When, in the construction of a just community, it is determined that justice includes that women participate in the same way as men in building up the community, this is not the result of appealing to a universal norm of justice. Far from it. Universal justice has been thought for millennia to be compatible with women's differential participation in an ideal community. This norm is being created in its enactment, and far from being eternal, what will result as it is recreated in other communities of which the students are members no one can say until it happens. This reevaluation of norms in light of their consequences is another of the aspects of a democratic process that is not found in hierarchical models, which dispense "eternal" norms "universally" understood. This is the theoretical basis for not just listening to, but taking seriously, the contributions of each member of the group. Students and teachers alike already have moral values. They do not need to interact with the group democratically to bring their own personal values more in line with "eternal" ones, although this is one means of seeming to do so. The Red Cells in China during Mao's reign were, by some accounts, quite effective in reeducating the individual's norms to the predetermined, official standards of a just society. What the democratic group situation gives them that no authoritarian system could is the opportunity to learn that no one has a monopoly on the determination of moral values, that noncoercive communities are built through cooperation, and that learning to work together means reevaluating one's values in relation to those of others so that the community will work and its members flourish.

The unpleasant practical consequences of trying to impose one's values on the group are immediately evident. The pleasures of participating for someone who has been alienated from school surroundings are also immediate and palpable. But we delude ourselves if we think that the more harmonious community which emerges is a result of individuals replacing their self-centered, immature values by universal ones like justice and community. They are learning the connections of certain means to ends, and since the experience is rewarding, it is hoped that they will try to recreate the process and structure in other circumstances. If, instead, they think that they are learning that their moral norms were false or immature and that now they have adopted mature, eternal, universal ones, then it is likely they will become more, not less, authoritarian in their interactions with others. In *The Quest For Certainty,* "A Study of the Relation of Knowledge and Action," Dewey explores in detail this connection of belief in absolute values with authoritarianism and of moral judgments, in principle revisable, made "on the basis of public, objective and shared consequences" with the spirit of cooperation (*LW*4:38).

The democratic process may or may not lead to less absolute certainty about the universality of norms, although it is notorious that those who deal sympathetically on a day-to-day basis with people having diverse cultural, ethnic, religious, or political norms of morality tend to be less rigid in insisting that they alone have access to eternal norms. But the operative word is "sympathetically." One can learn to be more rigid and autocratic if one sees others as inferiors. By learning to treat respectfully others for whom they may not initially care, the student participants also learn to respect what they say. Thus, students' tolerance for diversity may enlarge. Another issue that emerges is central to feminist discourse. Are the members of the "just" community learning to get along by modifying their own insights and moral stances to adopt some universal, shared norms? Or are they strengthening their own uniqueness through learning to value the unique perspectives of others without seeing them as a threat to their own?

4. CONTEXTUALISM AND FEMINISM

Relativistic approaches to morals entail the unwanted consequence that no one could logically demand that it is a moral duty for others to honor the conditions of their well-being. On the other hand, universalist and necessitarian approaches to morals ignore as irrelevant the particularity of persons and historical groups and the fortuitousness present in day-to-day living. But these are not the only two options. In pragmatism, values are categorized as relative to context but not relativistic, as applying to more situations than those in which they initially arose without falling into a false universalism, and as being objectively identifiable despite their origins in the uniqueness of each subject. Dewey developed this perspective in the greatest detail, and the pattern of his thinking can only be suggested. He often argued that philosophical theory has largely become irrelevant to the most pressing problems of our day as a direct result of its neglect of the context in which thinking takes place.[19] Philosophers should spend less time contemplating eternal values and more time criticizing, organizing, and testing the internal coherence of, and making explicit the consequences of, the "body of beliefs and of institutions and practices allied to them" at any given time in order to develop values that are understood as a projection of "a new perspective which leads to new surveys of possibilities" (*LW*6:18–19).

Neglect of context has prevented thinkers from realizing that "individuality in a social and moral sense" is not a given but an achievement. "It means initiative, inventiveness, varied resourcefulness, assumption of responsibility in choice of belief and conduct. . . . As achievements, they are not absolute but are relative to the use that is to be made of them. And this use varies with the environment." [20] Moral law is not an eternal set of principles but "is a formula of the way to respond when specified conditions present themselves" (*LW* 4:222). Such formulas have been derived experientially, but are nonetheless objectively grounded. "Any survey of the experiences in which ends-in-view are formed, and in which earlier impulsive tendencies are shaped through deliberation into a *chosen* desire, reveals that the object finally valued as an end to be reached is determined in its concrete makeup by appraisal of existing conditions as means." [21] Insofar as universalism is retained as a value, it is a goal to be achieved, not a precondition. "Communication, sharing, joint participation are the only actual ways of universalizing the moral law and end" (*LW* 12:197).

This perspective could be characterized as a variant of contextualism or constructivism, and Nona Lyons, Barbara Houston, and Nel Noddings all provide arguments supporting a feminist case for such a perspective. Lyons says that on the model that "all knowledge is contextual and constructed," then women, too, "are 'constructionists,' capable also of 'making theory.' " She finds that Gilligan's use of the metaphor *voice* captures the linkage between ideas of self and morality. When she questioned adolescent girls to systematically test Gilligan's hypotheses she found that "women were more likely to use response considerations while men were more likely to focus on considerations of equality and fairness in relationships." Self-images of interdependency and connectedness with others often link up with moral considerations of response or care, whereas a self-image of autonomy more frequently appeals to moral considerations of justice and fairness. These patterns of responses are different from, but not necessarily incompatible with, each other and may even coexist. Although more studies are needed to establish that thinking in terms of care is more frequently found in girls, Lyons suggests that teaching strategies should already be devised that speak to both patterns. Since "most schools tend to foster rule-oriented, rational, abstract thinking," then this means incorporating strategies congenial to a "logic of understanding." [22]

For Lyons, contextualism means paying more attention to women's care responses, since we already overemphasize the justice model. In this she supports Noddings's valorizing of the female. Noddings urges us to "analyze the structures and practices of our society from the perspective of women's experience and to begin the complex process of constructing a genuinely universal interpretation of culture." This articulation of a feminine morality rather than "an equity model" would emphasize the "mother model" as a counterweight to the masculine "warrior model." By drawing on "women's experience as a framework for the analysis of evil" the excesses of the warrior model can be tempered, and both men and women would "study and practice the womanly arts of caring." [23] Noddings equates the feminine with motherly caring and the masculine with warrior virtues.

Like Houston, Noddings recognizes that the so-called equity model is actually a model developed from masculine perspectives and therefore promotes domination and oppression. But Houston draws a very different conclusion from this insight. She warns against a premature move from an empirical claim of caring to a normative injunction. We should raise the question of what accounts for women's preference for care and what results from this orientation. By linking the valuing of caring with women's "historical context [and] the material conditions of most women's lives," she shows how men's inculcation of this as a value for women has contributed and continues to contribute to "women's condition of subordination." [24] Houston uses a broader notion of context than Lyons does, in that it includes the "economic, social and political contexts" in and through which women make moral decisions.

In a world in which women are exploited and dominated precisely through socializing them to unilaterally or disproportionately care for and service men, men's interests, and the needy in society in general, then it is not enough to try to educate men to also care. Women have to reconsider and reevaluate their commitment to caring, to develop a strong sense of self, and to be motivated to correct injustices they suffer.[25] Houston's challenge to the moral division of labor leads to the conclusion that further identification of women with a morality of care would itself be oppressive and would distract educators from the more immediately urgent task of helping women develop a strong sense of self precisely as a moral issue. Women's and men's very different socialization and ease of access to power means that the features of their moral development will and ought to differ accordingly. If it is true that society already contributes to an autonomous sense of self as a defining characteristic of the male and a connected and caring sense of self as a defining characteristic of the female, then this would constitute prima facie evidence that moral education should seek to develop those aspects of our ideal of humanity that the socialization process neglects with such dire consequences—that is, more autonomy for women and more connectedness for men.

5. GENDER-SPECIFIC OR GENDER-NEUTRAL VALUES?

Noddings quotes William James's "The Moral Equivalent of War" as instantiating the stereotype of the male warrior code, but what she does not point out is that James appeals to this model precisely to subvert it.[26] Since men's self-image in the nineteenth century—as in our own—was tied to a warrior model, James appealed to this socially constructed and reinforced model of masculinity as a gambit to redefine *fighting* from its primary denotation of physical combat to its metaphorical sense of fighting for values by peaceful means. In fact, he was trying to bridge the chasm that Victorians constructed between manly "warriors" and womanly "moralists" by arguing that it was masculine to be a fighter for morality. That he did not extend the same reversal to women is not surprising since he was a pacifist and condemned war as a means of settling disputes. Furthermore, far from denying the heroism contained in women's experience of mothering, as Noddings claims, James frequently extolled it in glowing terms and recommended it as a model to be emulated.[27] As was argued in chapter 6, this only indicates that he was unable to free himself from the Victorian stereotypes of masculinity and femininity, for, unless great care is exercised in the terms of the explanation, the glorification of motherhood as the source of women's strength reinforces a debilitating stereotype rather than being its antidote. But as a general practice James encouraged openness to perspectives neglected because of a bias in another direction. Thus he urged philosophers and theologians to incorporate the findings of science into their outlook and scientists to take seriously feelings and values.

I agree with Noddings that James's model of an "ideal type of human character," which he says has historically been thought to be instantiated in one of three types, the saint, the knight, or the gentleman, are drawn from male experience. We have seen that he explicitly talks about what constitutes "a certain type of man," namely, "the best man absolutely," and this heroic attitude is contrasted with "effeminacy." But then it is all the more remarkable that, despite being saddled with Victorian stereotypes and working out of his own masculine experiences, he reaches the conclusions that he does. Let us begin by recognizing his point of view and assume that he is primarily talking as a man to other men. First of all, he denies the legitimacy of appealing to "one intrinsically ideal type," even though this conception is "supposed by most persons." According to his radically empiricist philosophy, "all ideals are matters of relation." Rather than accepting uncritically an abstract, universal ideality, we should, he argues, turn to "the actual situation" and "particular circumstances" to discover the superiority of one type of conduct to another. He has already criticized the warrior mentality as barbarically de-

structive and irrational and has praised only the aspect of war that encourages "the strenuous life and heroism." But because he is not willing
to achieve these values at the cost that war exacts, he searches for its
"moral equivalent." Instead of "crushing weaker peoples," the heroic
strenuousness he advocates is better modeled on that required in voluntarily adopting poverty, because such freedom from material attachments would enable men to stop being the "propagators of corruption"
and instead "help to set free our generation" to devote themselves "to
unpopular causes" (*VRE,* 292–93, 297–98).

He turns to women for better models, since their power lies not in
brute force but, like the saint, in "gentleness in beauty." Although in
popular imagination such moral strength seems no match for the warrior's physical strength, James argues that it can actually be more effective. A society that lived out the warrior ideal would destroy itself through
unbridled aggressiveness. The saint as hero better realizes both the
means to and the end of a perfect society, which is conceived as one "in
which there would be no aggressiveness, but only sympathy and fairness"
(*VRE,* 296, 298). Furthermore, we already have living examples on a
small scale of what we are aiming for on a large scale: "any small community of true friends now realizes such a society." His reconstruction of
men's ideal of a properly masculine heroic strength thus involves a
double strategy: first, showing that brute force is less effective than peaceful means of combating evil of all kinds, and second, that a moral reconstruction of society can be at least as exciting as the martial arts. This
double strategy of both developing a moral ideal that will fire a man's
imagination and provide motive power and, at the same time, demonstrating its usefulness as a practical recourse and not merely an unattain-
able ideal is based on his analysis of practical rationality as constituted by
interactive aesthetic and practical aspects.

In turning from an abstract ideal of community to our actual societies we find that the exact mix of characteristics which will both be practically livable and still heroically ideal can vary a great deal, just as the
situations vary. What is called for in one situation is not necessarily trans-
ferable to a different one, even though we can agree in a preliminary way
what the characteristics are that are most admirable. In uncovering the
destructiveness of central concepts of masculinity that his society uncritically accepted and reconstructing a model of masculinity that incorporated what was commonly assigned to femininity, James provides us
with a model of analysis that is arguably worth appropriating, once it is
purged of those "special historic manifestations" that in hindsight are
no longer acceptable to us (*VRE,* 295). Finally, it is significant that in
holding up heroically saintly models for emulation he includes both men
and women, especially if one is assuming, as Noddings does, that he is

speaking as a man. By substituting the living model of a "community of true friends" small enough to be interactive for the oppressive machismo of the male warrior model, he is already proposing nonsexist explanations that can profitably be developed further by those of us for whom this move is central, not peripheral.

6. SYMPATHETIC CARING AS AN ORIGIN OF VALUES

In closing, I would like to propose an ethical perspective that places something very like care at the center of its value system as a model that other feminists might also find worthwhile reconstructing in the light of our present-day knowledge and interests. It is found in William James's essay, "On a Certain Blindness in Human Beings," where he argues that judgments of worth have their origins in feeling (*TT,* 132–49). If we had no feelings, ideals would not have any significance for us, and we would not separate them into values worth pursuing. But although feeling is a necessary condition, it is not a sufficient one, because we must still determine which of our predilections ought to be pursued in preference to others.

Since we are practical beings, our own situations and duties are of intense and constant interest, but we do not generally expect others to attach such importance to what concerns our inner life. Like us, they have their own vital interests. We therefore often misjudge the significance of lives different from our own. "Hence the falsity of our judgments, so far as they presume to decide in an absolute way on the value of other persons' conditions or ideals." This congenital blindness toward the feelings of peoples and creatures different from ourselves is the greatest obstacle to the ethical life. Without this basic sympathy we would have no motive for attributing an ideality to a way of life alien to our own. Since we are finite and practical creatures, the pursuit of those duties which constitute our vocation or situation in life tends to dull our sensitivity to the vital centers which animate others. It takes both a leap of the imagination and determined effort to recognize and sympathize with "the higher vision of inner significance" of others and to find "a new centre and a new perspective" extending the original boundaries of our own felt interests (*TT,* 132–38).

This sympathy goes beyond tolerance because it seeks to gain insight into the individuated worlds of experience of others and the values they hold that make these worlds cohere. This insight is only available from a perspective of caring. James calls it a "sympathetic, concrete observation" that understands more than is visible to disinterested scrutiny. It is a necessary precondition for concrete judgments of justice, as he argues in "The Moral Philosopher and the Moral Life" (*WB,* 141–62). Without it, justice is either so abstract that its practical meaning must still be determined through a process such as sympathetic concrete observation—that is, observation, reflection, appraisal, instantiation, and revision—or it merely imposes, with little regard to the specificity of the situation, a rigid moral outlook that is claimed to be universal but actually incorporates a particular world view and code of values.[28]

No philosophy of ethics is possible on the traditional model seeking to ground a system of abstract rules deduced from unrevisable, universal moral imperatives, "for every real dilemma is in literal strictness a unique situation; and the exact combination of ideals realized and ideals disappointed which each decision creates is always a universe without a precedent, and for which no adequate previous rule exists" (*WB*, 158). This is not to deny that in every actual moral deliberation predetermined rules and judgments of value have a vital role to play. But unless these rules and valuations themselves undergo intelligent modification through operational thinking, the gap between transcendent values and everyday life will eventually be so great as to negate any directive function. According to Dewey, "what is needed is intelligent examination of the consequences that are actually affected by inherited institutions and customs, in order that there may be intelligent consideration of the ways in which they are to be intentionally modified in behalf of generation of different consequences" (*LW* 4: 218).

This insistence on the irreducible value of each person's experience is also central to feminist theory. Both outlooks recognize that in this imperfect world of ours there are no guarantees that the moral choices we make are the right ones, and both insist that a place be found for each one's values in the total universe of values, insofar as this is possible. Since women, along with other oppressed groups, have suffered from the imposition of values falsely labeled universal, but developed in ignorance of our experiences, the criterion James gives for identifying mistaken moral choices should awaken curiosity about the possibility of appropriating his ethical outlook. He says that when we make a bad mistake "the cries of the wounded will soon inform [us] of the fact" (*WB*, 158). Thanks to recent advances in feminist and postcolonial achievements and scholarship, such cries are finally beginning to be heard.

Ten

Social Ethics

For pragmatists, social ethics is not a subset of ethics, but ethics itself. Believing that it is a travesty to reduce ethics to the mechanisms of a formal system or to a disembodied interior monologue, they start from the fact of human interrelationship, giving equal weight to subjectivity and to objective social relations. In an early essay John Dewey said the purpose of a method of moral deliberation that begins by "mentally constructing some actual scene of human interaction is "*the formation of a sympathetic imagination for human relations in action;* this is the ideal which is substituted for training in moral rules, or for analysis of one's sentiments and attitudes in conduct."[1]

In developing the implications of human association for the democratic ideal in *Democracy and Education,* Dewey recognizes the ambiguity of appeals to society and community. Not only do women and men associate in many different ways and for many purposes as specifically gendered, but each individual is associated in multiple ways—political, social, corporate, ethnic, and religious. Community as understood normatively in social philosophy emphasizes unity of purpose, loyalty to public ends, and mutuality of sympathy, while descriptively what one finds is a plurality of societies, bad ones as well as good. In order to hold up association as normative, some criteria must be designated. Two extremes to be avoided are ungrounded speculations about what constitutes an ideal society and mere replication of already existing societies (*MW*9:87–89).

The pragmatist method is to select those "desirable traits of forms of community life which actually exist, and employ them to criticize undesirable features and suggest improvement." It thus seeks to avoid ungrounded speculation and the tyranny of an impossible ideal wielded as a weapon against those who do not measure up, as well as a reactionary tyranny of enforcing conformity to some subset of already existing social conditions. Dewey begins by identifying two traits found in any social group: "some interest held in common" and "a certain amount of interaction and cooperative intercourse with other groups" (*MW* 9:89). From these he derives a standard by interpreting them from the perspective of what is required for the positive growth of socially intelligent human beings who exhibit continuity through renewal, as explicated in the six earlier chapters of *Democracy and Education*.

Accordingly, more numerous and varied interests consciously shared are preferable to fewer restricted ones, and full and free interactions with other groups are preferable to deprived and coercive ones. Cults and criminal gangs contribute less to human growth and development, according to these criteria, than a form of family life in which all participate in material, intellectual, and aesthetic interests, where all experience the growth of each member, where the family enters into intimate relationships with other social, cultural, and business groups, contributing to the political organization and being in turn supported by it. Dewey's model of a democracy as "a mode of associated living, of conjoint communicated experience" is obviously drawn from what is worthwhile in nonpatriarchal forms of family life, and he does not hesitate to apply lessons learned in the private sphere to the public sphere in order to condemn despotism in all its forms. In the larger society as well as in the myriad more intimate ones, the more that communities are truly democratic in that they educate members to understand their own interests and actions in relation to those of others, the more they will tend to break down the barriers that separate us, including those of class, race, national territory, gender, and sexual orientation (*MW* 9:89–93).

Even James, who holds that "the essence of good is simply to satisfy demand" and that "all demands as such are *prima facie* respectable," argues that in our tragically practical world demands will surely clash. Since no moralist has the right to impose her or his views on others, the guiding principle ought to be to satisfy at all times as many demands as possible and to prefer that solution which, even when prevailing, does some justice to the demands not met.[2] In an article on social science Dewey goes so far as to prevent misunderstanding by pointing out that he uses the word *moral* "for the human or 'social' in its most inclusive reach, not for any special region or segment" (*LW* 15:236, n. 7). Charlotte Perkins Gilman's definition of ethics is the same: "Ethics is the science of social relation, how persons and social forces work with and on one another."[3] Starting from a recognition of reciprocity and interdependence, pragmatist/feminist ethics criticizes exaggerated individualism, undermines appeals to privileged moral insight, and unmasks entrenched hierarchical relations. According to Jane Addams, for instance, Hull House was founded "on the theory that the dependence of classes on each other is reciprocal; and that as the social situation is essentially a reciprocal relation, it gives a form of expression that has a peculiar value." [4]

Influenced by Darwin to interpret present events as the result of change over time, the pragmatists, including pragmatist feminists, developed various genealogies of morals, which they usually called the genetic method.[5] According to Dewey, "The genetic standpoint makes us aware that the systems of the past are neither fraudulent impostures nor absolute revelations; but are the products of political, economic and scientific conditions whose change carries with it change of theoretical formulations" (*MW* 4:44). These genealogies provide a basis for a positive understanding of the origin of morals in relations that both reflect particular conditions, times, and places, and subject them to intelligent reconstruction. Like caudal appendages persisting through changes in bodily anatomy, present-day morality is not a purely a priori rational product but contains vestiges of unjust social relationships along with reflectively better moral insights and practices. Dewey's genealogy also provides a basis for a negative criticism of oppressive dualisms arising from classism and slavery that are still incorporated into moral theories. Gilman's, on the other hand, finds the origins of oppressive moral beliefs and practices in men's dominance over women, which resulted in an androcentric culture, defined as the male sex's monopoly of all human activities (in contrast to specifically female or male ones) and subsequent designation of them as "man's work." [6] She traces this process through the growth of the family into patriarchy, and names the androcentric prejudice by which males gradually monopolized art, sport, religion, education, law and government, politics and industry.

In his 1918 book, *The Ethics of Cooperation,* James Hayden Tufts argues for cooperation instead of competition or dominance as the guiding principle of social life.[7] And in the 1932 *Ethics* he coauthored with Dewey, Tufts denies that morality originates in physical or mental coercion or in a law or principle of Duty that splits human beings into two parts, sundering morality from relationship to our normal impulses and purposes. He instead argues "that the exercise of claims is as natural as anything else in a world in which persons are not isolated from one another but live in constant association and interaction." He generalizes from examples of the mutual claims of parents and children and of friends toward each other "to reach the conclusion that Right, law, duty, arise from the relations which human beings intimately sustain to one another, and that their authoritative force springs from the very nature of the relation that binds people together" (*LW* 7:217–19).

As is obvious from this brief review, the social interpretation of ethics was central to the pragmatism developed by both women and men.

Those facets of this mutually developed social ethics that can contribute to the growing field of feminist ethics will be explicated below. In the first section, the principle of reciprocity is developed by Dewey and Addams by considering which of the values learned in one's most enduring, intimate relationships should be retained and which rejected when such personal ties conflict with those of the larger community.

According to pragmatist ethics the concrete situation sets the problems that require reflection and reconstruction; hence, the second section explores some of the issues that have been addressed by pragmatists, particularly those concerning women and race. The third section issues a cautionary warning concerning some contemporary feminist efforts to privilege considerations of partiality over universalistic claims of impartiality. James demonstrates how easily such arguments for partiality can be used to deny women equality. By contrast, a more positive contribution is made by Addams and Dewey, who call for balancing the claims of both partiality and impartiality.

The pragmatist/feminist rejection of the legacy of the Western philosophical tradition of the dualisms of mind and body, theory and practice, is shown in the fourth section to be central to understanding the way that the recognition of the reciprocity of means and ends leads to an experimental construal of valuation. Explanations of the mutuality of disposition and the consequences incurred through action continue into the fifth section, which examines how considerations of sex and gender affect Dewey's naturalized morality as developed in *Human Nature and Conduct*. The chapter concludes by comparing the ethical issues of birth control raised by Gilman and Dewey as a way of showing what feminist and pragmatist analyses can contribute to each other.

1. THE TIES THAT BIND

Because individuals are interdependent, even physical and economic independence require cooperation and competition with others. Many of these relations are enduring, such as the "relations of friendship, of husband and wife, of parent and child, of citizen and nation . . . [, which] may be symbolized by terms or conceptions and then be stated in propositions. But they *exist* as actions and reactions in which things are modified" (*LW* 10:139). This is not to say that relationships cannot be perverted, as when obligations due to a parental or other office or situation are ignored and "they express merely one will in opposition to another, instead of proceeding from the tie which binds persons together." Legislators, judges, the police force do not officially act in their own person but as representatives of a community of interests and purposes. But civic and public officials frequently betray their obligations and use their power and prestige to advance their personal interests and private gains. This leads to resentment of all authority and "the feeling grows that all duties are limitations of personal freedom and arbitrary impositions of superior power" (*LW*7:227–29).

The wrongfulness of such acts stems not from contradictions of some abstract law of reason, as Kant would have it, but from the principle of reciprocity. Even the moral nonconformist does not deny the legitimacy of some moral claim by the community when she appeals to private advantage because such advantage supposedly contributes to the better welfare of all. The appeal is not to an abstract universality, however, but to a specific community. In asserting the rightfulness of her judgment over others, the moral nonconformist "is implicitly putting forth a social claim, something therefore to be tested and confirmed by further trial by others" (*LW*7:231). Addams goes even further: "We have learned to say that the good must be extended to all of society before it can be held secure by any one person or any one class; but we have not yet learned to add to that statement, that unless all men and all classes contribute to a good, we cannot even be sure that it is worth having." Ever the pragmatist, she adds: "In spite of many attempts we do not really act upon either statement." [8]

These conforming Others, in turn, have the duty of toleration, not in the sense of good-humored indifference but as "a positive willingness to permit reflection and inquiry to go on in the faith that the truly right will be rendered more secure through questioning and discussion, while things that have endured merely from custom will be amended" or discarded. The difficulty of such tolerance is shown by the alacrity with which censorship and force are used to suppress moral challenge. Those most insistent on Duty too often "think that the Right is made secure through the issuing of rules and regulations and by securing conformity to them" (*LW*7:226, 231).

Dewey begins a chapter on "Morals and Social Problems" in *Ethics* by putting together a series of quotations from the first four pages of Addams's first book, *Democracy and Social Ethics.* Not only does James also recognize this work of Addams as "one of the great books of our time" because of its "sympathetic interpretation to one another of the different classes of which society consists," but Dewey used it as a text in a course he taught and even invited Addams to lead class sessions with him.[9] In *Democracy and Social Ethics* he pointed out the inadequacy of a merely personal morality: "To attain personal morality in an age demanding social morality, to pride one's self upon the results of personal effort when the time demands social adjustment is utterly to fail to apprehend the situation." The situation is that social customs and institutions themselves are being questioned as to their moral worth, rather than blaming individual deviance for perceived failures. "All about us are men and women who have become unhappy in regard to their attitude toward the social order itself. The test which they would apply to their conduct is a social test." They demand a social morality: "They desire both a clearer definition of the code of morality applied to present day demands and a part in its fulfillment, both a creed and a practice of social morality." [10]

The difference between merely personal morality and social morality is clarified in two essays by Addams that expose and censure paternalism. "Filial Relations," a chapter in *Democracy and Social Ethics,* examines the conflicts evident around the turn of the century in the relation between parents and their grown-up daughters as young, middle-class women entered college in increasing numbers. "A Modern King Lear," which was not published until more than a decade after it was written because of its incendiary nature, examined the Pullman Strike of 1894 as an example of "the obsolescence of paternalism in the industrial order." [11] Although Addams thought peaceful conciliation would have been preferable to the legacy of distrust and bitterness that followed the rage and riot of the summer's social disorder, she nonetheless did not agree with those who blamed the workers for not being grateful for the philanthropy of the president of the Pullman Company, George M. Pullman. By comparing him to King Lear, she not only made an explicit connection between the tyranny of domestic and industrial paternalism, but she also linked grave social disorders to continued allegiance to personal morality when social morality was needed to properly address changes taking place in home and factory. [12]

According to Addams, although Pullman may originally have felt a glow of benevolence from designing and executing his model company town, how he appeared to his peers gradually became more important than measuring the usefulness of his benefits by the standard of the workers' own needs as they themselves saw them. In fact, it is the great and noble impulses of the benefactor role that gradually destroys the power to share in the equality of simple human relationships. Philanthropists who do not cultivate the moral life that springs from our common human experiences cause harm "so long as they are 'good to people,' rather than 'with them.'" [13] The Pullman Company president "lost the faculty of affectionate interpretation" and took on the attitudes of his class, despising the labor movement as full of deadbeats and agitators.

The labor-relations struggle between Pullman and his workers was at the same time a clash between the individual virtues that support capitalism—self-control, respect for property, sobriety, and hard work—and the social virtues, those that foster solidarity with others. Addams urged the workers on to an even more encompassing solidarity extending beyond the working class by holding up the ideal of social virtue according to which the emancipation of the workers must also include the emancipation of the employer. Pullman's idea of goodness was one that depended predominantly on one's own efforts and included such values as cleanliness, decency of living, thrift, and temperance, while the values motivating the workers required concerted action and included decent wages and working conditions and solidarity with other workers so that their own interests became tied to that of the working class. The loyalty of union workers, opposing 'scab' labor that kept wages at a starvation level for everyone is, to Addams, "a manifestation of moral power." [14]

Individual morality is also distinguished from social morality by their differing perspectives. The president of Pullman, for instance, consulted his own personal and commercial ends and could not view the situation from the social standpoint of "human affection and social justice which it involves." Those in power often think it enough to consult their own conscience and ideals unconnected with the consent of their fellow women and men. Such consent often means that a feasible right rather than an absolute right is all that can be accomplished by way of reform. Bringing along those to be benefited as participants in the process often means compromise and a groping toward a good neither group clearly envisioned beforehand. The effort to discover what people really want will most likely slow down progress and limit the goals attainable, but the outcome will be more lasting and worthwhile because it will not be dependent on one person's insights or efforts but will be "underpinned and upheld by the sentiments and aspirations of many others." [15]

Addams reinforces her distinction between morality conceived of as personal or as social in "Filial Relations," which begins by bemoaning the fact that the majority of people in society stick to traditional moral conventions and cannot "sympathetically interpret" efforts toward a higher social morality. This attitude particularly hinders those experiments and advances that depend on women's initiative because women are more sensitive to the individual and family claims, and their training reinforces these tendencies. As young women become more active in the life of their community through career or reform efforts as a result of the increasing democratization of relationships, the relation between parents and their grown-up daughters becomes increasingly strained. Young women who do not put their family claims before those of society at large are called selfish—a distinct contrast with parental attitudes toward sons, who are expected to be citizens and to pursue careers, so that the claims of family are urged much less strenuously.[16]

The tragic collision of interests between family and wider social claims instantiates rival moral claims, neither of which can be totally denied without impoverishing ethical life. But if the need and misery rampant in the world are recognized as legitimate social claims, then the daughter who answers these claims can be judged to be responding conscientiously, rather than neglecting primary duties. This recognition that the changes brought about by rapid industrialization require a social morality rather than an individual morality, and the family obligations, which are an extension of individual morality, may come through an emotion such as pity, "long before it is formulated and perceived by the intellect." [17]

The family and the state are best preserved as institutions through continuous reconstruction. To continue to enforce a morality developed on the basis of the needs of earlier periods of family life for which it was never designed, only results in misery and maladjustment.[18] "It is always difficult for the family to regard the daughter otherwise than as a family possession," and hard for them to acknowledge that she is an integral part of the social order and has social and political duties. When women's life outside the home was not recognized, education fitted her to fulfill only family obligations, but modern education was conceived to develop men's individuality and powers of independent action. When women educated in such a system act on its assumptions, they are often perplexed as to how to integrate it with traditional ideas of filial piety.[19]

Reacting with shock and stress, parents and daughters have hardly begun to analyze the situation nor to reconcile the conflicting claims of family and the larger society. Since the family claim is often strenuously and exclusively asserted, the daughter finds herself in a totally unnecessary conflict between social and family claims. Moreover, the social claim is often vague and nebulous while the family claim is concrete and definitely asserted, leading many young women to quietly submit even though they feel cheated. Long before Betty Friedan, Addams analyzed the plight of the unhappy woman constrained in the home, consumed with regrets and desires, vainly trying to lose herself in devotion to her family and her own self-improvement.[20] The conflict is not just between head and heart; emotions are tumultuously set against each other because the social claim is also an emotional one. Ignoring it suppresses not only her convictions but saps her energies in useless regrets as she lives a life of contradictions.

Higher education comes in for its share of blame for the inability of so many women to name and come to grips with their dilemma. Although colleges have often ethically taught that one's own rights can only be secured by working to secure those of others, the training has been singularly individualistic, stressing personal ambition and intellectual accumulation. It has not addressed women's special needs. The fact that experiences of community needs are not integrated into the curriculum affects women more than men because they are not expected to pursue postgraduate professional and career paths. Having been given neither an intellectual grasp of, nor a personal acquaintance with, larger social issues and societal problems, they are ill-prepared to understand what is required to address these problems or how to extend compassion or noble ambitions beyond an immediate circle to the larger society that shapes and influences the smaller domestic circle.[21]

A step in the right direction is the participation of young mothers in "Child Study" classes where they learn to view their children as related to the larger society and not just to the family. A better understanding of the social relation requires an intelligent grasp of the interests of those different from ourselves since many social misunderstandings and consequent conflicts are due to the fact that "our experiences have been so unlike that we cannot comprehend each other." Addams then draws on the same tragedy of King Lear that she used in her article on the Pullman Strike, this time emphasizing what went wrong between a father and his daughters. Lear illustrates the paternalism of the patriarchal family according to which the central and controlling moral obligation of daughters is to reverence and obey fathers and father surrogates. Against this individualistic ethics of women's subordination to the home, Cordelia asserts a wider social obligation. According to Lear's individualistic code of ethics, Cordelia was disrespectful and ungrateful, but according to her own code of social ethics she was striving to fulfill a larger conception of duty. Only when Lear was impoverished and bereft of authority, only when his experiences were not distanced by status and fortune from common, human experiences, only when he literally took the place of the other, as a poor naked wretch, could he begin to understand Cordelia. Addams concludes that we need to see the individual in relation to the family, and the family in relation to the society, according to a code of ethics that deals "with these larger relationships, instead of a code designed to apply so exclusively to relationships obtaining only between individuals."[22]

Although potentially liberating for the daughters of upper- and middle-class white families, Addams's chapter on filial relations, unlike her ones on "Charitable Effort" and "Household Adjustment" does not address the issues of poor women or other ethnic groups. In its focus on empowering women it does call into question some of the basic assumptions underlying what Patricia Hill Collins calls "the normative yardstick developed from the experiences of middle-class American and European nuclear families" that formed the basis of traditional social science research, but because it ignored the family experiences of African-American women, it is still deficient as a model of liberation. Even while recognizing and criticizing some aspects of a form of family life which disadvantages women, it reproduces other aspects of "the archetypal white, middle-class nuclear family [which] divides family life into two oppositional spheres: the 'male' sphere of economic providing and the 'female' sphere of affective nurturing." [23] This should not be surprising, because until such differently situated experiences as those of Collins and Addams's contemporary, Ida B. Wells-Barnett, are developed into theory and welcomed as necessary contributions to the ongoing discourse on women and families, what precisely is deficient in such necessarily limited analyses will not be recognized by those not so situated.

2. THE CONCRETE SITUATION

Pragmatists developed their theories of ethics in response to the great social, cultural, economic, and political upheavals of their time. They were not simply reactive, however, but developed their own complex and coherent ethical theories because none of the traditional ones were found adequate for dealing with new findings on individual developmental processes within a dynamic social situation and the changing conditions of life. It was this engagement with the pressing issues of the day that attracted women and blacks to pragmatist philosophy, and they utilized its resources to redress inequities that they could not ignore in their own lives. It has already been mentioned that Jesse Taft wrote a dissertation at the University of Chicago connecting the rise of industrialization to the oppression of women. According to Leonard Harris, Alain Locke, a black undergraduate studying philosophy at Harvard from 1904 to 1907, "maintained a high regard for [Josiah] Royce's uniqueness, as a Californian who was out of place among the Bostonians and other New Englanders at Harvard and as the only major American philosopher during the early 1900s to publish a book condemning racism," namely, *Race Question, Provincialism, and Other American Problems*.[24] W. E. B. Du Bois gave a brilliant commencement speech when he received a bachelor's degree in philosophy *cum laude* in 1890, deliberately choosing a subject that would force Harvard and the nation to acknowledge the connection between a cherished national and cultural ideal of individualism coupled with the rule of might and the perpetuation of slavery as illustrated in the person of Jefferson Davis. He drove home the point: "To say that a nation is in the way of civilization is a contradiction in terms and a system of human culture whose principle is the rise of one race on the ruins of another is a farce and a lie." [25]

In looking over Dewey's voluminous writings one is hard-pressed to find an issue that he did not address. It is this pervasive concern with the most pressing issues of the day, with the intention of radically transforming the conditions responsible for suffering and oppression, that contribute to the attraction pragmatism holds for feminism. Consider the following list from Dewey's *Ethics:*

> Nationalism and internationalism, capital and labor, war and peace, science and religious tradition, competition and cooperation, *laissez faire* and State planning in industry, democracy and dictatorship in government, rural and city life, personal work and control *versus* investment and vicarious riches through stocks and bonds, native born and alien, contact of Jew and Gentile, of white and colored, of Catholic and Protestant, and those of new religions: a multitude of such relationships have brought to the fore new moral problems with which neither old customs nor beliefs are competent to cope. (*LW*7:177)

Male/female and homosexual/heterosexual are two of the few areas missing as sites of conflict, although Dewey did mention now and then how a belief or practice unfairly impacted on women and although he spoke out publicly on such issues as birth control, higher education for women, women's suffrage, and empowerment of elementary school teachers.[26] The principles by which the other issues were addressed, however, are as applicable to issues involving women as to the others; for instance, that gender cannot be adequately understood in isolation from other factors such as class and race because relationships are multiple and interactive. This is not to imply that by reflecting on how ethical issues especially impact on women the terms of the debate will not be reconstructed. We have to turn to the women pragmatists for a sustained treatment of ethics and gender issues, just as we have to turn to W. E. B. Du Bois and Alain Locke among those who studied with the academic pragmatists and to social activists such as Ida B. Wells-Barnett and Mary McLeod Bethune for extensive critical analyses of racism and sexism.

All of Gilman's major works, beginning with her groundbreaking *Women and Economics* and continuing through *The Home, Human Work, The Man-Made World,* and *His Religion and Hers,* focused on liberating women. According to Gilman, "Our dawning social consciousness finds us bound, suffering, thwarted, starved, crippled in many ways. The more we see the possible joy of human living, the more painful become present conditions—if unchangeable. But they are changeable." In her shorter talks and articles she raised ethical issues: "The Ethics of Woman's Work" (1894), "Superfluous Women" (1900), "Domestic Economy" (1904), "Why Cooperative Housekeeping Fails" (1907), "Feminism" (ca. 1908), "Should Women Use Violence?" (1912), "Birth Control" (1915), "Maternity Benefits and Reformers" (1916), and "A Word with the Pacifists on How to End this War" (1916).[27] Unfortunately, her one book on ethics, *Social Ethics*, which was serialized in *The Forerunner*, is among her weakest. Like other pragmatists, she argues the need for getting beyond individualistic and family ethics to a more inclusive social ethics, criticizes empty generalizations in favor of studying antecedent influences on conduct as well as the particular conditions of "a given people in a given locality," and bases morality on the social nature of human development and the fact that "we are braided and woven together, a living tissue; and what one does is modified, inevitably, by what the others do."[28] However, the work is marred by her prejudices and Social Darwinist allegiances, as well as by the superficiality of some of her analyses and her suggestions for reform. She uncritically believes in the Lamarckian premise of the inheritance of acquired characteristics and in the inevitable progress of humanity, and she thinks of Jews, Africans, native Americans, and the poor as "primitives" who are lower on the evolutionary scale.

More consistently in tune with pragmatist principles, Jane Addams pays particular attention to women, ethnic minorities, and the often destitute working-class while covering a dizzying array of social issues in *Twenty Years at Hull-House*. Although national women's organizations were segregated and although white women reformers generally ignored issues important to blacks, Hull House seems an exception in interracial efforts: "In Chicago, for instance, white settlement and charity workers joined black reformers in campaigning for public services for dependent children, establishing the Chicago Urban League, and responding to the 1919 race riot."[29] In *The Second Twenty years at Hull-House* her concern for women and her multicultural interests expand to international ones, including, but not limited to, women's involvement in suffrage and peace movements. The first three chapters in *Democracy and Social Ethics* directly address ethical issues that arise in women's lives: "Charitable Effort," "Filial Relations," and "Household Adjustment." Nor are women ignored in the other three: "Industrial Amelioration," "Educational Methods," and "Political Reform." She emphasizes the "white-slave traffic" aspect of prostitution in *A New Conscience and an Ancient Evil.* Her active engagement and leadership in women's international peace movements is reflected in *Newer Ideals of Peace* and *Peace and Bread in Time of War.* Regrettably, there were occasional failures to listen to and take seriously the concerns of black women. Mary Church Terrell, for example, resigned from the executive board of the International League for Peace and Freedom, headed by Addams, because the league sponsored a petition calling for the removal from Germany of black soldiers for allegedly committing "terrible crimes against women," while ignoring the slaughter of almost 3,000 Haitians and the mass rape and murder of Haitian women perpetrated by white soldiers when the United States occupied Haiti.[30]

3. JAMES ON PARTIALITY AND IMPARTIALITY (*PP*, II, 1266–67)

Like many contemporary feminist moralists, William James argues against universal moral judgments derived from the application of abstract rules because such judgments unjustly ignore the web of relationships that constitutes the uniqueness of each person and her particular circumstances. Unlike contemporary feminists and the other pragmatists, however, he uses this criticism to undercut moral arguments for granting women equal rights. An examination of how James uses a defense of partiality to continue women's oppression and how Addams and Dewey relate it to the complementary value of impartiality to overcome oppression, should contribute to understanding what pragmatist feminists mean when they stress the priority of the concrete situation.

James says that we instinctively judge differently according to whether an issue pertains to us or to someone else. But this habitual way of thinking gets overturned as we learn to extend our judgment of what is right for us to others similarly placed. James thinks that extending this logical consistency in moral judgments so far that every difference is subsumed under some more general kind or class leads to fanaticism. A central problem of morality, therefore, is to determine when differences matter. There is no general rule in ethics that would automatically determine when a concrete case should be treated as unique and when it should be subsumed under a general kind, any more than there is a heuristic for identifying what marks of phenomena uniquely designate it and what are similar to others.

James, consistent with his pluralism, antireductionism, and concern for the value of each individual, no matter how much she or he differs from the norm, is more intent on defending difference than in extending the realm of universal judgments. He concedes that reasoning is immensely simplified the more that essential characteristics of being human are multiplied. With regard to that characteristic, we become substitutable for one another. If we are all equally human regardless of ethnicity, then a job cannot be ethically assigned on the basis that one of us is a Latino, another African-American, and a third of Irish descent. But instead of emphasizing the emancipatory aspects of such a disregard for difference as I just did in the example given, James dwells on its dangers.

A justice that subsumes all differences into abstract kinds, not distin-

guishing between or favoring Latinos or African-Americans or Eurameri-
cans, but considering them generically simply as members of the class of
'ethnicity,' represents "the Mephistophhelian point of view." This is ex-
emplified in the attitude of conquerors like Napoleon for whom the difference between German or Russian means nothing, since everyone can
be subsumed under a more general class of subject or citizen. "Pure rationalism, complete immunity from prejudice, consists in refusing to see
that the case before one is absolutely unique" (*PP,* II, 1267, n. 35). The
startling conclusion is that complete immunity from prejudice would
mean complete erasure of difference. James gives the example of the
history of the Jews and the Scots, with all their sectarian disputes, loyal-
ties, and patriotism evolving into a priceless heritage, often dramatically
represented by geniuses in story and song. Without their exclusions,
their refusals to assimilate, they would have no common heritage or
greatness as a people.

James thinks that the more judgments of justice or equity are extended to every facet of life, "the more wildly radical and unconditional
will be the justice aspired to." Individual facts, which are better assessed
through tact, are ignored in the mechanical application of a general rule
to a particular case. In a footnote he illustrates what he means by wildly
radical justice:

> A gentleman told me that he had a conclusive argument for opening the
> Harvard Medical School to women. It was this: "Are not women hu-
> man?"—which major premise of course had to be granted. "Then are they
> not entitled to all the rights of humanity?" My friend said that he had
> never met anyone who could successfully meet this reasoning (*PP,* II, 1266,
> n. 34).

James is afraid that in granting the abstract equality of women with men,
all that makes women unique and distinctively valuable as women will be
lost. Better to retain "the mists of affection," the "swamp-lights of sentimentality," than to embrace "naked equality" (*PP,* II, n. 35).

James's discussion of justice or equity versus partiality is compromised because it directly bears on his defense of women's subordination
to men. Appeals to equality deny the differences by which the privileged
justified their privilege. In arguing against abstract equality, he fears the
loss of his own uniqueness, since he would then be "substitutable for
other men." However, the actual example he gives of the negative outcome of blindly adhering to the value of equality is that of women being
admitted to medical school on an equal basis with men.

James criticizes the usual understanding of justice as universal because it leads to an impoverished sense of equality in which differences
are systematically eliminated until only what is held in common is re-

spected. He points out that nothing which constitutes women's distinctive qualities, situations, or values can be considered ethically relevant under such a definition of justice. But this would deny significant aspects of being human that follow from our nature as gendered individuals, and it cannot fail to diminish women's dignity and limit her redress of grievances. It is disconcerting to find James using the distinction between justice as equality and justice as recognizing relevant differences to argue for partiality precisely because it would prevent women from competing directly with men or from assuming many of their rights.

Lest there be any doubt that, like some feminists today, James is arguing for partiality as against impartiality as a better moral stance, there are two contiguous footnotes in *Principles* where he briefly develops a version of the conflict Gilligan characterizes as that of Kantian universalism versus caring (*PP,* II, 1266, n. 34 and 1267, n. 35). It is true that James's sexism distorts his conclusions and must be rejected, but the ways the issues are raised are worth recalling because they can still shed light on current debates. Purely rational determinations of justice end in fanaticism because they ignore what remains absolutely unique. The more general the heading under which individuals are classified, the more those differences that together constitute the person are lost. Sometimes the differences are relevant and sometimes they are not, but James cannot give any "general rule for deciding when it is morally useful to treat a concrete case as *sui generis,* and when to lump it with others in an abstract class" (*PP,* II, 1266–67).

Thanks in no small part to the struggles of blacks, lesbians, gays, feminists, and so on, we no longer consider the justice arrived at in the medical school example as being "wildly radical." Although it is only recently that women have been admitted to medical schools in great numbers, the more radical demands center on restructuring the whole medical system to be less authoritarian and more responsive to human needs. But, as James would also likely point out, the admission of women to medical schools is not due to the fact that the abstract logic of the case has now prevailed. Our attitudinal change is the direct result of new self-definitions, new social groupings, and many struggles to wrest power from those unwilling to relinquish it. Feminists in health care reform are also arguing that it is just to take women's different reproductive capacity into account when funding and treating medical needs.

None of the other pragmatists, women or men, draw the misogynistic conclusions that James does from recognizing that significant differences ought to counter the leveling effects of identifying justice with an abstract notion of equality. Jane Addams's statement that "self-righteousness is responsible for the most subtle forms of lawlessness" is similar to James's that "the logical stickler for justice always seems pedantic and mechanical to the man who goes by tact and the particular instance." They are also making similar points in that the statement is a commentary on a grisly incident in which a judge in his zeal that justice should prevail had condemned his son to death and then hanged him with his own hands when the other officials refused to do so, thus treating the young man as merely a specific instance of the genus *criminal* rather than as someone intimately related to him.[31]

In her chapter, "Efforts to Humanize Justice," Addams uses three specific examples of what she calls a trend to wider justice to show that taking into consideration the circumstances in which crimes are committed leads to a more humane understanding of justice. Differences are relevant because they help us to understand the social context of deviance, thus providing means both to more effectively remedy the conditions that contribute to it and to rehabilitate the offender. The three trends to a more intelligent justice are the establishment of a clinic for the psychiatric study of delinquent children in connection with the Juvenile Court in Chicago, the extension of legal protection to prostitutes, and attempts to extend justice to immigrants or 'aliens.' It turned out that the only examples Addams could find of the last trend are all negative. They include the imperialist expropriation of Mexican oil by United States corporations aided by the American government and the 1927 trial and execution of Sacco and Vanzetti. Addams, along with many people the world over, believed that the two Italians "were being tried on their religious, political or racial affiliations, which they instinctively realized has been the historic basis of intolerance."[32]

Differences are also relevant to a more humane justice because justice between individuals and nations can only come about through mutual understanding and goodwill. Typically, Addams draws parallels between local and international situations to illustrate her claim. Two institutional expressions of the sympathetic understanding that enlarges the sphere of justice were the establishment in 1899 of the first Juvenile Court because existing courts were not meeting the needs of children and of the World Court at The Hague in Holland to arbitrate international disputes instead of settling them by engaging in acts of aggression. The uniting of the distinctive ethnic points of view of judges drawn from the various nations held out the possibility of developing "a wider conception of justice than any one nation has as yet been able to obtain."[33]

Dewey reflects on partiality and impartiality in the context of his discussion of thinking, defined as "the intentional endeavor to discover *specific* connections between something which we do and the consequences which result, so that the two become continuous." Neither of its opposites—routine and capricious behavior—accepts the responsibility for the future consequences of present action that mark reflection. Thinking starts with something going on, but still incomplete and not yet fulfilled, and it projects possible or probable outcomes. "Reflection also implies concern with the issue—a certain sympathetic identification of our own destiny, if only dramatic, with the outcome of the course of events." But we are often flagrantly partisan, as shown in our tendency to identify ourselves with one course of action and reject others. If we cannot engage in overt action, we often take sides emotionally and imaginatively. In fact, were we to be totally indifferent to outcomes we would have no incentive at all for thinking about what is happening at all (*MW* 9:152–54).

This insight that thinking involves caring about outcomes leads to one of the chief paradoxes of thought: "Born in partiality, in order to accomplish its tasks it must achieve a certain detached impartiality." But emotional identification with one course of action can so affect our observations and interpretations of situations that we miscalculate. However, a distinction can be made between motive and value; that is, between recognizing "that the occasion of reflection lies in a personal sharing in what is going on" and that the value of reflection consists in detaching ourselves from it sufficiently to take a neutral stance. That this is so difficult is shown by the fact that thinking originates in situations where our attitudes are intended to influence the outcome and not just passively observe them.[34] Rather than conclude from the fact of the partiality of human reflection either that all thinking is hopelessly self-interested and will necessarily distort or to simply proceed as if we could adopt a neutral stance merely by willing to do so, Dewey concludes that "only gradually and with a widening of the area of vision through a growth of social sympathies does thinking develop to include what lies beyond our *direct* interests: a fact of great significance for education" (*MW* 9:154–55).

4. ETHICAL INSTRUMENTALISM: THE MEANS-ENDS CONTINUUM

If the majority of introductory ethics texts are any guide, ethics is often taught as a series of dichotomies: either hedonism or stoicism, either Kantian deontological ethics or consequentialist ethics like utilitarianism, either communitarianism or abstract individualism, either rule-governed behavior or a life incorporating virtue, and so on through debates over essentialism or relativism, subjectivism or objectivism, freedom or determination. Scholarly discourses reproduce these sharply etched dichotomies. One of the deepest divides is between motive and acts. Their differences have been transformed into an antithesis so strong that actions are often conceived as being irrelevant to the determination of moral goodness or badness. Take the example of dropping bombs on Dresden during the Second World War or of dropping atomic bombs on Hiroshima and Nagasaki. If one means well and intends no evil, then the fact that thousands, even hundreds of thousands, died as the result of one's decision is taken as being regrettable but not morally relevant. Contrast this moral judgment with the condemnation of the Vietnamese War actions that became known as the My Lai massacre. Although far fewer people died, the action was condemned as morally wrong because the soldiers were motivated by revenge and not by justice.

A strong, even dominant tradition in ethics argues that motives or dispositions constitute the essential moral act because actions are accidental, not completely under our control, and morally ambiguous. Deeply embedded in this thinking is the attractiveness of the spirituality of a hidden and inner life and a denigration of the physicality of bodily actions. The alternative is taken to be some variation of the naturalistic fallacy. The old chestnut of not deriving *ought* from *is* still surfaces in the repeated reminders that morality cannot be determined by any factual state of affairs.

This extreme dichotomizing is the result of a faulty psychology that can be traced back from modern times to Descartes. Susan Bordo attributes it to the exaggerated identification and achievement of masculine gender through opposition to the feminine, which was brought on by anxieties surfacing at a particular historical moment.[35] Marxists attribute it to the ideology of isolated individualism that resulted from the rise of capitalism. James, in pondering on the elimination of subjectivity from discourse that sought to be objective, attributes it to the success of the positivist understanding of science. Positivist science denigrated feeling as belonging to the unscientific half of existence, thus contributing to belief in a separate realm of inner states. Dewey attributes the separation of mind and matter, of elevating the ideal and the spiritual to the highest state and lowering esteem for material and worldly concerns to the economic and political class divisions of earlier eras, formalized in classical Greek philosophy.[36] Since slaves and artisans did all the physical work as a means to the good life of their masters, rational and theoretical knowledge was esteemed the proper concern of aristocrats and free citizens and was sharply distinguished from practical knowledge as menial labor.

Although we are no longer in a slave society or feudal era, Dewey argues that the consequences of the division between the ideal and the menial, theory and practice, continue to negatively affect our thinking. This claim is not only repeated in many of his writings, but his genealogical account of this fundamental dualism of spirit and matter, rational and practical knowledge, which is recounted in order to refute its basic premises, is absolutely central to revisioning philosophy in pragmatist terms. By its means he can account for and criticize the philosophical preoccupation with knowledge of Being or Reality rather than with knowledge attainable by the methods used by the special sciences. As a direct consequence of this fixation on Being, the chief problems of modern philosophers have for some time centered on the possibility of knowledge. They restrict their investigation to uncovering the conditions of knowing that must be satisfied to attain this Reality hidden behind particular instances of scientific knowledge, rather than employing what is already known to discovering and carrying out the task of philosophy. This task is taken by Dewey to be the ancient one of the search for wisdom, which he distinguishes from the search for knowledge "in being the application of what is known to intelligent conduct of the affairs of human life" (*LW* 15:157).

Given the crucial role that Dewey's deconstruction of the mind/body, theory/practice dualism as first formulated in Greek philosophy plays in his defense and explanation of pragmatic philosophy over the years, it is worth remarking that he is rather vague on why it is that this protean dualism survived and even generated more dualisms after the social and economic conditions that generated it no longer existed. According to Dewey, these and related distinctions have their origins in the need for slaveholders and citizens to distance themselves from the menial work of their slaves and artisans, but they were not seriously challenged until the rise of modern science. He says that although we have moved away from downright slavery and feudal serfdom, "the conditions of present life still perpetuate a division between activities which are relatively base and menial and those which are free and ideal" (*LW* 15:164).

But what these conditions are he does not make clear, beyond mentioning the fact that educators distinguish liberal studies from the mechanical arts, that economic theories isolate commercial and financial affairs from political and moral concerns, and that philosophers positively bristle with related dualisms. But surely these three examples are more effect than cause, more reflections of the original dualism than explanations for its surprising longevity. Gilman and Jessie Taft supply one of the missing links by showing that the same dualisms generated in slave societies were replicated in the relation of male to female, a relationship that has persisted into modern times. Wells-Barnett, Du Bois, Locke, and many other black theorists supply another by arguing that white society has not moved any great distance from slavery in regard to blacks and that colonialism is still another way of perpetuating the myth by which self-defined superior cultures can continue to appropriate the work and resources of those supposedly less advanced.

Dewey finds it ironic that as problems multiply in every aspect of modern life and require the attention of the best thinking we can muster if they are to be solved or alleviated, philosophers subordinate them more and more to an alleged problem of knowledge. Meanwhile scientific and technological breakthroughs change the conditions of everyday life so extensively that the more philosophers continue to question whether such knowledge has any foundation, the more esoteric and out of touch they seem to be to the general public. When so much is at stake, continued preoccupation with hoary problems of the *conditions* of knowledge seems strangely detached, if not actually reckless, in face of the vital problems of its *consequences* (*LW* 15 : 158).

Dewey finds it ironic that the more the sciences, such as economics, determine the conditions in which most of us live, the less they are reflectively used to determine humane and moral ends. But without such a free and systematic approach, actual determination of ends and values are left to "custom, prejudice, class interests, and traditions embodied in institutions whose results are mostly fixed by the superior power in possession of those who manage them" (*LW* 15 : 158). Philosophers encourage this state of affairs to the degree that they are preoccupied with a higher Reality, approached by way of quasi-mathematical symbolisms, and by continually rehashing issues, they neglect the search for wisdom.

Some philosophical approaches so subjectify values as private and personal affairs that they cannot be intelligently determined or judged on objective grounds. As intrinsic values or ends in themselves they are sharply demarcated from extrinsic or instrumental values. Instrumental values, when understood as mere means, can be the proper subject of scientific research, but "the 'ends' they serve (ends which are truly ends) are just matters of what groups, classes, sects, races, or whatever, happen irrationally to like or dislike" (*LW* 15 : 159). Meanwhile the actual conditions under which persons live, their relative advantage or disadvantage, happiness or misery, are decided by what this position would label a mere means, while their consequences are left to irrational habits, sectarian interests, religious fanaticism, and entrenched powers. If science instantiates only values that are merely means, then there is no significant difference between the use of atomic energy to destroy humans in war or to cure humans in medical applications.

In order to prepare the way for science and technology to perform a more humane and social function, philosophy has to purge itself of the doctrines originating in conditions of slavery that justify the continued separation of mind and matter and other pernicious dualisms. One that has had the worst consequences for ethics and social/political philosophy is the distinction of values that are intrinsic and final from those that are extrinsic and instrumental. Unless this prescientific, predemocratic assertion of the disjunction of the instrumental and the final is undermined, it will continue to hinder philosophers from taking an active part in utilizing the present scientific and technological resources to improve human affairs.[37] The entrenched habit of treating the economic situation, housework, childcare, and access to healthcare, as mere means with no intrinsic connection to ultimate or moral ends guarantees that solutions to social ills will be proposed that are so ideal as to be utopian and ineffective. Rather than walling off areas of utmost human concern from concrete investigations and restricting their moral cogency to personal exhortation or debate over principles and precepts, the initial step in solving them "demands systematic observation of the natural, the biological and societal, conditions by means of which knowing actually goes on" (*LW* 15:167).

When once means are recognized as means, that is, as intermediaries to some end, then to criticize a value as being merely instrumental because unconnected to ends no longer makes sense. When understood as a course of action that takes place over time, means can only be so in view of some end, just as ends are the conclusions of means. "The 'end' is merely a series of acts viewed at a remote stage; and a means is merely the series viewed at an earlier one." Means and ends are one reality, distinguished in judgment. To think of the end is to "extend and enlarge our view of the act to be performed." The result of denigrating means is to lessen the likelihood of realizing ends (*LW* 14:27–28).

The notion that there are ends in themselves distinct from ends that are mere means is a relic of a prescientific age, which did not have the resources, conceptual or technological, for realizing that there are no ends that are not also means. This continuum of means and ends is best shown in Dewey's theory of inquiry. It also demonstrates his otherwise puzzling assertion that moral ends are theoretically as subject to the same kind of "objective" factual determination as are technological ends (*LW* 15:165).[38]

Pragmatism, parting ways with a philosophical fixation on Reality and its epistemological and moral dualisms, affirms that the purpose of philosophy is the search for wisdom that consists in "search for the ends and values that give direction to our collective human activity" (*LW* 15:161). The best knowledge and methods we have available, namely scientific, are used in this search. Pragmatism is also called experimentalism or instrumentalism because it extends the scientific methodology and knowledge from physical matters to social and distinctively human affairs. Many of the remediable ills of the present time continue because the best insights and methods of science have not been brought to bear on them, but instead are left to power struggles and halfhearted hit-or-miss attempts at solutions.

Given this call for a shift in philosophical approach to the scientific projection of hypotheses as to the ways that social change may be brought about, it is extremely important to understand what pragmatists mean by science. A clue can be found when Dewey turns away from his negative criticism of the fundamental dualism of mind and matter to the constructive work of philosophy in bringing the best scientific resources to bear on social problems and conflicts. He says that philosophy cannot itself resolve such problems: "Only the associated members of the world can do this work in cooperative action." Philosophers can help by projecting leading ideas or plans of action and perfecting the tools used. "The initial step is to promote general recognition that knowing, including most emphatically scientific knowledge, is not outside social activity, but is itself a form of social behavior" (*LW* 15:166–67).

5. READING DEWEY'S NATURALIZED MORALITY FOR WHAT IT SAYS ABOUT WOMEN

My selective reading of Dewey's *Human Nature and Conduct* will explain only as much of his naturalized morality as is needed to understand the few direct references he makes to women or femaleness.[39] Even within these restrictive and therefore distorting parameters, it is possible to recognize the feminist potential of his project of historicizing human nature, of contextualizing human practices in an experimental morality, and his demonstration of the oppressiveness of moral claims to universality.

Dewey rejects the privatization of morality, whether this is taken to mean that moral good or virtue is something intrinsic and complete in itself or to consist in the cultivation of a certain feeling state. This interiorization deprives the agent of any objective criterion for determining the rightness or wrongness of acts. He appeals to our commonsense understanding of will as the initiator of action to debunk the Kantian noumenal will, which is unaffected by and essentially indifferent to the phenomenal world of physical events. Dewey, along with other pragmatists, defines dispositions, whether virtuous or not, as "tendencies to act." The tendency and its enactment form a temporal whole that can only be reflectively distinguished, either in prospect or retrospect. But both are needed to define a moral situation. "Consequences fix the moral quality of an act" and "on the whole, or in the long run but not unqualifiedly, consequences are what they are because of the nature of desire and disposition" (*MW* 14:33–34).

When once it is realized that absolute claims to privileged access to true reality or self-evident good are disguised forms of domination, then a morality freed of such delusions must be experimental. Since will means, concretely, habits, "and habits incorporate an environment within themselves," the fact that environments, especially social environments, change over time means that new habits can develop only by anticipating changes not yet fully realized. Such anticipations can best be characterized as "working hypotheses[,] corrected and developed by events as action proceeds" (*MW* 14:38–41).

Dewey connects the scientific revolution that began in the seventeenth century with a revolution in moral ideals. The revolutionary breakthrough was the recognition of the continuity in space and time of natural events with other events and the understanding of knowledge as experimental inquiries that reveal a multitude of minute, obscure, and interacting relationships. The same situation holds with respect to moral ideals of peace, justice, human sisterhood and brotherhood, and equality, none of which can simply be introspected, but which "can be known only by extensive and minute observation of consequences incurred in action." The psychology of the isolated self and the moral subjectivism predicated on it ignore this connection of habits, acts, and consequences, and therefore cannot defend the objectivity of morals. This false subjectivity also ignores what constitutes the moral relevance of the subject; that is, the power of desire and thought to break down old rigidities of habit and prepare the way for acts that re-create an environment (*MW* 14:41–42).

In *The Dewey School* Edwards emphasizes this pragmatic interaction of self and environment within a pragmatic hermeneutics of self and society by quoting Mead to the effect that "in a moral act, the will, the idea, and the consequences are all placed inside the act, and the act itself only within the larger activity of the individual in the society." She comments, "From this corollary to the theory's principle of growth it follows that mental and moral growth results from intelligent action only when action is motivated by social concern and directed to social ends." [40]

For Dewey ethical reflection begins with our situatedness within the world: "For practical purposes morals mean customs, folkways, established collective habits." Individual activity weaves itself out of its strands. "Customs . . . constitute moral standards [f]or they are active demands for certain ways of acting" (*MW* 14:54). Customs are preserved in the individual as habit. Since the routine of habit expresses continuity, breaches are often looked on as violations of right, and deviations as transgressions. Interfering with habitual ways of acting in a culture too often breeds resentment and avenging force.

Nonetheless, customs can and should be intelligently questioned. But reason is not simply the antithesis of custom; the real opposition is "between routine, unintelligent habit, and intelligent habit or art." Just as something has to exist before we perceive it, so moral reasoning "is the offspring of intercourse with objective adaptations and relations," and is not derivable from Platonic essences. Still, in recognizing the relation of facts to outcomes, reason does not just mirror preexisting conditions. "It sets up a heightened emotional appreciation and provides a new motive for fidelities previously blind. It sets up an attitude of criticism, of inquiry, and makes men sensitive to the brutalities and extravagancies of customs." Once customs are subjected to critical inquiry, as they were in ancient Greece, Dewey argues, new expectations arise, leading to the establishment of new customs, thus having a revolutionary potential. But in his time it is evident that women, industrial workers, and members of despised ethnic groups were among those most sensitized to the brutalities of customs and who therefore realized the revolutionary potential of critical inquiry (*MW* 14:55–56).

Since Plato located the source of the critique of customs in an ideal realm, with transcendental qualities and standards, he lost the connection between the everyday world of custom and a better way of life. Individual creative initiative becomes antithetical to its own conditions of growth and development, thus opening the door to unbridled extremism. Instead of redirecting forces, it often aims to eradicate them. Family life, like other social institutions, was not developed according to rational standards. Therefore, the mere fact that it exists according to a particular pattern does not have the sanction of rational justification. Yet it *is* a part of the fabric of life, and life does have a hold on us, one that rationalists tend to ignore.

Like all human organizations, the family can stagnate, retrogress, or progress; it can be suppressed or thoughtfully directed to better ends by employing better means. Dewey, Mead, and Tufts, for instance, questioned a form of family life that stunted women's and children's moral/ social growth, while Gilman, Addams, Jessie Taft, and Ethel Puffer Howes developed detailed criticisms of the subjection of women and children by traditional family forms and systematically developed alternatives. Gilman was the most explicit in identifying patriarchy as the cause of women's oppression and in incorporating this insight into her analyses and her concrete proposals for change. She says that "given a proprietary family, where the man holds the woman primarily for his satisfaction and service—then necessarily he shuts her up and keeps her for these purposes. Being so kept, she cannot develop humanly, as he has, through social contract, social service, true social life." She draws the unfortunate consequences: "It is not healthy to have a loving servant always ministering to one's desires. Less devotion and more knowledge, less affection and higher grade of skill, are needed." She goes on to draw even more fearsome consequences: "Neither do we realize that this constant ministering service to the personal desire of men in the home is responsible, to a terrible extent, for their helpless self-indulgence in the world outside.[41]

All the pragmatists link women's increasing dissatisfaction in the home to industrialization. Addams, who along with other women at Hull House worked daily among the immigrant poor, also includes the experiences of domestic workers in her criticisms of the family.[42] These working-class women who had to leave their own families in tenements to labor under onerous conditions in the homes of the wealthy were doubly oppressed. The traditional ethics of individual and family codes not only provided no guidance; it contributed to abusive conditions. Untouched by larger social forces or a social ethics, the household employer feels justified in disregarding even the basic human needs of her household workers, all the while fatuously praising the sanctity of the family— her own, of course. Because of the difference in power and status, even those women who do consciously have the goodwill of their servants at heart inevitably fail in practice; under such unequal conditions they can offer only "a simulacrum of companionship." Many other problems encountered by household workers stem from the social discrimination of isolating them from their own families and community life.[43] Addams argues vigorously that women employed in households are worse off than those working in factories—quite a damning accusation, given the miserable working conditions of factory life at the turn of the century.

As many black and hispanic feminists have pointed out, such attitudes and practices as Addams's indictment of the ethnic and class prejudices of middle- and upper-class women, her earnest attempts to understand the situation from the point of view of the working-class poor, and her practice of finding ways for poor women to speak for themselves— such attempts were unfortunately not common among white feminists.[44] Although Gilman consistently stressed the economic component of women's oppression, her attitudes were both racist and classist.[45] Not only does she fail to incorporate into her theories specific differences within and among the experiences of various class and ethnic groups; she often denigrates them. In her criticism of the patriarchal family she gives an example found "among certain more savage African tribes," and she says in another chapter of *The Man-Made World* that "the squaw belongs to a decadent race" and that "she too is subject to man."[46]

As living beings we are always already enmeshed in a web of relations. Critical intelligence is in the service of life when it questions the relative values of customs and seeks to intelligently adopt, direct, and transform them. To assume that an intelligent moral stance is not itself derivative from traditional practices leads paradoxically to deifying a particular tradition and raising it to an absolute, no longer subject to revisioning. In periods of great social change the appeal to immutable standards and purposes leads to "the most serious form of class warfare" (*LW* 14:58).

Segregation into classes evolves standards at variance with the dominant culture. Masculine and feminine virtues are given by Dewey as examples of the development of different working morals arising out of intertwined, but distinct, layers of social strata. With increased mobility these different standards come into conflict. Each side then appeals to its own standards as ultimate, on the one side the ultimateness of the old order, under which its own interests flourished, and on the other side the ultimateness of freedom as the necessary and just condition of change that will allow its submerged claims to be recognized and acted upon (*LW* 14:59).

In 1922 the three class struggles Dewey emphasized as erupting in open conflict were those between the propertied classes and wage earners, between men and women, and between young and old. These are in addition to the conflicts between races and nations. The times are said to be explosive because the various sides recognize no common ground of appeal, each appealing to its own standard of right as ultimate and unassailable and attributing to the other side only base motives "of personal desire, whim or obstinacy" (*LW* 14:59). Dewey does not reflect further on the nature of or solutions to the class conflicts he has brought up, but he ends chapter five abruptly by asserting that only intelligence can reconcile such conflicts. After provocatively raising the possibility of class warfare between women and men, he does not discuss women again in any detail until seven chapters later.

Dewey had, however, already attributed such conflicts as that between the propertied classes and wage earners and between women and men to their adherence to immutable standards. Such nonnegotiable standards develop when classes are rigidly segregated. Over time, the immobility of classes leads them to distinguish not only between noble virtues, such as power, glory, honor and magnificence, and plebian virtues, such as industry, obedience, abstinence, and humility; but also between masculine virtues, such as vigor, courage, energy, and enterprise, and feminine virtues such as submission, patience, charm, and personal fidelity. But as societies become more mobile and classes of various kinds mix, then the side whose interests are best served by the older order proclaim its virtues and the other side "proclaims its rights to freedom and identifies justice with its submerged claims" (*LW* 14:58–59).

Dewey thus gives a genealogy of class warfare and of values distinguished by class, including women as a class, which echoes Nietzsche's. He also argues that those who have a vested interest in present social arrangements are more likely to appeal to an innate human nature or to a natural feminine nature to forestall that reconstruction of self and environment with which morality ought to be concerned (*LW* 14:88). But he not only fails to follow up on his insight that those in power seek to retain it by preventing the very reconstruction of society for which he himself is calling; he actually undercuts the ability of the working class and of women to press the justice of their submerged claims because he does not accept their explanation that the ruling classes are willfully violating moral principles or that they are expressing self-interest or wielding superior might. He does so by not distinguishing between the legitimacy of the claims of the classes in power and those subject to that power, saying simply that both make such claims equally and does not question whether they are equally just in doing so. Dewey also fails to comment on the absurd implication that the subjugated classes have at their disposal the same superior power as those wielding economic, political, military, and patriarchal authority and power.

Finally, he thinks that a reconciliation brought about by intelligence will solve class warfare, where class is broadly construed as including gender. This solution is not as inappropriate as it sounds, given the fact that for him intelligence means effective transformation of the environment according to better ends, that the most important environment for human beings is formed by the activities of other human beings, and that "the most practical of all moral questions [is] the nature of freedom and the means of its achieving" (*LW* 14:8, 60). Nevertheless, downplaying the superior force and myriad means at the disposal of those in power and especially by underestimating the strength of their will to remain in power, Dewey does not provide a sufficient analysis of the conditions of oppression for it to be recognized for what it is and how it can be effectively overcome. In fact, although he had earlier decried the vested interests of the ruling classes of parents, priests, chiefs, and social censors who imposed their aims on reluctant subjects and of "men in authority [who] have turned moral rules into an agency of class supremacy," in neither case does he even name oppression as such, but refers only to conflicting interests (*LW* 14:4–5).

Later chapters undercut traditional appeals to a fixed human nature and to universal natural law by showing how customs and habits are not innate but develop in the socializing of infants. Dewey also draws on the findings of the new discipline of anthropology to illustrate the tremendous diversity of ways of being human. He redefines the nature of humanity as one of directed change over time, substituting continuous reconstruction for the theoretical extremes of appealing to a romantic improvised spontaneity or to a fixed nature or invariant tradition as the bulwark of universal morality.

In chapter 6 Dewey sums up the previous discussion of class conflict as discrediting the split between mind and body and of human beings from nature and as providing evidence for the understanding of the psychology of habit as objective and social, rather than as private and solipsistic. The individuality that has been traditionally ascribed to an ethereal mind is explained instead as a development out of a desire that conflicts with habitual custom. The deliberate assertion of such deviating impulses are the beginning of genuine individuality.

The theme of the alterability of human nature in chapter 9 provides grounds for denying that human nature is correctly defined by traits like aggressiveness, which are traditionally associated with masculinity: "Pugnacity and fear are no more native than are pity and sympathy" (*LW* 14: 79). These emotions are not sexually distinguished but are raised as part of an argument denying that war is inevitable as an expression of a native human aggressiveness and should instead be attributed to complex social interactions. War can only be eliminated as a means for settling disputes between nations when we take seriously enough the task of identifying and eliminating the precise conditions leading to it.

Although Dewey does not fall into the usual error of conflating masculine traits with human ones, neither does he recognize any connection of aggressiveness and war with masculinity, as both Gilman and Addams do, thus providing no insight into what is required to dismantle the social, political, and institutional processes that lead to the exaggeration of aggressiveness and continued recourse to war as a problem-solving technique in the first place. Gilman, on the other hand, distinguishes among traits common to masculinity, femininity, and humanity, and shows that in an androcentric culture like ours masculine traits masquerade as human ones. Her gender traits, on the other hand, are too rigidly construed and she sometimes falls into a biological determinism that could be eliminated by reflecting on Dewey's transactive view of human beings within a nature that is already social.

Having denied that war is inevitable, Dewey attacks the claim that capitalism is inevitable and is justified because it is built on private ownership, which is claimed to be an inexpugnable, because natural, human instinct. The assertion that "no system has ever as yet existed which did not in some form involve the exploitation of some human beings for the advantage of others" does not justify the unbridled competitive struggle for wealth. He directly challenges the Social Darwinism being used to justify the worst excesses of capitalistic exploitation and argues that possessiveness can be interpreted in many ways, not just as manifested in the historically specific economic institution of capitalism. We can imagine a state in which people derive as much proprietary satisfaction from sharing wealth with the community as from private ownership (*LW* 14:82–83). Personal gains might even become synonymous with group profit.

In any case, capitalism falsifies the complexity of the motives for (and satisfactions with) working to reduce them all to the single motive of private profit.

Dewey replaces the bifurcated explanations of human nature in terms of reason and instinct with the more dynamic notion of habit. Habits are not merely repetitive, they also conserve gains won through effort. They stabilize societies and eventually harden into rigid institutional structures, but they are also open to modification. Institutions often appear to be impervious to change, but they are still complexes of habits and as such can be intelligently redirected. Truly radical change cannot be brought about merely through replacing formal structures, however, drastic as such substitutions are. Habits of thought and desire must also change, and this is best effected in young people who have not yet been fully imbued with established customs. Dewey therefore turns to education as the preferred "leverage for changing institutions." The goal is not the replacement of one ideal or ideology for another but the formation of habits "which are more intelligent, more sensitively percipient, more informed with foresight, more aware what they are about, more direct and sincere, more flexibly responsive than those now current" (*LW* 14:88–90).

Against "the material error" that the self is fixed and simple, Dewey argues that selfhood "is in process of making, and that any self is capable of including within itself a number of inconsistent selves, of unharmonized dispositions." The unsubstantiated belief in a univocal self blinds us to the relative fluidity and diversity of the constituents of selfhood. A person can be sympathetically attentive in one situation and harshly arrogant in another. "There is no one ready-made self behind activities," but instead "complex, unstable, opposing attitudes, habits, impulses which gradually come to terms with one another" or else can acquire a deceptive consistency through rigid compartmentalization. The self is not ready-made, but continuously in the making through action, "an experiment in creating a self" (*LW* 14:96–97).

Dewey attacks the mythology of single causality, that is, reducing complex emotional states to a single origin. He gives us an example of this artificial simplification the claim that all instincts are grounded in sexuality, so that to understand conduct one has only to "*cherchez la femme* (under multitudinous symbolic disguises)" (*LW* 14:93). In denying the univocal correspondence between specific acts of fear, maternal love, and sexual desire and an underlying instinct, Dewey does not deny their reality. The stimulus-response model of alleged causal forces is only a lazy way of referring to a variety of complex occurences. The whole developing organism, along with an ever-changing environment, is engaged even in supposedly simple emotional states. Emotions are not just internal states; the expressiveness of emotions changes the situation in which they are expressed. The nature and value of emotional drives cannot be satisfactorily separated from the particulars of their interactive context. Most self-deception is due to taking immediate organic states, such as satisfaction or revulsion, for the value of an act. This ignores the objective effects of acts on others and judgment of the objective or social consequences by others (*LW* 14:104–6).

To illustrate the pragmatist method he has been developing, Dewey gives what can best be described as a feminist critique, one rare enough in his writings to be worth quoting in its entirety.

> The treatment of sex by psycho-analysts is most instructive, for it flagrantly exhibits both the consequences of artificial simplification and the transformation of social results into psychic causes. Writers, usually male, hold forth on the psychology of woman, as if they were dealing with a Platonic universal entity, although they habitually treat men as individual, varying with structure and environment. They treat phenomena which are peculiarly symptoms of the civilization of the West at the present time as if they were the necessary effects of fixed native impulses of human nature. Romantic love as its exists today, with all the varying perturbations it occasions, is as definitely a sign of specific historic conditions as are big battleships with turbines, internal-combustion engines, and electrically driven machines. It would be as sensible to treat the latter as effects of a single psychic cause as to attribute the phenomena of disturbance and conflict which accompany present sexual relations as manifestations of an original single psychic force or *Libido*. Upon this point at least a Marxian simplification is nearer the truth than that of Jung. (*LW* 14:106–7)

Instead of following up on these provocative insights, Dewey immediately turns to fear as his next example of an emotion that has been distorted by the reductive move. He gives so much astute criticism of the beliefs and social structures which oppress women that the reader feels a heightened sense of disappointment that he does not even categorize his analysis as one of exposing women's oppression, nor does he develop its radical implications. In fact, by giving his explanation the status of a mere example of the distortions that result from reductionism, he unwittingly reduces the complexity of his own analysis and defuses its revolutionary potential. A feminist perspective can usefully mine the resources offered in this passage. Grounds are given, for instance, for why what has been taken as private is really public. He shows how treating *woman* as a class while refusing to do the same for *man* exposes the masculinist perspective hidden behind supposedly neutral claims. He unmasks the ethnocentrism of romantic love and its claims for a universal human nature. Finally, even though they are still too simplistic, he should substitute economic explanations for his purely psychological ones, since they at least recognize the social dimensions of human behavior and open a space for moral reconstruction.

Although Dewey does not make the oppressiveness of women's condition a central theme in his work, he neither denies nor downplays it. He includes domestic arrangements in the public sphere as a matter of course, as when he criticizes unbridled capitalism: "Calculated pursuit of gain is in fact never what it is made out to be when economic action is separated from the rest of life, for in fact it is what it is because of a complex social environment involving scientific, legal, political and domestic conditions" (*LW* 14:153). Furthermore, he provides a framework for working out a feminist reconstruction of pragmatism. He regularly criticizes the injustice of contemporary social institutions and develops methods for cooperatively reconstructing a society that is not oppressive.

Dewey opposes revolution only because he believes that the violent overthrow of existing institutions "sweeps away customs and institutions in an undiscriminating avalanche," thus deferring rather than accelerating genuinely radical change (*LW* 14:116). "The short-cut revolutionist" fails to realize that institutions are embodied habits and that the habits of thoughts and feeling behind institutions are not easily altered. Political and legal institutions can be abolished while "the bulk of popular thought which has been shaped to their pattern persists" (*LW* 14:77). Moreover, he denies that violence is attributable only to revolutionists. The very fact of the presence of revolutionaries in a society testifies to the institutionalized violence of those in power, who encourage violent reaction by their refusal to respond positively as new needs emerge. "Life is perpetuated only by renewal." Only those who are themselves engaged in the positive reconstruction of society have the right to criticize those radicals who seek change through destructive means.

Finally, it does not take a great leap of the imagination to revision the supposedly neutral 'man' of the last two sentences of chapter 12 as referring to the androcentrism of those who oppose women's liberation: "Too often the man who should be criticizing institutions expends his energy in criticizing those who would re-form them. What he really objects to is any disturbance of his own vested securities, comforts and privileged powers" (*LW* 14:115).

6. BIRTH CONTROL

The advantages to be gained by reconstructing both feminist and pragmatist positions in response to the perspectives emphasized by each can be illustrated by comparing two articles on birth control, an issue that was as contentiously debated early in the twentieth century as abortion is at the end of it.[47] Gilman's article, "Birth Control," appeared in *The Fore-runner* in 1915 and Dewey's short article, "Education and Birth Control," in *The Nation* in 1932.[48] Both begin by relating birth control to a larger issue. In Gilman's case it is to the eventual threat of overpopulation, while Dewey somewhat melodramatically compares the opposition to the birth control movement to the struggle between darkness and knowledge. By this he means the ignorant, prejudiced opposition to science, particularly when its technological advances affect everyday practices in society.[49] Both appeal to intelligent control of blind natural forces and enlightenment of the public through education; both attribute opposition to unenlightened public sentiment, are against suppression and secrecy, and believe that having too many children too close together prevents the individual attention necessary for their beneficial physical, intellectual, and emotional growth.

Gilman would agree with Dewey that "because knowledge always means increased control" this "conflict between ignorance and knowledge becomes one between chance and control" (*LW* 6:147). But Gilman attributes the prejudice against preventing conception not to technological intrusiveness but to the influence of religious convictions and long-standing beliefs that sex is a natural instinct and should not be interfered with. She also emphasizes women's need to control their sexual activity, since abstinence is a value as well as a means for fertility control, while Dewey emphasizes technology as a new means of control in the area of fertility. In fact, Gilman spends over half of her much longer article arguing against what she takes to be the abnormality of unlimited indulgence in sex. She distances herself from a younger generation of feminists who demand a freer sex life for women by tying sexuality to procreation and criticizing what she sees as increasing indulgence in recreational sex. The biggest difference between the two articles, however, is that Gilman's is woman-centered, while Dewey manages to discuss birth control without ever mentioning women.

Gilman's support of birth control is more ambiguous than Dewey's, especially in her earlier articles. Most of her 1915 article actually argues against three reasons commonly given for supporting the deliberate limitation of offspring. She agrees with the bad effects of too frequent births but attributes them more to the conditions under which maternity is undertaken, rather than to the fact of childbearing itself. The first contention—that economics makes it difficult to raise large families responsibly—is not a natural condition, but one under human control. Resources should be more equitably distributed and a fair standard of living for all should be sought before we accept unjust economic conditions and resort to population control.

The second argument is that frequent childbearing injures women's health, especially when combined with unremitting hard work. Again, Gilman argues that women do not become ill from childbirth as a consequence of their natural infirmity but because of the conditions under which they bear children. Foremost is the fact that the majority of the population earn only subsistence wages, so that many women are underfed as well as overworked, and even middle-class women cannot find needed leisure time for themselves. Even while recommending that women look after their own health through exercise, a position that Gilman advocated early and often, she pointed out that the practical and personal problem remains for the individual mother, who already has many children, is in bad health, and worries that having more may kill her. Such women may legitimately determine that their duty to their families justifies refusing to have more children.

The third reason, which gives Gilman the most trouble, is that safe and free indulgence of the sex instinct is necessary for the perpetuation of the human race. While agreeing that sex has a psychological as well as biological function for humans, Gilman does not think that this entails regular indulgence nor that the main role of contraceptives is to permit such promiscuity. She advocates less frequent intercourse as healthier and preferable, and for those unfortunate women whose partners do not agree, she proposes that the proper methods of contraception be taught by competent physicians. She spends many pages showing that with proper education, the craving for indulgence in sex will decline so much that with no efforts at prevention, the birth rate will dwindle to two or three per family. This third position, common to the "social purity" movement of the 1890s, would find few supporters today.[50]

To counter the enormous preference for unrestrained sexuality, Gilman begins by pointing out that just because a majority of people hold a position does not make it right, nor does the fact that a few people claim to be more enlightened guarantee their position. The evidence she gives for these uncontroversial generalizations is the development of ideas over time. Advances in human history have often begun with one or a few persons going against the majority. Gilman is careful to point out that what she is advocating against the majority position is not better just because it is a minority opinion, but must still be discussed on its merits to determine if it is actually better. A hindrance to doing so is the enormous emotional attachment to traditional beliefs, so much so that Gilman says "the emotional responses of the mass of people are invariably reactionary."[51]

Like Dewey, Gilman distinguishes between the emotions and beliefs we have already, often the result of unreflective habits and traditions, and those that develop after inquiry. Appropriate emotional responses often follow, rather than precede, intellectual perception. Women and men, she says, can be forced by sheer reason and logic to admit the justice of equal suffrage and even act accordingly, yet even after this intellectual and moral stance is adopted, a "womanly woman" can continue to elicit warm feelings of approval, and an "unwomanly woman" cold aversion. Gilman does not elaborate on the prejudices implied in these designations, since she had already done so in great detail in earlier works, such as *The Home: Its Work and Influence, Human Work,* and *Man-Made World.*

Analysis of the many issues involved in birth control naturally brings to mind examples from other areas of concern theoretically and practically—in this case, equal suffrage. Unlike Dewey, who occasionally brings up feminist issues in his nonpolemical writings to illustrate some other point and then drops them, Gilman keeps her focus on women's liberation. She is also acutely aware of the role of feelings in encouraging or discouraging women's greater participation in their own emancipation. What good is it if women secure the vote but do not change their other behavior or attitudes under the continued influence of traditional feelings about women's roles?

Gilman's pragmatism includes the belief that human nature is second nature and that what is considered normal can be gradually modified to different emotional and functional demands. She speaks of a whole range of social emotions and functions which can be changed for the better through changing habits. Even in this area of shared convictions, her feminist outlook has her inventing a word, *e-feminate* to balance *emasculate,* using both words to refer to unwarranted fears raised by her call for changed sexual habits.[52] She argues that a psychology developed over the years through the arts, such as sculpture, stories, drama, and religion, not only reinforces the sex drive in humans, but it does so differentially for women and men, since it was elaborated "by the sex which has the most to gain and the least to lose by upholding such a standard."

In later testimony in a hearing by the Ways and Means Committee of the United States House of Representatives on a bill to allow doctors and medical institutions to use the mails to transmit contraceptive information, held in the same year Dewey's article appeared in The *Nation,* Gilman came out more strongly for birth control than she had previously. Her feminist focus on women is even more direct:

> I wish any of you would for the moment use your imagination and think of what it is to the woman, either by coercion or compulsion or persuasion to have forced upon her, as it were, another life within her to carry, to bear, to bring forth, to nurse, when she does not want to. When she does want to

she is free to. There is nothing to prevent her. The whole thing hinges on that; the woman who does not want more children must not be made to bear them.[53]

Dewey supported the bill in a short piece for the *People's Lobby Bulletin*. In "The Senate Birth Control" he uses the rhetorical device of borrowing from opponents their claim to be representing the conservative position, much as today's liberals claim that their proposals are more family-oriented than the vaunted family values of conservatives.[54] In an argument that could also be aimed at the Reagan-era gag rule forbidding doctors to discuss abortion as a birth control option with their patients, Dewey points out that the bill is already conservative in that it limits those authorized to give out information to medical societies, schools, and journals. He warns that the governmental prohibition of scientific information would one day be compared to earlier witch-hunts. The bill is also conservative in that it seeks to "conserve human life and well being, that of mothers, of children, of families." It aims at a birth control method that would lessen the need for abortions and encourage recourse to competent physicians rather than quacks. Dewey asks, "Can anything more absurd be imagined, than that clinics should be established for the care of women, and that a reputable physician should be guilty of a crime if he gives information as to the location of these clinics, to a woman needing care?" This complaint and a final statement are eerily prescient of today's abortion debate: "But it is un-American, undemocratic, and despotic, for those groups to attempt to use legislation to create crimes, in order to impose their special moral views upon others."[55]

Eleven

Cooperative Intelligence

I have struggled with various combinations and permutations of the relations of women and men who identified with pragmatist philosophy and of various formulations of feminism and pragmatism. I have been asking whether pragmatist-identified women were feminists, whether any feminists were pragmatists, what each has contributed to the other, and what each might find lacking in the other. It is now time to ask whether the distinctions can be dropped. In an effort to identify a common core of theoretical positions and concrete practices, is there finally any significant difference between a feminist pragmatism and a pragmatist feminism?

As the preceding chapters attest, feminist and pragmatist interests have historically both converged and diverged, and therefore it still makes sense to talk of feminists who were pragmatists and pragmatists who were feminists. But it should also be obvious that the pluralism and emancipatory goals of pragmatism require that feminist issues be addressed and incorporated into the continuous theoretical revisioning that arises from new cultural, political, and economic experiences. On the other hand, feminist theories are pluralist by default, if not always by intent, and pragmatism can be recognized as one promising variant. As with other varieties of feminism, it can also be used as a theoretical framework according to which the other varieties can be related as contributing perspectives.

Feminist theory at the end of the twentieth century is more vigorous and prolific than at the beginning of the century, but more fragmented than ever before. Despite the view from the outside that still tars feminism with one broad brush, there have always been divisions within feminism, and these divisions have made their way into many introductory texts and anthologies. This diversity has often been seen as a scandal.

Many still fervently hoped that with some modifications all the various positions would eventually coalesce into one coherent theory of women's oppression and liberation—either that, or others would eventually be convinced of the superiority of one's own position. But a few recent books may be a harbinger of a shift in expectations. Along with the proliferation of theories claiming to correct what has been wrong so far, mostly by complicating them through added complexity, a less ambitious note has been struck. A pragmatist recognition of the power of diversity is evident in such titles as *Theorizing Black Feminisms* and *Living With Contradictions*.

There is more willingness to live with differences and even welcome them as evidence of the continuing vitality of the feminist movement. While feminism itself continues to be for some the overarching theory and practice that encompasses all the rest, for others it has assumed the status of one liberatory perspective among others. While some still insist that their liberal or lesbian or third-world or Afrocentric, or whatever version of feminism is what truly defines feminism, others are beginning to recognize that the prolific, even chaotic, character of experience can never be adequately captured in any theory, no matter how complex or synthetic. In this increasing diversity of interests, values, and perspectives, feminism is coming to resemble less and less a single-minded theory or ideology and to reflect more and more the teeming multiplicity of the world from which it arises. At the same time, its emancipatory focus on women, however construed, relates the various strands of feminist theory to one another and provides grounds for challenging any particular preference of means and ends.

With these more recent perspectival shifts, many of the pragmatist/feminist themes gain in relevance.[1] Important contemporary issues seem to be merging with the feminist/pragmatist issues:

Fundamental to all of them is the recognition of the continuum of experience, knowledge, values, and praxis. This recognition is responsible for the rejection of philosophy as an epistemology industry and the development of it instead as an emancipatory process and transformative practice. Inquiry has a context; it is a function of experience, the dynamics of which are no longer ignored.

Exposure of the distortions and implications of sexism, racism, and classism, and homophobia has encouraged resistance to hegemonic impositions of solutions and efforts towards the empowerment of those traditionally excluded. Such empowerment includes concern with the conditions necessary for the growth of individuals as well as communities.

There is a cluster of issues around the rejection of empiricist emphases on the isolated individual and of idealist emphases on totalization.

Sympathetic apprehension of the point of view of others is taken as a condition of understanding that replaces the myth of neutrality. This opens up examination of the perspectivism and creativity that structure beliefs, making possible the constructive exploration of the multiplicity of relationships that dynamically constitute individuals actively involved in the world.

The democratization of organizations at all levels is an ongoing concern. It encourages the recognition of the importance of coalition building and community involvement in problem solving. The tragedy of the failure of public schools in the inner cities has forced recognition of the centrality of education to the health of a community and made obvious the folly of treating schools as independent entities that can be isolated from their community situation.

Emphasis on the ecological nature of our organism-environment interaction represents another cluster of interests. These include efforts to link scientific research with mutually agreed-upon values. The places of women, the poor, and third world countries in the increasingly technological and economic exploitation of natural and human resources have become litmus tests of the nature and value of global development.

Hopefully, the message of Jane Addams can allay the fears of feminists that their hard-won and still precarious identities as lesbian, as black or Latina, as non-Western or noncolonialist, will be submerged in a bland togetherness in the pragmatist goal of working together to first define and then solve common problems.

> It is difficult both to interpret sympathetically the motives and ideals of those who have acquired rules of conduct in experience widely different from our own, and also to take enough care in guarding the gains already made, and in valuing highly enough the imperfect good so painfully acquired and, at the best, so mixed with evil.[2]

Addams also has something to say to pragmatists who fear being swallowed up into radical feminist agendas that threaten their philosophical integrity. In praising Dewey's contributions to resolving troubling social problems of international as well as national scope, she picks out as emblematic the same passages of his that Joseph Ratner, as editor, chose for the title page of Dewey's *Characters and Events: Popular Essays in Social and Political Philosophy:*

> Better it is for philosophy to err in active participation in the living struggles and issues of its own age and times, than to maintain an immune monastic impeccability. To try to escape from the snares and pitfalls of time by recourse to traditional problems and interests—rather than that, let the dead bury their dead.[3]

In this concluding but not conclusive chapter, I would like to point out some of the ways that the early manifestations of a nascent feminism interacting with pragmatism in the Progressive era can challenge some contemporary feminist and pragmatist beliefs and theoretical categories. Pragmatism includes many complex and dynamic theories, ones that hopefully will displace such common misconceptions as those expressed by Barbara Sicherman, who says that Alice Hamilton was a pragmatist like Jane Addams because instead of joining the far left, in her commitment to public solutions for what were once considered private problems, she was "willing to accept half a loaf rather than no bread." The inference is that the practical exigencies of providing for the needy, a willingness to compromise over principles will at least result in ameliorating pressing problems. This echoes a common criticism of progressive reformers that they did not have "a consistently class-based or socialist analysis," but they somehow managed to link "their own fortunes with those of the socially deprived and often inarticulate groups for whom they worked." And despite the fact that women progressives "did not radically challenge the gender system," they successfully broke away from the stifling restrictions imposed on their gender and class to engage in pioneering career roles and unprecedented institutional changes, while seeking to include all women in their work.[4]

Understanding depends on context, and Sicherman's article on Alice Hamilton provides a richly detailed contextual analysis that can be used to open up new meanings when examined from the perspective of pragmatist feminism. In *Twenty Years at Hull-House* Jane Addams shrewdly undercuts the criticism that the radical reformers at Hull House were not ideologically pure enough by juxtaposing two chapters—"A Decade of Economic Discussion" and "Pioneer Labor Legislation." On the one hand, Hull House was harassed by the powerful right-wing political and economic forces in Chicago for providing a haven for left-wing radicals, including anarchists, Marxist socialists, and trade-unionists. But they were also criticized by these same radicals for not siding with any one of them, not helping them to develop their particular theory by showing the shortcomings of all the others, and dogmatically refusing to act if such an action could be construed as denying or watering down a single one of their principles. From the point of view of the women of Hull House, radical theoreticians tended either to be more concerned with developing the coherence and distinctiveness of the theory itself or, when it was imposed on practice, to be more worried about whether such actions perfectly modeled the theory than with whether situations were actually improved. In fact, a clear-cut theoretical victory was often preferred to a lesser outcome or a compromise that actually bettered the lives of individuals. Such impositions of theory on practice forget or deny that emancipatory theory arises out of practice as much as it reflects back on it. It is a tool for directing practice, not a privileged insight into reality. As a tool, it is instrumental to an outcome desired, rather than a hegemonic imposition of a predelineated order. Therefore, theories should be capable of revision as outcomes surpass or undercut expectations.

Pragmatist feminists refused in principle to subordinate flesh-and-blood human beings, in all their diversity, to the requirements of any theory, program, or institution. They were therefore sometimes criticized by radicals for being reformist rather than revolutionary, as though radicalism is determined by adherence to absolutist theories rather than by recognition of the extent and quality of change required to reconstruct society. Alice Hamilton neatly expresses the discrepancy, all too frequent, between radical theory and practice by telling a story about a Fabian socialist she was shepherding through the Hull House neighborhood. As he was eagerly telling her about the need for vacation schools for the slum children of London, they came to the Hull House courtyard, which was full of children. She remarks:

> He never saw them, at least not as slum children like those he was eager to help; he saw them only as obstacles in his way, and he pushed them aside impatiently as if they were so many chickens, all the time telling me about the pitiful children in London. I thought to myself, "You may love humanity, but you certainly do not love your fellow man." [5]

Feminist pragmatism rejects the a priori cookie-cutter model of knowledge and theory. Although anyone who wields a tool can judge its efficacy, theory for feminist pragmatists is modeled as inquiry directed toward changing situations, preeminently social situations, which always include human participants. Social situations cannot be resolved pragmatically if such resolutions satisfy only those with the power to force a resolution or if it excludes those for whom the situation is problematic in the first place. The usefulness of theory, therefore, is ultimately answerable to those whose lives are supposed to be bettered by it. Kimberle Crenshaw also argues that those currently marginalized should be placed as the center of theory and practice, thus justifying her criticism of the single issue and top-down approach to racial and sexist discrimination. She points out that if black liberationist politics and feminist theory are to include black women, "both movements must distance themselves from earlier approaches in which experiences are relevant only when they are related to certain clearly identifiable causes (for example, the oppression of blacks is significant when based on race, of women when based on gender). The praxis of both should be centered on the life chances and life situation of people who should be cared about without regard to the source of their difficulties." [6]

Discrimination is multidimensional. Authoritative, single-issue causal explanations can only distort the lived experience of those marginalized. Addams had already distanced the perspective of the Hull House activists from appeals to elitist privilege and such litmus tests of ideological purity by asking whose point of view is privileged in theory, anyway—those intellectuals who can formulate it or those whose victimization gives them a unique perspective on the systems that exploit them? Especially in academic settings, the intellectual perfecting of theory often takes precedence over applying it at all or dynamically reconstructing it in light of its effectiveness. As Addams succinctly put it:

> The decade between 1890–1900 was, in Chicago, a period of propaganda as over against constructive social effort; the moment for marching and carrying banners, for stating general principles and making a demonstration, rather than the time for uncovering the situation and for providing the legal measures and civic organization through which new social hopes might make themselves felt.[7]

Theory is not irrelevant, except as we make it so by succumbing to such purely aesthetic criteria as simplicity and coherence and ignore its connection to the ongoing struggles that generate the need for theory in the first place. "Uncovering the situation" requires pragmatist feminists to adhere to their theoretical conviction that those in the situation be heard and to participate in formulating the problem as well as the solution. In describing what it meant to say that the Hull House settlement was a way of life, Mary E. McDowell warned against the settlement movement becoming so professionalized that it would lose touch with the individuals in the neighborhood. She used an anecdote to illustrate the pragmatist feminist principle of sharing power *with* rather than exercising power *over* those with whom one works. McDowell had invited to dinner at Hull House a trade-union woman who told her in casual conversation of her feelings of bitterness as a young woman when she could not earn enough to support herself and her invalid mother. She had at first hesitated to accept the offer because she felt it was but another effort "to patronize a working girl." On arriving late, she reported that Jane Addams had risen to greet her just as if she were any other lady, and on seating her said: "I have asked you to come here and see what we could do with each other for the girls in your trade." McDowell explained that "she said that little word 'with' took the sting of bitterness out of her soul. 'If Miss Addams had said 'for you,' she continued, 'I would have said proudly, 'I want to do for myself,' but when she said 'with,' that made it different. I have been with her ever since.'"[8]

Hamilton believed that a scientist's responsibility does not end with the discovery, the publication in elite journals, and the notification of those funding the research that the radium used by industrial workers to paint luminous dials causes terrible sickness and death. She believed that as a professional scientist with access to privileged information she was responsible to the industrial workers being investigated and not just to the industrial owners who funded the research, and that helping them required arousing public opinion to force industry and government to intervene. Sicherman calls this faith in the value of publicity to bring about social change "the quintessential belief of a generation of progressive reformers."[9] But the use of publicity by the Hull House progressives was just one strategy in their efforts to enable the marginalized to take control of their own lives and exercise the power usually reserved for more elite segments of society.

Sicherman has shown that Hamilton—unlike most woman of her generation who managed to secure professional positions for themselves by participating in sex-segregated female work—spent most of her professional life in the male world of medicine, laboratory research, and investigating industrial factories. Instead of conforming to the male model of success that more recent research has shown is typical of token entrants into new fields, Hamilton creatively overcame the dichotomies of scientific exactness defined as detachment versus social involvement; the professional, public roles defined as male with the feminine world concerned with bodily well-being and health; and objectivity defined as not being involved with advocacy. Hamilton is an exemplar of the pragmatist feminist synthesis of scientific astuteness with social commitment to a better life for everyone, particularly those who are most vulnerable. She and the other women of Hull House were not only constructing new professional roles for themselves but were providing new exemplary models of professionalization, ones that directly challenged the dominant modes of professionalization and practice that were elitist and oppressive.

The tensions between community-based activists and academic theorists, present from the earliest days of the feminist movement and its offspring, women's studies, in the United States, has become more acute as more women successfully pursue academic careers involving feminist commitments. Colleges and universities traditionally reward those who single-mindedly pursue research, sometimes even feminist research, and look askance at those who challenge the system by innovative approaches to and combinations of research, community service, and teaching. Increasingly, feminist research has become more narrowly specialized along disciplinary lines, more distanced from community involvement, and more single-mindedly theoretical. It has reproduced the ideological divides of the scholarly community, and litmus tests for feminism too often depend on how closely one adheres to the standards set by postmodernist, socialist, lesbian or queer, black, Latina, or noncolonialist theories. Meanwhile, what changes? What difference does it make to the everyday world outside of higher education what version of feminism one adheres to when feminism itself is under attack and many of its causes are losing ground? Do our theoretical disputes set the agenda for feminist research or do the needs of women and those most vulnerable? Do our theories change in response to changing conditions of oppression or to changing intellectual fads?

Pragmatically speaking, the pluralistic proliferation of feminist points of view is a sign of health and vigor in feminism insofar as each perspective is contributing to the others, breaking down prejudices that thrive on isolation and ignorance, and developing a more encompassing understanding of our complexly interwoven human condition. To do so requires inventing imaginative ways for this sharing to take place. Resolving inter-theoretical disputes also requires going outside the theories themselves to collaboratively changing problematic situations for the better. It requires sensitivity to those involved who are not themselves theoreticians. It requires linking theory to practice in such a way that the practice is internalized in the theory itself.

What I am looking for in the lives and writings of the Hull House feminist pragmatists is to discover what they have done, theorized, or found out that would be helpful in working through the issues troubling feminists and pragmatists today. I do not want to judge whether they criticized oppressions based on gender in a way that would be called radical by today's standards, but whether and how their understanding of gender radically changed their lives and the lives of those with whom they worked. The "generic traits" that transcend situations are just those particular aspects of it that are identifiable as relationships that recur in a new context within other situations. The realization of similarity is motivated by the recognition that something about the earlier set of relations is found useful to understanding the later one. The recognition of discontinuities can be equally enlightening.[10] Nancy Cott is sensitive to both as she compares and contrasts two periods of mass movements of women, 1912–19 and 1967–74.[11] In her analysis of Hamilton and her generation, Sicherman is also careful to "locate female consciousness at a precise historical moment." She finds the attitude toward gender of the progressive generation of women to be paradoxical because they grew up at a time of extremely rigid stereotyping of behavioral norms, tightly bounded by gender, race, and class, but were nonetheless able to take advantage of new educational and vocational opportunities opening up to middle- and upper-class young women. "How they transmuted traditional values into new social and political norms, even as they gained a large measure of personal freedom, is the heart of their story."[12]

What did Addams, Hamilton, and other Hull House women reject of traditional understandings of gender? What did they retain? How does pragmatist theory explain their choices? Service of others was retained, but they gradually stripped away its class-based and gendered expressions of charity, moral absolutism, and self-abnegation. Their effective model of social change utilized new scientific methods of research. According to Sicherman, this was combined with their understanding of themselves as women, namely as serving others, and therefore their science was put to the service of society. But this was no mechanical combination of two different ideologies, femininity and science. Changes took place over time, the result of circumstance and opportunity, motivated by dissatisfaction with the approved models of womanhood and with the inequities in society, and intensified by choosing to live and work together in a women's community. Hamilton was able to find her way to fully embrace a scientific attitude and commitment and simultaneously fully embrace monumental tasks of social transformation not only because the Hull House women enthusiastically mentored each other but because they were participating in developing a pragmatist philosophy that emancipated them from an oppressive past while it provided a means of opening up the future.

Recently, white feminists have been criticized for single-mindedly pursuing feminist theory focused on the emancipation of women and the celebration of women's perspectives and accomplishments while ignoring or underestimating the role of other factors such as race and class. Earlier pragmatist feminists were acutely aware of class and ethnicity while ignoring or underestimating the pervasiveness of sexism and racism. The strengths and weaknesses of each perspective are thus surprisingly complementary, and insights can be gained by critically responding to both perspectives and learning from their successes and failures.

Finally, one of the most obvious differences between the ways that most pragmatists and feminists understand pluralism is how each commonly constructs the Other. It is more a matter of emphasis and style than of absolute opposition. Pragmatists are more likely to emphasize that everyone is significantly and valuably Other, while feminists often expose the controlling force exercised by those who have the power to construct the Other as a subject of domination. Consequently, pragmatists tend to celebrate otherness by seeking out and welcoming difference as an expression of creative subjectivity, while feminists tend to resist categorization as an alien and alienating otherness imposed from without. Of course, in order to embrace otherness, pragmatists have to criticize the forces of racism and classism and the structures of elitism that serve to alienate us from one another, and feminists have to develop positive models of otherness to replace the negative ones, such as developing an ethics of caring out of women's sensitivity to relationships. But the tone and style of argumentation are set by the initial starting points, ones so taken for granted, yet so differently positioned, that they can alienate those coming from the other perspective.

In *Pragmatism* James castigates philosophers who hide their perspectives by pretending that their system, at least, "is a picture of the great universe of God. What it is—and oh so flagrantly!—is the revelation of how intensely odd the personal flavor of some fellow creature is" (*PM*, 24). The singularity of each individual is a continual feast to be encouraged and celebrated. Contrast the feelings aroused by this positive celebration of otherness with those elicited by Kathryn Pauly Morgan: "And the Other is almost always affected by the dominant culture, which is male-supremacist, racist, ageist, heterosexist, anti-Semitic, ableist and class-biased."[13] The context of Morgan's remarks is alien to James's universe. She is criticizing the negative stereotyping of women which leads some of them to submit to cosmetic surgery. Both recognize that knowledge is perspectival and pluralistic, but one is optimistic about the effects of alterity or otherness and the other is pessimistic. Compare the feelings evoked by the title of another of James's books, *A Pluralistic Universe*, with the ones evoked by the title of one of Marjorie Miller's articles: "Feminism and Pragmatism: On the Arrival of a 'Ministry of Disturbance, a Regulated Source of Annoyance; a Destroyer of Routine; an Underminer of Complacency'." The phrase she quotes was actually used by Dewey but remained unnoticed for more than seventy years before Miller found it an appropriate expression of the engaged, critical voice that pragmatism can offer to the "passionate, wavering, tentative, even querulous voices" of women struggling to be feminists, for whom the usual philosophic voice fails to "articulate their confusion, frustration, anger, or terror."[14]

The difference of tone and style stems from the fact that the classical male pragmatists philosophized from the center, while feminists speak from the margin. There are different centers and margins, to be sure, as pragmatists are quick to point out in their attacks on mainstream, epistemologically-centered philosophies which marginalize philosophies of praxis. But although efforts were made by the early pragmatists to challenge rationalist authoritarianism and to be inclusive, and although Dewey even made these positions a condition of his democratically-oriented philosophy, their analyses were still centrally located securely, if somewhat uneasily, within a male-defined tradition of rationality. Women, marginalized by their femaleness, which could also be compounded by their ethnicity or sexual orientation or any of a number of other characteristics not considered relevant to the historically familiar identification of man as thinker, cannot take their positioning for granted. Or if they do, others soon remind them of their marginalized status. The early generation of pragmatist feminists and black pragmatists do not fit comfortably in either margin or center, although they partake of both, which makes their struggles to develop and express their experiences in theory so valuable to others still struggling to do the same.

Jane Addams points out that while Julia Lathrop enthusiastically supported the franchise for women, becoming president of the Illinois League of Women Voters in 1922, she was apprehensive that women would take the vote as the end of their actions and not one means among others to be used to effect needed social reforms. In her warning against the temptation to slacken off after winning the vote, Lathrop was deeply aware of how perception and action are affected by whether one's position is dominant or marginal: "It is not in human nature that any persons who possess power can be as active as those who are pursuing it." According to Addams, "she assured women that they were engaged in a revolution, for, she said, 'it is nothing less than a revolution that women have emerged from their kitchens to ask searching questions about the why and wherefore of the costs they and their husbands have ages-long accepted with fatalistic discontent.' "[15]

Standpoints only appear neutral if they are also the norm. It takes another perspective to recognize the bias of those whose privilege allows them to define bias as those interests one does not share or of which one does not approve. Patricia Hill Collins points out that "black women's concrete experiences as members of specific race, class, and gender groups as well as our concrete historical situations necessarily play significant roles in our perspectives on the world. No standpoint is neutral because no individual or group exists unembedded in the world. Knowledge is gained not by solitary individuals but by Black women as socially constituted members of a group."[16]

James rejects both absolute idealism, which overemphasizes connectedness to the exclusion of any genuine alterity, and empiricism, which overemphasizes discreteness by reducing everything to the smallest possible particles. He instead defends pluralism. In defining the term he says that "things are 'with' one another in many ways, but nothing includes everything, or dominates over everything. The word 'and' trails along after every sentence. Something always escapes." Collins, on the other hand, says that "portraying African-American women as stereotypical mammies, matriarchs, welfare recipients, and hot mammas has been essential to the political economy of domination fostering Black women's oppression. . . . As part of a generalized ideology of domination, these controlling images of Black womanhood take on special meaning because the authority to define these symbols is a major instrument of power."[17]

Not surprisingly for a professor of philosophy at an elite university, James's defense of pluralism is situated within a discussion of metaphysics. He alludes to the concept of domination in order to deny its force and assert that nothing "dominates over everything. . . . Something always escapes." The tone is hopeful. We are invited to celebrate diversity, to recognize that totalizing explanations always fail, and we are encouraged to resist universal claims that distort or ignore differences. Exactly what escapes is left deliberately vague, as befits a metaphysical context. Although hemmed in by his duties at Harvard, ill health, and insatiable wanderlust, James can nonetheless always escape into the privileged world of the nineteenth-century gentleman scholar.

Collins begins with diversity, with otherness, but the differences to which she calls our attention are not genuine, not self-chosen. They are distorted characterizations imposed on black women by those in a position of power to do so. Although she also refers to generalized ideologies, she leaves no doubt about the sources of the domination they exercise as she goes on to name those who are in a position to exercise power over black women—"elite white men." Otherness in this case is a means to dominate, not to escape hegemonic control, because it is deliberately constructed and imposed on black women in order to distance them from an acceptable model of humanity. Collins's tone is defiant; she challenges the controlling images and calls attention to the power hidden in the ability to manufacture and disseminate negative stereotypes and have them taken for the reality.

Pragmatist philosophers developed liberating theories about the pluralism and perspectivism of knowledge and reality. They sought to counter the fears that pushed differences to the margin by bringing the margins into the center as valued and necessary contributions to the central concerns of philosophers. They sought to undermine the hegemony of totalizing claims from within the tradition. Some feminist philosophers, who found little to celebrate in the differences assigned to them, emphasized women's common humanity with men and worked for the day when women's culturally limited perspectives would not differ from those of socially privileged men's. Others sought to celebrate women's distinctiveness and difference from men and to demonstrate how much women's unique perspectives can contribute to philosophical and social issues. But since women were judged to be less competent in virtue of their femaleness by the male philosophers who dominated departments of philosophy, both assimilationists and separatists had to reckon with the negativity of difference in a way that philosophers whose maleness was taken as the norm of rationality and humanity did not.

Feminists argue that differences are systematically distorted by being constructed within a male-defined (and heterosexist, white, colonialist, or other) order. Since pragmatist theorizing begins and ends with experience, it encourages and provides the means of justifying criticism of accepted beliefs and traditions based on one's different experiences, values, and points of view. But words like *suspicion, distortion, coercion, mystification,* and *manipulate* are seldom used because viewpoints are assumed to arise from experience, which is both individually lived through and culturally mediated, and initially accorded the respect due to persons.

Dorothy E. Smith also holds, as do pragmatists, "that the everyday world as the matrix of our experience is organized by relations tying it into larger processes in the world as well as by locally organized practices." But she goes on to develop a specifically feminist mode of inquiry, one that begins "with women's experience from women's standpoint" and then explores "how it is shaped in the extended relations of larger social and political relations." Since women have been systematically excluded from the making of our culture (or women's cultural contributions have been belittled or ignored), "the concerns, interests, and experiences forming 'our' culture are those of men in positions of dominance whose perspectives are built on the silence of women (and others)." After identifying a particular perspective and naming it as one of prejudice or sexism, she continues with the pragmatist methodology of exploring the consequences of women's exclusion. "What is there— spoken, sung, written, made emblematic in art—and treated as general, universal, unrelated to a particular position or a particular sex as its source and standpoint, is in fact partial, limited, located in a particular position, and permeated by special interests and concerns." Once it is realized that we are active participants in negotiating the constraints and possibilities of the cultural matrix through which the world appears as it does, then we are empowered to challenge it: "But we have assented to this authority and can withdraw our assent. Indeed this is essential to the making of knowledge, culture, and ideology based on the experiences and relevances of women." [18]

Smith criticizes standard sociology, which "claims objectivity not on the basis of its capacity to speak truthfully, but in terms of its specific capacity to exclude the presence and experience of particular subjectivities. Nonetheless, of course, they are there and must be." [19] But what does it mean to "speak truthfully"? Can any particular belief about the world we experience be other than exclusive, a part broken off from the whole? Is not the question one of determining what to exclude and what to include and to criticize the prejudicial basis of the exclusion, not the fact that all interpretations of reality are exclusive? Disciplinary exclusions on the basis of gender or race or any other less powerful collective, for instance, are wrong because these particular exclusionary practices are unfair and unjustified. Since, as perspectives, all our claims are partial, justice cannot consist in a neutral or omniscient point of view, but in the recognizing that different points of view are legitimate and assenting to the principle that other voices than the ones now privileged have a right to be heard. What is needed is thoughtful collaboration to develop strategies for supporting such active collaboration as an ongoing project. It means making and unmaking the world.

Smith offers Philippe Aries's *Centuries of Childhood* as an example of what is taken as supposedly neutral, objective scholarship about children but which actually embodies assumptions "of a world seen from men's position in it."[20] The problem is not that a unified, coherent point of view has been achieved on the basis of exclusions of other points of view. Such exclusions, whether deliberate or not, are unavoidable. The problem is that by hiding its perspectivism in a mask of neutrality, it closes rather than opens dialogue with other perspectives that might contribute to a fuller and more critically evolved view of childhood. The other extreme from a unification that rejects or diminishes plurality is that of a pluralism without enough unification to generate identification of those traits of experience on the basis of which generalizations are formulated and subsequently tested against other experiences.

Linda Pollock praises Shulamith Shahar's *Childhood in the Middle Ages* because, among other things, she "attempts to analyze childhood by gender and class, as well as taking disadvantaged children and child abuse into account." But she criticizes Shahar's methodology and exposition because of a superfluity of detail, paragraphs "crammed with diverse items of information, creating a sense of dizziness." Although her sensitivity to ambiguities and complexities is laudable, "her tendency to clutter every generalization with caveats and 'on the other hand' means one cannot grasp the main point." More than stylistic failure is at issue. Pollock says that those looking for information on subjects hitherto overlooked are finding reams of information. She complains that with the prodigious expansion of knowledge "the past is becoming murkier rather than more distinct with each new book" and that what is needed is a synthesis that can integrate the vast compendium of knowledge.[21]

Her criticism is well taken to the extent that the mere proliferation of detail without any end-in-view precludes recognizing and testing explanatory hypotheses. But this very desire for synthesis can also be an expression of a drive toward totalization. Every unification requires rejection, and just what is rejected and how and by whom should always be subject to criticism and open to revision. Meanwhile, our experiences overflow any container meant to hold them.

One way feminist pragmatists join pluralism and perspectivism is by drawing attention to the diversity found throughout the world and throughout history. There is by now overwhelming historical, literary, an-

thropological, sociological, and psychological evidence of many different types of thinking, many hierarchies of values, and many beliefs
about the world. However suitable these may be for different purposes
and situations, they may still conflict with one another. None can claim
to encompass the entire truth without ignoring, rejecting, or belittling
contrary claims. Pragmatists explain this pluralism of points of view as
evidence that all theories are instrumental. They are cognitive means of
handling experiences satisfactorily for our purposes. Such satisfaction is
transactive. It must succeed in joining our already funded experience
with the present physical and social situation as guided by our ends-in-
view.[22] Funded experience, that is, those cognitive structures, embodied
habits, and emotional reserves which we bring to the situation, will either
be found adequate or will be adapted, revised, or rejected until the situation is satisfactorily resolved. Situations are no more static than are our
appropriations, and they lend themselves partially, fully, or not at all to
our attempts at organizational understanding.

Truth does not mean for pragmatists a correspondence to an independent reality but the outcome of a satisfactory organization of experience. Satisfaction refers to (but is not limited to) a standard of values
maximally inclusive of the fullest development of persons. And the reality encompassed in truth claims is the concrete reality as we variously
experience and interpret it at different times. Dewey's terminology,
which substitutes "warranted beliefs" for "truth" and "experience" or
"situation" for "reality," encapsulates this pragmatist rejection of correspondence theories of truth and presentist representations of reality.
James seemingly likens pragmatism to a promiscuous woman, one

> willing to take anything, to follow either logic or the senses, and to count
> the humblest and most personal experiences. . . . She will take a God who
> lives in the very dirt of private fact—if that should seem a likely place to
> find him. Her only test of probable truth is what works best in the way of
> leading us, what fits every part of life best and combines with the collectivity
> of experience's demands, nothing being omitted. . . . What other kind of
> truth could there be, for her, than all this agreement with concrete reality?
> (*PM*, 44)

Since experiences can be organized in different ways, depending on
our intentions and on the malleability of the situation, the beliefs we call
truths are pluralistic. But these differences are not relativistic because
such pragmatist truths must mediate between the funded character of
experience and emergent situations. They must fulfill their instrumen-
talist function by emancipating us from distorting or prejudicial beliefs
disguised as already determined facts and must empower us to organize
experiences satisfactorily in light of their multiple relations and indi-

vidual and social needs. Pragmatists also recognize that agreement about the parameters of relevant experiences will limit the possibility of warranted solutions, sometimes even to a single one. Rigorous initiation into the standards of the sciences and the varied paradigms within the humanities is supposed to produce just such agreement about a predelimited subject area. But such standards are always contestable and should be challenged insofar as they fall short of pragmatist feminist goals. Although skepticism has exercised philosophers from the beginning of the philosophical tradition originating in ancient Greece, women's skepticism of claims that seemed to them to be male-biased has not been welcomed into the classical debates because it challenges the very framework of skepticism or acceptable parameters of it. Lorraine Code attributes some of the negative reviews of her first book, *Epistemic Responsibility,* to the fact that her explorations of "how subjectivity contributes to the production of knowledge" did not conform "to the metaphilosophical requirements of the Anglo-American epistemological mainstream." This criticism for not conforming to "the rhetoric that confirms philosophical respectability" is all the more striking because, like much of the writings of pragmatists, it was not explicitly feminist, as was her second book, *What Can She Know?*[23]

Feminist pragmatists argue that truth claims are oppressive when they illicitly extend what is found to be true within predetermined and situated limits to reality as such. Since all truth claims incorporate a point of view and include unspecified assumptions and values, the failure to recognize these constraints often leads to false claims. Dewey developed the most comprehensive explanation of the dynamics of determining warranted beliefs in *Logic, the Theory of Inquiry* and demonstrated how including the points of view of everyone affected by truth claims is necessary for there to be truths or warranted beliefs at all. Such inclusiveness of all the actual perspectives involved is not just a charitable or political move. For one thing, situations do not identify themselves, and to even begin delineating the problematic situation that our truth claims are supposed to recognize, philosophers must draw on the insights of all those who help constitute the problematic situation in question. Persons and situations are related not as hand to glove but as organism to environment. The boundaries are permeable: air is environing, but it is also constitutive of the cells which make up the living organism. It requires a decision and not just a description in order to determine its proper sphere, that is, to determine whether air is part of the organism or the environment. For what purpose is the distinction being made? Who decides? By what warrant? How is it determined whether it is the best or even the better explanation?

Coming from a feminist pragmatist perspective, I am surprised that feminists often conflate consensus with coercion. Lee Quinby's attack on the politics of totalization in "Ecofeminism and the Politics of Resistance" is a case in point. Though it is generally in keeping with pragmatist theory, she confuses consensus with the oppression of the majority over the minority: "The move toward orthodoxy is complicitous with the tendency of power to totalize, to demand consensus, to authorize certain alliances and to exclude others—in short, to limit political creativity." [24] But demanding consensus is an oxymoron because coercion is by definition not consensual, that is, freely offered participatory agreement. Consensus can only come from the bottom up and not from the top down.

Majority rule can be coercive, and it often is in practice. This was already realized two hundred years ago in the debates surrounding the ratification of the Constitution of the United States, and it prompted a demand for a Bill of Rights to protect the minority from oppression by the majority. But consensus is a process that seeks to subvert majority rule—meaning a ratio of anything over fifty percent of a relevant group—by providing a mechanism by which the majority can be no less than every single participant. As long as there remains a minority of even one dissenter, consensus has not yet been achieved.

But why need consensus be achieved? It is one of the fundamental values of pragmatist feminist philosophy because social problems require concerted action to be solved equitably and efficaciously. Such consensus is temporary, revisable, strategic, and directed toward specific ends-in-view. Consensus is obviously an ideal very seldom achieved, but an ideal nonetheless. According to Cott, the contradictions that have emerged from the increasing emphasis by some feminists on the diversity of women, while other feminists emphasize the similar socialization of women and men, can be overcome by acknowledging how multifaceted women are. Such "acknowledgement allows coalition building, the only realistic political 'unity' women have or will have." [25] Feminist pragmatists try to figure out what mechanisms—social, institutional, educational, political, and cultural—open possibilities of consensual decision making and revisioning in light of desired, eventual, concrete outcomes and which ones preclude or diminish it. It is this insistence on "prioritizing actual over hypothetical consensus—and so actual over hypothetical dialogue" that distinguishes pragmatist feminism from "most Anglo-American ethics." [26] Consensus does not mean avoiding conflicts or denying differences, as is clear from bell hook's theory about "Sisterhood: Political Solidarity between Women." [27]

hooks criticizes the historically exclusionary sisterly bonding of "bourgeois women's liberationists" over issues of shared victimization. Instead, she advocates "working together to expose, examine, and eliminate sexist socialization in ourselves," including overcoming barriers of racism and classism. White privilege and class privilege are as real as sexual discrimination. In a perception that leads right back to the early years of Hull House, hooks points out that "most poor and working class women or even individual bourgeois nonwhite women would not have assumed that they could launch a feminist movement without first having the support and participation of diverse groups of women." Unlearning racist socialization cannot take place only in dialogue, although dialogue is a necessary means, but must include "actively struggling to resist racist oppression in our society." Unless insights eventuate in action, which in turn influences our thinking, no learning has really taken place. Hooks does not downplay the fact that truly pluralistic dialogues and classroom practices which actively confront and deal with multiple prejudices will generate pain before they generate understanding. She says that "to experience solidarity, we must have a community of interests, shared beliefs and goals around which to unite, to build Sisterhood." But she also recognizes that such solidarity is an outcome that can only be achieved gradually and not a predetermined condition. Differences do not have to be eradicated to achieve a shared solidarity of interests, beliefs, and political action.[28]

Notes

ONE

1. William James, *The Principles of Psychology* (hereafter *PP*), vol. 1 (Cambridge: Harvard University Press, 1991), 19.

2. See, for example, *What Is Feminism?* ed. Juliet Mitchell and Ann Oakley (Oxford: Basil Blackwell, 1986).

3. Nancy Fraser, *Unruly Practices: Power, Discourse, and Gender in Contemporary Social Theory* (Minneapolis: University of Minnesota Press, 1989); Margaret Jane Radin, "The Pragmatist and the Feminist," *Southern California Law Review* 63/6 (1990): 1699–1726; and the eighth annual Comparative Literature Symposium on "Pragmatism and the Politics of Culture," March 25–28, 1993.

4. *Pragmatism* is too often understood as referring to a narrow instrumentalism. I am using the term to refer to a historically specific philosophical movement also sometimes called Classical American Philosophy. This latter term avoids the negative connotations of the former, designates a particular historical locus, and denotes philosophical positions more encompassing than pragmatic methodology, but it has also been extended to include philosophers such as George Santayana and Justus Buchler, whose positions were not notably pragmatic. I use *pragmatism* to refer to a range of positions originating in the classical period of American philosophy that challenge the traditional philosophical privileging of theory at the expense of practice.

5. Preliminary dialogues have already taken place, such as papers given at meetings of the Society for Women in Philosophy in February, 1990, and of the Society for the Advancement of American Philosophy in March, 1990, which form the basis for the second chapter; a plenary symposium on pragmatism and feminism at the meetings of the Society for the Advancement of American Philosophy, March 1–2, 1991; a symposium on American philosophy and feminist perspectives at the American Philosophical Association, April 23–25, 1992; and a special issue on feminism and pragmatism in *Hypatia* 8/2 (1993).

6. James, *Essays in Philosophy* (*EPH*) (Cambridge: Harvard University Press, 1978), 17.

7. For an explanation of James's hermeneutics of cooperation, see Charlene

Haddock Seigfried, *William James's Radical Reconstruction of Philosophy* (Albany: State University of New York, 1990), 181–83.

8. See, for instance, Barbara J. Berg, *The Remembered Gate* (New York: Oxford University Press, 1978); and Gerda Lerner, *The Creation of Feminist Consciousness* (New York: Oxford University Press, 1983).

9. This intriguing phrase was used as the title of *Before Their Time,* ed. Katharine M. Rogers (New York: Ungar, 1979). See also Rosalind Delmar, who raises similar concerns if feminism is simply equated with social movements: "What Is Feminism?" in *What Is Feminism?* ed. Mitchell and Oakley, 14–24.

10. Robert B. Westbrook, for example, says: "Strictly speaking, pragmatism is a set of notions about knowledge, meaning, and truth; it is an epistemological argument." "A New Pragmatism," *American Quarterly* 45/3 (1993): 439.

11. Richard Rorty, *Consequences of Pragmatism* (Minneapolis: University of Minnesota Press, 1982), 191–210, 213–14.

12. This definition of pragmatism is taken from my contribution to *The Cambridge Dictionary of Philosophy,* ed. Robert Audi (Cambridge University Press, forthcoming).

13. John J. Stuhr, ed., *Classical American Philosophy* (New York: Oxford University Press, 1987), 4–11.

14. James, *The Will to Believe (WB)* (Cambridge, Harvard University Press, 1979), 224.

15. Simone de Beauvoir, *The Second Sex,* trans. H. M. Parshley (New York: Vintage Books, 1974), 791.

16. "Books: The World of Science Fiction," *Ms.,* November/December 1990, 54.

17. See Nadya Aisenberg and Mona Harrington, *Women of Academe* (Amherst: University of Massachusetts Press, 1988).

18. For an interpretation of Dewey's philosophy from the perspective of his "biosocial psychology" see Elizabeth Flower and Murray G. Murphey, *A History of Philosophy in America,* vol. 2 (New York: Capricorn Books, 1977), 811–87.

19. Giles Gunn, *Thinking across the American Grain* (Chicago: University of Chicago Press, 1992), 196–97.

20. Rose M. Brewer, "Theorizing Race, Class, and Gender," in *Theorizing Black Feminisms,* ed. Stanlie M. James and Abena P. A. Busia (London: Routledge, 1993), 13. According to Beverly Guy-Sheftall, "Some of the most significant reforms in American higher education over the past three decades have come as a result of the Black Studies and Women's Studies movements," and the last decade has seen the development of a new field of study—Black Women's Studies. "A Black Feminist Perspective on Transforming the Academy," *Theorizing Black Feminisms,* 77.

21. Mead's interdisciplinary interests joined philosophy, sociology, and psychology. *Philosophy, Social Theory, and the Thought of George Herbert Mead,* ed. Mitchell Aboulafia (Albany: State University of New York Press, 1991), x.

22. David L. Miller, *George Herbert Mead* (Chicago: University of Chicago Press, 1973), xxiii.

23. James, *Pragmatism (PM)* (Cambridge: Harvard University Press, 1975), 31.

24. Dewey, "Some Implications of Anti-Intellectualism," *MW*6:88.

25. James, *PM,* 9–10, 11, 17–18.

26. See Cornel West, *The American Evasion of Philosophy* (Madison: University of Wisconsin Press, 1989); Nancy Muller Milligan, "W. E. B. Du Bois' American Pragmatism," *Journal of American Culture* 8/2 (1985): 31–37; and Leonard Harris, ed., *The Philosophy of Alain Locke* (Philadelphia: Temple University Press, 1989). As Locke reports, "Verily paradox has followed me the rest of my days: at Harvard, clinging to the genteel tradition of Palmer, Royce and Münsterberg, yet attracted by the disillusion of Santayana and the radical protest of James; again in 1916 I returned to work under Royce but was destined to take my doctorate in Value Theory under [Ralph Barton] Perry." Harris, *Alain Locke,* 16.

27. Thelma Z. Lavine, "Pragmatism and the Constitution in the Culture of Modernism," *Transactions of the Charles S. Peirce Society* 20/1 (1984): 7–8.

28. Lavine, "Pragmatism," 10, 16. I should say that I do not agree with Lavine's later article, "American Philosophy, Socialism, and the Contradictions of Modernity," in which she argues that the end of the cold war demonstrates that Dewey's arguments for political and economic socialism have been defeated, along with totalitarian versions of socialism, and that socialism has been reduced to the symbolic, merely symbolizing "the search for the self, for community, and for spiritual transcendence; the concern for minorities, the weak and oppressed; and a sensitivity to cruelties and pain." To sever these aspirations from actual economic and political institutions and practices would deny Dewey's many analyses of how they mutually interact to bring about oppressive or liberatory situations and leave only a generalized utopian hope, a form of reflection he repeatedly and cogently rejected. *Philosophy and the Reconstruction of Culture,* ed. John J. Stuhr (Albany: State University of New York Press, 1993), 13.

29. Gerald E. Myers, introduction to *Principles of Psychology* (*PP*), vol. 1, xxxvii.

30. These characteristics would also be reasons for the lesser status accorded to James's more humanistic psychology by those who adopted a positivistic scientism. According to Carolyn Wood Sherif this positivistic bias contributed to the failure to acknowledge the male-centeredness of psychology until very recently: "Bias in Psychology," in *Feminism and Methodology,* ed. Sandra Harding (Bloomington: Indiana University Press, 1987), 37–56. See also *Reinterpreting the Legacy of William James,* ed. Margaret Donnelly (Washington, DC: American Psychological Association, 1992); and *Reflections on "The Principles of Psychology,"* ed. Michael G. Johnson and Tracy B. Henley (Hillsdale, NJ: Lawrence Erlbaum, 1990).

31. See James Campbell, *John Dewey* (Urbana: University of Illinois Press, 1995), and *The Community Reconstructs* (Urbana: University of Illinois Press, 1992). See also Robert B. Westbrook, *John Dewey and American Democracy* (Ithaca: Cornell University Press, 1991).

32. See John Dewey, *Individualism, Old and New, LW* 5: 41–123, *Freedom and Culture, LW* 13: 65–188; and George Herbert Mead, "The Philosophies of Royce, James, and Dewey in Their American Setting," *International Journal of Ethics* 40 (1930), 211–31, reprinted in *Selected Writings: George Herbert Mead,* ed. Andrew J. Reck (Indianapolis: Bobbs-Merrill, 1964), 371–91.

TWO

1. Gina M. Scuteri, Seminar on Liberalism and American Social Institutions, Purdue University, Spring, 1989. This chapter combines two articles I have written on the same topic. The first, "Where Are All the Pragmatist Feminists?" *Hypatia* 6/2 (1991): 1–20, already joins two papers that differed in emphasis only because they were addressed to two different audiences with two different areas of interest and knowledge. One was originally read in February, 1990, at the Midwest meeting of the Society for Women in Philosophy, and the other in March, 1990, at the annual meeting of the Society for the Advancement of American Philosophy. The second article, "The Missing Perspective," published in *Charles S. Peirce Society* 27/4 (1991): 405–16, introduces articles by Eugenie Gatens-Robinson, Marcia K. Moen, Felicia E. Kruse, and Marjorie Miller. Aside from combining the two articles, dropping some material, and adding a few new references, I have edited the chapter only slightly because it represents an earlier state of affairs in which feminists and pragmatists largely ignored one another. Not only are subsequent chapters meant to remedy this situation, but subsequent events have begun to do so: "Where Are All the Pragmatist Feminists?" has been excerpted in the third edition of *Philosophy of Woman,* ed. Mary Briody Mahowald (Indianapolis: Hackett, 1994), 425–42.

2. As a result, the special issue of *Hypatia* 8/2 (1993) on feminism and pragmatism was conceived as a way to generate interest in pursuing the connections between the two.

3. See Gary Brodsky, "Rorty's Interpretation of Pragmatism," *Charles S. Peirce Society* 18/4 (1982): 311–37; John J. McDermott, R. W. Sleeper, A. Edel, and R. Rorty, "Symposium on Rorty's *Consequences of Pragmatism,*" *Charles S. Peirce Society,* 21/1 (1985): 1–48; Richard J. Bernstein, "One Step Forward, Two Steps Backward," *Political Theory* 15/4 (1987): 538–63; and "Rorty's Liberal Utopia," *Social Research* 57/1 (1990): 31–72.

4. See, for instance, Richard Rorty, *Philosophy and the Mirror of Nature* (Princeton: Princeton University Press, 1979) and *Consequences of Pragmatism,* especially 214–30; and Robert Schwartz, "Whatever Happened to Pragmatism?" in *Values and Value Theory in Twentieth-Century America,* ed. Murray G. Murphey and Ivar Berg (Philadelphia: Temple University Press, 1988), 37–45.

5. Denise Riley, *"Am I That Name?"* (Minneapolis: University of Minnesota Press, 1988), 112, uses *pragmatism* in the broader sense. But I first heard this claim from Mary Mahowald at the American Philosophical Association's "Symposium on American Philosophy and Feminist Perspectives," Louisville, April, 1992. Jane Duran also writes that "most women are pragmatists" in "The Intersection of Pragmatism and Feminism," *Hypatia* 8/2 (1993): 169.

6. I am deliberately excluding women from the pantheon of pragmatist philosophers to make both a historical and a political point. Historically, Classical American philosophy—as it has been handed down in publications and taught in the universities—excludes female pragmatists. Until I began this project, I was not even aware that there were any beyond my own immediate contemporaries. I begin with this tradition in which women are invisible as a heuristic device that enables me to subvert it as the article develops. On the level of theory and in my

own development as a philosopher, however, what comes from feminist and what from pragmatist sensibilities cannot easily be distinguished.

7. Joe R. Burnett, "Whatever Happened to John Dewey?" *Philosophy of Education Since Mid-century,* ed. Jonas F. Soltis (New York: Teachers College Press, 1981), 64–82; and Larry A. Hickman, *John Dewey's Pragmatic Technology* (Bloomington: Indiana University Press, 1990).

8. Katherine Camp Mayhew and Anna Camp Edwards, *The Dewey School* (New York: D. Appleton-Century, 1936), v.

9. See notes 1 and 2. Among those articles published before 1990 and not mentioned elsewhere in this chapter are Maryann Ayim, "The Implications of Sexually Stereotypic Language as Seen through Peirce's Theory of Signs," *Charles S. Peirce Society* 19/2 (1983): 183–97; Lisa Heldke, "John Dewey and Evelyn Fox Keller" *Hypatia* 2/3 (1987): 129–40, and "Recipes for Theory Making," *Hypatia* 3/2 (1988): 15–29; and Wilma R. Miranda, "Implications in Dewey for Feminist Theory in Education," *Educational Horizons,* 58 (1980): 197–202.

10. Alison Jaggar, *Feminist Politics and Human Nature* (Totowa, NJ: Rowman and Allenheld, 1983).

11. Rosemarie Tong, *Feminist Thought* (Boulder: Westview, 1989).

12. Jaggar, *Feminist Politics,* 354–55.

13. Pierre Bourdieu, *Language and Symbolic Power,* ed. John B. Thompson, trans. Gino Raymond and Matthew Adamson (Cambridge: Harvard University Press, 1991).

14. James, *A Pluralistic Universe (PU)* (Cambridge: Harvard University Press, 1977), 32. Coincidentally, Giles Gunn points out James's influence on Bourdieu in *Thinking across the American Grain,* 6–7.

15. See H. S. Thayer, *Meaning and Action,* 2d ed. (Indianapolis: Hackett, 1981); John E. Smith, *The Spirit of American Philosophy,* rev. ed. (Albany: State University of New York Press, 1983); and Richard J. Bernstein, *Beyond Objectivism and Relativism* (Philadelphia: University of Pennsylvania Press, 1983).

16. Thomas McCarthy, "Philosophy and Social Practice: Avoiding the Ethnocentric Predicament," paper presented at a symposium on "Analysis, Interpretation, and the End of Philosophy," Purdue University, March 17, 1989.

17. West, *The American Evasion of Philosophy,* 113.

18. James, *Essays, Comments, and Reviews* (ECR) (Cambridge: Harvard University Press, 1987), 67–74.

19. See Thomas M. Alexander, *John Dewey's Theory of Art, Experience, and Nature* (Albany: State University of New York Press, 1987), 119–82; Seigfried, "Extending the Darwinian Model: James's Struggle with Royce and Spencer," *Idealistic Studies,* 14 (September, 1984), 259–72; and "Poetic Invention and Scientific Observation," *Charles S. Peirce Society,* 26/1 (1990): 115–30.

20. Peirce's infatuation with arcane technical language and elaborate system-building is one reason why he hardly figures in my own reconstruction of pragmatism.

21. Marilyn French, "Is There a Feminist Aesthetic?" *Hypatia* 5/2 (1990): 33–42. French begins addressing this issue by asserting that "a third feminist principle, to which I myself am committed, is accessibility, language and style that aim at comprehensibility" 39.

22. Quoted in Ralph Barton Perry, *The Thought and Character of William James,* vol. 2 (Boston: Little, Brown, 1935), 387.

23. Dewey, *The Public and Its Problems* (*LW* 2:343).

24. This "*we*" is a diverse lot. Beverly Guy-Sheftall, for instance, recounts a similar story of graduating from Spellman College, the oldest and best-known college for Black women in America, in 1966, "with no understanding of patriarchy or colonialism or apartheid." After her return to Spellman as a faculty member in 1971, she and Roseann Bell worked five years to find material for *Sturdy Black Bridges,* the first anthology of Black women's literature published in the United States. Guy-Sheftall also helped found the Spellman College Women's Center and developed courses in Black Women's Studies and Black Feminism so that students would not leave Spellman today with the same gaps in their knowledge that she had had twenty-five years earlier. Guy-Sheftall, "A Black Feminist Perspective on Transforming the Academy," in *Black Feminisms,* 77–89.

25. See Dale Spender, *Women of Ideas* (London: Ark, 1983); and Joanna Russ, *How to Suppress Women's Writing* (Austin: University of Texas Press, 1983).

26. In his conclusion to his book, *Dewey's New Logic,* Tom Burke says that "it seems clear that . . . ideological differences served as barriers to Russell's giving Dewey an honest reading. To a larger extent than should have to be admitted, the early rejection of Dewey's logical theory was due not to any unusual obscurity on Dewey's part, but rather to the fact that he was not saying what logical theorists wanted to hear at the time." (Chicago: University of Chicago Press, 1994), 267.

27. For corroboration in regard to philosophy, see Daniel J. Wilson, *Science, Community, and the Transformation of American Philosophy, 1860–1930* (Chicago: University of Chicago Press, 1990). In "The Plural Worlds of Educational Research," *History of Education Quarterly* 29/2 (1989): 185–214, Ellen Condliffe Lagemann details the virtual erasure of Dewey's legacy to education from the institutional memory of the University of Chicago and the consequent displacement of a socially engaged model of scientific experimentation with a positivist model.

28. I was introduced to this approach by Margaret Simons in "Simone de Beauvoir: Gender, Politics, and Truth," a talk delivered at the American Philosophical Association meetings, Chicago, April 30–May 2, 1987. She effectively used the technique to demonstrate Simone de Beauvoir's exclusion from histories and critical discussions of existentialism and Continental philosophy generally. See Simons, "Sexism and the Philosophical Canon," *Journal of the History of Ideas* 51 (1990): 487–504.

29. Herbert W. Schneider, *A History of American Philosophy* (New York: Columbia University Press, 1963). Orig. 1946.

30. Flower and Murphey, *History of Philosophy in America,* 3. Quotations in text are given by volume number and page.

31. In focusing on the importance of the debate between realism and nominalism, Susan Haack does not comment on the irony of giving as a motto at the beginning of her article a quotation from Chauncey Wright that assumes the philosophical intellect is male: ". . . the question of nominalism and realism— that question on which each new-fledged masculine intellect likes to try its pow-

ers of disputation" " 'Extreme Scholastic Realism': Its Relevance to Philosophy of Science Today," *Charles S. Peirce Society,* 28/1 (1992): 19.

32. The index in the second edition was not revised to include the new entries in "Some Recent Literature" published since the first edition. Flower and Murphey's *History* is added, as well as books by Carolyn Eisele (ed.), Charlene Haddock Seigfried, Jo Ann Boydston (ed.), and Sandra B. Rosenthal.

33. Linda Lopez McAlister, for instance, recalls her disappointment on discovering that the *Encyclopedia of Philosophy,* ed. Paul Edwards (New York: Macmillan, 1967), which had just been published, contained not a single article on a female philosopher, although many obscure male figures merited short articles. "Some Remarks on Exploring the History of Women in Philosophy," *Hypatia* 4/1 (1989): 1.

34. Since this claim was first made in a paper in 1990, the situation has changed, and at least a beginning of a pragmatist/feminist dialogue has begun, including responses to the neopragmatism of Richard Rorty's "Feminism and Pragmatism," *Michigan Quarterly Review* 30/2 (1991): 231–58, rpt. *Radical Philosophy* 59 (Autumn, 1991).

35. Robin May Schott, *Cognition and Eros* (Boston: Beacon Press, 1988).

36. John Dewey, "Is Co-Education Injurious to Girls?" *Ladies' Home Journal* 28 (1911), 60–61. Rpt. *MW* 6:161.

37. Susan Laird points out the masculinist biases of the *Ladies' Home Journal* article in "Women and Gender in John Dewey's Philosophy of Education," *Educational Theory* 38/1 (1988): 111–29. Her major criticism, however, is that Dewey's support of coeducation was wrong because contemporary empirical studies show that single-sex education is more beneficial for women. Criticizing Dewey because he did not know empirical facts that were not established until after he wrote is unacceptable methodologically. His remarks have to be put into the context of the differing curricula and educational goals of women's colleges and coeducational ones as well as the reasons given at the time for supporting or attacking either one. For further information concerning Dewey's support of coeducation in the context of feminist issues of the time, see Seigfried, "Shared Communities of Interest," *Hypatia* 8/2 (1993): 3–5.

38. For a short, powerful explanation of the negative effects on women of men's different experiences and valuations, see Russ, *How to Suppress Women's Writing.* By contrast, Dewey at least recognized that women's ways of experiencing the world means they would have distinctive contributions to make to philosophy.

39. "Is There a Feminist Method?" in *Feminism and Methodology,* ed. Sandra Harding (Bloomington: Indiana University Press, 1987), 11.

40. Nicholas Lemann, *The Promised Land* (New York: Knopf, 1991). As reviewed in *New York Times Book Review,* 24 February 1991, 24.

41. Blanche Wiesen Cook, "Books: The Womanly Art of Biography," *Ms.,* November/December 1991, 61. But see Mary Jo Deegan, *Jane Addams and the Men of the Chicago School, 1892–1918* (New Brunswick: Transaction Books, 1988); and Ellen Condliffe Lagemann, "Jane Addams: An Educational Biography," in *Jane Addams on Education,* ed. Lagemann (New York: Teachers College Press, 1985), 1–48.

42. Lynn D. Gordon, "Pursing Equality, Achieving Change: Women Challenge American Higher Education," *American Quarterly* (1989): 385–90.

43. Mary Mahowald, "A Majority Perspective" *Cross Currents* 36/4 (1987): 416.

44. Lynne M. Adrian, "Emma Goldman and the Spirit of Artful Living," paper presented at the Frontiers in American Philosophy Conference, Texas A & M, June, 1988. Published in *Frontiers in American Philosophy*, ed. Robert W. Burch and Herman J. Saatkamp Jr. (College Station: Texas A & M University Press, 1992), 191–99.

45. David L. Miller, *George Herbert Mead*, xxxi, xxxiv.

46. For confirmation, see Jane P. Tomkins, ed., *Reader-Response Criticism* (Baltimore: Johns Hopkins University Press, 1980), x and xxvi, n.1). Louise M. Rosenblatt, *Literature as Exploration* (New York: Appleton Century, 1938) and *The Reader the Text the Poem* (Carbondale: Southern Illinois University Press, 1978).

47. See Judith Fetterly, *The Resisting Reader* (Indianapolis: Indiana University Press, 1978).

48. Dewey, *Experience and Education* (New York: Macmillan, 1938), 43–44. Also *LW* 13: 25.

49. Seigfried, "Feminist Aesthetics and Marginality," *Resources for Feminist Research*, 16/4 (1987): 10–15. Rosenblatt's critical reputation survived in literary criticism, if not in philosophical circles. *Literature as Exploration* has remained continuously in print since 1938. The Modern Language Association published a fourth edition in 1983 and has proposed a fifth edition. *The Reader, the Text, The Poem* has been reissued in paperback with a new preface and epilogue (Carbondale and Edwardsville: Southern Illinois University Press, 1994).

50. Maureen Egan, "Evolutionary Theory in the Social Philosophy of Charlotte Perkins Gilman," *Hypatia* 4/1 (1989): 103.

51. Gilman, *His Religion and Hers* in *Charlotte Perkins Gilman*, ed. Larry Ceplair (New York: Columbia University Press, 1991), 301.

52. Mahowald, "Majority Perspective," 413, 415.

53. Kimberle Crenshaw, "Demarginalizing the Intersection of Race and Sex," in *Living with Contradictions*, ed. Alison M. Jaggar (Boulder: Westview Press, 1994), 39–52. See also Paula Giddings, *When and Where I Enter* (William Morrow, 1984).

54. James, *Essays in Philosophy* (EPH), 168; and Seigfried, *William James's Radical Reconstruction*, 181–83.

55. For a pragmatist analysis of the intertwining of biological and normative descriptions of gender, see Seigfried, "*Second Sex:* Second Thoughts" (1985), rpt. *Hypatia Reborn: Essays in Feminist Philosophy*, ed. Azizah al-Hibri and Margaret E. Simons (Bloomington: Indiana University Press, 1990), 305–22.

56. Susan Bordo, *The Flight to Objectivity* (Albany: State University of New York Press, 1987), 6–7.

57. Thomas Nagel, *The View from Nowhere* (Oxford: Oxford University Press, 1986).

58. Bordo, *Flight*, 58.

59. Seigfried, "Vagueness and the Adequacy of Concepts," *Philosophy Today* 26 (1982): 357–67.

60. Quoted in Richard J. Bernstein, *John Dewey* (Atascadero, CA: Ridgeview, 1966), 12.

61. For the importance of metaphors in structuring thinking, see Mark Johnson, *The Body in the Mind* (Chicago: University of Chicago Press, 1987); George Lakoff and M. Johnson, *Metaphors We Live By* (Chicago: University of Chicago Press, 1980); and Lakoff, *Women, Fire, and Dangerous Things* (Chicago: University of Chicago Press, 1987). Steven A. Fesmire emphasizes Dewey's notion of interaction as the key to understanding the nature of metaphorical structure in "What Is 'Cognitive' about Cognitive Linguistics?" *Metaphor and Symbolic Activity,* 9/2 (1994), 149–54.

62. To take just one page of *Art as Experience* for illustration, Dewey's language shows few traces of the exaggerated ego boundaries often said to distinguish masculinity from femininity: "fused with all the other properties of the work of art," "synthesis or fusion," "harmonious merging," "this interfusion of all properties," "Only when all means are diffused through one another does the whole suffuse the parts so as to constitute an experience that is unified through inclusion instead of by exclusion," "union of qualities of direct sensuous vividness," and "Sense qualities are the carriers of meanings, not as vehicles carry goods but as a mother carries a baby when the baby is part of her own organism. Works of art, like words, are literally pregnant with meaning" (*LW* 10: 122).

63. William James, *The Varieties of Religious Experience* (*VRE*) (Cambridge: Harvard University Press, 1985), 394. See also Lisa Heldke, "Recipes for Theory Making," *Hypatia* 3/2 (1988): 15–29.

64. Klaus Oehler, "Notes on the Reception of American Pragmatism in Germany, 1899–1952," *Charles S. Peirce Society,* 17/1 (1981): 33. Oehler explains how Heidegger shared a widespread German prejudice against "Americanism" and regularly confused pragmatism with positivism.

65. Dewey, *Reconstruction in Philosophy* (*MW* 12: 77–201).

66. Harding, *Feminism,* 6–9.

67. For the pragmatists' use of *concrete* as an important modifier see chap. 7, n.25.

68. "Thinking takes place in a scale of degrees of distance from the urgencies of an immediate situation in which something is to be done. The greater the degree of remoteness, the greater is the danger that a temporary and legitimate failure of express reference to context will be converted into a virtual denial of its place and import. Thinking is always thinking, but philosophic thinking is, upon the whole, at the extreme end of the scale of distance from the active urgency of concrete situations" (*LW* 6: 17).

69. West, *American Evasion,* 181. After writing this, West participated in an innovative dialogue with an American black woman intellectual, bell hooks, who does indeed draw on her own experiences and speak for herself. bell hooks and Cornel West, *Breaking Bread* (Boston, MA: South End Press, 1991).

THREE

1. Charlotte Perkins Gilman, *The Man-Made World; or, Our Androcentric Culture,* 3d ed. (New York: Charlton, 1914), 16–17. Originally serialized in Gilman's magazine, *The Forerunner,* in 1910, it was published as a book in 1911.

2. Maureen L. Egan, "Evolutionary Theory in the Social Philosophy of Charlotte Perkins Gilman," *Hypatia* 4/1 (1989): 102–19.

3. Jane S. Upin, "Charlotte Perkins Gilman: Instrumentalism beyond Dewey," *Hypatia* 8/2 (1993): 38, 56.

4. See, for example, Ann J. Lane, *To Herland and Beyond* (New York: Meridian, 1991; and *The Captive Imagination: A Casebook* on "The Yellow Wallpaper," ed. Catherine Golden (New York: Feminist Press, 1992).

5. For exceptions see, besides Egan and Upin, Mary A. Hill, *Charlotte Perkins Gilman* (Philadelphia: Temple University Press, 1980); Polly Wynn Allen, *Building Domestic Liberty* (Amherst: University of Massachusetts Press, 1988); Ann Pameri, "Charlotte Perkins Gilman," in *Discovering Reality*, ed. Sandra Harding and Merrill B. Hintikka (Dordrecht, Holland: D. Reidel, 1983); Nancy J. Holland, *Is Women's Philosophy Possible?* (Savage: Rowman and Littlefield, 1990).

6. Gilman, *Women and Economics* (Boston: Small, Maynard, 1898).

7. Charlotte Perkins Gilman, *The Living of Charlotte Perkins Gilman: An Autobiography* (New York: D. Appleton-Century, 1935), 182.

8. Gilman, *Mad-Made World*, 139.

9. William Gavin, *William James and the Reinstatement of the Vague* (Philadelphia, Temple University Press, 1992), 189.

10. Max H. Fisch, *Peirce, Semiotic, and Pragmatism*, ed. Kenneth Laine Ketner and Christian J. W. Kloesel (Bloomington: Indiana University Press, 1986), 110.

11. This is particularly true for those elite institutions most likely to have an impact on the direction scholarship takes. Although I have no figures for philosophers, Ellen Fitzpatrick reports that "of the nine women who earned doctorates in sociology, political science, and political economy during [the University of] Chicago's first fifteen years, not a single one secured a regular faculty appointment at a coeducational university upon her graduation." *Endless Crusade* (New York: Oxford University Press, 1990), 72.

12. Fisch also includes Chauncey Wright and—somewhat inexplicably—Elijah Jordan: *Peirce, Semiotic, and Pragmatism*, 111. Thayer includes C. I. Lewis but excludes Royce, *Meaning and Action*, 68. Stuhr includes George Santayana: *Classical American Philosophy*, 3.

13. See Lynn D. Gordon, *Gender and Higher Education in the Progressive Era* (New Haven: Yale University Press, 1990).

14. Addams is acknowledged to the extent that her association with Dewey and Mead is duly recorded, both by them and in subsequent histories of American philosophy, but her specific contributions to the development of pragmatism as a philosophical theory are never discussed.

15. Morton White, *Documents in the History of American Philosophy* (New York: Oxford UP, 1972). Women philosophers are absent from all the collections of American philosophy texts that I know, with the lone exception of Barbara MacKinnon's *American Philosophy* (Albany: State University of New York Press, 1985), which includes one woman, Ruth Macklin, among thirty-five men.

16. Mary Jo Deegan, *Jane Addams and the Men of the Chicago School, 1892–1918* (New Brunswick: Transaction Books, 1988), 13.

17. Addams exchanged ideas with the Cambridge pragmatists as well as with those at Chicago. See Deegan, *Jane Addams and the Men*, 13, 253; and William

James, "Review of Jane Addams, *The Spirit of Youth and the City Streets*," *American Journal of Sociology*, 15/4 (1910): 553.

18. Gordon, *Gender and Higher Education*, 85–120. Gordon says that Dewey, Veblen, Thomas, Angell, and Mead, all at Chicago, "supported their women graduate students and sponsored exciting research on sex differences," 102.

19. Deegan, *Jane Addams and the Men*, 5–6.

20. In *Endless Crusade* Fitzpatrick remedies this lack of attention in regard to four pioneering political scientists, Edith Abbott, Sophonisba Breckinridge, Katherine Bement Davis, and Frances Kellor, all of whom were graduate students at the University of Chicago during its first decade (1892–1902). "Abbott and Breckenridge also belonged to a tight group of University of Chicago professors who had high visibility in municipal reform circles," xii–xiii, 192.

21. Elizabeth Scarborough and Laurel Furumoto, *Untold Lives* (New York: Columbia University Press, 1987), 17–51; Seigfried, "Archive: 1895 Letter from Harvard Philosophy Department," *Hypatia* 8/2 (1993).

22. Thomas C. Cadwallader and Joyce V. Cadwallader, "Christine Ladd-Franklin (1847–1930)," in *Women in Psychology: A Bio-bibliographical Sourcebook*, ed. Agnes N. O'Connell and Nancy Felipe Russo (New York: Greenwood, 1990), 220–29.

23. Deegan, *Jane Addams and the Men*, 209. The dissertation, which was later published (Menhasa, WI: Collegiate Press, George Banta, 1915), is summarized in Seigfried, "Introduction to Jessie Taft, 'The Woman Movement from the Point of View of Social Consciousness.'" The second chapter of the dissertation is reprinted in the Archive section of *Hypatia* 8/2 (1993): 215–29.

24. Rosalind Rosenberg, *Beyond Separate Spheres* (New Haven: Yale University Press, 1982), 139.

25. Mary Jo Deegan, "The Clinical Sociology of Jessie Taft," *Clinical Sociology Review*, 4 (1986): 30–45.

26. For Calkins's and Puffer's differing reasons, see Seigfried, "1895 Letter from Harvard Philosophy Department," *Hypatia* 8/2 (1993): 230–31.

27. Ethel Puffer Howes, "The Golden Age," *Radcliffe Quarterly*, 21/2 (1937): 14–16.

28. Scarborough and Furumoto, *Untold Lives*, 71–90.

29. Howes, "The Meaning of Progress in the Woman's Movement," *Annals of the American Academy of Political and Social Science* 143/232 (1929), 14–20; and, among others, "We Women," and "The Revolt of Mother," *Woman's Home Companion*, February/December, 1923.

30. Mitchell, for instance, was profoundly influenced by Jane Addams, who "represented an amalgam of all the professional and personal attributes Lucy found in her other mentors." Joyce Antler, *Lucy Sprague Mitchell* (New Haven: Yale University Press, 1987), 158.

31. Information on Clapp was gathered from the Clapp Papers, Special Collections of the Southern Illinois University at Carbondale Library, no. 2111.

32. Sidney Ratner and Jules Altman, eds., *John Dewey and Arthur F. Bentley* (New Brunswick, NJ: Rutgers University Press, 1964), 11.

33. Jane M. Dewey, "Biography of John Dewey," in *The Philosophy of John Dewey*, ed. Paul Arthur Schilpp (Evanston: Northwestern University Press, 1939),

37. Schilpp says that "in the emphasis on varied influences and in the philosophical portions it may be regarded as an autobiography," 3. The fact that the earliest, most explicit recognition of the influence of various women on John Dewey's intellectual career appears in a biography edited by his daughter may not be a coincidence, however. Jo Ann Boydston, editor of the critical edition of John Dewey's writings, has pointed out to me that Jane Dewey was especially concerned that her mother's influence on her father's life and thought was not sufficiently recognized in professional publications.

34. Jane Dewey, "Biography of John Dewey," 28–30.

35. Dewey says, in the published versions of his 1899 presidential address before the American Psychological Association, that he owes a specific point "(as well as others more generally) to my friend and colleague, Mrs. Ella Flagg Young," "Psychology and Social Practice," (*MW* 1: 134, n.2). He also refers twice to Young's *Isolation in the School,* University of Chicago Contributions to Education, no. 1 (Chicago: University of Chicago Press, 1901), in an article on the elementary school: "As Concerns the Elementary School," (*MW* 1: 269, n.1, and 272, n.2). He mentions this indebtedness to Young's *Scientific Method in Education* (University of Chicago Decennial Publications) in a footnote to an article first published in *Third Yearbook* of the National Society for the Scientific Study of Education, 1904 (*MW* 3: 263, n.4). Historians might read Dewey's praise of Young in "The School and Society," a book review in *New Republic,* 10 April 1929, 231–32, but few philosophers would come upon it (*LW* 5: 371–74). If it were not for the publication of Dewey's Collected Works by the Southern Illinois University Press, these references would still not be accessible to the majority of scholars who are familiar with Dewey's major works.

36. Deegan, *Jane Addams and the Men,* 253.

37. Christopher Lasch, ed., *The Social Thought of Jane Addams* (Indianapolis: Bobbs-Merrill, 1965), 176.

38. In *John Dewey and American Democracy,* 556, Robert B. Westbrook does include substantial discussions of Mayhew and Edwards's account of the Laboratory School, and in his critical review of Dewey scholarship he says that "no library of Dewey basics is complete without Katherine Camp Mayhew and Anna Camp Edwards, *The Dewey School.*" However, none of the (anonymous) teachers or members of the school community are portrayed as contributing anything to pragmatist educational theory, but rather as simply carrying out Dewey's creative vision.

39. Dewey to Elsie Ripley Clapp, September 2, 1911, Clapp Papers.

40. Anne S. Sharpe, ed., *Index, John Dewey, The Collected Works, 1882–1953* (Carbondale and Edwardsville: Southern Illinois University Press, 1991).

41. Clapp Papers, 21/1/15, 21/1/17, 21/1/20.

42. Clapp Papers, 21/1/20.

43. Joseph P. Lash, "Mrs. Roosevelt's 'Baby'—Arthurdale," *Eleanor and Franklin* (New York: W. W. Norton, 1971), 393–417.

44. Elsie Clapp, *Community Schools in Action* (New York: Viking, 1939).

45. Clapp Papers, collection 21.

46. Clapp, *Community Schools,* 48, v.

47. Clapp Papers, 2/1/5.

48. Information on Mitchell is from Antler, *Lucy Sprague Mitchell.*

49. Antler, *Lucy Sprague Mitchell*, 207.

50. Lucy Sprague Mitchell, *Two Lives* (New York: Simon and Schuster, 1953), 192, 119–22.

51. Mitchell, *Two Lives*, 122.

52. Mitchell, *Two Lives*, 137.

53. Gordon, *Gender and Higher Education*, 52–84. Peixotto, "a brilliant student, . . . received the second doctorate awarded by Berkeley to a woman in 1900. She became the university's first female faculty member as an instructor in political economy in 1904 and its first female full professor in 1918," 62.

54. Mitchell, *Two Lives*, 193, 121.

55. Mitchell, *Two Lives*, 210.

56. Antler, *Lucy Sprague Mitchell*, xiv–xv.

67. Wesley Clair Mitchell was a distinguished economist, an authority on business cycles and a founding member of the New School for Social Research, the National Bureau of Economic Research, and the Social Science Research Council. Lucy first met him briefly when he was a graduate student at the University of Chicago, but their relationship developed only later when he was teaching economics at Berkeley. At Chicago Mitchell came under the influence of both Dewey and Thorstein Veblen.

58. In an unusual hybrid autobiography/biography in which Lucy tells of the life she and Wesley shared, Lucy emphasizes how important it was to both of them that she continue her professional life after marriage. Mitchell, *Two Lives*, xviii, 221–36.

59. Mitchell, *Two Lives*, 74, 60.

60. Antler, *Lucy Sprague Mitchell*, 66.

61. Mitchell, *Two Lives*, 191. Interestingly, Myrtle B. McGraw, who pioneered the "methodology of studying overt behavior development in infants" makes an almost identical claim: "The thirties had been a glorious decade when the babies had been my teacher," in *Models of Achievement*, ed. Agnes N. O'Connell and Nancy Felipe Russo (New York: Columbia University Press, 1983), 49, 51.

62. Harriet Johnson was also unconventional in her lifestyle. She "shared her personal life with Harriet Forbes" and in 1916 adopted a baby girl with her. Johnson and Forbes were affectionately referred to as "the Harriets" by the Mitchells. Antler, *Lucy Sprague Mitchell*, 209–210, 250–51.

63. Jane M. Dewey, "Biography of John Dewey," 30.

64. Jane Addams, *Twenty Years at Hull-House* (New York: Macmillan, 1910), and "The Settlement as a Way of Life," *Neighborhood* 2 (July 1929), 139–46; and Mary McDowell, "The Settlement as a Way of Life," *Neighborhood*, 2 (July 1929), 146–58.

65. Jane M. Dewey, "Biography of John Dewey," 29.

66. Allen F. Davis and Mary Lynn McCree, eds., *Eighty Years at Hull-House* (Chicago: Quadrangle Books, 1969), 100. Alice Hamilton left in 1919 to become the first woman professor at Harvard Medical School.

67. Deegan, *Jane Addams and the Men*, 39, 41. Deegan also refers to Mead's article, "The Working Hypothesis in Social Reform," *American Journal of Sociology* 5 (March, 1899): 369–71.

68. Clapp, *Community Schools,* 67.

69. This practice is an organizing theme in Addams's *Twenty Years.*

70. See Julia Lathrop, "Hull-House as a Laboratory of Sociological Investigation," *Proceedings of the Twenty-First National Conference of Charities,* 21 (1984), 313–20.

71. Dewey, in Mayhew and Edwards, *Dewey School,* 7. Also *LW* 11: 195.

72. Gary Bullert says that Wesley Mitchell and Thorstein Veblen were "Dewey's two closest associates among academic economists." Lucy Mitchell is not mentioned in any context. *The Politics of John Dewey* (Buffalo, New York: Prometheus Books, 1983), 26.

73. Mitchell, *Two Lives,* 87–88. Given women's exclusion from elite university faculties and in view of Dewey's and Mead's mentoring and active support of female academics and of women's issues, Lucy Mitchell's gibe at Dewey's male academic followers as "lesser folk" seems particularly apt.

74. Jane M. Dewey, "Biography of John Dewey," 37.

75. Deegan, *Jane Addams and the Men,* 2.

76. Deegan, "The Clinical Sociology of Jessie Taft." Information on Taft is taken from this source.

77. Deegan, *Jane Addams and the Men,* 2.

78. Myrtle B. McGraw, autobiographical sketch in O'Connell and Russo, *Models of Achievement,* 50. Dewey also wrote an introduction to McGraw's *Growth: A Study of Johnny and Jimmy* (New York: D. Appleton-Century Co., 1935). Rpt. *LW* 11: 510–14.

79. The John Dewey Society for the Study of Education and Culture, Special Collections, Southern Illinois University at Carbondale.

80. McGraw, quoted in O'Connell and Russo, *Models of Achievement,* 48–49.

81. Talbot was one of the first women members of the sociology department and the Dean of Women at the University of Chicago, having been recruited in 1892 from Wellesley College. Mary Jo Deegan, "Sociology at Wellesley College: 1900–1919," *Journal of the History of Sociology,* 5/1 (1983): 91–115.

82. Scarborough and Furumoto, *Untold Lives,* 43. Calkins was hired at Wellesley by Alice Freeman (Palmer). Ladd-Franklin was appointed yearly as a part-time lecturer at Johns Hopkins from 1904 to 1909 and at Columbia University from 1915 until she died in 1930. No complete bibliography for Ladd-Franklin exists, and the only writings on women's issues I have found are a short article, "College Life for Women" (October 24, 1889), and two reviews, one on Mary Wollstonecraft, *A Vindication of the Rights of Woman* (February 19, 1891) and one on Ch. Letourneau, *The Evolution of Marriage* (July 16, 1891), all published anonymously in *The Nation;* and "Endowed Professorships for Women," *Association for Collegiate Alumnae Bulletin,* Series 3, no. 9 (February, 1904), 53–61. O'Connell and Russo, *Models of Achievement,* 220, 226.

83. For the importance of support networks for women, see Blanche Wiesen Cook, "Female Support Networks and Political Activism: Lillian Wald, Crystal Eastman, Emma Goldman," *Chrysalis,* 3 (1977): 43–61.

84. In the Progressive era "Chicago offered not only similar intellectual influences but a chance to participate in an unusually well defined and self-conscious

community of academic women," Fitzpatrick, *Endless Crusade*, xiii. The location of the University of Chicago "in a center of urban reform, its commitment to graduate education, connections between women faculty, social reformers, and feminists, and the determination of Marion Talbot made possible women's achievements," Gordon, *Gender and Higher Education*, 120.

85. Taft cites Charlotte Perkins Gilman, *Women and Economics* and *Our Androcentric Culture;* and Edith Abbott, *Women in Industry* (New York: D. Appleton, 1910).

86. Calkins cherished her introduction to psychology via a private seminar with James on his newly published *Principles of Psychology*. The other three students, all male, dropped out in the early weeks of the Fall of 1890, and "it is just possible that Calkins' presence in James' seminar quite literally drove the men students out." Scarborough and Furumoto, *Untold Lives*, 36.

87. Scarborough and Furumoto, *Untold Lives*, 84, 88–90.

88. Lucy Sprague Mitchell, *Know Your Children in School* (New York: Macmillan, 1954), 14.

89. Antler, *Lucy Sprague Mitchell*, xx. See also Antler, "Feminism as Life Process: The Life and Career of Lucy Sprague Mitchell," *Feminist Studies* 7 (Spring 1981): 134–57.

90. The professional careers of these women philosophers paralleled those of other women who pursued graduate study in the decades before and after the turn of the century. They "faced unparalleled opportunities in American higher education and persistent constraints in realizing professional goals." Edith Abbott, Sophonisba P. Breckinridge, Katherine Bement Davis, and Frances Kellor never became professors in their fields of study. "Rather, they applied their education as social scientists to new areas of social activism." Fitzpatrick, *Endless Crusade*, xii–viii.

91. Mitchell, *Two Lives*, 121.

FOUR

1. Rosenberg, *Beyond Separate Spheres*, 115–16.

2. First under Dewey's leadership and then under Tuft's and Mead's, undergraduates as well as graduates at the University of Chicago were influenced by the pragmatist school of thought centered in the interdisciplinary philosophy department. The Chicago school of pragmatism persisted until 1931, when President Robert M. Hutchins succeeded in forcing on the department his view of philosophy as limited to the traditional canon, detached from current social problems. See David L. Miller, *George Herbert Mead*, xxxvii–xxxviii. So great were Dewey's contributions that his influence on faculty and students persisted as long as the pragmatist school of philosophy lasted at Chicago. Darnell Rucker, *The Chicago Pragmatists* (Minneapolis: University of Minnesota Press, 1960), ix.

3. Rosenberg, *Separate Spheres*, 110.

4. Wilson, *Science, Community, and the Transformation of American Philosophy, 1860–1930*, 194.

5. See James T. Kloppenberg, *Uncertain Victory* (New York: Oxford University Press, 1986).

6. Vernon J. Williams Jr., "Franz U. Boas and the Conflict between Science and Values, 1894–1915," *American Philosophical Association Newsletter on Philosophy and the Black Experience,* ed. Leonard Harris, 92/1 (1993): 7–16.

7. Rosenberg, *Separate Spheres,* 53 and 52, n. 52.

8. Rucker, *Chicago Pragmatists,* 162.

9. Max Eastman points out how central Alice Chipman's influence was in getting John Dewey involved in practical social and political issues. At the time they met at the University of Michigan, Eastman describes Alice as "a strong-minded girl, descended from a family of radicals and freethinkers, an ardent woman suffragist, deeply religious but of no church, and brilliantly intolerant of 'bunk.'" *Great Companions* (New York: Farrar, Straus and Cudahy, 1959), 264.

10. Rosenberg, *Separate Spheres,* 66.

11. Rosenberg, *Separate Spheres,* 48–51.

12. Her thesis was later published: Helen Bradford Thompson (Woolley), *The Mental Traits of Sex: An Experimental Investigation of the Normal Mind in Men and Women* (Chicago: University of Chicago Press, 1903), 167–68. Information about Helen Thompson Woolley is taken from Rosenberg, chap. 3.

13. Mary W. Calkins, "Community of Ideas of Men and Women," *Psychological Review* 3 (July, 1896): 426. As quoted in Rosenberg, *Separate Spheres,* 74.

14. Rosenberg, *Separate Spheres,* 80. As Dewey also emphasized, it is fallacious to assume that analyzing an arbitrary segment of experience could provide accurate data which could then be summed up as the scientific facts of the case. No social study can be scientific that ignores "the conditioning antecedents and the consequences which are the inevitable outcome of what is locally and immediately at hand." "Liberating the Social Scientist," *LW* 15: 227–28.

15. Rosenberg, *Separate Spheres,* 81.

16. Rosenberg, *Separate Spheres,* 81.

17. W. E. B. Du Bois, *The Autobiography of W. E. B. Du Bois* (New York: International, 1980, 148. Orig. 1968. Although the advice in both cases was kindly meant to prevent the frustration of pursuing a nearly impossible goal, and was taken by the advisees as such, we can question in hindsight whether such practical realism did not inadvertently contribute to the prejudiced perception that blacks and women were inappropriate vehicles for the transmission of the culture's rational values. In thus preserving the status quo rather than challenging it and publicly supporting the entrance of discriminated groups into the philosophical professorate, the pragmatist principles of inclusiveness and empowerment were subverted.

18. Rosenberg, *Separate Spheres,* 83.

19. Mayhew and Edwards, *Dewey School,* 7.

20. *John Dewey and Arthur F. Bentley,* ed. Ratner and Altman, 10.

21. Cornel West, *American Evasion,* 6, 12, 14–18, 28.

22. Alice and John Dewey, for example, named one of their daughters Jane Mary after Jane Addams and her close friend Mary Rozet Smith, as reported in George Dykhuizen, *The Life and Mind of John Dewey* (Carbondale and Edwardsville: Southern Illinois University Press, 1973), 106. In Smith's intimate friendship with Addams, she took on the role of a wife. Robyn Muncy, *Creating a Female Dominion in American Reform 1890–1935* (New York: Oxford University Press, 1991), 16.

23. Dykhuizen days of Dewey's encounters with Hull House that "his contacts with people with more radical and extreme views than his deepened and sharpened his own ideas." *Life and Mind of Dewey*, 105.

24. Rosenberg, *Separate Spheres*, 34.

25. Dewey, quoted in Paul Kellogg, "Twice Twenty Years at Hull-House," in *Eighty Years*, 171.

26. Francis Hackett, "Hull-House—A Souvenir," *Eighty Years*, 73.

27. Lois Rudnick, "A Feminist American Success Myth: Jane Addams's *Twenty Years at Hull-House*," in *Tradition and the Talents of Women*, ed. Florence Howe (Urbana: University of Illinois Press, 1991), 146.

28. Addams, *Twenty Years*, 58, 236.

29. For Addams's speech, see "A Toast to John Dewey," *The Social Thought of Jane Addams*, 175–83.

30. Addams, quoted in *LW* 15: 196.

31. Addams, *Twenty Years*, 237.

32. Hamilton, quoted in Hackett, *Eighty Years*, 76, 74.

33. Hamilton, "Hull-House Within and Without," *Eighty Years*, 100, 102. Excerpted from her autobiography, *Exploring the Dangerous Trades* (Boston, 1943), 68–87.

34. W. E. B. Du Bois, *Darkwater* (New York: Harcourt, Brace and Howe, 1920), 140.

35. Hamilton, "Hull-House," *Eighty Years*, 103.

36. Davis and McCree, *Eighty Years*, 22.

37. Lagemann, *Jane Addams on Education*, 25–26. See also Florence Kelley, "I Go to Work," *Survey* 58, 5 (1927), 271–74. Kelley's description of "The Women of Hull House" is excerpted in *Women's America: Refocusing the Past*, 3d ed., ed. Linda K. Kerber and Jane Sherron De Hart (New York: Oxford University Press, 1991), 302–6.

38. John C. Farrell, *Beloved Lady* (Baltimore: Johns Hopkins University Press, 1967), 69.

39. Anne Phillips, *Engendering Democracy* (University Park, PA: Pennsylvania State University Press, 1991), 112.

40. Ella Flagg Young, *Isolation in the School* (Chicago: University of Chicago Press, 1900).

41. According to Mayhew and Edwards, in the first years of the Laboratory School both staff and students were small in number, and because of the close cooperation of directors and teachers, administrative lines were not sharply drawn. Because of the growth from 1900 to 1902 the organization became less haphazard and more formal, largely thanks to Young's administrative skills. John continued as director, Ella became supervisor of instruction, and Alice's "previous informal connection now became official as principal of the school" from 1901 to 1903. No specific date is given for Young. *Dewey School*, 8–9. John T. McManis says that Young became a supervisor in 1900. *Ella Flagg Young and a Half-Century of the Chicago Public Schools* (Chicago: A. C. McClurg, 1916), 109. The critical edition lists 1901 as the date John appointed both Ella and Alice (*LW* 11:199).

42. The department of pedagogy is given on the title page of Young's disser-

tation as the department of her affiliation. But according to John T. McManis, she was dissatisfied with that choice and was instrumental in changing it to the department of education. McManis, *Ella Flagg Young,* 116.

43. McManis, *Ella Flagg Young,* 116.

44. Young, "Isolation in the School" (no. 1, 1901), "Ethics in the School" (no. 4, 1906), and "Some Types of Modern Educational Theory" (no. 6, 1909); Dewey, "Psychology and Social Practice" (no. 2, 1901), "The Educational Situation" (no. 3, 1902), and "The Child and the Curriculum" (no. 5, 1902). *Contributions to Education,* (University of Chicago Press). Series found in the Newberry Library, Chicago. While at the University of Chicago Young also wrote *Scientific Method in Education,* First series, vol. 3 of *Decennial Publications* (Chicago: University of Chicago Press, 1903). Unless otherwise noted, information in this paragraph and the previous one is taken from McManis, *Ella Flagg Young,* 101–16.

45. Dewey letter in McManis, *Ella Flagg Young,* 119–20.

46. This thorough integration of their experience of the interactive character of learning into theories of knowledge and value seems to have been a particular contribution of women teachers to pragmatism. Louise M. Rosenblatt, for instance, says: "My classroom experiences made me realize that essential to the assimilation of such social insights was a personally experienced evocation of the literary work rather than the traditional text-oriented promulgation of an interpretation by a teacher. And I had observed the value of interchange among students as a stimulant to the development of critical and self-critical reading, essential to citizens of a democracy." *The Reader the Text the Poem,* 180.

47. McManis, *Ella Flagg Young,* 121.

48. McManis, *Ella Flagg Young,* 119–20.

49. McManis, *Ella Flagg Young,* 121–22. Presumably Dewey was speaking of Eleanor Roosevelt.

50. Dewey, "The School and Society," review of *School and Society in Chicago* by George S. Counts (New York: Harcourt, Brace, 1928), first published in *New Republic,* 10 April 1929, 231–32, (*LW* 5: 371–74).

51. "The exclusion of black women from the white women's clubs and the ignoring or trivializing of life-and-death black issues, such as lynching, have been amply documented." Linda Gordon, "Black and White Visions of Welfare: Women's Welfare Activism, 1890–1945," *Journal of American History* 78/2 (1991): 564.

52. Information about the battle over coeducation is taken from Rosenberg, *Separate Spheres,* 43–51.

53. "Is Co-Education Injurious to Girls?" (*MW* 6: 155–64). Originally published in *Ladies' Home Journal,* 28 (1911), 22, 60–61.

54. Cornel West, *American Evasion,* 85.

55. Ratner and Altman, *John Dewey and Arthur F. Bentley,* 10.

56. Westbrook, *John Dewey and American Democracy,* 112–13.

57. James Miller, "The Common Faith," *Nation,* 14 October 1991, 452.

58. Mayhew, *Dewey School,* 14, 17, 18.

59. "Essay," in John D. Buenker, John C. Burnham, and Robert M. Crunden, *Progressivism* (Cambridge, MA: Schenkman, 1977), 103, n. 44.

60. Robert L. McCaul, "Dewey and the University of Chicago," *School and Society,* Part I: July, 1894–March, 1902 (March 25, 1961), 152–57; Part II: April, 1902–May, 1903 (April 8, 1961), 179–83; Part III: September, 1903–June, 1904

(April 22, 1961), 202–6. Jo Ann Boydston pointed out this source in "The Chicago Years: Breaking Away," given at the conference, John Dewey in Illinois, Center for Dewey Studies, Southern Illinois University at Carbondale, October 8, 1994. George Dykhuizen's account in *Life and Mind of Dewey* also draws heavily on McCaul's. See pp. 107–115 and 353, n. 52.

61. McCaul, Part I, 152, 205.

62. McCaul, Part II, 181. McCaul gives the details of Dewey's relations with the two schools throughout the article.

63. McCaul, Part III, 203.

64. Alice's decisions, according to Eastman, "were swift, direct, and harshly realistic." He also says that John was aware that "she was not a good mixer. She had an uncanny gift of seeing through people who were faking, and made such witty game of them that she alarmed even those who were not faking—or, at least, not faking very much." So there does not seem to be extra-archival evidence of friction with her teachers. Eastman, *Great Companions,* 273 and 277.

65. McCaul, Part III, 203.

66. McCaul, Part III, 204.

67. McCaul, Part III, 205.

68. Dewey's resignation over issues of governance parallels Young's own principled resignation from the position of superintendent in the public schools because the increased centralization of power was eroding the freedom of teachers to make crucial decisions regarding education. One can speculate that her resignation some five years earlier, protesting the erosion of democratic governance in the organizational changes instituted following the recommendations for a consolidation of power made by the Harper Commission, inspired Dewey's own decision, which was also precipitated by President Harper. McManis, *Ella Flagg Young,* 104–7.

69. Eastman, *Great Companions,* 277. Eastman maintains that without Alice there would not even have been a Dewey School. He says that she "would grab Dewey's ideas—and grab him—and insist that something be done. . . . Dewey's views of his wife's influence is that she put 'guts and stuffing' into what had been with him mere intellectual conclusions," 273.

70. See Joe R. Burnett, Introduction (*MW* 1: xxii).

71. After searching through the documents at the archives of the University of Chicago, McCaul hints at an even more sinister explanation: "Perhaps the housecleaning of several generations of archivists has resulted in a deposit slanted in Harper's favor or, less likely, in Dewey's favor." Part I, 153.

72. McCaul, Part III, 205–6.

73. Eastman, *Great Companions,* 274.

74. Eastman, *Great Companions,* 278.

FIVE

1. Conversely, without an awareness of Dewey's other writings, "his aesthetics and consequently his pedagogy" will be misunderstood. At some point the hermeneutic circle must be entered if a beginning of understanding is to be made, but Dewey's positions more than those of most thinkers cannot be compartmentalized nor adequately understood from only one angle. John J. McDermott, "The Gamble for Excellence: Dewey's Pedagogy of Experience," in *Values and*

Value Theory in Twentieth-Century America: Essays in Honor of Elizabeth Flower, ed. Murray G. Murphey and Ivar Berg (Philadelphia: Temple University Press, 1988), 108.

2. Dewey's remarks were originally made in "From Absolutism to Experimentalism," *Contemporary American Philosophy,* ed. George Plimpton Adams and William Pepperell Montague, vol. 2 (New York: Macmillan, 1930), 13–27; rpt. *LW* 5:147–160. In 1939, when he was eighty years old, Dewey once again emphasized the centrality of education to his thought by linking the central concept of pragmatism with it in *Experience and Education* (*LW* 13:1–62).

3. See "What Is the Matter with Teaching?" (*LW* 2:116–23); and Mayhew, *Dewey School,* 372–73; rpt. *LW* 11:199–200.

4. Jane Addams remarked that only the unbreakable walls of division in the different departments of the United States government rivaled the gulf between departments of philosophy and education, one which the pragmatists at the University of Chicago nonetheless successfully bridged. *The Social Thought of Jane Addams,* ed. Lasch, 179.

5. Richard Rorty, "The Priority of Democracy to Philosophy," in *The Virginia Statute for Religious Freedom,* ed. Merrill D. Peterson and Robert C. Vaughan (Cambridge, England: Cambridge University Press, 1988), 261–63, 273, 275.

6. Sidney Hook, for example, rejects a metaphysical interpretation of Dewey's *Experience and Nature,* calling it instead "a philosophical anthropology" that stresses "the interactions and transactions between the human organism and its environment" (*LW* 1:xvi). Westbrook also takes issue with Rorty's remark about philosophical anthropology. *John Dewey and American Democracy,* 367, n. 37.

7. Judith W. Kay, "Politics Without Human Nature?" *Hypatia* 9/1 (1994): 21.

8. Mayhew shows, for instance, how easily Dewey mingled the public and the private and how important it was for the development of his philosophy, especially his idea of experiment: "The early flowering of Mr. Dewey's philosophy into practice was stimulated by a twofold desire for a laboratory to test his educational philosophy and to provide opportunity for growth and development in his own children." Not only did Dewey turn to educational philosophy "mainly on account of the children," but "his own nursery was his laboratory wherein to test [his] theories" about the function of thought, feelings, and activity in growth and development. "The educational possibilities of the fundamental activities of the home and especially of farm life interested him greatly," and when the parents of one of his students moved with their four children from the city to the country Dewey took it as an experiment in education. "The father of the family treasured in his old age Mr. Dewey's acknowledgment of the value of this experiment in the formulating of his educational theories." Mayhew, *Dewey School,* 446–47.

9. Westbrook also suggests reading *Experience and Nature* and *The Quest for Certainty* as fulfilling the program laid out in *Philosophy and Democracy. John Dewey,* 366.

10. See Dewey, "The Influence of Darwinism on Philosophy," *MW* 4:3–14.

11. Helen E. Longino, *Science as Social Knowledge* (Princeton: Princeton University Press, 1990), 214–15.

12. Virginia Held, *Rights and Goods* (New York: Free Press, 1984), 272.

13. Dewey, *Individualism, Old and New* (1929), *LW* 5:81–83.

14. Held, *Rights and Goods*, 60.

15. Ross continues: "That meant that it was as natural for a thing to be known as it was for it to grow, and as natural for it to be changed purposely as a result of its being known as it was for it to decay or erode. It also meant that mind and consciousness lost any non-natural spiritual quality and became organic functions or relations of knowing and awareness, rather than private entities." Introduction, *MW* 7 : xi–xii.

16. Virginia Held, *Feminist Morality* (University of Chicago Press, 1993), 6–8.

17. *Individualism Old and New, LW* 5 : 41 – 123; *The Public and its Problems, LW* 2 : 235 – 372; and *Liberalism and Social Action, LW* 11 : 1 – 65.

18. Dewey, *Living Philosophies* (New York: Simon and Schuster, 1931), 32 – 33. I am grateful to Phillip W. Jackson for calling my attention to these passages. Rpt. *LW* 5 : 276.

19. W. E. B. Du Bois, *Darkwater*, intro. Herbert Aptheker (Millwood, NY: Kraus-Thomson Organization, 1991), 20–21. Orig. 1920.

20. Patricia Hill Collins, "Mammies, Matriarchs, and Other Controlling Images," in *Feminist Philosophies*, ed. Janet A. Kourany, James P. Sterba, and Rosemarie Tong (NJ: Prentice Hall, 1992), 119–28.

21. See chap. 3, n. 62.

22. Laggemann, "The Plural Worlds of Educational Research," 204–7.

23. Dewey letters to Scudder Klyce, 5 July 1915, 8 May 1920. The Center for Dewey Studies, Southern Illinois University, Carbondale.

24. Nellie Y. McKay, "The Souls of Black Women Folk in the Writings of W. E. B. Du Bois," *Reading Black, Reading Feminist*, ed. Henry Louis Gates Jr. (New York: A Meridian Book, 1990), 237–38. McKay examines Du Bois's work from the perspective of feminist autobiography: "Using the criteria of inclusiveness of experience, and an awareness of race and gender oppression as aspects of the composition of feminist autobiography, Du Bois comes closer to consciously repudiating the intellectual/emotional, mind/body split than many other writers of intellectual autobiography," 229. The citations to *Darkwater* in the quotation are in McKay's text.

25. Du Bois's positions are taken from "The Damnation of Women," *Darkwater*, 163–86.

26. Du Bois is, of course, giving a black man's view of black women, whose perspectives will inevitably differ in significant ways. This difference in critical perspective is evident in McKay's article, which goes beyond the one essay on "The Damnation of Women." Even in this one essay I notice the erasure of contemporary black women intellectuals; for example, when he introduces a striking quote by the phrase "As one of our women writes," without identifying who the woman is. *Darkwater*, 173.

27. See bell hooks, "Sisterhood: Political Solidarity between Women," *Feminist Philosophies*, 391–404.

28. Even today, Frank B. Dilley reports that of 273 philosophy doctoral dissertations written in the United States and Canada in 1991–1992, only 18 (fewer than 7 percent) were directed by women. He also says that nearly 30 percent of new doctoral degrees are awarded to women, and continues: "A possible explanation of the discrepancy between the number of women members of the profes-

sion and the number of dissertation advisers who are women is that women philosophers tend to be clustered at the lower ranks and located at institutions where there are not large numbers of graduate students." Letter to the Editor, *Proceedings and Addresses of the American Philosophical Association* 67/6 (1994): 59. For statistics of the number of women philosophers with Ph.D.'s, numbers employed, academic rank, and so forth, see Helen E. Longino, "Report from the Chair," *APA Newsletter on Feminism and Philosophy* 94/1 (Fall, 1994): 52–53.

29. A beginning to recognizing such absences is found in Steven A. Fesmire's remark in his review of a book of interviews with American philosophers: "Although one suspects a randomness in [the author's] choices (as evidenced by her unfortunate omission of women), the result is an intriguing blend of harmonies and tensions." Review of *The American Philosophers: Conversations with Quine, Davidson, Putnam, Nozik, Danto, Rorty, Cavell, Macintyre, and Kuhn*, by Giovanna Borradori, trans. Rosanna Crocitto (Chicago: University of Chicago Press, 1994), in *Newsletter of the Society for the Advancement of American Philosophy*, 68 (June, 1994), 37. For documentation of the narrow range of people in the philosophical profession—"the American philosophy professoriate is still very much a matter of live white males teaching about dead ones"—see Nicholas Rescher, "American Philosophy Today," *Review of Metaphysics* 46 (June, 1993): 717–45.

SIX

1. George Cotkin also points out a "certain blindness" in James in regard to the "inner realities" of the working class. *William James, Public Philosopher* (Baltimore, Johns Hopkins University Press, 1990), 111.

2. Addams, *Twenty Years at Hull-House, The Long Road of Women's Memory* (New York: Macmillan, 1916), *Democracy and Social Ethics* (New York: Macmillan, 1902); and *Who Cares?* ed. Mary M. Brabeck, *Theory, Research, and Educational Implications of the Ethic of Care*, ed. Mary M. Brabeck (New York: Praeger, 1990).

3. Jane Addams, "Why Women Should Vote," "If Men Were Seeking the Franchise," "Utilization of Women in City Government," "The World's Food Supply and Woman's Obligation," *Jane Addams: A Centennial Reader*, ed. Emily Cooper Johnson (New York: Macmillan, 1960), 104–7, 107–13, 113–23; 130–35; Deegan, *Jane Addams and the Men of the Chicago School, 1892–1918*, 230–33.

4. Marion Talbot and Lois Kimball Matthews Rosenberry, *The History of the American Association of University Women, 1881–1931* (Cambridge, MA: Houghton Mifflin, 1931); and Mabel Newcomer, *A Century of Higher Education for American Women* (New York: Harper Brothers, 1959).

5. See James's discussion, for instance, concerning the fact that "there are innumerable consciousnesses of emptiness, no one of which taken in itself has a name, but all different from each other" *PPI*, 243.

6. See, for instance, Sandra Harding, "Why Has the Sex-Gender System Become Visible Only Now?" in *Discovering Reality*, ed. Harding and Hintikka.

7. Nancy Tuana says that women reading the canonical philosophers often experience an alienation that is amorphous rather than focused because the source of the unease, the uncritical assumption by the philosopher of women as Other, is pervasive and explicit only in asides that do not seem to affect the main

arguments put forth. *Woman and the History of Philosophy* (New York: Paragon House, 1992), 4–5.

8. Naomi Scheman, "Changing the Subject," *Newsletter on Feminism and Philosophy* 92/1 (1993): 47.

9. See Howard McGary, "Philosophy and Diversity: The Inclusion of African and African-American Materials," *Newsletter on Feminism and Philosophy* 92/1 (1993): 51.

10. Virginia Woolf, *A Room of One's Own* (London: Hogarth Press, 1928).

11. Examples of "James's enlightened attitude toward women" can be found in Gerald E. Myers, *William James: His Life and Thought* (New Haven: Yale University Press, 1986), 428–29.

12. See Ann Douglas, *The Feminization of American Culture* (New York: Avon Books, 1977).

13. Tuana, *Woman*, 7, 10.

14. For fringe/horizon see Seigfried, *William James's Radical Reconstruction*, 79–81, 184–85, 203–4, 277–78.

15. Morris Grossman, review of *The Creation of Chaos*, by Frederick J. Ruf (Albany: State University of New York Press, 1991), *Charles S. Peirce Society* 28/4 (1992): 890–91.

16. James (*ECR*), 246–56. The review originally appeared in *North American Review* 109 (October, 1869): 556–65.

17. See Linda A. Bell's criticism of James's arguments for the dependency of women in marriage: "Does Marriage Require a Head? Some Historical Arguments," *Hypatia* 4/1 (1989): 148–49.

18. A clue to James's conception of women's mental capacity can be gathered from his 1887 review of Henry T. Finck's *Romantic Love and Personal Beauty*, in which he ends a series of direct quotations that celebrate and help confirm "the ideal of American young people" with this remark: "Nor would female education be any longer neglected, were it fully understood how essential it is to Personal Beauty and true Romantic Love, the basis of happy conjugal life" (*ECR*, 407).

19. Myers, however, refers to others who did recognize James's sexism, particularly George A. Garrison and Edward H. Madden, "William James—Warts and All," *American Quarterly* 29 (1977): 212–21. *William James*, 597, n. 109, 424–27.

20. Myers, *William James*, 425.

21. Myers, *William James*, 426.

22. James, *The Meaning of Truth* (*MT*) (Cambridge: Harvard University Press, 1975), 103, n. 2.

23. See William R. Woodward, Introduction, to *Essays in Psychology* (*EPS*) (Cambridge: Harvard University Press, 1983), xiv–xvii.

24. This linking of "lower races" and women as natural examples of inferior intelligence was still prevalent thirty years later. See Vernon J. Williams Jr., "Franz U. Boas and the Conflict between Science and Values, 1894–1915," *APA Newsletter on Philosophy and the Black Experience* 92/1 (1993): 7–16, especially, 14.

25. "On a Certain Blindness in Human Beings" and "What Makes a Life Significant," *Talks to Teachers on Psychology TT* (Cambridge: Harvard University Press, 1983).

26. See Brabeck, *Who Cares?*

27. The ethics of care is discussed in chap. 9.

28. Dewey came to the same conclusion about an earlier passage of James's (*PPI*, 305) about mothers' instinctive love for their babies, which Dewey characterizes as "a natural response to a particular situation, and one lacking in moral quality as far as it is wholly unreflective, not involving the ideal of *any* end, good or bad" (*LW* 7: 294).

29. Interestingly, this passage occurs in the chapter "The Perception of Reality." James is illustrating his contention that human credulity has psychological roots. He continues: "Blame, dread, and hope are thus the great belief-inspiring passions, and cover among them the future, the present, and the past."

30. William James's son, Henry, confirms that William's wife, Alice, lived up to his high moral expectations, which may help account for why he was so enamored of the role of women as selfless servant: "His wife, who entered into all his plans and undertakings with unfailing understanding and high spirit, stood guard over his library door, protected him from interruptions and distractions, managed the household and the children and family business, helped him to order his day and to see and entertain his friends at convenient times, sped him off on occasional much-needed vacations, and encouraged him to all his major undertakings, with a sustaining skill and cheer which need not be described to anyone who knew his household. . . . If consulted, she would not tolerate even this allusion." Henry James, *The Letters of William James,* vol. 1 (Boston: Atlantic Monthly Press, 1920), 193.

31. Men's natural pugnacity, love of war, and will to overcome others is the underlying theme of all James's writings on pacifism. See "Robert Gould Shaw: Oration by Professor William James," "Remarks at Peace Banquet," and "The Moral Equivalent of War," *Essays in Religion and Morality* (*ERM*) (Harvard University Press, 1982).

32. James's equation of heroic male characteristics with human characteristics is found in such statements as "Our permanent enemy is the noted bellicosity of human nature. Man, biologically considered, and whatever else he may be in the bargain, is simply the most formidable of all beasts of prey" (*ERM*, 121).

33. James further contributes to the misogynist tradition of warning young men against the snares of women's sexuality and domesticity by quoting "a worldly-wise old friend" in a note in *Varieties of Religious Experience:* "Woman's heart and love are a shrewd device of Nature, a trap which she sets for the average man, to force him into working. But the wise man will always prefer work chosen by himself." (Cambridge: Harvard University Press, 1985), 121–22, n.10.

34. Compare this ideal with the remarks made by Peter Alden in George Santayana's *The Last Puritan,* explaining why he will marry Caroline: "She has consciously undertaken to heal me, to do the mother in the wife" (New York: Charles Scribner's Sons, 1936), 64. Santayana, a Harvard colleague of James, subtitled his book "A Memoir in the Form of a Novel."

35. Letter of 1882 to his wife, Alice, in Henry James, *Letters,* vol. 1, 211.

36. The phrase "alien lives" occurs on p. 165.

37. Ralph Waldo Emerson, *Nature,* in *Emerson on Transcendentalism,* ed. Edward L. Ericson (New York: Ungar, 1987), 36.

38. Emerson, *Nature,* 45–46.

39. James's position provides evidence for some recent feminist evaluations of literature, typified by Elaine Showalter and Carolyn Heilbrun, who argue that "Western culture was no longer seen as a republic of letters to which both sexes were equal heirs but as a state in which the rulers were usurping men who had recreated women in alienated terms as nature, inspiration or chaos." Janet Todd, *Feminist Literary History* (New York: Routledge, 1988), 27.

40. James, *Manuscript Lectures* (*ML*) (Cambridge: Harvard University Press, 1988), 63.

41. The pervasiveness and ambiguity of James's appeals to gender as a basic ordering device can be seen in his characterization of the spirit of Greek classicism as "too essentially masculine for pessimism to be elaborated" in contrast to the tragic character of life experienced by "races more complex, and (so to speak) more feminine than the Hellenes had attained to" (*VRE,* 120–21, n. 9).

42. For an insightful discussion of the central problems surrounding the metaphorical gendering of reason, see Phyllis Rooney, "Gendered Reason: Sex Metaphor and Conceptions of Reason," *Hypatia* 6/2 (1991): 77–103.

43. "The Energies of Men" (*ERM,* 129–46) is a sustained appeal to scientific men to recognize and utilize "the mystical portions of our nature freely" (*ERM,* 131). James invokes the story of his friend with breast cancer as an example of the power of mind over matter and explicitly links women, saintliness, mysticism, expansiveness, and powers that make intellectual men uncomfortable. He says that men inhibited by their scientific respectability are like persons who work with only one finger, refusing to utilize a greater range of organic powers, and urges them to get in touch with their mystical side. Scientists should utilize historical and biographical material rather than laboratory experimentation in order "to get a topographic survey made of the limits of human power . . . and we ought then to construct a methodical inventory of the paths of access, or keys . . . to the different kinds of power" (*ERM,* 145).

44. The extreme masculinizing of human virtues is most apparent in "The Moral Equivalent of War" (*ERM,* 162–73). Although James dissociates himself from the cruelty and rapaciousness of war, he admires the militaristic strenuousness that scorns co-education and "feminism unabashed" as breeding softness and insipidity (*ERM,* 166).

45. James's defense of religion at a time when intellectual fashions were turning toward positivistic science and religion was becoming women's special province seems to be a factor in his continuing worries over his masculinity and intellectual rigor. In an 1882 letter to Thomas Davidson, for instance, he says that by dropping the dogma of God's all-exclusive reality and adopting the hypothesis of a primordial pluralism, "piety forthwith ceases to be incompatible with manliness, and religious 'faith' with intellectual rectitude." Ralph Barton Perry, *The Thought and Character of William James,* vol. 1 (Boston: Little, Brown, 1935), 738.

46. Dale Spender argues that such appropriations are the rule rather than the exception in *Women of Ideas.*

47. See Seigfried, *William James's Radical Reconstruction,* 61–64.

48. Germaine Greer says that according to the stereotype of the Eternal Feminine a woman "need achieve nothing, for she is the reward of achievement. . . .

The matter is solely one of male rivalry." "The Stereotype," in *Philosophy of Woman*, 2d. ed., ed. Mahowald, 9.

49. See Jean Strouse, *Alice James: A Biography* (Boston: Houghton Mifflin, 1980). One can wonder whether William's intimate knowledge of Alice's nervous prostrations and life of invalidism influenced his advocacy of exercise for women as a way of overcoming nervous disorders and engaging in a fuller, more productive life. In "The Gospel of Relaxation" (1899) he points out that women's lives in Norway have been revolutionized by their participation in the new sport of skiing. What had happened since his review of *Subjection of Women* in 1869 for William James to ridicule as an "old-fashioned ideal of femininity, the 'domestic angel,' the 'gentle and refining influence' sort of thing"? The daring Norwegian women who donned skis to defy darkness and heights are reported as not only rejecting "the traditional feminine pallor and delicacy of constitution, but actually taking the lead in every educational and social reform" (*TT*, 119–20).

50. Quoted in Ruth Bernard Yeazell, *The Death and Letters of Alice James* (Berkeley: University of California, 1981), 107.

51. Yeazell, *Death and Letters*, 121.

52. John J. McDermott, ed., *The Writings of William James* (New York: Modern Library, 1968), 448–49.

53. See, for example, how Marjorie C. Miller's feminist reading brings out the structural and functional misogyny of Santayana's writings in "Essence and Identity: Santayana and the Category 'Women,'" *Charles S. Peirce Society* 30/1 (1994): 33–50.

54. As James goes on to say, "to some of us it proves a most inspiring notion," and philosophers have indeed praised these texts as examples of James's doctrine of the Promethean self. In commenting on his espousal of heroism and strenuosity, George Cotkin defends James against the charge of imperialism, to which the language lends itself. But by paraphrasing James's remarks as addressed to women as well as men, he ignores the issue of its masculinist bias. *William James, Public Philosopher*, 170–71.

55. See, for instance, the special issue on "Teaching in Ways That Attract Women and Minorities to the Profession," ed. Hilda Hein, *APA Newsletter on Feminism and Philosophy*, 92/1 (Spring, 1993), 44–64.

56. James, "The True Harvard (1903)," *ECR*, 77.

57. James, *Psychology: Briefer Course* (*PBC*) (Cambridge: Harvard University Press), 132–38. *The Freshman Girl: A Guide to College Life*, ed. Kate W. Jameson and Frank C. Lockwood (Boston: D. C. Heath, 1925. The authors are, besides seven deans, three present or retired college presidents: Mary E. Woolley of Mount Holyoke College, Ada Louise Comstock of Radcliffe College, and Le Baron Russell Briggs, former president of Radcliffe College; one M.D.; two professors, Vida D. Scudder of Wellesley College and Sarah M. Sturtevant of Columbia; an unaffiliated woman who writes on "Dancing"; and James's posthumous contribution.

58. This is not to say that the sexist tone is deliberate. The vehemence expressed might well reflect James's own lifelong ambivalence about being torn between an unstructured life of sentiment and a rigorous life of scientific thought. Perry assumes that "James's exhortation to action was addressed primar-

ily to himself" because of his "very definite tendency to brooding melancholy." Perry, *Thought and Character*, vol. 2, 674. Nonetheless, the valuations are expressed within a horizon of sexism that informs what is said as well as how it is said.

59. See Genevieve Lloyd, *The Man of Reason: 'Male' and 'Female' in Western Philosophy* (Minneapolis: University of Minnesota Press, 1984); Susan Bordo, *Flight to Objectivity;* Robin Schott, *Cognition and Eros;* and Karen J. Warren, "Male-Gender Bias and Western Conceptions of Reasons and Rationality," *APA Newsletter on Feminism and Philosophy*, 88/2 (1989): 48–58.

SEVEN

1. Harriet A. Jacobs, *Incidents in the Life of a Slave Girl Written by Herself*, ed. L. Maria Child (Cambridge: Harvard University Press, 1987), xiii, xx.

2. Carolyn Whitbeck, "A Different Reality" in *Women, Knowledge, and Reality*, ed. A. Garry and Marilyn Pearsall (Boston: Unwin Hyman, 1989), 69, n. 1.

3. "Perilous Balance: The Complex, Beleaguered Lives of Soviet Women," *Chicago Tribune*, 25 March 1990, sec. 14, p. 3.

4. See also Linda Alcoff, "Cultural Feminism Versus Poststructuralism," in *Feminist Theory in Practice and Process*, ed. Micheline R. Malson (Chicago: University of Chicago Press, 1989).

5. Riley, *"Am I That Name?"* 13. A recent example can be found in Sheila Ruth, *Issues in Feminism*, 2d ed., (Mountain View, CA: Mayfield, 1990), 413: "How, generations of women have asked, can one integrate claims to full equality with a sense of women's special identity?"

6. Riley, *"Am I That Name?"* 99, 114.

7. Riley, *"Am I That Name?"* 112–13.

8. *Art as Experience* (*LW* 10: 224).

9. *Experience and Nature* (*LW* 1: 67).

10. *The Quest for Certainty* (*LW* 4: 175).

11. "Context and Thought," (*LW* 6: 4).

12. "Valid Knowledge and the 'Subjectivity' of Experience" (*MW* 6: 80).

13. Patricia Hill Collins, *Black Feminist Thought* (New York: Routledge, 1991), 28–29.

14. A brief literature survey of feminist critiques of dualism is included in Whitbeck's "A Different Reality," *Women, Knowledge, and Reality*, 69, n.1.

15. Susan Sherwin, "Philosophical Methodology and Feminist Methodology: Are they Compatible?" in *Women, Knowledge, and Reality*, 32.

16. Stephanie Rieger, *Signs* 19 (Winter, 1994), 514–15.

17. See Seigfried, "Like Bridges Without Piers," in *Antifoundationalism, Old and New*, ed. Tom Rockmore and Beth J. Singer (Philadelphia: Temple University Press, 1992), 143–64.

18. For the pernicious effects of the construction of racial and gender differentiation and a call for a reconstruction of difference, see Paula Rothenberg, "The Construction, Deconstruction, and Reconstruction of Difference," *Hypatia* 5/1 (1990): 42–57.

19. See bell hooks, *Ain't I a Woman* (Boston: South End Press, 1981); Collins, *Black Feminist Thought;* Jill Johnston, *Lesbian Nation* (New York: Simon and Schus-

ter, 1974); Nancy Myron and Charlotte Bunch, eds., (*Lesbianism and the Women's Movement,* ed. Nancy Myron and Charlotte Bunch (Baltimore, MD: Diana Press, 1975); Maria Lugones and Elizabeth V. Spelman, "Have We Got a Theory For You! Feminist Theory, Cultural Imperialism, and the Demand for 'The Woman's Voice,'" in *Women and Values,* ed. Marilyn Pearsall (Belmont, CA: Wadsworth, 1986), 19–32.

20. Ellyn Kaschak, *Engendered Lives* (New York: Basic Books, 1992).

21. Judith Lewis Herman, "Seeing for Ourselves," *Women's Review of Books,* 10/5 (1993), 9–10.

22. David L. Miller, ed., *The Individual and the Social Self* (Chicago: University of Chicago Press, 1982), 73.

23. Jacobs, *Life of a Slave Girl,* xx–xxi.

24. Collins, *Black Feminist Thought,* 33.

25. For an analysis of pragmatist appeals to concrete experience, see Seigfried, *William James's Radical Reconstruction,* 75–116, 183–90, 263–68, 299–306, 317–24, and 356–60; and Dewey, *MW* 12: 166, 187–88, *MW* 6: 286–92, *LW* 8: 293–300.

26. Lorraine Code, *What Can She Know?* (Ithaca: Cornell University Press, 1991); Sandra Harding, *Whose Science? Whose Knowledge?* (Ithaca: Cornell University Press, 1991); Bell Hooks, *Feminist Theory from Margin to Center* (Boston, MA: South End Press, 1984); and Lynn Hankinson Nelson, *Who Knows? From Quine to a Feminist Empiricism* (Philadelphia: Temple University Press, 1990).

27. Dorothy E. Smith, *The Everyday World as Problematic* (Boston: Northeastern University Press, 1987), 109–10.

28. Smith, *Everyday World,* 109.

29. Linda Holler also argues for an embodied rationality in "Thinking with the Weight of the Earth," *Hypatia* 5/1 (1990): 1–23.

30. "Experience is emotional but there are no separate things called emotions in it" (*LW* 10: 48).

31. Lloyd, *Man of Reason,* 116, 126.

32. In keeping with my feminist reconstruction, I have changed *his* to *her.*

33. Dewey, "Philosophy and Civilization," in *Philosophy and Civilization* (New York: Peter Smith, 1968), 9.

34. Beauvoir, *The Second Sex,* 161.

35. Ruth, *Issues in Feminism,* 469–70. For contemporary accounts of how women are still being molded to men's ideals, see Sandra Lee Bartky, *Femininity and Domination: Studies in the Phenomenology of Oppression* (New York: Routledge, 1990); Rita Freedman, *Beauty Bound* (Lexington, MA: D. C. Heath 1986); and Jenijoy LaBelle, *Herself Beheld: The Literature of the Looking Glass* (Ithaca: Cornell University Press, 1989).

36. *Newsweek,* 22 April 1991, 69.

37. Eugenie Gatens-Robinson uses this criterion (but not the citation) to criticize the applicability of the ethics of "rights" to the morality of abortion, of surrogate mother contracts, and of marriage contracts on the grounds that it distorts or silences the experiences it is meant to clarify. "A Defense of Women's Choice: Abortion and the Ethics of Care," *Southern Journal of Philosophy* 30/3 (1992): 39–66. She arrives at this criterion from a feminist rather than a prag-

matist perspective, but Marjorie C. Miller and Raymond D. Boisvert independently quote this Dewey passage in a feminist context. Miller, "Feminism and Pragmatism," *Monist,* 75/4 (1992), 448; and Boisvert, "Heteronomous Freedom," *Philosophy and the Reconstruction of Culture,* ed. J. Stuhr, 140.

EIGHT

1. John Lachs, "Aristotle and Dewey on the Rat Race," *Philosophy and the Reconstruction of Culture,* ed. Stuhr, 101.

2. Fraser, *Unruly Practices,* 94.

3. Rucker, *The Chicago Pragmatists,* 163.

4. Alain Locke seems unaware of the extent to which Dewey rejects the epistemological turn, with its denigration of feeling and values, in his understanding of science. According to Leonard Harris, Locke rejected Dewey's position in *Quest for Certainty* because of what he took to be his focus on "the field of truth and knowledge," with a "logico-experiential slant" that makes "common cause with the current scientific attitude." "The Legitimation Crisis in American Philosophy," *Social Science Information* 26/1 (March, 1987): 63. But the passage that Locke attributes to Dewey in *Quest for Certainty* (*LW* 4: 17–18) to back up this claim states a position that Dewey specifically rejects as following from a non-experimental metaphysics of Being. Locke, "Values and Imperatives," *American Philosophy Today and Tomorrow,* ed. Horace M. Kallen and Sidney Hook (Freeport, NY: Books for Libraries Press, 1968), 317, n. 2.

5. For a feminist appropriation of Dewey's logic, see Carroll Guen Hart, "'Power in the service of love,'" *Hypatia* 8/2 (1993): 190–214.

6. Donna Haraway, "Situated Knowledges," *Feminist Studies* 14/3 (1988): 575–99.

7. Simone de Beauvoir shared these earlier expectations. Her analysis of the emancipatory power of science replicates many pragmatist themes, including the anti-dogmatic fallibilism of scientific methodology, the interrelation of science and art, the centrality of the means-ends continuum, and scientific emphasis on changing concrete situations. *The Ethics of Ambiguity,* trans. Bernard Frechtman (Secaucus, NJ: Citadel Press, 1948), chap. 3, secs. 4, 5.

8. Muncy, *Creating a Female Dominion,* 72, 76–77.

9. Muncy, 188, n. 29, 82.

10. Muncy, 82, 75.

11. Jane S. Upin, "Charlotte Perkins Gilman: Instrumentalism beyond Dewey," *Hypatia* 8/2 (1993): 45–46, 58, n. 6.

12. Phillips, *Engendering Democracy,* 113.

13. Longino, *Science as Social Knowledge,* 220–21.

14. "The Development of American Pragmatism," (*LW* 2: 19).

15. Nelson, "Addelson: The Politics of Knowledge," *Who Knows?* 137–85. See also Kathryn Pine Addelson, "The Man of Professional Wisdom," *Discovering Reality,* ed. Harding and Hintikka; and Holland, *Is Women's Philosophy Possible?*

16. See Seigfried, chap. 6, "Natural History Methodology and Artistic Vision," *William James's Radical Reconstruction.*

17. "Appendix 1," letters dated 1908 and 1909, *The Letters of William James,* ed. Henry James, vol. 2 (Boston: Atlantic Monthly Press, 1920), 353–56.

18. Henry James, *Letters*, vol. 2, 355.

19. The first article, which deconstructs the aesthetic dimension of rationality, was published in *Mind*, 4 (1879), 317–46 and reprinted in *Essays in Philosophy* (1978), 32–70. The second, which begins with extracts from the first one, develops the practical dimension of rationality. It was first published in *Princeton Review* (July, 1882) and reprinted in *The Will to Believe* (1979), 57–89.

20. Whereas Dewey and James are also explicit in calling for the enlargement of the relevant community of investigators, Peirce typically emphasizes the expertise of (male) scientists. See, for example, his division of "all human lives" into three groups: the "devotees of enjoyment," those who embrace "a life of action," and "the men of science." In accordance with his penchant for classification and technical language, the latter are further subdivided into *taxospudists, prattospudists,* and *herospudists.* "The Nature of Science," *Classical American Philosophy*, ed. Stuhr, 46–48.

21. Longino, *Science as Social Knowledge*, 72–74, 214.

22. Nelson, *Who Knows?* 3–19.

23. To give just one example, Dewey argues that "in genuine scientific inquiry . . . the frame of reference is a *working* matter . . . a product of previous knowings as well as a directive of further inquiries." Those whose positivist understanding of science leads them to take this frame as prior to and outside inquiry do not subject their own experimental assumptions to critical inquiry. Consequently, what is merely the result of a narrow slice of historical experience—the established order or status quo—is given scientific warrant. Science is perverted from its function of "liberation from conditions previously fixed" to the extent that the "dangerous delusion" spreads that scientific inquiries are more objective to the extent that they ignore their economic, social, and ideological conditions. "Liberating the Social Scientist," *LW* 15: 226–27.

24. *When Peoples Meet*, ed. Alain Locke and Bernhard J. Stern (New York: Hinds, Hayden and Eldredge, 1942, rev. ed. 1949), 3–4. Although two editors are given, I have assumed that the section introductions from which the quotations from this book are taken are those of Locke because in the foreword the editors say that "the project was initially conceived by Alain Locke, who prepared the original outline" and "Alain Locke is primarily responsible for the text commentary," xi.

25. Locke, *When Peoples Meet*, 5–6.

26. In addition to citing many positive published reports, Du Bois mentions that William James commended his "splendid scientific work" in a 1907 letter, and Jane Addams attended a 1908 conference he helped organize. Du Bois, *Autobiography*, 218.

27. Du Bois, *Autobiography*, 205, 225, 227–28.

28. Du Bois, *Autobiography*, 236, 256, 296, 303, 337–39.

29. Locke, *When Peoples Meet*, 6.

30. Locke, *When Peoples Meet*, 30, 236.

31. Locke, *When Peoples Meet*, 302, 684, 686.

32. This emphasis may account for Dewey's concern to relate values and science, and to interpret the individual within a more socially and politically engaged version of pragmatism as compared to Peirce's, which is "little more than

a description of a typical (generalized) laboratory experimenter's procedure." Kenneth Laine Ketner, "Introduction to Charles Sanders Peirce," *Classical American Philosophy*, 20.

33. *Ferment* is a good word because it suggests that Dewey did not simply take over James's whole outlook, but critically engaged his writings to develop his own position. As I realized, too, in working through James's psychologically grounded philosophy, Dewey points out two unreconciled strains in his *Psychology* and remarks on how difficult it is to develop a new vocabulary to intelligibly convey genuinely new ideas (*LW* 5: 157). See Seigfried, *William James's Radical Reconstruction of Philosophy*.

34. Once again, the central role that the "distinctively human" plays for Dewey distances his position from Rorty, who wants to restrict questions about the point of human existence to the private sphere.

35. Rucker, *Chicago Pragmatists*, 53. Rucker quotes from Moore's *Pragmatism and Its Critics* (Chicago: University of Chicago Press, 1910), 19.

36. Sandra Harding and Nelson, for example, explore the consequences of privileging biology or the social sciences instead of physics as the model for philosophical thinking. Harding, *The Science Question in Feminism* (New York: Cornell University Press, 1986), 44–47; Nelson, *Who Knows?* 249–54. Nelson also says that she cannot predict prior to its occurrence what a new logic that accepted the implications of Quine's argument against the analytic/synthetic distinction would be like or even if one would be developed. I think that Dewey had already developed one that fulfills her criteria in *Logic, The Theory of Inquiry* (*LW* 12).

37. Rucker, *Chicago Pragmatists*, 94–95.

38. Dewey, "Experiment in Education," *MW* 10: 122–23.

39. Mayhew and Edwards, *Dewey School*, v–vii. In his introduction to *LW:* 11, John J. McDermott briefly explains how in the 1930s, the decade in which the book was written, the American dream became a nightmare, xi–xii.

40. In his introduction Dewey says that the school was "animated by a desire to discover in administration, selection of subject-matter, methods of learning, teaching, and discipline, how a school could become a coöperative community while developing in individuals their own capacities and satisfying their own needs." All the areas mentioned were carried out by women who were both administrators and teachers. Mayhew and Edwards, *Dewey School*, xvi. Among many such references in *Twenty Years at Hull-House*, Jane Addams says: "Our next coöperative experiment was much more successful, perhaps because it was much more spontaneous." By *spontaneous* she means that women shoe-factory workers, who were particularly vulnerable in strikes because loss of wages meant that they would be thrown out of their rented rooms, themselves proposed setting up a boarding club at Hull House, 105.

41. Mayhew and Edwards, *Dewey School*, 365, See vii for the division of authorship in the book.

42. Mayhew and Edwards, *Dewey School*, 271. The following account is taken from Mayhew's concise explanation of Dewey's principles of education in "Appendix I: The Evolution of Mr. Dewey's Principles of Education," 445–62.

43. Mayhew and Edwards, *Dewey School*, 450. Quotation is taken from Dewey, "Principles of Mental Development in Early Infancy," rpt. *MW* 1: 175–91.

44. Mayhew and Edwards, *Dewey School,* 449–52.

45. Mayhew and Edwards, 453.

46. Mayhew and Edwards, *Dewey School,* 454–58. George Herbert Mead, "The Philosophies of Royce, James, and Dewey in Their American Setting," *International Journal of Ethics* (January, 1930).

47. Mayhew and Edwards, *Dewey School,* 462.

48. Joe R. Burnett, Introduction, *MW* 1: xxii–xxiii.

49. Alice Hamilton, for example, learned a deep suspicion and fear of the police while at Hull House because of experiences of police prejudices against and brutality toward the immigrant poor and laborers, including killing them and denying them their civil rights. She reports that these actions were condoned from the highest levels of city government on down through the ranks. She also acquired a hostility toward newspaper reporters because the press so often stirred up public opinion against Hull House, employing scare tactics and publishing half-truths and outright lies to do so. "Hull House Within and Without," *Eighty Years at Hull-House,* ed. Davis and McCree, 103. Orig. *Exploring the Dangerous Trades* (Boston, 1943), 68–87.

50. Addams reports that the Hull House Social Science Club "convinced the residents that no one so poignantly realizes the failures in the social structure as the man at the bottom, who has been most directly in contact with those failures and has suffered most." *Twenty Years at Hull-House,* 137.

51. Addams, *Twenty Years,* xviii.

52. Addams tells the story of a young woman who lived in a neighboring tenement and helped out at Hull-House and who was invariably questioned by upper-class visitors about "those people" without suspecting that they were talking to one of "them." Addams says she learned a lesson from the incident; thereafter "I never addressed a Chicago audience on the subject of the Settlement and its vicinity without inviting a neighbor to go with me, that I might curb any hasty generalization by the consciousness that I had an auditor who knew the conditions more intimately than I could hope to do so." *Twenty Years,* 80.

53. Addams, *Twenty Years,* 42, 44, 56–57, 72, 76.

54. Westbrook, *John Dewey,* 188. For an astute discussion of the criticisms of progressivism and its defense, see also 182–94.

55. Addams, *Democracy and Social Ethics* (1902), 13–70. Addams shows how class privilege causes young college women engaged in charity work to misjudge the situation and motives of the recipients of their charity, and how differently the interaction looks when seen from the perspective of the recipients. She graphically illustrates the impossibility of arriving at an unbiased judgment of the situation when the economic and social conditions influencing it, with which the lower classes are all too familiar, remain outside the charity visitor's experience and knowledge. The Dewey quotation is from *Ethics* (*MW* 5: 276); it is also quoted in Westbrook, *John Dewey,* 185.

NINE

1. Carol Gilligan, *In a Different Voice* (Cambridge: Harvard University Press, 1982). This chapter, slightly modified, first appeared as "Pragmatism, Feminism, and Sensitivity to Context," in *Who Cares?* ed. Brabeck, 63–83.

2. It is a constant complaint of black, Latina, and third-world feminists that middle-class white women theorists tend to universalize women's experiences on the basis of their own.

3. Muriel J. Bebeau and Mary M. Brabeck, "Integrating Care and Justice Issues in Professional Moral Education: A Gender Perspective, *Journal of Moral Education* (1987), 16.

4. See *Experience and Nature* (*LW:* 1) on the generic traits of experience. A good overview of this theme, including what appears in his other works, is provided by Lewis E. Hahn in *Guide to the Works of John Dewey*, ed. Jo Ann Boydston (Carbondale: Southern Illinois University Press, 1970), 43–48. See also Dewey's definition of *situation* or *context* in *Experience and Education* (New York: Collier Books, 1963), 43–44.

5. According to Bebeau and Brabeck, "Research has shown that differential socialization . . . has led women to place greater emphasis on interpersonal relationships. Females have also been found to be more accurate than males in decoding nonverbal cues about another person's affective state." "Ethical Sensitivity and Moral Reasoning among Men and Women in the Professions," in *Who Cares?* 152.

6. Bebeau and Brabeck, 156, 158.

7. Seigfried, "*Second Sex:* Second Thoughts," in *Hypatia Reborn*, 305–22.

8. Beauvoir, *Second Sex*, 288.

9. See Seigfried, "Gender-Specific Values," *Philosophical Forum* 15 (1984): 425–42.

10. "The Objectivism-Subjectivism of Modern Philosophy" (*LW* 14: 199–200).

11. Seigfried, "Vagueness and the Adequacy of Concepts," 357–67.

12. Beauvoir, *Second Sex*, xviii.

13. See, for example, Annette Baier, *Moral Prejudices* (Cambridge: Harvard University Press, 1994); and Richard Rorty, "Why Can't a Man Be More like a Woman, and Other Problems in Moral Philosophy," *London Review of Books* 24 (February, 1994), 3, 6.

14. "The Construction of Good" (*LW* 4: 203–28).

15. Bebeau and Brabeck, *Who Cares?* 158.

16. See Elisabeth D. Däumer, "Queer Ethics; or, the Challenge of Bisexuality to Lesbian Ethics," *Hypatia* 7/4 (1992): 91–105; Judith Butler, *Gender Trouble* (New York: Routledge, 1990); Claudia Card, *Intimacy and Responsibility* (Madison: Institute for Legal Studies, University of Wisconsin-Madison Law School, 1987); Marilyn Frye, *The Politics of Reality* (Trumansburg, New York: Crossing Press, 1983); and Sarah Lucia Hoagland, *Lesbian Ethics* (Palo Alto: Institute of Lesbian Studies, 1988).

17. Noddings, "Educating Moral People," *Who Cares?* 224.

18. Higgins, "The Just Community Educational Program," in *Who Cares?* 202, 205, 208, 210.

19. "Context and Thought" (*LW* 6: 1–21).

20. *Reconstruction in Philosophy* (*LW* 12: 191).

21. *Theory of Valuation* (*LW* 13: 213).

22. Nona Lyons, "Ways of Knowing, Learning, and Making Moral Choices," *Who Knows?* 104–5, 122–23.

23. Noddings, *Who Cares?* 224, 226–30.

24. Houston, "Prolegomena to Future Caring," *Who Cares?* 89.

25. Houston, "Prolegomena," 89.

26. The passage mentioning "the moral equivalent of war" can be found in William James, *The Varieties of Religious Experience* (1902), (Cambridge: Harvard University Press, 1985). For the earlier paper with this title, see *ERM*, 162–73. My remarks refer to both.

27. James, *PP* II: 1055–56; and *The Letters of William James*, vol. 1, ed. Henry James, 210–11.

28. For an explanation of sympathetic concrete observation, see Seigfried, *William James's Radical Reconstruction*, 139–170.

TEN

1. Dewey, "Teaching Ethics in the High School" (*EW* 4: 57).

2. James, "The Moral Philosopher and the Moral Life (1891)," (*WB* 153–55). For an explication of the social dimensions of James's personalistic ethics, see Seigfried, "Sympathetic Apprehension of the Point of View of the Other," in *Classical American Pragmatism*, ed. Douglas Anderson, Carl Hausman, and Sandra Rosenthal (University of Illinois Press, forthcoming).

3. Gilman, *The Man-Made World*, 126.

4. Jane Addams, *Twenty Years at Hull-House*, 91. There is no more *a* pragmatist ethics than there is *a* feminist ethics, as is evident in a book edited by Alison M. Jaggar titled *Living with Contradictions* (Boulder: Westview Press, 1994). I an constructing similarities and differences between some pragmatist and feminist approaches to ethics by emphasizing certain aspects of their writings that could be helpful in understanding an earlier stage of pragmatist and feminist insights as well as offering possibilities for further development of a pragmatist feminist approach to ethics.

5. Abraham Kaplan, for instance, says that "pragmatism applies the genetic method to philosophy," meaning that "ideas are to be understood in terms of their historical origins and their social functions, as Marx and Nietzsche had already emphasized." Introduction to *Art as Experience* (*LW* 10: xi). And Lewis E. Hahn calls "a naturalistic experimental approach from the genetic standpoint" one of the major themes of Dewey's pragmatic philosophy. Introduction to *MW* 4: xi.

6. Gilman sharply distinguishes the nature and characteristics of the masculine, the feminine, and the human. Masculine and feminine are both biological categories, while the human is a social or cultural one. Along with other pragmatists, she was a Reform Darwinist who rejected the laissez-faire perspective of the Social Darwinists. But because of his "gynaecocentric theory," she also drew more on Lester Ward's version of evolutionism than on Darwin's. She emphasizes that women have been unnaturally stymied in their growth because of their economic dependence on men. But unlike the other pragmatists, her evolutionary explanations are deterministic, and she thinks that progress is inevitable. See *Women and Economics*. For her relationship to Ward, see Hill, *Charlotte Perkins Gilman*, 264–72. The other pragmatists take Darwinian evolutionary theory as re-

futing determinism and disclosing the play of chance, opening the way for the possible failure of the human species as well as for possible advances. See Dewey, "The Influence of Darwinism on Philosophy," (*MW* 4: 3–14).

7. James H. Tufts, *The Ethics of Cooperation* (Boston: Houghton Mifflin, 1918).

8. Addams, *Democracy and Social Ethics*, 220.

9. James, quoted in *The Social Thought of Jane Addams*, ed. Lasch, 62. Information about Dewey comes from Lagemann, "The Plural Worlds of Educational Research," 194.

10. Addams, *Democracy and Social Ethics*, 1–4, quoted in *LW* 7: 315.

11. When the workers at the Pullman Palace Car Company in Illinois struck after five successive wage reductions, Eugene Debs's American Railway Union organized a sympathetic boycott of all Pullman train cars, and rioting broke out. President Cleveland sent federal troops into Illinois to suppress it. Since Pullman had been regarded as a model employer who built a model company town for his workers, their rejection of his paternal benevolence as well as of his wage scale revealed the depth of the worker's alienation from middle-class norms and raised the spectacle of class war. *Social Thought*, ed. Lasch, 105–6.

12. See also "Industrial Amelioration," *Social Ethics*, ed. Lasch, 137–77.

13. Addams, "A Modern King Lear," *Social Thought*, ed. Lasch, 119.

14. Addams, "A Modern King Lear," 112–15, 120.

15. Addams, "A Modern King Lear," 121–22.

16. Addams, "Filial Relations," *Democracy and Social Ethics*, 71–74.

17. Addams seems here to be recalling her own difficulty in trying to define a life for herself and the obstacles encountered in the need to invent a social service career at a time when morally good women were expected to be either wives and mothers or members of religious societies.

18. This was a central contention of Jessie Taft, who traced the contemporary bind in which women found themselves in the early twentieth century to the societal expectation that they continue familial patterns formed in feudal times in the changed conditions of an industrial society. *The Woman Movement From the Point of View of Social Consciousness* (Menasha, Wisconsin: Collegiate Press, George Banta Publishing Co., 1915), chap. 2, "The Woman Movement as Part of the Larger Social Situation," rpt. *Hypatia* 8/2 (1993), 219–29. See also in the same issue Seigfried, "Introduction to Jessie Taft," 213–18.

19. Addams, "Filial Relations," 82–84.

20. Friedan, *The Feminine Mystique* (New York: W. W. Norton, 1963). Jessie Taft also analyzed the plight of the "uneasy woman" in *The Woman Movement*.

21. Addams, "Filial Relations," 88.

22. Addams, "Filial Relations," 92–93, 101.

23. Collins, *Black Feminist Thought*, 46.

24. Royce, *Race Questions* (New York: Macmillan, 1908). Harris, ed., *The Philosophy of Alain Locke*, 3–4, 26.

25. Du Bois, *Autobiography*, 146–47.

26. Dewey participated in a symposium on women's suffrage with Gilman and others in 1911 (*MW* 6:153–54). Given the paucity of references in philosophical writings to women's intellectual contributions, it is significant that the two areas

in which Dewey cites women are ethics and education. Besides the long quotation in the 1932 *Ethics,* Addams is mentioned in the 1908 *Ethics* as showing the difficulties clan loyalty poses for democracy (*MW:* 5,136). In the highlighted General Literature for part 3: The World of Action, two of her books are cited in both editions: *Democracy and Social Ethics* (1902), and *Newer Ideals of Peace* (1907) (*MW* 5:382; *LW* 7:313). In the first edition Addams's *Philanthropy and Social Progress* is also a bibliographic entry (*MW* 5:434). *Some Ethical Gains Through Legislation,* ed. Richard T. Ely, (1905) by another Hull-House resident, Florence Kelly, is mentioned as showing that in regard to corporate bodies, results count, not motives unaccompanied by responsible action: "The value of good motives and moral purpose is in this case located in those who strive to secure and execute progressive legislation for the public good, and in the personal spirit with which this is accepted and carried out by officials" (*MW* 5:466). Other references to books written by women on ethical issues are found in the various bibliographies at the ends of chapters.

But neither Kelly nor Elsie Clews Parsons, whose book, *The Family: An Ethnological and Historical Outline* (Putnam's Sons, 1906), is also referred to, makes it into the second edition. Two other ethics books by women are mentioned in both editions: Edith J. Simcox, *Natural Law: An Essay in Ethics* (London: Trübner, 1877) and Cora May Williams, *A Review of the Systems of Ethics Founded on the Theory of Evolution* (Macmillan, 1893). Two women whose books appeared too late for the first edition are mentioned in the second: Mary Calkins, *The Good Man and the Good* (1918) (*LW:* 7:234), and Ellen Karolina Sofia Key, *Love and Marriage* (Putnam's Sons, 1911). (Both Gilman and Howe criticize Key for supporting an unemancipated version of motherhood, but Jessie Taft reports favorably on her writings.) Dewey also wrote a foreword to Helen Edna Davis's *Tolstoy and Nietzsche: A Problem in Biographical Ethics,* in which he praises her new approach to ethics.

Mead reviewed one of Addams's books: "Jane Addams, *The Newer Ideals of Peace,*" *American Journal of Sociology* 13 (1907), 121–28, and he wrote about another Hull-House resident: "Mary McDowell," *Neighborhood* 2 (April, 1929), 77–78. He defended Ella Flagg Young in "A Heckling School Board and an Educational Stateswoman," *Survey* 31 (10 January 1914): 443–44.

27. Gilman, "A Summary of Purpose," *The Forerunner* 7 (November 1916), in *Charlotte Perkins Gilman,* ed. Ceplair, 203. The list is taken from Ceplair, vii–viii.

28. Gilman, *Social Ethics* in *The Forerunner* 5, nos. 1–12 (1914), rpt. New York: Greenwood Reprint Corporation, 1968, 103, 105.

29. Gordon, "Black and White Visions of Welfare," *Journal of American History* 78/2 (1991): 564.

30. Letter of Mary Church Terrell to Jane Addams, Mary Church Terrel Papers (Library of Congress, Washington, D.C.), cited in Giddings, *When and Where I Enter,* 179–180.

31. Addams, *Second Twenty Years,* 336, and PP,II, 1266–67.

32. Addams, *Second Twenty Years,* 334.

33. Addams, *Second Twenty Years,* 341–42.

34. For an extended analysis of the pragmatist position that although all or-

ganizations of experience, including the intellectual, express interests and particular perspectives, criteria of objectivity can nonetheless be legitimately derived, see Seigfried, *William James's Radical Reconstruction of Philosophy*.

35. Bordo, *Flight to Objectivity*.

36. Introduction to *Problems of Men* (*LW* 15: 163–164).

37. Abraham Edel has long followed Dewey in showing the relevance of the biological and social sciences to ethical issues. See *Ethical Judgment: The Use of Science in Ethics* (New Brunswick, NJ: Transaction, 1994), *In Search of the Ethical: Twentieth-Century Moral Theory Science, Ideology, and Value, Vol. 5* (New Brunswick, NJ: Transaction, 1993), and *Science and the Structure of Ethics*. Scientific ethics is central to Dewey, according to Darnell Rucker, because it "will relieve philosophic ethics from its dependence upon fixed values and standards and relieve ethics as an art from its search for specific rules of conduct, replacing both set ideals and rules with *methods* for analysis of moral problems." "Dewey's Ethics, Part Two," *Guide to the Works of John Dewey*, ed. Boydston, 113.

38. Dewey puts 'objective' and 'subjective' in scare quotes to signal that he rejects a metaphysics that assumes an ontological distinction between a private, inner self and an outer, public world. Human beings are "part of the world, not something set over against it" (*LW* 15:165).

39. Dewey, *Human Nature and Conduct* in *Middle Works, vol. 14: 1922*.

40. Mayhew and Edwards, *The Dewey School*, 417.

41. Gilman, *Man-Made World*, 39, 67–68.

42. Addams, "Household Adjustment," *Democracy and Social Ethics*, 102–136.

43. For the importance of social networks for the family life of black women forced to work in adverse circumstances, see Patricia Hill Collins, "Black Women and Motherhood," in *Living With Contradictions*, ed. Jaggar, 450–61.

44. A few among the many: bell hooks, *Feminist Theory;* Gloria T. Hull, Patricia Bell Scott, and Barbara Smith, eds., *All the Women Are White, All the Blacks Are Men, But Some of Us Are Brave* (New York: Feminist Press, 1982); Chandra Talpade Mohanty, Ann Russo, and Lourdes Torres, eds., *Third World Women and the Politics of Feminism* (Bloomington: Indiana University Press, 1991); and Karen Sacks, "The Class Roots of Feminism," *Issues in Feminism*, ed. Ruth, 485–95.

45. Hill, *Charlotte*, 172–74; *Charlotte*, ed. Ceplair, 7.

46. Gilman, *Man-Made World*, 31, 53.

47. In 1906, for instance, "a full decade before Margaret Sanger's birth-control movement gained notoriety," Elsie Clews Parsons suggested that contraception would soon become widely accepted in America. See Rosenberg, *Beyond Separate Spheres*, 161.

48. Gilman, "Birth Control," rpt. *Charlotte*, ed. Ceplair, 249–56; Dewey, "Education and Birth Control," rpt. *LW* 6:146–148.

49. In regard to issues of class rather than of contraception, Peter Manicas criticizes Dewey's appeal to the opposition to science as the source of prejudice: "But Dewey's idea that 'coercion and oppression on a large scale exist' because 'of the perpetuation of old institutions and patterns not touched by scientific method' is patently fallacious. Indeed, in the text already quoted from *Individualism Old and New*, he had it right: 'There is a difference and a choice between

blind, chaotic and unplanned determinism, issuing from business conducted for pecuniary profit, and the determination of a socially planned and ordered development,' between 'a socialism that is public and one that is capitalistic.'" It is true that in both contexts Dewey too simplistically reduces the complexity and virulence of prejudice. I think, however, that when a sympathetic interpretation of his understanding of science is brought to his more concrete analyses of specific prejudices, such as the one from *Individualism,* then a more satisfactory explanation emerges. "A socialism that is public," for instance, is a democratic socialism opposed to monopoly by capitalists that, like science, (1) assumes that the world is open to cooperative experimentation and therefore rejects determinism and (2) is "public" because all its members can in principle subject any organization to inquiry and further development. Dewey is not so much giving a causal analysis of particular prejudices as he is explaining why prejudices flourish when a scientific ideal of community participation, questioning of presuppositions, and openness to intelligently directed social reconstruction is rejected. Peter Manicas, "Dewey and the Class Struggle," in *Values and Value Theory,* ed. Murphey and Berg, 77.

50. Hill, *Charlotte,* 181–82.

51. *Charlotte,* ed. Ceplair, 252.

52. *Charlotte,* ed. Ceplair, 253.

53. *Charlotte,* ed. Ceplair, 274.

54. Dewey, "The Senate Birth Control Bill," *People's Lobby Bulletin,* 2 (May, 1932), 1–2; rpt. *LW* 6:388–89.

55. For an alternative to the rights paradigm so common in feminist discussions of abortion, see an approach that stresses the biological and experiential realities of pregnancy in a pragmatist feminist spirit, Eugenie Gatens-Robinson, "A Defense of Women's Choice: Abortion and the Ethics of Care," *Southern Journal of Philosophy,* 30/3 (1992), 39–66.

ELEVEN

1. The slash indicates that the position is held by both pragmatist feminists and feminist pragmatists. Besides those for whom feminism and pragmatism constitute one seamless philosophical perspective, so also can there be feminists who use pragmatism as their only or major theoretical and methodological resource, but whose primary interests and referents are feminist, just as there can be pragmatists who incorporate feminist theoretical and methodological resources into their pragmatism, but whose primary interests and referents are drawn from the pragmatist tradition.

2. Addams, *Democracy and Social Ethics,* 222.

3. Dewey, *Characters and Events,* ed. Ratner (New York: Henry Holt, 1929). Jane Addams, "A Toast to John Dewey," (1929) in *The Social Thought of Jane Addams,* ed. Lasch, 183. The first sentence of the quotation is also given in *John Dewey: the Political Writings,* ed. Morris and Shapiro (Indianapolis: Hackett, 1993), xi.

4. Barbara Sicherman, "Working It Out: Gender, Profession, and Reform in the Career of Alice Hamilton," in *Gender, Class, Race, and Reform in the Progressive*

Era, ed. Noralee Frankel and Nancy S. Dye (Lexington: University Press of Kentucky, 1991), 134, 142–143.

5. Hamilton, "Hull-House Within and Without," *Eighty Years at Hull-House,* ed. Davis and McCree, 106.

6. Crenshaw, "Demarginalizing the Intersection of Race and Sex," in *Living with Contradictions,* ed. Jaggar, 48.

7. Jane Addams, *Twenty Years,* 133.

8. McDowell, "The Settlement as a Way of Life," 156–57.

9. Sicherman, "Career of Alice Hamilton," 136.

10. Dewey's complex discussion of the generic traits of experience that emerge in the transactions of individuals with their environment is central to understanding how values are related to facts. See *Experience and Nature* (*LW* 1: 67, 198–203, 250, 308, 314). See also his discussion of practical judgments on the importance of the continuity of means and ends in identifying relevant traits within and among situations in "The Logic of Judgments of Practice," *MW* 8:14–82. For the role of aesthetics in identifying relevant aspects of situations, see *LW* 5: 248–62.

11. Nancy F. Cott, "Feminist Theory and Feminist Movements: the Past before Us," in *What is Feminism?* ed. Mitchell and Oakley, 49–62.

12. Sicherman, "Career of Alice Hamilton," 128–30.

13. Kathryn Pauly Morgan, "Women and the Knife: Cosmetic Surgery and the Colonization of Women's Bodies," *Hypatia* 6/3 (1991): 38.

14. *The Monist,* 75/4 (1992), 445–57.

15. Jane Addams, *My Friend Julia Lathrop* (New York: Macmillan, 1935), 59–60.

16. Collins, *Black Feminist Thought,* 33.

17. Collins, "Mammies, Matriarchs, and Other Controlling Images," in *Feminist Philosophies,* ed. Kourany, Sterba, and Tong (Englewood Cliffs, NJ: Prentice Hall, 1992), 119–28.

18. Dorothy E. Smith, *The Everyday World as Problematic,* 10, 18–22.

19. Smith, *Everyday World,* 2.

20. Philippe Aries, *Centuries of Childhood* (Harmondsworth, England: Penguin Books, 1975), 22.

21. Linda Pollock, *Times Literary Supplement,* November 9–15, 1990, 1212.

22. For an explanation of truth as ongoing negotiations between funded and present experiences, see James, *Pragmatism,* chap. 6.

23. Lorraine Code, "Responsibility and Rhetoric," *Hypatia* 9/1 (Winter, 1994): 1–20.

24. Lee Quinby, "Ecofeminism and the Politics of Resistance," in *Reweaving the World: The Emergence of Eco-Feminism,* ed. Irene Diamond and Gloria Fenman Orenstein (San Francisco: Sierra Club Books, 1990), 122.

25. Cott, "Feminist Theory and Feminist Movements," *What Is Feminism?* 59–60.

26. Alison M. Jaggar argues that such prioritizing is required, given feminist analyses showing the inadequacy of theories that ignore "'actually existing' difference and 'actually existing' domination" in their advocacy of an idealized hy-

pothetical consensus. I am pointing out that pragmatist feminism is an exception to her remark that the view advocated "is foreign to most Anglo-American ethics." "Feminist Ethics: Projects, Problems, Prospects," in *Feminist Ethics,* ed. Claudia Card (Lawrence: University Press of Kansas, 1991), 99–100.

27. In *Feminist Philosophies,* 391–404.

28. hooks, *Feminist Philosophies,* 392–93, 397–98, 404.

Bibliography

Abbott, Edith. *Women in Industry*. New York: D. Appleton-Century, 1910.

Aboulafia, Mitchell. "Was George Herbert Mead a Feminist?" *Hypatia* 8/2 (Spring, 1993): 145–58.

——, ed. *Philosophy, Social Theory, and the Thought of George Herbert Mead*. Albany: State University of New York Press, 1991.

Addams, Jane. *Democracy and Social Ethics*. New York: Macmillan, 1902.

——. *Newer Ideals of Peace*. New York: Macmillan, 1907.

——. *The Spirit of Youth and City Streets*. New York: Macmillan, 1909.

——. *Twenty Years at Hull-House*. New York: Macmillan, 1910.

——. *The Long Road of Women's Memory*. New York: Macmillan, 1916.

——. *Peace and Bread in Time of War*. New York: Macmillan, 1922. Intro. John Dewey. Boston: Hall, 1960.

——. "The Settlement as a Way of Life." *Neighborhood* 2 (July, 1929): 139–46.

——. *The Second Twenty Years at Hull-House*. New York: Macmillan, 1930.

——. "John Dewey and Social Welfare." In *John Dewey: The Man and His Philosophy*, ed. Henry W. Holmes, 140–51. Cambridge: Harvard University Press, 1930.

——. "Aspects of the Woman's Movement." *Survey* 8 (August, 1930): 113–23.

——. *The Excellent Becomes the Permanent*. New York: Macmillan, 1932.

——. *My Friend, Julia Lathrop*. New York: Macmillan, 1932.

——. *Jane Addams: A Centennial Reader*, ed. Emily Cooper Johnson. New York: Macmillan, 1960.

——. *The Social Thought of Jane Addams*, ed. Christopher Lasch. Indianapolis: Bobbs-Merrill, 1965.

Addams, Jane, Emily Greene Balch, and Alice Hamilton. *The Women at the Hague*. New York: Macmillan, 1915.

Adrian, Lynne M. "Emma Goldman and the Spirit of Artful Living: Philosophy and Politics in the Classical American Period." In *Frontiers in American Philosophy*, ed. Robert W. Burch and Herman J. Saatkamp Jr., 191–99. College Station: Texas A & M University Press, 1992.

Aisenberg, Nadya, and Mona Harrington. *Women of Academe: Outsiders in the Sacred Grove.* Amherst: University of Massachusetts Press, 1988.

Alexander, Thomas M. *John Dewey's Theory of Art, Experience, and Nature: The Horizons of Feeling.* New York: State University of New York Press, 1987.

al-Hibri, Azizah, and Margaret A. Simons, eds. *Hypatia Reborn: Essays in Feminist Philosophy.* Bloomington: Indiana University Press, 1990.

Allen, Polly Wynn. *Building Domestic Liberty: Charlotte Perkins Gilman's Architectural Feminism.* Amherst: University of Massachusetts Press, 1988.

Antler, Joyce. *Lucy Sprague Mitchell: The Making of a Modern Woman.* New Haven: Yale University Press, 1987.

———. *The Educated Woman and Professionalization: The Struggle for a New Feminine Identity, 1890–1920.* New York: Garland, 1987.

———. "Feminism as Life Process: The Life and Career of Lucy Sprague Mitchell," *Feminist Studies* 7 (Spring, 1981): 134–57.

Ayim, Maryann. "The Implications of Sexually Stereotypic Language as Seen through Peirce's Theory of Signs." *Transactions of the Charles S. Peirce Society* 19 (Spring, 1983): 183–98.

Baier, Annette. *Moral Prejudices: Essays on Ethics.* Cambridge: Harvard University Press, 1994.

Bartky, Sandra. *Femininity and Domination: Studies in the Phenomenology of Oppression.* New York: Routledge, 1990.

Beauvoir, Simone de. *The Second Sex,* trans. H. M. Parshley. New York: Vintage Books, 1974.

———. *The Ethics of Ambiguity,* trans. Bernard Frechtman. Secaucus, N.J.: Cidadel, 1948.

Bebeau, Muriel J., and Mary M. Brabeck. "Integrating Care and Justice Issues in Professional Moral Education: A Gender Perspective. *Journal of Moral Education* (1987).

Bell, Linda A. "Does Marriage Require a Head? Some Historical Arguments." *Hypatia* 4/1 (Spring, 1989): 148–49.

Benhabib, Seyla, and Drucilla Cornell, eds. *Feminism as Critique: On the Politics of Gender.* Minneapolis: University of Minnesota Press, 1987.

Bernstein, Richard J. *John Dewey.* Atascadero, CA: Ridgeview, 1966.

———. *Beyond Objectivism and Relativism: Science, Hermeneutics, and Praxis.* University of Pennsylvania Press, 1983.

Bordo, Susan. *The Flight to Objectivity.* Albany: State University of New York Press, 1987.

Boydston, Jo Ann. "John Dewey and the New Feminism." *Teachers College Record* 76/3 (February, 1975): 442–48.

———, ed. *Guide to the Works of John Dewey.* Carbondale: Southern Illinois Press, 1970.

Brabeck, Mary M., ed. *Who Cares? Theory, Research, and Educational Implications of the Ethic of Care.* New York: Praeger, 1990.

Bullert, Gary. *The Politics of John Dewey.* Buffalo, N.Y.: Prometheus Books, 1983.

Burke, Tom. *Dewey's New Logic: A Reply to Russell.* Chicago: University of Chicago Press, 1994.

Burnett, Joe R. "Whatever Happened to John Dewey?" *Philosophy of Education Since Midcentury*, ed. Jonas F. Soltis, 64–82. New York: Teachers College Press, 1981.

Butler, Judith. *Gender Trouble*. New York: Routledge, 1990.

Cadwallader, Thomas C., and Joyce V. Cadwallader. "Christine Ladd-Franklin (1847–1930)." In *Women in Psychology: A Bio-bibliographical Source Book*, ed. Agnes N. O'Connell and Nancy Felipe Russo. New York: Greenwood, 1990.

Calkins, Mary W. "Community of Ideas of Men and Women." *Psychological Review* 3 (July, 1896).

Campbell, Barbara Kuhn. *The "Liberated" Woman of 1914: Prominent Women in the Progressive Era*. Ann Arbor: UMI Research Press, 1979.

Campbell, James. *The Community Reconstructs: The Meaning of Pragmatic Social Thought*. Urbana: University of Illinois Press, 1992.

———. *John Dewey*. Urbana: University of Illinois Press, 1995.

Card, Claudia. *Intimacy and Responsibility: What Lesbians Do*. Madison: Institute for Legal Studies, University of Wisconsin-Madison Law School, 1987.

———, ed. *Feminist Ethics*. Lawrence: University Press of Kansas, 1991.

Clapp, Elsie Ripley. *Community Schools in Action*. New York: Viking, 1939.

———. *The Use of Resources in Education*. New York: Harper, 1952.

———. Clapp Papers. Special Collections of the Southern Illinois University at Carbondale Library.

Code, Lorraine. "Responsibility and Rhetoric." *Hypatia* 9/1 (Winter, 1994): 1–20.

———. *What Can She Know? Feminist Theory and the Construction of Knowledge*. Ithaca: Cornell University Press, 1991.

———. *Epistemic Responsibility*. Hanover, NH: University Press of New England, 1987.

Collins, Patricia Hill. *Black Feminist Thought: Knowledge, Consciousness, and the Politics of Empowerment*. New York: Routledge, 1991.

———. "Mammies, Matriarchs, and Other Controlling Images." In *Feminist Philosophies*, ed. Kourany, Sterba, and Tong, 119–28. Englewood Cliffs: Prentice Hall, 1992.

Cotkin, George. *William James, Public Philosopher*. Baltimore: Johns Hopkins Press, 1990.

Cott, Nancy F. "Feminist Theory and Feminist Movements: The Past before Us." In *What is Feminism?* Mitchell and Oakley, 49–62.

Crenshaw, Kimberle. "Demarginalizing the Intersection of Race and Sex: A Black Feminist Critique of Antidiscrimination Doctrine, Feminist Theory, and Antiracist Politics." In *Living with Contradictions*, ed. Jaggar, 39–52.

Curti, Merle. "Jane Addams on Human Nature." *Journal of the History of Ideas* 22 (April–June 1961): 240–53.

Davis, Allen F., and Mary Lynn McCree, eds. *Eighty Years at Hull-House*. Chicago: Quadrangle Books, 1969.

Deegan, Mary Jo. "Sociology at Wellesley College: 1900–1919." *Journal of the History of Sociology* 5/1 (Spring 1983): 91–115.

———. "The Clinical Sociology of Jessie Taft." *Clinical Sociology Review* 4 (1986), 30–45.

————. *Jane Addams and the Men of the Chicago School, 1892–1918.* New Brunswick: Transaction Books, 1988.

————. "W. E. B. Du Bois and the Women of Hull House, 1895–1899." *American Sociologist* 19/4 (Winter, 1988): 301–11.

Dewey, Jane M. "Biography of John Dewey." In *The Philosophy of John Dewey,* ed. Schilpp.

Dewey, John. (See List of Abbreviations)

————. "Education and the Health of Women" (1885), 64–68; and "Health and Sex in Higher Education" (1886), 69–80. In *Early Works, 1: 1882–1888.*

————. "The School as Social Centre" 80–93; "Memorandum to President Harper on Coeducation," 105–7; and "Letter to A. K. Parker on Coeducation," 108–16. In *Middle Works, 2: 1902–1903.*

————. "A Symposium on Woman's Suffrage" 153–54; and "Is Co-Education Injurious to Girls?" 155–64. In *Middle Works, 6: 1910–1911.*

————. "Philosophy and Democracy" 41–53. In *Middle Works, 11: 1918–1919.*

————. "What is the Matter with Teaching?" 116–23. In *Later Works, 2: 1925–27.*

————. "A Critique of American Civilization" 133–44; and "Why I Am a Member of the Teachers Union," 269–75. In *Later Works, 3: 1927–28.*

————. "The School and Society." Review of George S. Counts's *School and Society in Chicago,"* 371–74; and "Foreword to Helen Edna Davis's *Tolstoy and Nietzsche: A Problem in Biographical Ethics,"* 398–400. In *Later Works, 5: 1929–1930.*

————. "Context and Thought," 1–28; "Education and Birth Control" 146–48; "Senate Birth Control Bill," 388–89; and "Address to the National Association for the Advancement of Colored People," 224–30. In *Later Works, 6: 1927–28.*

————. "Introduction to *Growth: A Study of Johnny and Jimmy,* 510–14. In *Later Works, 11: 1935–37.* First published in McGraw, *Growth.*

————. "Democratic Versus Coercive International Organization: The Realism of Jane Addams," 192–98. In *Later Works, 15: 1942–48.* First published in Addams, *Peace and Bread in Time of War.*

————. "The Health of Women and Higher Education," 7–9; "In Defense of Mary Ware Dennett's *The Sex Side of Life,"* 127; "Emily Greene Balch," 149–150; and "Child Health and Protection," 511–19. In *Later Works, 17: 1885–1953.*

————. *Reconstruction in Philosophy.* In *Middle Works, 12: 1920.*

Dewey, John [with Evelyn Dewey]. *Schools of Tomorrow.* In *Middle Works, 8: 1915.*

Dewey, John, with Alice Chipman Dewey. *Letters from China and Japan,* ed. Evelyn Dewey. New York: E. P. Dutton, 1920.

Diner, Steven J. "George Herbert Mead's Ideas on Women and Careers: A Letter to His Daughter-in-Law, 1920." *Signs* 4 (1978), 407–9.

Donnelly, Margaret E., ed. *Reinterpreting the Legacy of William James.* Washington, D.C.: American Psychological Association, 1992.

Donovan, Josephine. *Feminist Theory: The Intellectual Traditions of American Feminism.* New York: Ungar, 1985.

Douglas, Ann. *The Feminization of American Culture.* New York: Avon Books, 1977.

Du Bois, W. E. B. *Darkwater: Voices from within the Veil.* New York: Harcourt, Brace and Howe, 1920.

————. *The Autobiography of W. E. B. Du Bois.* New York: International, 1980.

Duran, Jane. "The Intersection of Pragmatism and Feminism," *Hypatia* 8/2 (Spring, 1993): 159–71.

Dykhuizen, George. *The Life and Mind of John Dewey.* Carbondale and Edwardsville: Southern Illinois University Press, 1973.

Eastman, Max. *Great Companions.* New York: Farrar, Straus, and Cudahy, 1959.

Egan, Maureen. "Evolutionary Theory in the Social Philosophy of Charlotte Perkins Gilman." *Hypatia* 4/1 (Spring, 1989): 102–19.

Eisenstein, Zillah R. *The Color of Gender: Reimaging Democracy.* Berkeley: University of California Press, 1994.

Emerson, Ralph Waldo. "Nature." *Emerson on Transcendentalism,* ed. Edward L. Ericson. New York: Ungar, 1987.

Farrell, John C. *Beloved Lady: A History of Jane Addams's Ideas on Reform and Peace.* Baltimore: Johns Hopkins University Press, 1967.

Fee, Elizabeth. "Is Feminism a Threat to Objectivity? *International Journal of Women's Studies* 4 (1981): 378–92.

Ferguson, Kathy E. *Self, Society, and Womankind.* Westport: Greenwood, 1980.

Fetterly, Judith. *The Resisting Reader.* Indianapolis: Indiana University Press, 1978.

Fisch, Max H. *Peirce, Semiotic, and Pragmatism,* ed. Kenneth Laine Ketner and Christian J. W. Kloesel. Bloomington: University of Indiana Press, 1986.

Fitzpatrick, Ellen. *Endless Crusade: Women Social Scientists and Progressive Reform.* New York: Oxford University Press, 1990.

Flax, Jane. "Postmodernism and Gender-Relations in Feminist Theory," *Signs,* 11/4 (1987).

Flower, Elizabeth, and Murray G. Murphey. *A History of Philosophy in America.* 2 vols. New York: Capricorn Books, 1977.

Fonow, Mary Margaret, and Judith A. Cook, eds. *Beyond Methodology: Feminist Scholarship and Lived Research.* Bloomington: Indiana University Press, 1991.

Fontinell, Eugene. *Self, God, and Immortality: A Jamesean Investigation.* Philadelphia: Temple University Press, 1986.

Francis, Leslie. "The Reentry of Pragmatism." *Newsletter on Philosophy and Law* 90/2 (Winter, 1991), 124–29.

Frankel, Noralee, and Nancy S. Dye, eds. *Gender, Class, Race, and Reform in the Progressive Era.* Lexington: University Press of Kentucky, 1991.

Frankenberry, Nancy. *Religion and Radical Empiricism.* Albany: State University of New York Press, 1987.

Fraser, Nancy. "Solidarity or Singularity? Richard Rorty between Romanticism and Technocracy." *Praxis International* 8/3 (1988): 257–72.

————. *Unruly Practices: Power, Discourse, and Gender in Contemporary Social Theory.* Minneapolis: University of Minnesota Press, 1989.

————. "From Irony to Prophecy to Politics: A Response to Richard Rorty." *Michigan Quarterly Review* 30/2 (Spring, 1991), 259–66.

French, Marilyn. "Is There a Feminist Aesthetic?" *Hypatia* 5/2 (1990): 33–42.

Frye, Marilyn. *The Politics of Reality: Essays in Feminist Theory.* Trumansburg, NY: Crossing Press, 1983.

Garrison, A., and Edward H. Madden. "William James—Warts and All." *American Quarterly* 29 (Summer, 1987): 212–21.

Garry, Ann, and Marilyn Pearsall. *Women, Knowledge, and Reality.* Boston: Unwin Hyman, 1989.

Gatens, Moira. *Feminism and Philosophy: Perspectives on Difference and Equality.* Oxford: Basil Blackwell Polity Press, 1991.

Gatens-Robinson, Eugenie. "Dewey and the Feminist Successor Science Project." *Transactions of the Charles S. Peirce Society* 27/4 (Fall, 1991): 417–33.

———. "A Defense of Women's Choice: Abortion and the Ethics of Care." *Southern Journal of Philosophy* 30/3 (1992): 39–66.

Gates, Henry Louis Jr., ed. *Reading Black, Reading Feminist: A Critical Anthology.* New York: Meridian, 1990.

Gavin, William Joseph. *William James and the Reinstatement of the Vague.* Philadelphia: Temple University Press, 1992.

Giarelli, James M., and J. J. Chambliss. "John Dewey on Moral Development and Education: Context, Conception and Legacy." *Discourse* 9/2 (April, 1989): 83–103.

Giddings, Paula. *When and Where I Enter: The Impact of Black Women on Race and Sex in America.* William Morrow, 1984.

Gilligan, Carol. *In a Different Voice: Psychological Theory and Women's Development.* Cambridge: Harvard University Press, 1982.

Gilman, Charlotte Perkins. "The Yellow Wallpaper." *New England Magazine* 5 (January, 1892): 647–59. Rpt. New York: Feminist Press, 1973.

———. *Women and Economics: A Study of the Economic Relation between Men and Women as a Factor in Social Evolution.* Boston: Small, Maynard, 1898. Rpt., with a foreword by Carl N. Degler, New York: Harper and Row, 1966.

———. *The Home: Its Work and Influence.* New York: McClure, Phillips, 1903. Rpt. Urbana: University of Illinois, 1972.

———. *The Forerunner.* New York: Charlton, 1909–1916. Rpt. Westport: Greenwood, 1966.

———. *The Man-Made World; or, Our Androcentric Culture.* New York: Charlton, 1911. Rpt. Minneapolis: University of Minnesota Series in American Studies, 1971.

———. *Herland.* Serialized in *Forerunner,* 1915. New York: Random House, 1979.

———. *His Religion and Hers: A Study of the Faith of Our Fathers and the Work of Our Mothers.* New York: Century Co., 1923. Rpt. Westport: Hyperion, 1976.

———. *The Living of Charlotte Perkins Gilman: An Autobiography.* New York: D. Appleton-Century, 1935. Rpt. New York: Arno, 1972.

———. *Charlotte Perkins Gilman,* ed. Larry Ceplair. New York: Columbia University Press, 1991.

Gordon, Lynn D. "Pursuing Equality, Achieving Change: Women Challenge American Higher Education." *American Quarterly* (1989): 385–90.

———. *Gender and Higher Education in the Progressive Era.* New Haven: Yale University Press, 1990.

———. "Black and White Visions of Welfare: Women's Welfare Activism, 1890–1945." *Journal of American History* 78/2 (September, 1991).

Gouinlock, James. *Excellence in Public Discourse*. New York: Teachers College Press, 1986.

Guen Hart, Carroll. *Grounding Without Foundations: A Conversation between Richard Rorty and John Dewey to Ascertain Their Kinship*. Toronto, Canada: Patmos Press, 1993.

Gunn, Giles. *Thinking across the American Grain: Ideology, Intellect, and the New Pragmatism*. Chicago: University of Chicago Press, 1992.

Guy-Sheftall, Beverly. "A Black Feminist Perspective on Transforming the Academy: The Case of Spellman College." In *Theorizing Black Feminisms*, ed. James and Busia, 77–89.

Hamilton, Alice. *Exploring the Dangerous Trades*. Boston, 1943.

———. "Hull-House Within and Without." In *Eighty Years at Hull-House*, ed. Davis and McCree, 100–07. Chicago: Quadrangle Books, 1969.

Haraway, Donna. "Situated Knowledges: The Science Question in Feminism and the Privilege of Partial Perspective." *Feminist Studies* 14/3 (Fall, 1988): 575–99.

Harding, Sandra. "Why Has the Sex-Gender System Become Visible Only Now?" In *Discovering Reality*, ed. Harding and Hintikka.

———. "The Instability of the Analytical Categories of Feminist Theory." *Signs* 11/4 (1986).

———. *The Science Question in Feminism*. Ithaca: Cornell University Press, 1986.

———. "Conclusion: Epistemological Questions." In *Feminism and Methodology*, ed. Harding and Hintikka, 181–90.

———. *Whose Science? Whose Knowledge? Thinking from Women's Lives*. Ithaca: Cornell University Press, 1991.

———, ed. *Feminism and Methodology: Social Science Issues*. Bloomington: Indiana University Press, 1987.

Harding, Sandra, and Merrill B. Hintikka, eds. *Discovering Reality: Feminist Perspectives on Epistemology, Metaphysics, Methodology, and Philosophy of Science*. Dordrecht, Holland: D. Reidel, 1983.

Harris, Leonard. "The Legitimation Crisis in American Philosophy: Crisis Resolution from the Standpoint of the Afro-American Tradition of Philosophy." *Social Science Information* 26/1 (1987), 57–73.

———, ed. *The Philosophy of Alain Locke: Harlem Renaissance and Beyond*. Philadelphia: Temple University Press, 1989.

Held, Virginia. *Rights and Goods: Justifying Social Action*. New York: Free Press, 1984.

———. *Feminist Morality: Transforming Culture, Society, and Politics*. University of Chicago Press, 1993.

Heldke, Lisa. "John Dewey and Evelyn Fox Keller: A Shared Epistemological Tradition." *Hypatia* 2/3 (Fall, 1987): 129–40.

———. "Recipes for Theory Making." *Hypatia: A Journal of Feminist Philosophy* 3/2 (Summer, 1988): 15–29.

Hickman, Larry A. *John Dewey's Pragmatic Technology*. Indiana University Press, 1990.

Hill, Mary A. *Charlotte Perkins Gilman: The Making of a Radical Feminist, 1860–1896*. Philadelphia: Temple University Press, 1980.

Hoagland, Sarah Lucia. *Lesbian Ethics: Toward New Value.* Palo Alto: Institute of Lesbian Studies, 1988.

Holland, Nancy J. *Is Women's Philosophy Possible?* Savage: Rowman and Littlefield, 1990.

Holler, Linda. "Thinking with the Weight of the Earth: Feminist Contributions to an Epistemology of Concreteness." *Hypatia* 5/1 (Spring, 1990): 1–23.

hooks, bell. *Ain't I a Woman? Black Women and Feminism.* Boston: South End Press, 1981.

———. *Feminist Theory from Margin to Center.* Boston: South End Press, 1984.

———. "Sisterhood: Political Solidarity between Women." In *Feminist Philosophies,* ed. Kourany, Sterba, and Tong, 391–404.

hooks, bell, and Cornel West. *Breaking Bread: Insurgent Black Intellectual Life.* Boston: South End Press, 1991.

Howe, Florence, ed. *Tradition and the Talents of Women.* Urbana and Chicago: University of Illinois Press, 1991.

Howes, Ethel Puffer. "True and Substantial Happiness," "The Revolt of Mother," "We Women." *Woman's Home Companion,* February–December, 1923.

———. "The Meaning of Progress in the Woman Movement." *Annals of the American Academy of Political and Social Science,* vol. 143 (May, 1929), 14–20.

———. "The Golden Age." *Radcliffe Quarterly* 21/2 (May, 1937), 14–16.

Jacobs, Harriet A. *Incidents in the Life of a Slave Girl Written by Herself,* ed. L. Maria Child. Cambridge: Harvard University Press, 1987.

Jaggar, Alison M. *Feminist Politics and Human Nature.* Totowa, NJ: Rowman and Alleheld, 1983.

———, ed. *Living with Contradictions: Controversies in Feminist Social Ethics.* Boulder: Westview Press, 1994.

James, Stanlie M., and Abena P. A. Busia, ed. *Theorizing Black Feminisms: The Visionary Pragmatism of Black Women.* London: Routledge, 1993.

James, William. (See List of Abbreviations)

———. Review of Horace Bushnell, *Women's Suffrage* and John Stuart Mill, *Subjection of Women, North American Review* 109 (1869): 556–65. Also in *ECR,* 246–56.

———. Review of *Romantic Love and Personal Beauty,* by Henry T. Finck. In *Nation* 45 (1887), 238. Also in *ECR,* 402–7.

———. "Brute and Human Intellect." EPS, 1–37.

———. Review of *Spirit of Youth* by Jane Addams, *American Journal of Sociology* 15/4 (1910): 553.

———. *Letters of William James,* 2 vols. ed. Henry James, Boston: Atlantic Monthly Press, 1920.

Jameson, Kate W., and Frank C. Lockwood, eds. *Freshman Girl: A Guide to College Life.* Boston: D. C. Heath, 1925.

Joas, Hans. *George Herbert Mead: A Contemporary Re–examination of His Thought.* Trans. Raymond Meyer. Cambridge: MIT Press, 1985. Orig. Frankfurt: Suhrkamp Verlag, 1980.

Johnson, Michael G., and Tracy B. Henley, eds. *Reflections on* "The Principles of Psychology." Hillsdale: Lawrence Erlbaum, 1990.

Johnston, Jill. *Lesbian Nation: The Feminist Solution.* New York: Simon and Schuster, 1974.

Kallen, Horace M., and Sidney Hook, eds. *American Philosophy Today and Tomorrow.* Freeport, NY: Books for Libraries Press, 1968.

Kaschak, Ellyn. *Engendered Lives: A New Psychology of Women's Experiences.* New York: Basic Books, 1992.

Kay, Judith W. "Politics without Human Nature? Reconstructing a Common Humanity." *Hypatia* 9/1 (Winter, 1994): 21–22.

Kelley, Florence. *Some Ethical Gains through Legislation,* ed. Richard T. Ely. New York: Macmillan, 1905.

————. "I Go to Work." *Survey* 58/5 (June 1, 1927): 271–74.

Kerber, Linda K., and Jane Sherron De Hart, eds. *Women's America: Refocusing the Past.* 3d ed. New York: Oxford University Press, 1991.

Kloppenberg, James T. *Uncertain Victory: Social Democracy and Progressivism in European and American Thought.* New York: Oxford University Press, 1986.

Kourany, Janet A., James P. Sterba, and Rosemarie Tong, eds. *Feminist Philosophies.* New Jersey: Prentice Hall, 1992.

Kruse, Felicia E. "Luce Irigaray's *Parler Femme* and American Metaphysics." *Transactions Charles S. Peirce Society* 27/4 (Fall, 1991): 451–64.

Lachs, John. "Aristotle and Dewey on the Rat Race." In *Philosophy and the Reconstruction of Culture,* ed. Stuhr, 97–110.

[Ladd-Franklin, Christine.] "A Revived Classic." Unsigned review of Mary Wollstonecraft, *A Vindication of the Rights of Woman.* In *Nation* 52: 1338 (February 19, 1891), 163–64.

————. "The Evolution of Marriage." Review of Letourneau, *The Evolution of Marriage.* In *Nation* 53: 1359 (July 16, 1891), 52–53.

————. "College Life for Women." *Nation* 49: 1269, 24 October 1889, 326–27.

————. "Endowed Professorships for Women." *Association for Collegiate Alumnae Bulletin,* series 3, no. 90 (February, 1904), 53–61.

Lagemann, Ellen Condliffe. "The Challenge of Jane Addams: A Research Note." *History of Education Annual,* vol. 6 (University of Rochester, 1986), 51–61.

————. "The Plural Worlds of Educational Research." *History of Education Quarterly* 29/2 (Summer, 1989): 185–214.

————, ed. "Jane Addams: An Educational Biography." In *Jane Addams on Education.* New York: Teachers College Press, 1985.

Laird, Susan. "Women and Gender in John Dewey's Philosophy of Education." *Educational Theory* 38/1 (Winter, 1988): 111–29.

Lane, Ann J. *To Herland and Beyond: The Life and Work of Charlotte Perkins Gilman.* New York: Meridian, 1991.

Langsdorf, Lenore, and Andrew R. Smith, eds. *Recovering Pragmatism's Voice: The Classical Tradition, Rorty, and the Philosophy of Communication.* Albany: State University of New York Press, 1995.

Lash, Joseph P. *Eleanor and Franklin.* New York: W. W. Norton, 1971.

Lathrop, Julia. "Hull-House as a Laboratory of Sociological Investigation." *Proceedings of the Twenty-First National Conference of Charities* 21 (1894), 313–20.

Lavine, Thelma Z. "Ideas of Revolution in the Women's Movement." *American Behavioral Scientist* 20/4 (March/April, 1977): 535–66.

————. "Pragmatism and the Constitution in the Culture of Modernism." *Transactions of the Charles S. Peirce Society* 20/1 (Winter, 1984): 1–19.

————. "American Philosophy, Socialism, and the Contradictions of Modernity." In *Philosophy and the Reconstruction of Culture*, ed. Stuhr, 1–15.

Lerner, Gerda. *The Creation of Feminist Consciousness: From the Middle Ages to Eighteen-Seventy*. Oxford University Press, 1983.

Levine, Daniel. *Jane Addams and the Liberal Tradition*. Madison: State Historical Society of Wisconsin, 1971.

Locke, Alain. "Values and Imperatives." In *American Philosophy Today and Tomorrow*, ed. Kallen and Hook, 313–33.

Locke, Alain, and Bernhard J. Stern, eds. *When Peoples Meet: A Study in Race and Cultural Contacts*. New York: Hinds, Hayden and Eldredge, 1942. Rev. ed. 1949.

Lloyd, Genevieve. *Man of Reason: "Male" and "Female" in Western Philosophy*. Minneapolis: University of Minnesota Press, 1984.

Longino, Helen E. *Science as Social Knowledge: Values and Objectivity in Scientific Inquiry*. Princeton: Princeton University Press, 1990.

Lovibond, Sabina. "Feminism and Pragmatism: A Reply to Richard Rorty." *New Left Review* 193 (May/June, 1992), 56–74.

Lynd, Staughton. "Jane Addams and the Radical Impulse." *Commentary* 32 (July 1961), 54–59.

McAlister, Linda Lopez. "Some Remarks on Exploring the History of Women in Philosophy." *Hypatia* 4/1 (Spring, 1989): 1–5.

McCaul, Robert L. "Dewey and the University of Chicago." *School and Society*. Part I: July, 1894–March, 1902 (March 25, 1961), 152–57; Part II: April, 1902–May, 1903 (April 8, 1961), 179–183; Part III: September, 1903–June, 1904 (April 22, 1961), 202–6.

McDermott, John J. "A Metaphysics of Relations: James' Anticipation of Contemporary Experience." In *The Philosophy of William James*, ed. W. R. Corti, 81–99. Hamburg: Felix Meiner, 1976.

————. *Streams of Experience: Reflections on the History and Philosophy of American Culture*. Amherst: University of Massachusetts Press, 1986.

————. "The Gamble for Excellence: Dewey's Pedagogy of Experience." In *Values and Value Theory*, ed. Murphey and Berg, 101–21.

————, ed. *Writings of William James*. New York: Modern Library, 1968.

McDowell, Mary. "The Settlement as a Way of Life." *Neighborhood* 2 (July 1929), 146–58.

McGary, Howard. "Philosophy and Diversity: The Inclusion of African and African-American Materials." *Newsletter on Feminism and Philosophy* 92/1 (Spring, 1993), 51–55.

McGraw, Myrtle Byram. *Growth: A Study of Jimmy and Johnny*. Intro. John Dewey, New York: D. Appleton-Century, 1935.

————. *Models of Achievement*, ed. Agnes N. O'Connell and Nancy Felipe Russo. New York: Columbia University Press, 1983.

McKay, Nellie Y. "The Souls of Black Women Folk in the Writings of W. E. B. Du Bois." In *Reading Black, Reading Feminist*, ed. Gates.

McManis, John T. *Ella Flagg Young and a Half-century of the Chicago Public Schools*. Chicago: A. C. McClurg, 1916.

Mahowald, Mary Briody. "A Majority Perspective: Feminine and Feminist Elements in American Philosophy." *Cross Currents* (Winter, 1986–87), 410–17.

————, ed. *Philosophy of Woman*. 3d ed. Indianapolis: Hackett, 1994.

Mailloux, Steven. "The Turns of Reader-Response Criticism." *Conversations: Contemporary Critical Theory and the Teaching of Literature,* ed. Charles Moran and Elizabeth Penfield. Urbana: National Council of Teachers of English, 1990, 38–54.

————, ed. *Rhetoric, Sophistry, Pragmatism*. Cambridge: Cambridge University Press, 1995.

Manicas, Peter. "Dewey and the Class Struggle." In *Values and Value Theory,* ed. Murphey and Berg, 67–81.

Mayhew, Katherine Camp and Anna Camp Edwards. *The Dewey School: The Laboratory School of the University of Chicago, 1896–1903.* New York: D. Appleton-Century, 1936.

Mead, George Herbert. "The Working Hypothesis in Social Reform." *American Journal of Sociology* 5/3 (November, 1899): 367–71. Reprinted in part in *Selected Writings: George Herbert Mead,* ed. Andrew J. Reck, 3–5. Indianapolis: Bobbs-Merrill, 1964.

————. Review of *The Newer Ideals of Peace,* by Jane Addams. In *American Journal of Sociology* 13 (1907): 121–28.

————. "The Social Settlement: Its Basis and Function." *University [of Chicago] Record* 12 (1908), 108–110.

————. "The Social Self." *Journal of Philosophy, Psychology, and Scientific Methods* 10 (1913), 374–80. Reprinted in Reck, ed., *Selected Writings,* 142–49.

————. "A Heckling School Board and an Educational Stateswoman." *Survey* 31/15 (10 January 1914), 443–44.

————. "The Objective Reality of Perspectives." *Proceedings of the Sixth International Congress of Philosophy,* ed. Edgar Sheffield Brightman, 75–85. New York: Longmans, Green, 1927. Rpt. Reck, ed., *Selected Writings,* 306–19.

————. "Mary McDowell." *Neighborhood* 2 (April 1929), 77–78.

————. "The Philosophies of Royce, James, and Dewey in Their American Setting." *International Journal of Ethics* 40 (January, 1930), 211–31. Rpt. Reck, ed., *Selected Writings,* 371–91.

Miller, David L. *George Herbert Mead: Self, Language, and the World.* Chicago: University of Chicago Press, 1973.

————, ed. *The Individual and the Social Self: Unpublished Work of George Herbert Mead.* Chicago: University of Chicago Press, 1982.

Miller, Marjorie C. "Response to Eugenie Gatens-Robinson, Marcia K. Moen, Felicia Kruse." *Transactions of the Charles S. Peirce Society* 27/4 (Fall, 1991): 465–74.

————. "Feminism and Pragmatism: On the Arrival of A 'Ministry of Disturbance, A Regulated Source of Annoyance; A Destroyer of Routine; An Underminer of Complacency.'" *Monist* 75/4 (October, 1992), 445–57.

————. "Essence and Identity: Santayana and the Category 'Women.'" *Transactions of the Charles S. Peirce Society* 30/1 (Winter, 1994): 33–50.

Milligan, Nancy Muller. "W. E. B. Du Bois's American Pragmatism." *Journal of American Culture* 8/2 (1985), 31–37.

Miranda, Wilma R. "Implications in Dewey for Feminist Theory in Education." *Educational Horizons* 58 (Summer, 1980): 197–202.

Mitchell, Juliet, and Ann Oakley, eds. *What is Feminism?* Oxford: Basil Blackwell, 1986.

Mitchell, Lucy Sprague. *Two Lives: The Story of Wesley Clair Mitchell and Myself.* New York: Simon and Schuster, 1953.

———. *Know Your Children in School.* New York: Macmillan, 1954.

Moen, Marcia K. "Peirce's Pragmatism as Resource for Feminism." *Transactions of the Charles S. Peirce Society* 27/4 (Fall, 1991): 435–50.

Morgan, Kathryn Pauly. "Women and the Knife: Cosmetic Surgery and the Colonization of Women's Bodies." *Hypatia* 6/3 (Fall, 1991): 25–53.

Morris, Debra, and Ian Shapiro, eds. *John Dewey: the Political Writings.* Indianapolis: Hackett, 1993.

Muncy, Robyn. *Creating a Female Dominion in American Reform 1890–1935.* New York: Oxford University Press, 1991.

Murphey, Murray G., and Ivar Berg, eds. *Values and Value Theory in Twentieth-Century America: Essays in Honor of Elizabeth Flower.* Philadelphia: Temple University Press, 1988.

Myers, Gerald E. *William James: His Life and Thought.* New Haven: Yale University Press, 1986.

Myron, Nancy, and Charlotte Bunch, eds. *Lesbianism and the Women's Movement.* Baltimore: Diana Press, 1975.

Nelson, Lynn Hankinson. *Who Knows? From Quine to a Feminist Empiricism.* Philadelphia: Temple University Press, 1990.

Newcomer, Mabel. *A Century of Higher Education for American Women.* New York: Harper Brothers, 1959.

O'Connell, Agnes N., and Nancy Felipe Russo, eds. *Models of Achievement.* New York: Columbia University Press, 1983.

Oehler, Klaus. "Notes on the Reception of American Pragmatism in Germany, 1899–1952." *Transactions of the Charles S. Peirce Society* 17/1 (Winter, 1981), 25–35.

Pameri, Ann. "Charlotte Perkins Gilman: Forerunner of a Feminist Social Science," In *Discovering Reality,* ed. Harding and Hintikka.

Pappas, Gregory Fernando. "Dewey and Feminism: The Affective and Relationships in Dewey's Ethics." *Hypatia* 8/2 (Spring, 1993): 78–95.

Peirce, Charles Sanders. *The Collected Papers of Charles Sanders Peirce,* ed. Charles Hartshorne, Paul Weiss, and Arthur W. Burks. 8 vols. Cambridge: Harvard University Press, 1931–1958.

———. "The Nature of Science." In *Classical American Philosophy,* ed. Stuhr, 46–48.

Perry, Ralph Barton. *The Thought and Character of William James.* 2 vols. Boston: Little, Brown, 1935.

Phillips, Anne. *Engendering Democracy.* University Park: The Pennsylvania State University Press, 1991.

Radin, Margaret Jane. "The Pragmatist and the Feminist." *Southern California Law Review* 63/6 (1990): 1699–1726. Rpt. *Readings in the Philosophy of Law,* ed. John Arthur and William H. Shaw. Englewood Cliffs: Prentice Hall, 1993.

Randall, M. M. *John Dewey and Jane Addams.* Jane Addams House, Philadelphia: Women's International League for Peace and Freedom, 1959.

Ratner, Joseph, ed. *Characters and Events: Popular Essays in Social and Political Philosophy.* New York: Henry Holt, 1929.

Ratner, Sidney, and Jules Altman, eds. *John Dewey and Arthur F. Bentley: A Philosophical Correspondence, 1932–1951.* New Brunswick: Rutgers University Press, 1964.

Rescher, Nicholas. "American Philosophy Today." *Review of Metaphysics* 46 (June, 1993): 717–45.

Riley, Denise. *"Am I That Name?": Feminism and the Category of 'Women' in History.* Minnesota: University of Minnesota Press, 1988.

Rockmore, Tom, and Beth J. Singer, eds. *Anti-Foundationalism Old and New.* Philadelphia: Temple University Press, 1992.

Rogers, Katharine M., ed. *Before Their Time: Six Women Writers of the Eighteenth Century.* New York: Ungar, 1979.

Rooney, Phyllis. "Gendered Reason: Sex Metaphor and Conceptions of Reason. *Hypatia* 6/2 (Summer, 1991): 77–103.

Rorty, Richard. *Philosophy and the Mirror of Nature.* Princeton: Princeton University Press, 1979.

———. *Consequences of Pragmatism.* Minneapolis: University of Minnesota Press, 1982.

———. "The Priority of Democracy to Philosophy." In *The Virginia Statute for Religious Freedom,* ed. Merrill D. Peterson and Robert C. Vaughan, 257–82. Cambridge, England: Cambridge University Press, 1988.

———. "Feminism and Pragmatism." *Michigan Quarterly Review* 30/2 (Spring, 1991): 231–58. Rpt. *Radical Philosophy* 59 (Autumn, 1991).

———. "Feminism, Ideology, and Deconstruction: A Pragmatist View." *Hypatia* 8 (Spring, 1993): 96–103.

———. "Why Can't a Man Be More Like a Woman, and Other Problems in Moral Philosophy." Review of *Moral Prejudices: Essays on Ethics,* by Annette Baier. *London Review of Books,* 24 February 1994, 3.

Rosenberg, Rosalind. *Beyond Separate Spheres: The Intellectual Roots of Modern Feminism.* New Haven: Yale University Press, 1982.

Rosenblatt, Louise M. *The Reader the Text the Poem: The Transactional Theory of the Literary Work.* Carbondale and Edwardsville: Southern Illinois University Press, 1978. Rev. ed., 1994.

———. *Literature as Exploration.* New York: Appleton-Century, 1938. 3d ed. New York: Modern Language Association, 1983.

———. "Viewpoints: Transaction Versus Interaction—A Terminological Rescue Operation." *Research in the Teaching of English,* February, 1985, 96–107.

Rosenthal, Sandra B. *Charles Peirce's Pragmatic Pluralism.* State University of New York Press, 1994.

Rosenthal, Sandra B., and Patrick L. Bourgeois. *Mead and Merleau-Ponty: Toward a Common Vision.* Albany: State University of New York Press, 1991.

Rothenberg, Paula. "The Construction, Deconstruction, and Reconstruction of Difference." *Hypatia* 5/1 (Spring, 1990): 42–57.

Royce, Josiah. *Race Questions, Provincialism, And Other American Problems.* New York: Macmillan, 1908.

Rucker, Darnell. *The Chicago Pragmatists.* Minneapolis: University of Minnesota Press, 1969.

Rucki, Elizabeth. "Philosophical Interplay between James's Pragmatic Method and Feminism." Master's thesis, Queens University, Kingston, Canada, 1987.

Rudnick, Lois. "A Feminist American Success Myth: Jane Addams's *Twenty Years at Hull-House.*" In *Tradition and the Talents of Women,* ed. Howe.

Russ, Joanna. *How to Suppress Women's Writing.* Austin: University of Texas Press, 1983.

Ruth, Sheila. *Issues in Feminism.* 2nd ed. Mountain View: Mayfield, 1990.

Scarborough, Elizabeth, and Laurel Furomoto. *Untold Lives: The First Generation of American Women Psychologists.* New York: Columbia University Press, 1987.

Scheman, Naomi. "Changing the Subject." *Newsletter on Feminism and Philosophy* 92/1 (Spring, 1993), 45–47.

Schilpp, Paul Arthur, ed. *The Philosophy of John Dewey.* Evanston: Northwestern University Press, 1939.

Schneider, Herbert W. *A History of American Philosophy.* New York: Columbia University Press, 1963. Orig. 1946.

Schott, Robin May. *Cognition and Eros: A Critique of the Kantian Paradigm.* Boston: Beacon Press, 1988.

Seigfried, Charlene Haddock. *Chaos and Context: A Study in William James.* Athens, OH: Ohio University Press, 1978.

———. "Vagueness and the Adequacy of Concepts." *Philosophy Today* 26 (Winter, 1982): 357–67. Rpt. *Twentieth Century Literary Criticism,* vol. 32, 337–41. Gale Research, 1989.

———. "Gender-Specific Values." *Philosophical Forum* 15 (Summer, 1984): 425–42.

———. "*Second Sex:* Second Thoughts." *Hypatia: Women's Studies International Forum* 8/3 (1985): 219–29. Rpt. in *Hypatia Reborn,* ed. al-Hibri and Simons, 305–22.

———. "Feminist Aesthetics and Marginality." *Resources for Feminist Research: Documentation sur la Recherche Feministe.* Special Issue: New Feminist Research 16/4 (December, 1987), 10–15.

———. "Pragmatism, Feminism, and Sensitivity to Context." In *Who Cares?* ed. Brabeck, 1989, 63–83.

———. "Weaving Chaos into Order: A Radically Pragmatic Aesthetic." *Philosophy and Literature* 14/1 (1990): 108–16.

———. "Poetic Invention and Scientific Observation: James's Model of 'Sympathetic Concrete Observation.'" *Transactions of the Charles S. Peirce Society* 26/1 (Winter, 1990): 117–32.

———. *William James's Radical Reconstruction of Philosophy.* Albany: State University of New York Press, 1990.

———. "Where Are All the Pragmatist Feminists?" *Hypatia* 6/2 (Summer, 1991): 1–20.

———. "The Missing Perspective: Feminist Pragmatism." *Transactions of the Charles S. Peirce Society* 27/4 (Fall, 1991): 405–16.

———. "Like Bridges without Piers: Beyond the Foundationalist Metaphor." In Rockmore and Singer, eds., 143–64. *Anti-Foundationalism Old and New,* 1992.

———. "Classical American Philosophy's Invisible Women." *Canadian Review of American Studies.* Special Issue, Part 1 (1992): 83–116.

———. "Validating Women's Experiences Pragmatically." *Philosophy and the Reconstruction of Culture,* ed. Stuhr, 111–29.

———, ed. Feminism and Pragmatism Special Issue. *Hypatia* 8/2 (Spring, 1993).

Seigfried, Charlene Haddock, and Hans Seigfried. "Individual Feeling and Universal Validity." In *Rhetoric, Sophistry, Pragmatism,* ed. Mailloux, 139–54.

Sicherman, Barbara. "Working It Out: Gender, Profession, and Reform in the Career of Alice Hamilton." In *Gender, Class, Race, and Reform in the Progressive Era,* ed. Frankel and Dye.

Simons, Margaret. "Sexism and the Philosophical Canon: On Reading Beauvoir's *The Second Sex." Journal of the History of Ideas* 51 (1990): 487–504.

Sklar, Kathryn Kish. "Hull House in the 1890s: A Community of Women Reformers." *Signs* 10 (Summer, 1985): 658–77.

Small, Albion W. "Scholarship and Social Agitation." *American Journal of Sociology* 1 (March, 1896): 564–82.

———. "The Social Mission of College Women." *The Independent* 54 (January 30, 1902): 261–63.

———. "Coeducation at the University of Chicago." *Proceedings of the National Education Association* (1903), 265–96.

Smith, Dorothy E. *The Everyday World as Problematic: A Feminist Sociology.* Boston: Northeastern University Press, 1987.

Smith, John E. *The Spirit of American Philosophy.* Rev. ed. Albany: State University of New York Press, 1983.

Smith, Patricia. "Feminist Jurisprudence." *APA Newsletter on Philosophy and Law* 90/1 (Fall, 1990), 152–60.

Spender, Dale. *Women of Ideas (And What Men Have Done to Them).* London: Ark, 1983.

Strouse, Jean. *Alice James: A Biography.* Boston: Houghton Mifflin, 1980.

Stuhr, John J., ed. *Classical American Philosophy.* New York: Oxford University Press, 1987.

———, ed. *Philosophy and the Reconstruction of Culture: Pragmatic Essays after Dewey.* Albany: State University Press of New York, 1993.

Taft, Jessie. *The Woman Movement from the Point of View of Social Consciousness.* Menhasa, WI: Collegiate Press, George Banta, 1915.

Talbot, Marion. *More than Lore: Reminiscences of Marion Talbot.* Chicago: University of Chicago Press, 1936.

Talbot, Marion, and Lois Kimball Mathews Rosenberry. *The History of the American Association of University Women, 1881–1931.* Cambridge: Houghton Mifflin, 1931.

Thayer, H. S. *Meaning and Action: A Critical History of Pragmatism.* 2d ed. Indianapolis: Hackett, 1981.

Thompson (Woolley), Helen Bradford. *The Mental Traits of Sex: An Experimental Investigation of the Normal Mind in Men and Women.* Chicago: University of Chicago Press, 1903.

Tomkins, Jane P., ed. *Reader-Response Criticism.* Baltimore: Johns Hopkins University Press, 1980.

Tong, Rosemarie. *Feminist Thought.* Boulder: Westview, 1989.

Tuana, Nancy. *Woman and the History of Philosophy.* New York: Paragon House, 1992.

Tufts, James H. "The Family," *Ethics.* In *The Middle Works, Vol. 5, 1908.* Carbondale and Edwardsville: Southern Illinois University Press, 1976, 510–40. Revised as "Marriage and the Family," in *Ethics, The Late Works, Vol. 7: 1932,* 438–62.

———. *Ethics of Cooperation.* Boston: Houghton Mifflin, 1918.

Turner, Victor W., and Edward M. Bruner, eds. *The Anthropology of Experience.* Urbana and Chicago: University of Illinois, 1986.

Upin, Jane S. "Charlotte Perkins Gilman: Instrumentalism beyond Dewey." *Hypatia* 8/2 (Spring, 1993): 38–63.

Warren, Karen J. "Male-Gender Bias and Western Conceptions of Reasons and Rationality." *American Philosophical Association Newsletter on Feminism and Philosophy* 88/2 (March, 1989), 48–58.

West, Cornel. *The American Evasion of Philosophy: A Genealogy of Pragmatism.* Madison: University of Wisconsin, 1989.

West, Robin. "Liberalism Rediscovered: A Pragmatic Defininition of the Liberal Vision." *University of Pittsburgh Law Review* 46 (1984), 673–738.

Westbrook, Robert B. *John Dewey and American Democracy.* Ithaca: Cornell University Press, 1991.

White, Morton. *Documents in the History of American Philosophy: From Jonathan Edwards to John Dewey.* New York: Oxford University Press, 1980.

White, Morton, and Lucia White. "Pragmatism and Social Work: William James and Jane Addams." In *The Intellectual Versus the City.* Cambridge: Harvard University and MIT Presses, 1963.

Williams, Jr., Vernon J. "Franz U. Boas and the Conflict Between Science and Values, 1894–1915." *American Philosophical Association Newsletter on Philosophy and the Black Experience,* ed. Leonard Harris 92/1 (Spring, 1993), 7–16.

Wilson, Daniel J. *Science, Community, and the Transformation of American Philosophy, 1860–1930.* Chicago: University of Chicago Press, 1990.

Yeazell, Ruth Bernard. *The Death and Letters of Alice James.* Berkeley: University of California, 1981.

Young, Ella Flagg, and John Dewey. *Contributions to Education* series. University of Chicago.

No. 1: Young, *Isolation in the School.* 1901.

No. 2: Dewey, *Psychology and Social Practice.* 1901.

No. 3: Dewey, *The Educational Situation.* 1902.

No. 4: Young, *Ethics in the School.* 1906.

No. 5: Dewey, *The Child and the Curriculum.* 1902.

No. 6: Young, *Some Types of Modern Educational Theory.* 1909.

———. *Scientific Method in Education.* 1st series, vol. 3, *Decennial Publications.* Chicago: University of Chicago Press, 1903.

Young, Iris Marion. *Justice and the Politics of Difference.* Princeton: Princeton University Press, 1990.

———. *Throwing Like a Girl and Other Essays in Feminist Philosophy and Social Theory.* Bloomington: Indiana University Press, 1990.

Index

Abbott, Edith, 64, 181–82
Addams, Jane, 58–59, 63, 73–79,
199–200, 247, 251, 261–62, 267,
269; *Democracy and Social Ethics*,
228–29; and hermeneutics of cooperation, 4, 197; influence on
Dewey of, 29–30, 45, 48–49, 58–
59, 73–78, 286n. 14; and James,
111, 135, 138, 228; and pacifi-
cism, 75–76; and partiality in
ethics, 238–39; as pragmatist, 44–
45, 65, 74–78, 228; and pragmatist canon, 44–45; and racism,
235–36, 248; and reciprocity, 78,
225–26, 228, 264, 308nn. 52, 55;
and Smith, 292n. 22; and social
ethics, 228–33; and sociology, 11,
44, 59, 181; and sympathetic understanding, 200, 239. *See also*
Hull House Settlement
Adrian, Lynne, 30,
Alexander, Thomas, 281n. 19
Alienation, 101
Analogy, reasoning by, 121–23
Angell, James Rowland, 11, 44, 71,
69–70, 82, 86
Anthropology: and philosophy, 159,
161, 250
Antler, Joyce, 53, 65
Ariès, Philippe, 272

Aristotle, 177
Art, moral function of, 186–87
Art as Experience (Dewey), 145, 186
Assertions, warranted, 7

Beauvoir, Simone de, 9, 112, 170,
207, 209; and science, 305n. 7
Bebeau, Muriel J., 205, 211
Behaviorism, 71, 198
Being-in-the-world, 39, 114
Bethune, Mary McLeod, 234
Birth control, 254–58
Body-mind, 162–63. *See also* Subject
Bordo, Susan, 34–35, 241
Brabeck, Mary, 205, 211
Breckinridge, Sophonisba, 44, 181–82
Burke, Tom, 282n. 26
Burnett, Joe R., 50, 199

Calkins, Mary Whiton, 30, 45–46, 63–
65, 70, 138; and James, 45, 291n. 86
Campbell, James, 279n. 31
Canon, challenges to the, 29–31,
40–41, 44–45, 56, 64
Clapp, Elsie Ripley, 45–52, 59, 61,
65, 91
Classical American philosophy, 3,
6–7, 56, 277n. 4; invisibility of
women in, 280n. 6. *See also*
Pragmatism

Classism, 123, 139–40, 150, 160–61, 226

Code, Lorraine, 274

Coeducation, Dewey on, 27–28, 82–83

Collins, Patricia Hill, 103, 146, 156, 232–33, 269–70

Colonialism, 191

Communication, 93–94, 145; and ethics, 218; transactive, 163–64

Community, 57–58, 93; and Chicago school of pragmatism, 69; and democracy, 91; and education, 51–52, 65; just, approach, 214–17; living in, as reformers, 58–59; as normative, 224–26; and social intelligence, 96–97; versus autonomy, 32

Concreteness, 32, 285n. 67; of black women's experiences, 269; in ethics, 233–36; as feminine and pragmatic, 35; of feminism and pragmatism, 37–39, 236; of the lived world, 11–12, 92, 157, 160; and radical empiricism, 11

Conflict, class, 249–52

Consensus, 275; cooperative, 97, 275

Context: of experience, 144–45, 160, 211; and gender, 205, 207, 209; neglect of, 38–39, 218; and thought, 36; and values, 213–19, 221

Control, social, 98

Cooperation, 90–101; Addams's emphasis on, 75; in communication, 145; in education, 196–97, 199, 307n. 40; in ethics, 201, 207, 226, 245

Cotkin, George, 298n. 1, 302n. 54

Cott, Nancy, 266, 275

Counts, George S., 81

Crenshaw, Kimberle, 33, 263, 284n. 53

Critical theory, 3, 14

Crunden, Robert M., 84

Daniels, Ruby Lee, 29

Darwin, Charles, 177

Davidson, Thomas, 120

Deegan, Mary Jo, 44, 49, 60

Democracy, 79, 201; and education, 91–92; as noncoercive, 75–76; social, 91; as a way of life, 58, 74; and women, 129

Democracy and Education (Dewey), 50–51, 53, 62, 90–91, 224–25

Democracy and Social Ethics (Addams), 228–29

Descartes, René, 35, 164

Dewey, Alice Chipman, 82; influence of, on John Dewey, 48–49, 59, 69, 72–73, 292n. 9, 295n. 69; resignation of, 83–89

Dewey, Jane, 47, 60

Dewey, John: and anti-essentialism, 91; on birth control, 255, 257–58; citations of women by, 311–12n. 26; and Clapp, 47–52, 59; and coeducation, 27–28, 82–83; 283n. 37; feminine style in, 285n. 62; and feminism, 105, 234, 253–54; and genetic method, 147, 226, 241–42, 249–50; graduate students of, 47; and Hull House, 58, 73–77; influenced by Addams, 45, 48, 58–59, 74–75; and James, 111, 141; and Marx, 13; as mentor of women, 52, 53, 55–56, 61–63; on partiality in ethics, 239–40; personal influences on, 47–52, 59, 69–70; resignation of, 83–89; and sexism, 62–64, 102–3, 149–50, 151, 247, 249–50; and truth, 7; on women's experiences, 12–13, 101, 144, 149–50; and Young, 48–49; 288n. 35. See also *Art as Experience;* Democracy; *Democracy and Education;* Education; Ethics; Experience; *Experience and Nature; Human Nature and Conduct*

Dewey School (Edwards and Mayhew), 19, 196–99

Dispositions, 96, 98, 100

Disrobing, intellectual, 157

Doings and undergoings, 156–57,

165–69; gendered, 166–69. *See also* Experience
Dualisms: criticisms of, 100, 104, 146–50, 159–60; in ethics, 240–42; sexual 133
Du Bois, W. E. B., 12, 21, 71, 189, 233, 242; and anti-elitism, 77; and pragmatist science, 192; and racism, 102, 191–92; and sexism and racism, 106–7, 234, 297n. 24

Eastman, Max, 87, 292n. 9, 295n. 69
Edman, Irwin, 47
Education: Dewey and, 58–60, 194–201; and domestic sphere, 94, 96–97, 99, 101; experimental, 56, 58–60, 194–201; James on, 116, 139–40; as radical transformation, 58, 100, 252; as social, 197–99; theory of, 92–94
Edwards, Anna Camp, 19, 49, 84, 196–97, 246
Egan, Maureen L., 40
Elitism, anti-, 22
Emancipation, as pragmatist goal, 9, 11, 21, 60, 152, 157, 160, 173
Emerson, Ralph Waldo, 73–74, 130–31
Emotions, 256–57; of anger, 167–69; in experience, 164–69; gendered, 251; and knowledge, 113–14, 148, 159, 186; objectivity of, 165, 252–53; and radical reform, 58. *See also* Feelings
Ends-in-view, 6, 57, 96–97, 114, 206, 218, 272–73, 275; pragmatist, 147–49
Environment. *See* Organism
Epistemology: pragmatist, 147–49; pragmatist criticisms of, 11–12, 100, 144–45, 175–76; pragmatist and feminist, 121, 274; and science, 185, 274
Ethics: and art, 186–87; of care, 111, 202, 206–12; cooperative, 201, 207, 226, 245; developmental, 32; of domination, 207; and feelings,

222–23, 240; individual versus social, 228–33, 235, 240, 248; in James, 119–20, 123–26; and just community, 213–17; means and ends in, 240–45; naturalistic, 97–98; partiality in, 236–40; pragmatist, 7
Ethnocentrism, 190–94, 236–37. *See also* Sexism: and ethnocentrism
Evolution, Darwinian, 176; impact on philosophy of, 177–79
Experience: concrete, 11–12; and emotions, 164–69; as experimental, 160; feminist theory and, 98, 142–44; as inferential, 176; lesbian, 153–54; lived, 9, 145, 156–61; and reality, 150–56; reconstruction of, 53, 92–93, 166, 195; and selective interest, 121–23; as starting point, 11–12, 151, 154; and theory, 9, 57–58, 173; transactive, 145–46, 165–67; women's, 63, 142–43, 171, 269, 271; women's, and pragmatism, 12–13, 56, 143–44, 154–56, 158–59. *See also* Concreteness; Doings and undergoings; Organism; Transaction
Experience and Nature (Dewey), 159, 162, 170, 184, 296n. 6
Experimentalism, 182; in education, 194–207; in ethics, 184–86; in experience, 160, in knowledge, 57; as transactive, 57; as transformative, 183, 197
Experiments: in community living, 58; in cooperation, 91
Exploitation, 191–93

Fallacy, great intellectual, 144
Family, analysis of, 230–33, 247–48
Feelings: as cognitive, 161–64; and values, 222–23. *See also* Emotions
Feminine: in James, 114–15, 122–23, 125–29, 131–35, 141
Feminity. *See* Gender
Feminism: and the academy, 265–66; branches of, 10, 204; common

Feminism (*cont.*),
  traits of, and pragmatism, 37–39,
  102–8, 197; contribution of, to
  pragmatism, 59; definition of, 4–
  5, 8, 23; liberal, 17; and perspec-
  tivism, 152–56; and pragmatism,
  267–69; pragmatist reconstruc-
  tion of, 6, 151–52, 263; and
  psychoanalysis, 15; and racism,
  106–7; social, 20
Feminist theory. *See* Feminism.
Fesmire, Steven J., 285n. 61, 298n. 29
Fisch, Max H., 43
Fitzpatrick, Ellen, 44, 286n. 11,
  287n. 20
Flower, Elizabeth, 24–25
Forbes, Harriet, 103
Foucault, Michel, 14–15, 151
Fraser, Nancy, 3, 175
Freeman, Alice, 44
French, Marilyn, 22
Freud, Sigmund, 15
Friedan, Betty, 15
Friendship, 97, 117–18, 169, 222
Fuller, Margaret, 44

Gallagher, Buell G., 192
Gatens-Robinson, Eugenie, 304n. 37
Gavin, William Joseph, 42
Gender, 32–37, 147, 154–55, 251;
  social nature of, 203–6, 208,
  210–12
Genetic method. See Method:
  genetic
Genealogy: class-based, 147, 249–50;
  in James, 13. *See also* Method,
  genetic
Gilligan, Carol, 111, 123, 202, 204,
  206, 209–10, 218, 238
Gilman, Charlotte Perkins, 64, 103,
  105, 177, 234–35, 242, 248; on
  androcentric culture, 40, 63, 112,
  226, 247–48; on birth control,
  255–58; and evolution, 310n. 6;
  on gender differences, 32–33,
  251; as philosopher, 41; as pragmatist, 31, 40–41, 65, 225, 257

Golden age of philosophy at Harvard,
  46
Goldman, Emma, 30
Gordon, Lynn D., 30, 44, 289n. 53
Gray, Francine du Pressix, 142
Grossman, Morris, 114
Growth: for Lucy Sprague Mitchell,
  53; obstacles to, 166–69; as ulti-
  mate value, 7, 41, 198, 225
Gunn, Giles, 278n. 19; on James and
  Bourdieu, 281n. 14
Guy-Sheftall, Beverly, on black wom-
  en's studies, 278n. 20, 282n. 24

Haack, Susan, 282n. 31
Habermas, Jürgen, 14–15
Habits, 98–100, 102, 196, 251–52,
  257; in ethics, 245–46
Hamilton, Alice, 44, 58–59, 76–77,
  262, 263–67, 308n. 49
Harding, Sandra, 37, 307n. 36; on
  male feminists, 28
Harper, William Rainey, 79–80, 82–88
Harraway, Donna, 179
Harris, Leonard, 233, 305n. 4
Heidegger, Martin, 14, 285n. 64
Held, Virginia, 95; on ethical natural-
  ism, 97–98
Herman, Judith Lewis, 155
Hermeneutics of cooperation,
  pragmatist, 4
Hickman, Larry, 281n. 7
Higgins, Ann, 213–15
History of American Philosophy
  (Schneider), 24
History of Philosophy in America
  (Flower and Murphey), 25
Holmes, Oliver Wendell, 215
Hook, Sidney, 43, 47
hooks, bell, 275–76, 285n. 68
Houston, Barbara, 218–19
Howes, Ethel Pufer, 138, 247; as
  feminist, 46, 63–65, 103; at
  Harvard, 46
Hull House Settlement, 56, 58–59,
  63–64, 73–79, 197, 199–200,
  248, 262–65, 276; center for re-

form and research, 77–78; and
Dewey, 48, 58, 73–77, 293n. 23;
residents of, 44, 59, 265; as working model, 77, 266–67
Human nature, 91–92, 125–29,
249–52; as social, 94–97, 205–6,
257; and women, 111, 116–117,
122–23, 125–31, 143–44, 205–
6, 250, 253. *See also* Habits
Human Nature and Conduct (Dewey),
91, 245–54; as social psychology,
22

Imagination: and radical reform, 58,
176, 186–87; and ethics, 224
Individual. *See* Subject
Individualism, 99
Inquiry: community-based, 4, 32; and
truth, 7
Instrumentalism, 273; in education,
194–201; in ethics, 240–45; as
nonoppressive, 193–94; recon-
struction of, 36; and values, 183–
86. *See also* Means-ends continuum
Intelligence: social, 95–101; and
consequences of behavior, 96–97;
reconstruction of, 186
Interaction, in feminist theory, 185.
See also Transaction
Interdependence, 95–101, 162
Interdisciplinary studies, 10–11,
291n. 2
Interest, selective. *See* Selective
interest
Interests, aesthetic and practical, 121

Jackman, Wilbert S., 83, 85–86
Jacobs, Harriet A., 142, 155
Jaggar, Alison, 19–20, 315n. 26
James, Alice (sister of William), 135–
36, 302n. 49
James, Alice (wife of William), 300n.
30
James, William, 3–6; and Addams,
111, 135, 138, 228; and automatic
sweetheart, 119–20; and Calkins,
45, 291n. 86; and Dewey, 194–95;

and Du Bois, 71–72; and ethics of
care, 123–26; and ethnocentrism
and sexism, 122–23, 125–29,
131, 135–40, 236–38; feminine
style of, 33, 114–15; on gendered
instincts, 125–28; influence of
women on, 138–41; and masculinity, 116–21, 301nn. 41, 44, 45;
and Mitchell, 53; and Nietzsche,
13; on partiality and impartiality,
236–38; and philosophy, 187–89;
and rationality, 188–89; and psychology, 15, 279n. 30; and saintliness, 133–36, 221; on science and
women, 131–36; and *Subjection of
Women,* 115–19; and subjectivity,
113–14; and sympathetic understanding, 222–23, 310n. 2; and
truth, 7; and women, 111–41; on
women's equality, 118–19, 302n.
49; *See also* Feminine; Mysticism;
Principles of Psychology; Radical
Empiricism
Jefferson, Thomas, 215
Johnson, Harriet, 57, 103; and
Harriet Forbes, 289n. 62
Judd, Charles Hubbard, 104

Kallen, Horace M., 43
Kaschak, Ellyn, 154–55
Kay, Judith W., 92
Kelley, Florence, 44, 77–78, 181
Kloppenberg, James T., 291n. 5
Klyce, Scudder, 105
Knowledge: dualistic, 147–49; and
emotions, 114; experimental, 57;
guided by interests, 7, 97, 121–
22; as instrumental, 7, 96–97;
and values, 31–32, 97–98, 148

Laboratory School of the University
of Chicago, 19, 48–50, 59, 83–
89, 196–99; named by Young, 60;
organization of, 293n. 41
Lachs, John, 174
Ladd-Franklin, Christine, 45–46, 63,
290n. 82; and Peirce, 30

Laggemann, Ellen Condliffe, 104, 282n. 27
Laird, Susan, 283n. 37
Lasch, Christopher, 49
Lathrop, Julia, 44, 77–78, 181, 269
Lavine, Thelma Z., 13, on symbolic socialism, 279n. 28
Leadership, nonhegemonic, 76
Le Guin, Ursela K., 9
Lemann, Nicolas, 29
Liberalism, 91–92, 99, 175; Mill on, 119
Lloyd, Genevieve, 164
Locke, Alain, 12, 189, 242, 305n. 4; at Harvard, 279n. 26; on science and racism, 190–94, 234
Logic: radical transformation of, 178–79, 282n. 26; and psychology, 194–95
Logic, the Theory of Inquiry (Dewey), 274
Longino, Helen, 93, 185; on social dimension of sciences, 189–90
Lyons, Nona, 218

Mahowald, Mary, 30, 33
Manicas, Peter, 313–14n. 49
Marriage, 100–101
Marx, Karl, 13
Masculinity. *See* Gender
Maureen L. Egan, 31
Mayhew, Katherine Camp, 19, 49, 84, 196–99
McAlister, Linda Lopez, 283n. 33
McCaul, Robert L., 84–89
McDermott, John J., 295n. 1
McDowell, Mary E., 264
McGraw, Myrtle B., 61, 63–64
McKay, Nellie Y., 105–6, 297nn. 24, 26
McManis, John T., 80
Mead, George Herbert, 6, 44, 46, 64–65, 86, 198, 246; and community of inquiry, 4; and generalized Other, 13, 155; and sociology, 11; and women's issues, 30, 61, 69, 82, 247; and working hypothesis, 59

Mead, Irene Tufts, 30
Meaning: behavioral, 145–46; as use, 96, 185
Meaning and Action (Thayer), 25–26
Means-ends continuum, 183–86; as moral criterion, 75, 201, 240–45
Meinong, Alexius, 187
Metaphors, pragmatic, 35–36
Metaphysics: of Being, 150, 159, 208, 242, 244, 313n. 38; evolutionary critique of, 178–79
Method: experimental, as empowering women, 58–60; genetic, 226, 241–42, 310n. 5; pragmatic, 5; and prejudice, 58–60
Midwife, Socratic, 101–8
Mill, John Stuart, 27; and *Subjection of Women*, 115–19, 124
Miller, James, 84
Miller, Marjorie, 268, 302n. 53
Mills, C. Wright, 21
Mind. *See* Body-mind
Misogyny, 34
Mitchell, Lucy Sprague, 29–30, 45, 47; 52–57, 59–60, 61, 65–66, 103; and Dewey, 51, 53–57, 290n. 73; as feminist, 54–55; and Harvard, 53; imitating philosophy professors, 53
Mitchell, Wesley Clair, 55, 60, 289nn. 57, 58, 290n. 72
Modernism, enlightenment and romantic, 13–14
Moore, G. E., 187
Morgan, Kathryn Pauly, 268
Movements, feminist, 8
Multiculturalism, 94, 160, 195; of Hull House residents, 75–77; Locke on, 190–94
Muncy, Robin, 181
Münsterberg, Hugo, 45, 50, 53
Murphey, Murray G., 25
Myers, Gerald E., 117–19
Mysticism, James on, 131–35, 301n. 43

Nagel, Ernest, 47
Naturalism, 100, 297n. 15; in ethics,

97–98, 241; in rationality, 121–23

Nelson, Lynn Hankinson, 190, 307n. 36

Nepotism, 83–89

Nietzsche, Friedrich, 13, 134

Noddings, Nel, 111, 209, 213, 128–19, 220–21

Objectivity. *See* Subjectivity

Observation, sympathetic concrete, 114, 187, 222–23

Oppression, 38, 150, 152–53, 156, 201, 226, 234, 257–58, 274–76; of black women, 269–70, 275–76; recognition of, 167–69, 171–73, 250

Organism, 162–63; and environment, 164–67

Other, the, 267–70, 298n. 7; taking the place of, 93, 97, 134

Overholser, Geneva, 172

Pacifism, 75–76, 220–21

Palmer, Alice Freeman, 53–55

Palmer, George Herbert, 53

Partiality and impartiality: in ethics, 210–11, 236–40; of perspectives, 152–54

Peirce, Charles Sanders, 5, 6, 45–46, 50, 177, 306nn. 20, 32; architectonic style of, 4, 19, 281n. 20; and feminism, 114; and semiotics, 13

Peirce, Melusina Fay, 30

Peixotto, Jessica Blanche, 54

Perception, active 166. *See* Perspectivism

Perry, Ralph Barton, 43

Perspectives, gendered, 29, 114, 120, 126–27, 129, 131–32, 136–40, 149, 151–56, 170–72, 209–10; racist, 191–92, 213, 219

Perspectivism, 8, 10, 79, 217, 268–69, 272–74; of Addams, 76; James on, 114, 121–23, 131–32, 268; partiality of, 152–54. *See also* Perspectives, gendered; Pluralism

Petroski, Catherine, 142–43

Phillips, Anne, 185

Philosophy, Chicago School of, 11, 291n. 2; Dewey on women's contributions to, 29; task of, 38; and social science, 195

Pluralism, 9–11, 113, 133, 154, 259–60, 266, 268–70, 272–73, 276; of Addams, 76; in ethics, 211–12, 224–25; and Locke, 192; and Nietzsche, 13. *See also* Perspectivism

Point of view. *See* Perspectivism

Political science, pragmatist women in, 287n. 20

Pollock, Linda, 272

Positivism: logical, 18, 34, 188; pragmatist criticism of, 22, 31–32, 36, 57, 187–189, 208–9, 241

Pragmatism: and analytic philosophy, 21; and the canon, 64; Chicago school of, 291n. 2; common traits of, and feminism, 37–39, 46, 57–60, 69, 78–79, 107–8, 190, 197; definition of, 5–8, 277n. 4; eclipse of, 18–24, 175; feminist reconstruction of, 6, 9–11, 149–50, 157–58, 161, 165–69, 170–72, 253–54, 267, 294n. 46; interdisciplinary character of, 64, 69; as masculinist, 56, 62–63; the origins of, at Hull House, 44; and sexism, 62–64; strengths of, 21; and women's experiences, 56; and women's oppression, 45, 63, 106–7, 267–69. *See also* Emancipation; Pragmatists

Pragmatists: loss of women, 24–29; 60–66, 107–8; two generations of, 43

Praxis, 45

Prejudice: hooks on, 275–76; Dewey on, 313–14n. 49; Du Bois on, 191–92; James on, 113; Locke on, 190–94; overcome by experimental method, 58–60, 79, 273; recognition of, 165, 187

Principles of Psychology (James), 22; as feminist resource, 15; influence of, on Dewey, 194–95, 307n. 33; influence of, on Edmund Husserl and Ludwig Wittgenstein, 15

Problem solving, cooperative, 58–59, 74, 182

Problematic situation. *See* Situation, problematic

Process, 159–60, 212

Professionalism: criticism of, 187–88; and specialized jargon, 22; and taking the place of the Other, 58–59, 264; and women, 68, 70, 104, 107–8, 181–82, 265, 291n. 90, 297n. 28

Progressive era, 44, 68, 100, 104–5, 200–201, 262, 266

Psychology: pragmatist, and logic, 194–95; developmental, 197–99

Public and private spheres, 64, 92, 103, 225, 244, 296n. 8; Addams on, 229–33; James on, 111, 116–17, 129, 140

Puffer, Ethel. *See* Howes

Pullman, George M., 229–30

Pullman strike, 229–30, 311n. 11

Putnam, Hilary, 190

Quest for Certainty (Dewey), 146
Quinby, Lee, 275

Racism, 102, 106–7, 139, 150, 267, 275–76; and femininity, 33, 155–56

Radical Epiricism, 11

Randell, John H. Jr., 47

Rationality, 147–49, 237; as masculine, 121–23, 131–35, 136–40, 270; naturalized, 121–23, 164–65, 175, 178–79, 188–89

Ratner, Joseph, 47, 72, 83, 261

Rawls, John, 91, 210

Reader-response theory, 30–31

Reading as a woman. *See* Perspectives

Realism: criticism of, 144–45, 148–49, 152; and experience, 150–56

Reciprocity: in ethics, 228; in human relations, 199–200, 209–10, 276; of theory and praxis, 7

Reconstruction. *See* Experience

Resources in education, 52

Revolution, 254, 263, 269

Reweaving the social fabric, 93

Riley, Denise, 143–44

Robinson, Virginia, 67

Roosevelt, Eleanor, 51

Rorty, Richard, 5, 91–92; and neo-pragmatism, 18, 175; and post-modernism, 13

Rosenberg, Rosalind, 67, 68, 70, 72, 74

Rosenblatt, Louise M., 30–31, 284n. 49, 294n. 46

Ross, Ralph, 98

Rousseau, 210

Royce, Josiah, 6, 50, 53; and Calkins, 30, 45; and community, 33; on racism, 233

Rucker, Darnell, 69

Rudnick, Lois, 74

Russell, Bertrand, 187–88

Santayana, George, 53, 300n. 34, 302n. 53; and feminism, 114

Scheman, Naomie, 112

Schneider, Herbert W., 24, 43, 47

Schott, Robin May, 27

Science: as cooperative, 182; as emancipatory, 71, 179–80, 184, 193–94, 306n. 25; and everyday life, 180–81; experimental, 57, 193; feminist theories of, 93, 179, 182, 185; as masculine, 131–33; myth of the neutrality of, 185, 187, 208–9; in pragmatism and positivism, 72, 183, 187; and racism, 190–94; and reform, 181–82, 265, 267; as social activity, 72, 245; and values, 183–86, 194, 242–45, 313n. 37

Selective interest, 38, 121–23, 161

Sexism, 62–64, 102–8, 112–14, 131; and ethnocentrism, 122–23, 128–29, 139, 267

Sexual differences, 70–71
Sexuality, 252–53, 255–57; and James, 15, 125–28, 300n. 33
Sherif, Carolyn Wood, 279n. 30
Sherwin, Susan, 146
Sicherman, Barbara, 262, 265–67
Simons, Margaret, 282n. 28
Situation, problematic, 7, 160, 264, 266, 274
Situation, concrete, 38. *See also* Context
Skepticism, 274
Small, Albion, 86
Smith, Dorothy E., 160, 271–72
Smith, Mary Rozet, 292n. 22
Social Darwinism, 251
Social sciences, 72, 174, 181–82, 195, 292n. 14; and sex-segregation, 61
Society for the Advancement of American Philosophy, 9
Sociology, 271; and experience, 160; feminist, 160–61, 271
Sprague, Lucy. *See* Mitchell
Stanton, Elizabeth Cady, 170–71
Starr, Ellen Gates, 44, 77; and Mead, 30
Stuhr, John J., 7
Style: pragmatism as exhibiting feminine, 31–37
Subject, the, 158–59, 166–67, 198, 252; as body-mind, 162–63; interdependency of, 162
Subjection of Women (Mill), 115–19, 124
Subjectivity: James on, 13–14; and objectivity, 145–46, 152–54, 58–59, 208
Sympathetic understanding. *See* Understanding

Taft, Jessie, 61, 63–66, 67, 105, 233, 242, 247; dissertation of, on women's movement, 46, 287n. 23, 311n. 18
Talbot, Marion, 44, 63, 82
Technology, 184–85, 193; and birth control, 255

Temporality, 7, 101–3; of emotions, 165
Terrell, Mary Church, 235–36
Thayer, H. S., 25
Theory: and practice, 59, 64–65, 148–50, 262–66; feminist, branches of, 10; pragmatist and feminist, 10–11, 147
Thinking, strategic, 38
Thomas, W. I., 44
Thompson, Helen. *See* Woolley
Tolerance, 228
Tong, Rosemarie, 20
Transaction: in education, 58, 294n. 46; of experience, 145–46, 165–67, 273; and gender, 205–7; of organism and environment, 6; and reader-response theory, 30–31; in science, 57
Truth: as inquiry, 7; instrumental theory of, 273–74; as perspectival, 137–38, 273
Tuana, Nancy, 114, 298n. 7
Tufts, James Hayden, 11, 46, 64, 226, 247

Understanding, sympathetic, 93, 200, 217, 222–23, 224, 239–40; interactive character of, 93–94
Universalism, 390n. 2; in ethics, 213–14, 236–40; fallacy of, in ethics, 207, 209, 215–19
Upin, Jane, 183

Vagueness, 3
Values: definition of, 7; in experience, 97–98. *See also* Ethics
Veblen, Thorstein, 44

Wald, Lillian, 181
Ward, Lester F., 115
Warranted assertions, 7
Watson, James B., 71
Wells-Barnett, Ida B. 115, 233–34, 242
West, Cornel, 21, 29, 39, 73–74

Westbrook, Robert B., 83, 201, 288n.
38; on pragmatism as epistemology, 278n. 10
Whitbeck, Carolyn, 142, 144
White, Morton, 44
Williams, Vernon J., 299n. 24
Wilson, Daniel J., 68
Women, 106–7; academic status of,
64–66, 71; and associated life,
100–101, 290n. 84; in the history
of American philosophy, 24–29;
the influence of, on pragmatism,
12–13, 59, 196; and nature, 130–
31, 135, 300n. 39; standpoint of
black, 146; theorizing own experience; 12, 66, 142–43, 152–56,
171
Woolf, Virginia, 113
Woolley, Helen Thompson, 70–72,
103

Young, Ella Flagg, 79–82, 89, 293n.
42; influence of, on Dewey, 48–
49, 59–60, 72–73, 80, 288n. 35;
resignation of, 295n. 68